React Native Cookbook
Second Edition

Recipes for solving common React Native development problems

Dan Ward

BIRMINGHAM - MUMBAI

React Native Cookbook
Second Edition

Commissioning Editor: Amarabhab Banerjee
Acquisition Editor: Trusha Shriyan
Content Development Editor: Arun Nadar
Technical Editor: Leena Patil
Copy Editor: Safis Editing
Project Coordinator: Kinjal Bari
Proofreader: Safis Editing
Indexer: Tejal Daruwale Soni
Graphics: Alishon Mendonsa
Production Coordinator: Arvindkumar Gupta

First published: December 2016

Second edition: January 2019

Production reference: 2080419

Published by Packt Publishing Ltd.
Livery Place
35 Livery Street
Birmingham
B3 2PB, UK.

ISBN 978-1-78899-192-6

www.packtpub.com

`mapt.io`

Mapt is an online digital library that gives you full access to over 5,000 books and videos, as well as industry leading tools to help you plan your personal development and advance your career. For more information, please visit our website.

Why subscribe?

- Spend less time learning and more time coding with practical eBooks and Videos from over 4,000 industry professionals

- Improve your learning with Skill Plans built especially for you

- Get a free eBook or video every month

- Mapt is fully searchable

- Copy and paste, print, and bookmark content

Packt.com

Did you know that Packt offers eBook versions of every book published, with PDF and ePub files available? You can upgrade to the eBook version at `www.packt.com` and as a print book customer, you are entitled to a discount on the eBook copy. Get in touch with us at `customercare@packtpub.com` for more details.

At `www.packt.com`, you can also read a collection of free technical articles, sign up for a range of free newsletters, and receive exclusive discounts and offers on Packt books and eBooks.

Contributors

About the author

Dan Ward is a full-stack developer and web technology consultant who has a number of years of experience working on mobile applications with React Native, and developing web applications with React, Vue, and Angular. He's also a co-founder at gitconnected, and co-editor at the associated Medium publication. His professional interests include React Native development, modern web development, and technical writing. He also has a BA in English Literature from Florida State University.

About the reviewer

Ashok Kumar S has been working in the mobile development domain for about six years. In his early days, he was a JavaScript and Node.js developer. Thanks to his strong web development skills, he mastered web and mobile development. He is a Google-certified engineer, a speaker at global-scale conferences, including DroidCon Berlin and MODS, and also runs a YouTube channel called AndroidABCD for Android developers. He also contributes to open source heavily with a view to improving his e-karma. He has written books on Wear OS programming and Mastering Firebase Toolchain. He has also reviewed books on mobile and web development, namely, *Mastering JUnit5*, *Android Programming for Beginners*, and *Building Enterprise JavaScript Applications*.

> *I would like to thank my family, mostly my mother, for her infinite support in every possible way, as well as family members Shylaja, Sumitra, Krishna, and Vinisha, and my fiancee, Geetha Shree.*

Packt is searching for authors like you

If you're interested in becoming an author for Packt, please visit `authors.packtpub.com` and apply today. We have worked with thousands of developers and tech professionals, just like you, to help them share their insight with the global tech community. You can make a general application, apply for a specific hot topic that we are recruiting an author for, or submit your own idea.

Table of Contents

Preface

Parts of this book require software that is only available for macOS. While React Native development can be done on a Windows machine, certain aspects, such as running your applications on iOS devices and in the iOS simulator, or editing native code with Xcode, can only be done with a Mac.

There are many ways for a developer to build an app for iOS or Android. React Native stands out as one of the most stable, performant, and developer-friendly options for building hybrid mobile apps. Developing mobile apps with React Native allows developers to build iOS and Android apps in a single code base, with the added ability for code-sharing between the two platforms.

Even better, a developer with experience in building web apps in React will be ahead of the game, since many of the same patterns and conventions are carried over into React Native. If you've had experience of building web apps with React, or another framework based on **Model**, **View**, **Component** (**MVC**), you'll feel right at home building mobile apps in React Native.

There are currently two widely-used ways to create and develop a React Native app: with pure React Native using the React Native CLI, or with Expo (`www.expo.io`), which is a comprehensive set of tools, libraries, and services for developing React Native applications. Unless you need access to certain, often more advanced features of React Native, Expo is my recommendation for React Native development. Expo has many features that improve the development experience, such as access to more native functionality via the Expo SDK, a more flexible and friendly CLI, and a browser-based GUI for common dev tasks. This is why all of the recipes in this book that do not require pure React Native are implemented using Expo. For more on the differences between React Native and Expo, check out the *React Native development tools* section in `Chapter 10`, *App Workflow and Third-Party Plugins*.

This book is intended to serve as a go-to reference for solutions to common problems you'll likely face when building a wide variety of apps. Each chapter is presented as a series of step-by-step recipes that each explain how to build a single feature of an overall app.

React Native is an evolving language. At the time of writing, it's still in the 0.5x stage of the development life cycle, so there are some things that will change in the months and years to come. Best practices could morph into stale ideas, or the open source packages highlighted here could fall out of favor. Every recipe in this book has been updated and revised from its counterpart in the first edition, both to account for updates to the development process and to improve clarity. I've done all I could to keep this text as up to date as possible, but technology moves fast, so it's impossible for a book to keep up by itself. The repository for all of the code covered in this book is hosted on GitHub at . If you find anything in the code here that doesn't seem to be working correctly, you can submit an issue. Or, if you've got a better way to do something, consider submitting a pull request!

Any time there's an update to anything in this book, you will be able to find the details and changes in the GitHub repository.

I hope you find this book helpful on your way through the land of React Native. Happy developing!

Who this book is for

This book has been designed with beginner to intermediate level React Native developers in mind. Even if you don't have a lot of experience with web development, the JavaScript found in this book should hopefully never be over your head. I've tried to avoid complexity wherever possible, to keep the focus on the lesson being taught within a given recipe.

This book also assumes the developer works on a computer running macOS. While it is technically possible to develop React Native apps using Windows or Linux, there are a number of limitations that make macOS machines much more preferable for React Native development, including the abilities to work with native iOS code via Xcode, run iOS code on the iOS simulator, and work with the most robust development tools for React Native app development.

What this book covers

Chapter 1, *Setting Up Your Environment*, covers the different software we'll be installing to get started on the development of React Native apps.

Chapter 2, *Creating a Simple React Native App*, covers the basics of building layouts and navigation. The recipes in the chapter serve as an introduction to React Native development, and cover the basic functionality found in most any mobile app.

Chapter 3, *Implementing Complex User Interfaces – Part I*, covers features including custom fonts and custom reusable themes.

Chapter 4, *Implementing Complex User Interfaces – Part II*, continues with more recipes based on UI features. It covers features such as handling screen orientation changes and building user forms.

Chapter 5, *Implementing Complex User Interfaces – Part III*, covers other common features you'll likely need when building complex UIs. This chapter covers adding map support, implementing browser-based authentication, and creating an audio player.

Chapter 6, *Adding Basic Animations to Your App*, covers the basics of creating animations.

Chapter 7, *Adding Advanced Animations to Your App*, continues building on the previous chapter, with more advanced features.

Chapter 8, *Working with Application Logic and Data*, introduces us to building apps that handle data. We'll cover topics including storing data locally and handling network loss gracefully.

Chapter 9, *Implementing Redux*, covers implementing the Flux data patter using the Redux library. Redux is a battle-tested way to handle data flow in React apps, and works just as well in React Native.

Chapter 10, *App Workflow and Third-Party Plugins*, covers the different methods a developer can use to build an app, along with how to build apps using open source code. This will also cover the differences between building applications with pure React Native (using the React Native CLI) and building applications with Expo (a comprehensive development).

Chapter 11, *Adding Native Functionalities – Part I*, covers the basics of working with native iOS and Android code in a React Native app.

Chapter 12, *Adding Native Functionalities – Part II*, covers more complex techniques for communicating between the React Native and native layers.

Chapter 13, *Integration with Native Applications*, covers integrating React Native with an existing native app. Not every app can be built from scratch. These recipes should be helpful for developers who need to integrate their work with an app already in the App Store.

Chapter 14, *Deploying Your App*, covers the basic process of deploying a React Native app, as well as details for using HockeyApp to track the metrics of your app.

Chapter 15, *Optimizing the Performance of Your App*, covers some tips, tricks, and best practices for writing performant React Native code.

To get the most out of this book

It is assumed that you have the following levels of understanding:

- You have some basic programming knowledge.
- You are familiar with web development basics.

It will be helpful if you also have the following:

- React, Vue, or Angular experience
- At least an intermediate level of experience with JavaScript

Download the example code files

You can download the example code files for this book from your account at www.packt.com. If you purchased this book elsewhere, you can visit www.packt.com/support and register to have the files emailed directly to you.

You can download the code files by following these steps:

1. Log in or register at www.packt.com.
2. Select the **SUPPORT** tab.
3. Click on **Code Downloads & Errata**.
4. Enter the name of the book in the **Search** box and follow the onscreen instructions.

Once the file is downloaded, please make sure that you unzip or extract the folder using the latest version of:

- WinRAR/7-Zip for Windows
- Zipeg/iZip/UnRarX for Mac
- 7-Zip/PeaZip for Linux

The code bundle for the book is also hosted on GitHub at `https://github.com/warlyware/react-native-cookbook`. In case there's an update to the code, it will be updated on the existing GitHub repository.

We also have other code bundles from our rich catalog of books and videos available at `https://github.com/PacktPublishing/`. Check them out!

Download the color images

We also provide a PDF file that has color images of the screenshots/diagrams used in this book. You can download it here: `https://www.packtpub.com/sites/default/files/downloads/9781788991926_ColorImages.pdf`.

Conventions used

There are a number of text conventions used throughout this book.

`CodeInText`: Indicates code words in text, database table names, folder names, filenames, file extensions, pathnames, dummy URLs, user input, and Twitter handles. Here is an example: "We'll use a `state` object with a `liked` Boolean property for this purpose."

A block of code is set as follows:

```
export default class App extends React.Component {
  state = {
    liked: false,
  };

  handleButtonPress = () => {
    // We'll define the content on step 6
  }
```

When we wish to draw your attention to a particular part of a code block, the relevant lines or items are set in bold:

```
onst styles = StyleSheet.create({
  container: {
    flex: 1,
  },
  topSection: {
    flexGrow: 3,
    backgroundColor: '#5BC2C1',
    alignItems: 'center',
  },
```

Any command-line input or output is written as follows:

```
expo init project-name
```

Bold: Indicates a new term, an important word, or words that you see onscreen. For example, words in menus or dialog boxes appear in the text like this. Here is an example: "Click the **Components** tab, and install a simulator from the list of provided simulators."

 Warnings or important notes appear like this.

 Tips and tricks appear like this.

Sections

In this book, you will find several headings that appear frequently (*Getting ready, How to do it..., How it works..., There's more...,* and *See also*).

To give clear instructions on how to complete a recipe, use these sections as follows:

Getting ready

This section tells you what to expect in the recipe and describes how to set up any software or any preliminary settings required for the recipe.

How to do it...

This section contains the steps required to follow the recipe.

How it works...

This section usually consists of a detailed explanation of what happened in the previous section.

There's more...

This section consists of additional information about the recipe in order to make you more knowledgeable about the recipe.

See also

This section provides helpful links to other useful information for the recipe.

Get in touch

Feedback from our readers is always welcome.

General feedback: If you have questions about any aspect of this book, mention the book title in the subject of your message and email us at customercare@packtpub.com.

Errata: Although we have taken every care to ensure the accuracy of our content, mistakes do happen. If you have found a mistake in this book, we would be grateful if you would report this to us. Please visit www.packt.com/submit-errata, selecting your book, clicking on the Errata Submission Form link, and entering the details.

Piracy: If you come across any illegal copies of our works in any form on the Internet, we would be grateful if you would provide us with the location address or website name. Please contact us at copyright@packt.com with a link to the material.

If you are interested in becoming an author: If there is a topic that you have expertise in and you are interested in either writing or contributing to a book, please visit authors.packtpub.com.

Reviews

Please leave a review. Once you have read and used this book, why not leave a review on the site that you purchased it from? Potential readers can then see and use your unbiased opinion to make purchase decisions, we at Packt can understand what you think about our products, and our authors can see your feedback on their book. Thank you!

For more information about Packt, please visit packt.com.

Setting Up Your Environment

1

The React Native ecosystem has evolved quite a bit since the first edition. The open source tool Expo.io, in particular, has streamlined both the project initialization and development phases, making working in React Native even more of a pleasure than it already was in version 0.36.

With the Expo workflow, you'll be able to build native iOS and Android applications using only JavaScript, work in the iOS simulator and Android emulator with live reload, and effortlessly test your app on any real-world device via Expo's app. Until you need access to native code (say, to integrate with legacy native code from a separate code base), you can develop your application entirely in JavaScript without ever needing to use Xcode or Android Studio. If your project ever evolves into an app that must support native code, Expo provides the ability to eject your project, which changes your app into native code for use in Xcode and Android Studio. For more information on ejecting your Expo project, please see `Chapter 10`, *App Workflow and Third-Party Plugins*.

Expo is an awesome way to build fully featured apps for Android and iOS devices, without ever having to deal with native code. Let's get started!

We will cover the following topics in this chapter:

- Installing dependencies
- Initializing your first application
- Running your application in a simulator/emulator
- Running your application on a real device

Technical requirements

This chapter will cover installing the tools you'll be using throughout this book. They include:

- Expo
- Xcode (for iOS simulator, macOS only)
- Android Studio
- Node.js
- Watchman

Installing dependencies

The first step toward building our first React Native application is installing the dependencies in order to get started.

Installing Xcode

As mentioned in the introduction of this chapter, Expo provides us with a workflow in which we can avoid working in Xcode and Android Studio altogether, so we can develop solely in JavaScript. However, in order to run your app in the iOS simulator, you will need to have Xcode installed.

 Xcode requires macOS, and therefore running your React Native application in an iOS simulator is only possible on macOS.

Xcode should be downloaded from the App Store. You can search the App Store for Xcode, or use the following link:
`https://itunes.apple.com/app/xcode/id497799835`.

Xcode is a sizable download, so expect this part to take a little while. Once you have installed Xcode via the App Store, you can run it via the `Applications` folder in the Finder:

1. This is the first screen you will see when launching Xcode. Note, if this is the first time you've installed Xcode, you will not see recent projects listed down the right-hand side:

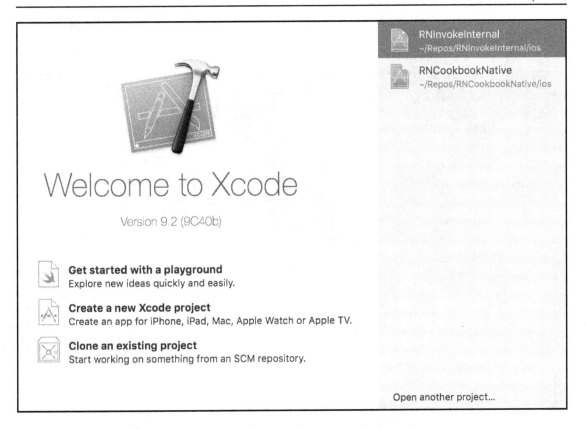

2. From the menu bar, choose **Xcode | Preferences...** as follows:

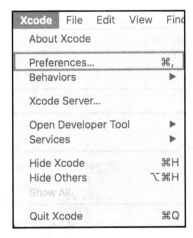

3. Click the **Components** tab, and install a simulator from the list of provided simulators:

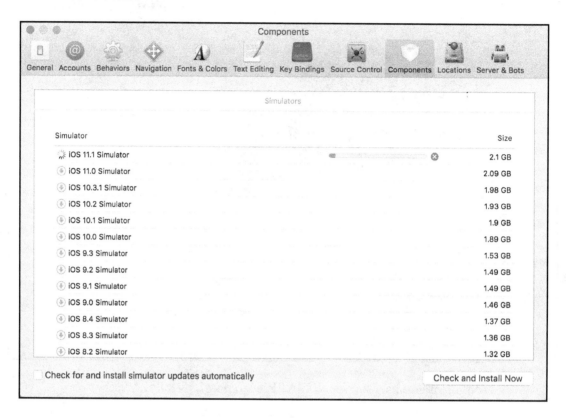

4. Once installed, you can open the simulator from the menu bar: **Xcode | Open Developer Tool | Simulator**:

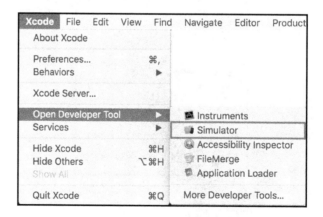

Installing Android Studio

Android Studio comes with the official Android emulator, which is the emulator that Expo recommends for use during development.

How to do it...

1. Download Android Studio from `https://developer.android.com/studio/`.
2. Open the downloaded file and drag the **Android Studio.app** icon to the **Applications** folder icon:

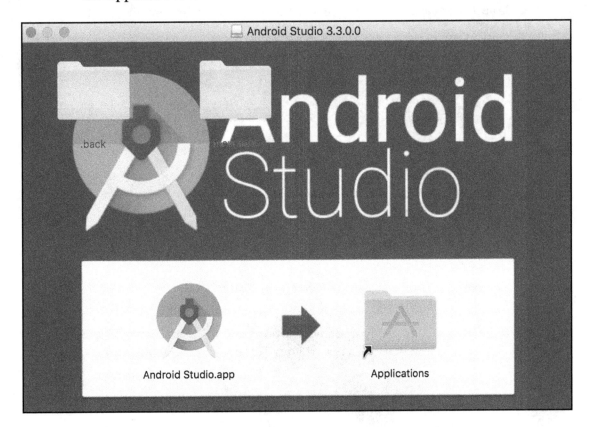

3. Once installed, we'll need to change the Android Studio preferences. Open Android Studio, and then open **Preferences** from the Android Studio menu in the system bar. In the **Preferences** submenus, select **Appearance & Behavior** | **System Settings** | **Android SDK**. Under the **SDK Tools** tab, ensure that you have some version of Android SDK Build-Tools installed, and install it if isn't installed already.

4. We'll also need to add the Android SDK location to the system PATH by editing ~/.bash_profile or ~/.bashrc. You can do this by adding the following line:

   ```
   export PATH=$PATH:/Users/MY_USER_NAME/Library/Android/sdk
   ```

   Be sure to replace MY_USER_NAME with your system username.

5. On macOS, you will also need to add platform-tools to your PATH in ~/.bash_profile or ~/.bashrc. You can do this by adding the following line:

   ```
   PATH=$PATH:/Users/MY_USER_NAME/Library/Android/platform-tools
   ```

   Be sure to replace MY_USER_NAME with your system username.

   If you've never edited a .bash_profile or .bashrc file before, or aren't familiar with PATH, you can get more information on what purpose they serve and how to work with them from the following resources:

   - https://www.rc.fas.harvard.edu/resources/documentation/editing-your-bashrc/
   - https://www.cyberciti.biz/faq/appleosx-bash-unix-change-set-path-environment-variable/

6. If the PATH was correctly updated, the adb command should work in the Terminal. You may have to restart your Terminal for the changes to take effect.

7. On a fresh install of Android Studio, you'll see a welcome screen. Start a new app to fully open the software. Then, select the AVD Manager from the buttons in the top -right corner of the window, as indicated in the following steps:

8. Press **Create Virtual Device** in the opened modal.
9. Select a device in the **Select Hardware** screen, and then press **Next**:

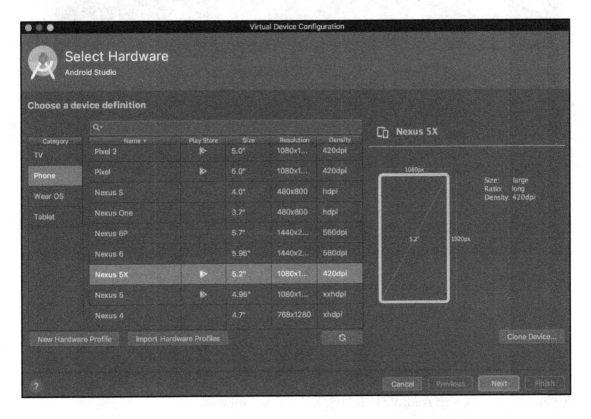

10. Download one of the system images under the **Recommended** tab of the **System Image** screen:

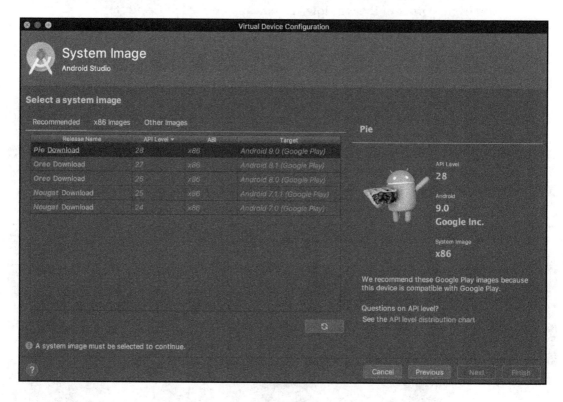

11. Press **Finish** on the final screen and Android Studio will create your new virtual device. The device can be run at any time by pressing the play button in the row of buttons in the top-right corner:

To run your app on an Android emulator during development, Expo used to recommend using the excellent third-party emulator Genymotion. As of Expo version 29, however, they now recommend using the official emulator that ships with Android Studio.

You can follow the step-by-step guide provided in the official Expo documentation to ensure that Android Studio is set up to work properly with your Expo development workflow. The guide can be found at `https://docs.expo.io/versions/latest/workflow/android-studio-emulator`.

This is all the setup you need to get started developing your first React Native app using Expo! There are, however, a few extra steps you'll need to perform for working with pure React Native applications (non-Expo applications). Pure React Native app development will be covered in depth in `Chapter 10`, *App Workflow and Third-Party Plugins*. Since this setup process is a little more involved and subject to change, I recommend referring to the official guide. You can find these instructions in the React Native: **Getting Started** guide, located at `https://facebook.github.io/react-native/docs/getting-started.html` under the **Building Projects with Native Code tab** section.

Once Simulator is open, select your desired iOS device via the menu bar: **Hardware** | **Device** | **[IOS Version]** | **[iOS Device]**. When running Expo applications in Simulator in the future, the same device should be used automatically.

The app can be started with the Expo CLI in your Terminal if you run the following command:

```
expo start
```

The command will build your app and open the Expo Developer Tools in your web browser. In the Expo Developer Tools, select **Run on iOS Simulator**.

There's more...

Once you have launched an app in the simulator, you'll be able to press the **Run on iOS Simulator** button without opening Simulator from Xcode. It should also remember your device choice. Opening Simulator from Xcode provides an easy way to choose your preferred iOS device to simulate.

If you followed the steps in the Expo guide, which can be found in the *Installing Android Studio* section, you would have also seen that it covered installing a virtual device that we can run as our emulator. To start your app on the emulator, just open the Android Virtual Device you installed in Android Studio, run the `expo start` command in your Terminal, and select **Run on Android device/emulator**.

Installing Node.js

Node.js is a JavaScript runtime built on Chrome's V8 JavaScript engine, and is designed to build scalable network applications. Node allows JavaScript to be executed in a Terminal, and is an indispensable tool for any web developer. For more information on what Node.js is, you can read the project's *About Node.js* page at `https://nodejs.org/en/about/`.

According to the Expo installation documentation, Node.js is not technically required, but as soon as you start actually building something, you'll want to have it. Node.js itself is outside the scope of this book, but you can check out the *Further reading* section at the end of this chapter for more resources on working with Node.js.

There are numerous methods to install Node.js, and it is therefore difficult to recommend a particular installation method. On macOS, you can install Node.js in one of the following ways:

- Downloading and installing Node.js from the project's site at `https://nodejs.org/en/download/`.
- Installing via Homebrew. If you are familiar with Homebrew, this process is explained succinctly at `https://medium.com/@katopz/how-to-install-specific-nodejs-version-c6e1cec8aa11`.
- Installing via Node Version Manager (NVM; `https://github.com/creationix/nvm`). NVM allows you to install multiple versions of Node.js and easily switch between them. Use the instructions provided in the repository's README to install NVM. This is the recommended method, due to its flexibility, as long as you're comfortable working in the Terminal.

Installing Expo

The Expo project used to have a GUI-based development environment called the Expo XDE, which has been replaced with a browser-based GUI called the Expo Developer Tools. Since the Expo XDE has been deprecated, creating new Expo apps is now always done using the Expo CLI. This can be installed using npm (Node Package Manager, which comes as part of Node.js) via the Terminal with the following command:

```
npm install expo-cli -g
```

We'll be using Expo quite a bit throughout this book to create and build out React Native applications, particularly those apps that do not need access to native iOS or Android code. Applications built with Expo have some very nice advantages for development, helping obfuscate native code, streamlining app publishing and push notifications, and providing a lot of useful functionality built into the Expo SDK. For more information on how Expo works, and how it fits into the bigger picture of React Native development, see Chapter 10, *App Workflow and Third-Party Plugins*.

Installing Watchman

Watchman is a tool used internally by React Native. Its purpose is to watch files for updates, and trigger responses (such as live reloading) when changes occur. The Expo documentation recommends installing Watchman, since it has been reported that some macOS users have run into issues without it. The recommended method for installing Watchman is via Homebrew. The missing package manager for macOS, Homebrew allows you to install a wide array of useful programs straight from your Terminal. It's an indispensable tool that should be in every developer's tool bag:

1. If you don't have Homebrew installed already, run the following command in the Terminal to install it (you can read more about it and view the official documentation at `https://brew.sh/`):

   ```
   /usr/bin/ruby -e "$(curl -fsSL
   https://raw.githubusercontent.com/Homebrew/install/master/install)"
   ```

2. Once Homebrew has been installed, run the following two commands in Terminal to install `watchman`:

   ```
   brew update
   brew install watchman
   ```

Initializing your first app

This is all the setup you need in order to get started developing your first React Native app using Expo! There are however a few extra steps you'll need to perform for working with pure React Native apps (non-Expo apps). Pure React Native app development will be covered in depth in `Chapter 10`, *App Workflow and Third-Party Plugins*. Since this setup process is a little more involved and subject to change, I recommend referring to the official guide. You can find these instructions in the **React Native | Getting Started** guide located at `https://facebook.github.io/react-native/docs/getting-started.html` under the **Building Projects with Native Code** tab. From here on out, we can use the magic provided by Expo to easily create new apps for development.

We'll create our first app using Expo via the Expo CLI. Making a new application is as simple as running the following:

```
expo init project-name
```

Running this command will first prompt you which type of app you'd like to create: either a blank app, which has no functionality added, or a tabs app, which will create a new app with minimal tab navigation. For the recipes in this book, we'll be using the blank app option.

Once you've selected your preferred application type, a new, empty Expo-powered React Native app in a new project-name directory is created, along with all of the dependencies needed to start developing right away. All you need to do is begin editing the App.js file in the new project directory to get to work.

To run our new app, we can cd into the directory, then use the expo start command. This will automatically build and serve the app, and open a new browser window with the Expo Developer Tools for your in-development React Native app.

For a list of all of the available commands for the Expo CLI, check out the documentation at https://docs.expo.io/versions/latest/guides/expo-cli.html.

With our first application created, let's move on to running the application in an iOS simulator and/or Android emulator.

Running your app in a simulator/emulator

You have created a new project, and started running that project with Expo in the last step. Once we start making changes to our React Native code, wouldn't it be nice to see the results of those changes? Thanks to Expo, running your project in the installed iOS simulator or Android emulator has also been streamlined.

Running your app on an iOS simulator

Running your app in the Xcode simulator only takes a few clicks.

1. Open Xcode.
2. Open the **Simulator** from the menu bar: **Xcode** | **Open Developer Tool** | **Simulator**:

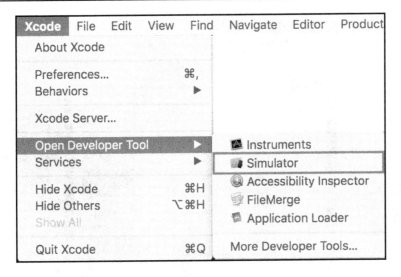

3. The app can be started with the Expo CLI in your Terminal if you run the following command:

```
expo start
```

The command will build your app and open the Expo Developer Tools in your web browser. In the Expo Developer Tools, select **Run on iOS Simulator**.

4. The first time you run a React Native app on the iOS simulator via **Run on iOS Simulator**, the Expo app will be installed on the simulator, and your app will automatically be opened within the Expo app. The simulated iOS will ask if you want to **Open in "Expo"?**. Choose **Open**:

5. Upon loading, you will see the Expo Developer menu. You can toggle between this menu and your React Native app by pressing *command* key + *D* on your keyboard:

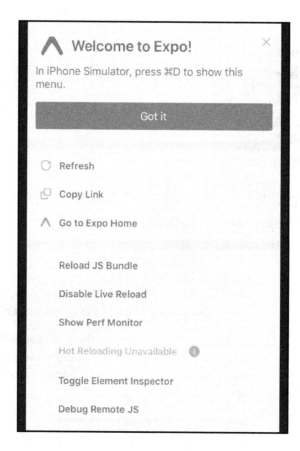

There's more...

Once you have launched an app in the simulator, you'll be able to press the **Run on iOS Simulator** button without opening Simulator from Xcode. It should also remember your device choice. Opening Simulator from Xcode provides an easy way to choose your preferred iOS device to simulate.

You can toggle between your React Native app and the Expo Developer menu, a list of helpful features for development, by pressing *command* key + *M* on your keyboard. The Expo Developer menu should look something like this:

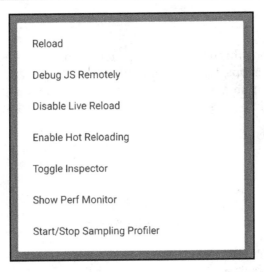

Running your app on a real device

Running your development app on a real device as easy as running your app on a simulator. With the clever combination of the native Expo app and a QR code, running on a real device is only a few clicks and taps away!

Running your app on an iPhone or Android

You can get the in-development app running on your phone in three simple steps:

1. Open the App Store on your iPhone, or the Google Play Store on your Android device.
2. Search for and download the Expo Client app.
3. While your app is running on your development machine, you should also have the Expo Developer Tools open in a browser. You should see a QR code at the bottom of the left-hand side menu of the Expo Developer Tools. Use the iPhone's native Camera app, or the **Scan QR Code** button in the Expo Client app on Android, to scan the QR code. This will open your in-development app on the device within the Expo Client app.

Your React Native app should now be running on your real device, fully equipped with live reload! You can also shake the device to toggle between your React Native app and the Expo Developer menu.

Summary

In this chapter, we've gone through all the steps required for getting started with developing React Native apps, including initializing a new project, emulating running your new project on your computer, and running your development app on real-world devices. Thanks to the power of Expo, it's easier to jump in and start working than ever before.

Now that you've got everything set up, it's time to start building!

Further reading

Here's a list of other resources covering similar topics:

- The Expo installation documentation at `https://docs.expo.io/versions/latest/introduction/installation.html`.
- *Node.js Web Development* at `https://www.packtpub.com/mapt/book/web_development/9781785881503`
- *Introducing Hot Reloading - React Native* at `https://facebook.github.io/react-native/blog/2016/03/24/introducing-hot-reloading.html`. This blog post from the React Native team describes how Hot Reloading works in depth.
- *Publishing with Expo* at `https://docs.expo.io/versions/latest/guides/publishing.html`. Expo has a publish feature that allows you to share your in-development React Native application with fellow developers by creating a persistent URL.
- Expo Snack at `https://snack.expo.io`. Similar to `codepen.io` or `jsfiddle.net`, Snack lets you live edit a React Native app in the browser!

Creating a Simple React Native App

2

In this chapter, we'll cover the following recipes:

- Adding styles to elements
- Using images to mimic a video player
- Creating a toggle button
- Displaying a list of items
- Using flexbox to create a layout
- Setting up and using navigation

React Native is a fast-growing library. Over the last few years it has become very popular among the open source community. There's often a new release every other week that improves performance, adds new components, or provides access to new APIs on the device.

In this chapter, we'll learn about the most common components in the library. To step through all of the recipes in this chapter, we'll have to create a new application, so make sure you have your environment up and running.

Adding styles to elements

We have several components at our disposal, but containers and text are the most common and useful components to create layouts or other components. In this recipe, we'll see how to use containers and text, but most importantly we'll see how styles work in React Native.

Getting ready

Follow the instructions in the previous chapter in order to create a new application. We'll name this application `fake-music-player`.

When creating a new application with Expo, a small amount of boilerplate code will be added to the `App.js` file in the `root` folder. This will be the starting point of any React Native application you build. Feel free to remove all boilerplate at the beginning of each recipe, as all code (including what's used in the `App.js` boilerplate) will be discussed.

How to do it...

1. In the `App.js` file, we're going to create a stateless component. This component will mimic a small music player. It will only display the name of the song and a bar to show the progress. The first step is importing our dependencies:

```
import React from 'react';
import { StyleSheet, Text, View } from 'react-native';
```

2. Once we've imported the dependencies, we can build out the component:

```
export default class App extends React.Component {
  render() {
    const name = '01 - Blue Behind Green Bloches';

    return (
      <View style={styles.container}>
        <View style={styles.innerContainer} />
        <Text style={styles.title}>
          <Text style={styles.subtitle}>Playing:</Text> {name}
        </Text>
      </View>
    );
  }
}
```

3. We have our component ready, so now we need to add some styles, to add colors and fonts:

```
const styles = StyleSheet.create({
  container: {
    margin: 10,
    marginTop: 100,
    backgroundColor: '#e67e22',
    borderRadius: 5,
  },
  innerContainer: {
    backgroundColor: '#d35400',
    height: 50,
    width: 150,
    borderTopLeftRadius: 5,
    borderBottomLeftRadius: 5,
  },
  title: {
    fontSize: 18,
    fontWeight: '200',
    color: '#fff',
    position: 'absolute',
    backgroundColor: 'transparent',
    top: 12,
    left: 10,
  },
  subtitle: {
    fontWeight: 'bold',
  },
});
```

4. As long as our simulator and emulator are running our application, we should see the changes:

How it works...

In *step 1*, we included the dependencies of our component. In this case, we used `View`, which is a container. If you're familiar with web development, `View` is similar to `div`. We could add more `Views` inside other `Views`, `Texts`, `Lists`, and any other custom component that we create or import from a third-party library.

If you're familiar with React you'll notice that, this is a stateless component, which means it doesn't have any state; it's a pure function and doesn't support any of the life cycle methods.

We're defining a `name` constant in the component, but in real-world applications this data should come from the props. In the return, we're defining the **JavaScript XML (JSX)** that we're going to need to render our component, along with a reference to the styles.

Each component has a attribute called `style`. This property receives an object with all of the styles that we want to apply to the given component. Styles are not inherited (except for the `Text` component) by the child components, which means we need to set individual styles for each component.

In *step 3*, we defined the styles for our component. We're using the `StyleSheet` API to create all of our styles. We could have used a plain object containing the styles, but by using the `StyleSheet` API instead of an object, we gain some performance optimizations, as the styles will be reused for every renderer, as opposed to creating an object every time the render method gets executed.

There's more...

I'd like to call your attention to the definition of the title style in *step 3*. Here, we've defined a property called `backgroundColor` and set `transparent` as its value. As a good exercise, let's comment this line of code and see the result:

On iOS, the text will have an orange background color and it might not be what we really want to happen in our UI. In order to fix this, we need to set the background color of the text as transparent. But the question is, why is this happening? The reason is that React Native adds some optimizations to the text by setting the color from the parent's background color. This will improve the rendering performance because the rendering engine won't have to calculate the pixels around each letter of the text and the rendering will be executed faster.

 Think carefully when setting the background color to transparent. If the component is going to be updating the content very frequently, there might be some performance issues with text, especially if the text is too long.

Using images to mimic a video player

Images are an important part of any UI, whether we use them to display icons, avatars, or pictures. In this recipe, we'll use images to create a mock video player. We'll also display the icons from the local device and a large image from a remote server (hosted by Flickr).

Getting ready

In order to follow the steps in this recipe, let's create a new application. We're going to name it fake-video-player.

We're going to display a few images in our application to mimic a video player, so you'll need corresponding images for your application. I recommend using the icons I used by downloading them from the repository for this recipe on GitHub at https://github.com/warlyware/react-native-cookbook/tree/master/chapter-2/fake-video-player/images.

How to do it...

1. The first thing we're going to do is create a new folder called Images in the root of the project. Add the images you've downloaded to the new folder.

2. In the App.js file, we include all of the dependencies we'll need for this component:

```
import React from 'react';
import { StyleSheet, View, Image } from 'react-native';
```

3. We need to `require` the images that'll be displayed in our component. By defining them in constants, we can use the same image in different places:

```
const playIcon = require('./images/play.png');
const volumeIcon = require('./images/sound.png');
const hdIcon = require('./images/hd-sign.png');
const fullScreenIcon = require('./images/full-screen.png');
const flower = require('./images/flower.jpg');
const remoteImage = { uri:
`https://farm5.staticflickr.com/4702/24825836327_bb2e0fc39b_b.jpg`
};
```

4. We're going to use a stateless component to render the JSX. We'll use all of the images we've declared in the previous step:

```
export default class App extends React.Component {
  render() {
    return (
      <View style={styles.appContainer}>
        <ImageBackground source={remoteImage} style=
          {styles.videoContainer} resizeMode="contain">
          <View style={styles.controlsContainer}>
            <Image source={volumeIcon} style={styles.icon} />
            <View style={styles.progress}>
              <View style={styles.progressBar} />
            </View>
            <Image source={hdIcon} style={styles.icon} />
            <Image source={fullScreenIcon} style={styles.icon} />
          </View>
        </ImageBackground>
      </View>
    );
  }
};
```

5. Once we have the elements that we're going to render, we need to define the styles for each element:

```
const styles = StyleSheet.create({
  flower: {
    flex: 1,
  },
  appContainer: {
    flex: 1,
    justifyContent: 'center',
    alignItems: 'center',
  },
  videoContainer: {
```

```
      backgroundColor: '#000',
      flexDirection: 'row',
      flex: 1,
      justifyContent: 'center',
      alignItems: 'center',
    },
    controlsContainer: {
      padding: 10,
      backgroundColor: '#202020',
      flexDirection: 'row',
      alignItems: 'center',
      marginTop: 175,
    },
    icon: {
      tintColor: '#fff',
      height: 16,
      width: 16,
      marginLeft: 5,
      marginRight: 5,
    },
    progress: {
      backgroundColor: '#000',
      borderRadius: 7,
      flex: 1,
      height: 14,
      margin: 4,
    },
    progressBar: {
      backgroundColor: '#bf161c',
      borderRadius: 5,
      height: 10,
      margin: 2,
      paddingTop: 3,
      width: 80,
      alignItems: 'center',
      flexDirection: 'row',
    },
});
```

6. We're done! Now, when you view the application, you should see something like the following:

How it works...

In *step 2*, we required the `Image` component. This is the component responsible for rendering images from the local filesystem on the device or from a remote server.

In *step 3*, we required all of the images. It's good practice to require the images outside of the component in order to only require them once. On every renderer, React Native will use the same image. If we were dealing with dynamic images from a remote server, then we'd need to require them on every renderer.

The `require` function accepts the path of the image as a parameter. The path is relative to the folder that our class is in. For remote images, we need to use an object defining `uri` for where our file is.

In *step 4*, a stateless component was declared. We used `remoteImage` as the background of our application via an `ImageBackground` element, since `Image` elements cannot have child elements. This element acts similarly to the `background-url` property in CSS.

The `source` property of `Image` accepts an object to load remote images or a reference to the required file. It's very important to explicitly require every image that we want to use because when we prepare our application for distribution, images will be added to the bundle automatically. This is the reason we should avoid doing anything dynamic, such as the following:

```
const iconName = playing ? 'pause' : 'play';
const icon = require(iconName);
```

The preceding code won't include the images in the final bundle. As a result, we'll have errors when trying to access these images. Instead, we should refactor our code to something like this:

```
const pause = require('pause');
const play = require('playing');
const icon = playing ? pause : play;
```

This way, the bundle will include both images when preparing our application for distribution, and we can decide which image to display dynamically at runtime.

In *step 5*, we defined the styles. Most of the properties are self-explanatory. Even though the images we're using for icons are white, I've added the `tintColor` property to show how it can be used to color images. Give it a try! Change `tintColor` to `#f00` and watch the icons turn red.

Flexbox is being used to align different portions of the layout. Flexbox in React Native behaves essentially the same as it does in web development. We'll discuss flexbox more in the *Using flexbox to create a layout* recipe later in this chapter, but the complexities of flexbox itself are outside the scope of this book.

Creating a toggle button

Buttons are an essential UI component in every application. In this recipe, we'll create a toggle button, which will be unselected by default. When the user taps on it, we'll change the styles applied to the button to make it appear selected.

We'll learn how to detect the tap event, use an image as the UI, keep the state of the button, and add styles based on the component state.

Getting ready

Let's create a new app. We're going to name it `toggle-button`. We're going to use one image in this recipe. You can download the assets for this recipe from the corresponding repository hosted on GitHub at `https://github.com/warlyware/react-native-cookbook/tree/master/chapter-2/toggle-button/images`.

How to do it...

1. We're going to create a new folder called `images` in the root of the project and add the heart image to the new folder.

2. Let's import the dependencies for this class next:

```
import React, { Component } from 'react';
import {
  StyleSheet,
  View,
  Image,
  Text,
  TouchableHighlight,
} from 'react-native';

const heartIcon = require('./images/heart.png');
```

3. For this recipe, we need to keep track of whether the button has been pressed. We'll use a `state` object with a `liked` Boolean property for this purpose. The initial class should look like this:

```
export default class App extends React.Component {
  state = {
    liked: false,
  };

  handleButtonPress = () => {
    // Defined in a later step
  }

  render() {
    // Defined in a later step
  }
}
```

4. We need to define the content of our new component inside the `render` method. Here, we're going to define the `Image` button and a `Text` element underneath it:

```
export default class App extends React.Component {
  state = {
    liked: false,
  };

  handleButtonPress = () => {
    // Defined in a later step
  }

  render() {
    return (
      <View style={styles.container}>
        <TouchableHighlight
          style={styles.button}
```

```
                  underlayColor="#fefefe"
              >
                <Image
                  source={heartIcon}
                  style={styles.icon}
                />
              </TouchableHighlight>
              <Text style={styles.text}>Do you like this app?</Text>
          </View>
        );
      }
    }
```

5. Let's define some styles to set dimensions, position, margins, colors, and so on:

```
const styles = StyleSheet.create({
  container: {
    marginTop: 50,
    alignItems: 'center',
  },
  button: {
    borderRadius: 5,
    padding: 10,
  },
  icon: {
    width: 180,
    height: 180,
    tintColor: '#f1f1f1',
  },
  liked: {
    tintColor: '#e74c3c',
  },
  text: {
    marginTop: 20,
  },
});
```

6. When we run the project on the simulators, we should have something similar to the following screenshot:

7. In order to respond to the tap event, we need to define the content of the
   `handleButtonPress` function and assign it as a callback to the
   `onPress` property:

```
handleButtonPress = () => {
  this.setState({
    liked: !this.state.liked,
  });
}

render() {
  return (
    <View style={styles.container}>
      <TouchableHighlight
        onPress={this.handleButtonPress}
        style={styles.button}
        underlayColor="#fefefe"
      >
        <Image
          source={heartIcon}
          style={styles.icon}
        />
      </TouchableHighlight>
      <Text style={styles.text}>Do you like this app?</Text>
    </View>
  );
}
```

8. If we test our code, we won't see anything changing on the UI, even though the state on the component changes when we press the button. Let's add a different color to the image when the state changes. That way, we'll be able to see a response from the UI:

```
render() {
    const likedStyles = this.state.liked ? styles.liked :
undefined;

    return (
      <View style={styles.container}>
        <TouchableHighlight
          onPress={this.handleButtonPress}
          style={styles.button}
          underlayColor="#fefefe"
        >
          <Image
            source={heartIcon}
            style={[styles.icon, likedStyles]}
          />
        </TouchableHighlight>
        <Text style={styles.text}>Do you like this app?</Text>
      </View>
    );
}
```

How it works...

In *step 2*, we imported the `TouchableHighlight` component. This is the component responsible for handling the touch event. When the user touches the active area, the content will be highlighted based on the `underlayColor` value we have set.

In *step 3*, we defined the state of `Component`. In this case, there's only one property on the state, but we can add as many as needed. In `Chapter 3`, *Implementing Complex User Interfaces – Part I*, we'll see more recipes about handling the state in more complex scenarios.

In *step 6*, we used the `setState` method to change the value of the `liked` property. This method is inherited from the `Component` class that we're extending.

In *step 7*, based on the current state of the `liked` property, we used the styles to set the color of the image to red or we returned `undefined` to avoid applying any styles. When assigning the styles to the `Image` component, we used an array to assign many objects. This is very handy because the component will merge all of the styles into one single object internally. The objects with the highest index will overwrite the properties with the lowest object index in the array:

There's more...

In a real application, we're going to use several buttons, sometimes with an icon aligned to the left, a label, different sizes, colors, and so on. It's highly recommended to create a reusable component to avoid duplicating code all over our app. In Chapter 3, *Implementing Complex User Interfaces – Part I*, we'll create a button component to handle some of these scenarios.

Displaying a list of items

Lists are everywhere: a list of orders in the user's history, a list of available items in a store, a list of songs to play. Nearly any application will need to display some kind of information in a list.

For this recipe, we're going to display several items in a list component. We're going to define a JSON file with some data, then we're going to load this file using a simple require to finally render each item with a nice but simple layout.

Getting ready

Let's start by creating an empty app. We'll name this application list-items. We're going to need an icon to display on each item. The easiest way to get images is to download them from this recipe's repository hosted on GitHub at https://github.com/warlyware/react-native-cookbook/tree/master/chapter-2/list-items/images.

How to do it...

1. We'll start by creating an images folder and adding basket.png to it. Also, create an empty file in the root of the project called sales.json.

2. Inside the `sales.json` file, we'll define the data that we're going to display in the list. Here's some sample data:

```
[
  {
    "items": 5,
    "address": "140 Broadway, New York, NY 11101",
    "total": 38,
    "date": "May 15, 2016"
  }
]
```

3. To avoid cluttering the pages of this book, I've only defined one record, but go ahead and add more content to the array. Copying and pasting the same object multiple times will do the trick. In addition, you could change some values on the data so that each item displays unique data in the UI.

4. In our `App.js` file, let's import the dependencies we'll need:

```
import React, { Component } from 'react'; import {
  StyleSheet,
  View,
  ListView,
  Image,
  Text,
} from 'react-native';
import data from './sales.json';

const basketIcon = require('./images/basket.png');
```

5. Now, we need to create the class to render the list of items. We're going to keep the sales data on the state; that way, we could insert or remove elements easily:

```
export default class App extends React.Component {
  constructor(props) {
    super(props);
    const dataSource = new ListView.DataSource({
      rowHasChanged: (r1, r2) => r1 !== r2
    });

    this.state = {
      dataSource: dataSource.cloneWithRows(data),
    };
  }

  renderRow(record) {
    // Defined in a later step
```

```
  }

  render() {
    // Defined in a later step
  }
}
```

6. In the `render` method, we need to define the `ListView` component and we'll use the `renderRow` method to render each item. The `dataSource` property defines the array of elements that we're going to render on the list:

```
render() {
  return (
    <View style={styles.mainContainer}>
      <Text style={styles.title}>Sales</Text>
      <ListView dataSource={this.state.dataSource}
renderRow={this.renderRow} />
    </View>
  );
}
```

7. Now, we can define the contents of `renderRow`. This method receives each object containing all of the information we need. We're going to display the data in three columns. In the first column, we'll show an icon; in the second column, we'll show the number of items for each sale and the address where this order will ship; and the third column will display the date and the total:

```
    return (
      <View style={styles.row}>
        <View style={styles.iconContainer}>
          <Image source={basketIcon} style={styles.icon} />
        </View>
        <View style={styles.info}>
          <Text style={styles.items}>{record.items} Items</Text>
          <Text style={styles.address}>{record.address}</Text>
        </View>
        <View style={styles.total}>
          <Text style={styles.date}>{record.date}</Text>
          <Text style={styles.price}>${record.total}</Text>
        </View>
      </View>
    );
```

8. Once we have the JSX defined, it's time to add the styles. First, we'll define colors, margins, paddings, and so on for the main container, title, and row container. In order to create the three columns for each row, we need to use the flexDirection: 'row' property. We'll learn more about this property in the *Using flexbox to create a layout* recipe later in this chapter:

```
const styles = StyleSheet.create({
  mainContainer: {
    flex: 1,
    backgroundColor: '#fff',
  },
  title: {
    backgroundColor: '#0f1b29',
    color: '#fff',
    fontSize: 18,
    fontWeight: 'bold',
    padding: 10,
    paddingTop: 40,
    textAlign: 'center',
  },
  row: {
    borderColor: '#f1f1f1',
    borderBottomWidth: 1,
    flexDirection: 'row',
    marginLeft: 10,
    marginRight: 10,
    paddingTop: 20,
    paddingBottom: 20,
  },
});
```

9. If we refresh the simulators, we should see something similar to the following screenshot:

10. Now, inside the `StyleSheet` definition, let's add styles for the icon. We're going to add a yellow circle as the background and change the color of the icon to white:

```
iconContainer: {
  alignItems: 'center',
  backgroundColor: '#feb401',
  borderColor: '#feaf12',
```

```
        borderRadius: 25,
        borderWidth: 1,
        justifyContent: 'center',
        height: 50,
        width: 50,
      },
      icon: {
        tintColor: '#fff',
        height: 22,
        width: 22,
      },
```

11. After this change, we'll see a nice icon on the left side of each row, as shown in the following screenshot:

12. Finally, we'll add the styles for the text. We need to set `color`, `size`, `fontWeight`, `padding`, and a few other properties:

```
info: {
  flex: 1,
  paddingLeft: 25,
  paddingRight: 25,
},
items: {
  fontWeight: 'bold',
  fontSize: 16,
  marginBottom: 5,
},
address: {
  color: '#ccc',
  fontSize: 14,
},
total: {
  width: 80,
},
date: {
  fontSize: 12,
  marginBottom: 5,
},
price: {
  color: '#1cad61',
  fontSize: 25,
  fontWeight: 'bold',
}
```

13. The end result should look similar to the following screenshot:

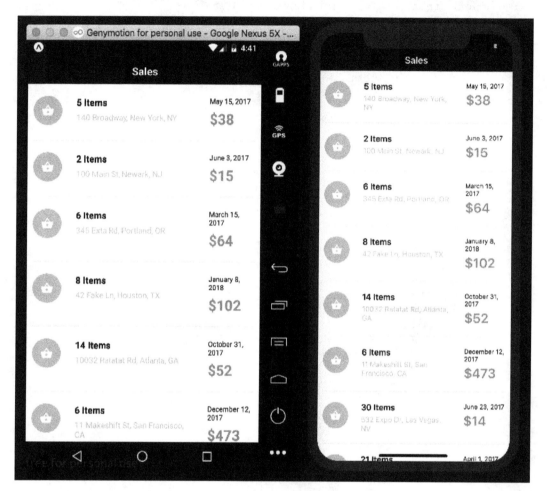

How it works...

In *step 5*, we created the data source and added data to the state. The `ListView.DataSource` class implements performance data processing for the `ListView` component. The `rowHasChanged` property is required, and it should be a function to compare the next element. In our case, if the changes are different from the current data, which is represented as `(r1, r2) => r1 !== r2`, then React Native will know to respond and re-render the UI.

When filling up the data source with data, we need to call the `cloneWithRows` method and send an array of records.

If we want to add more data, we should call the `cloneWithRows` method again with an array containing the previous and new data. The data source will make sure to compute the differences and re-render the list as necessary.

In *step 7*, we define the JSX to render the list. Only two properties are required for the list: the data source we already have from *step 6* and `renderRow`.

The `renderRow` property accepts a function as a value. This function needs to return the JSX for each row.

There's more...

We've created a simple layout using flexbox; however, there's another recipe in this chapter where we'll dive into more detail about using flexbox.

Once we have our list, chances are that we're going to need to see the detail of each order. You can use the `TouchableHighlight` component as the main container for each row, so go ahead and give it a try. If you are not sure how to use the `TouchableHighlight` component, take a look at the *Creating a toggle button* recipe from earlier in this chapter.

Using flexbox to create a layout

In this recipe, we'll learn about flexbox. In the previous recipes in this chapter, we've been using flexbox to create layouts, but in this recipe, we'll focus on the properties we have at our disposal by recreating the layout from a random name generator application on the App Store called *Nominazer* (`https://itunes.apple.com/us/app/nominazer/id765422087?mt=8`).

Working in flexbox in React Native is essentially the same as working with flexbox in CSS. This means if you're comfortable developing websites with a flexbox layout, then you already know how to create layouts in React Native! This exercise will cover the basics of working with flexbox in React Native, but for a list of all of the layout props you can use, refer to the documentation on Layout Props (`https://facebook.github.io/react-native/docs/layout-props.html`).

Getting ready

Let's begin by creating a new blank app. We'll name it `flexbox-layout`.

How to do it...

1. In `App.js`, let's import the dependencies we'll need for our app:

```
import React from 'react';
import { StyleSheet, Text, View } from 'react-native';
```

2. Our application only needs a `render` method since we're building a static layout. The rendered layout consists of a container `View` element and three child `View` elements for each colored section of the app:

```
export default class App extends React.Component {
  render() {
    return (
      <View style={styles.container}>
        <View style={styles.topSection}> </View>
        <View style={styles.middleSection}></View>
        <View style={styles.bottomSection}></View>
      </View> );
    }
  }
```

3. Next, we can begin adding our styles. The first style we'll add will be applied to the `View` element that wraps our entire app. Setting the `flex` property to 1 will cause all children elements to fill all empty space:

```
const styles = StyleSheet.create({
  container: {
    flex: 1,
  }
});
```

4. Now, we can add the styles for the three child `View` elements. Each section has a `flexGrow` property applied to it, which dictates how much of the available space each element should take up. `topSection` and `bottomSection` are both set to 3, so they'll take up the same amount of space. Since the `middleSection` has the `flexGrow` property set to 1, this element will take up one third of the space that `topSection` and `bottomSection` take up:

```
topSection: {
```

```
      flexGrow: 3,
      backgroundColor: '#5BC2C1',
    },
    middleSection: {
      flexGrow: 1,
      backgroundColor: '#FFF',
    },
    bottomSection: {
      flexGrow: 3,
      backgroundColor: '#FD909E',
    },
```

5. If we open our application in the simulators, we should already be able to see the basic layout taking shape:

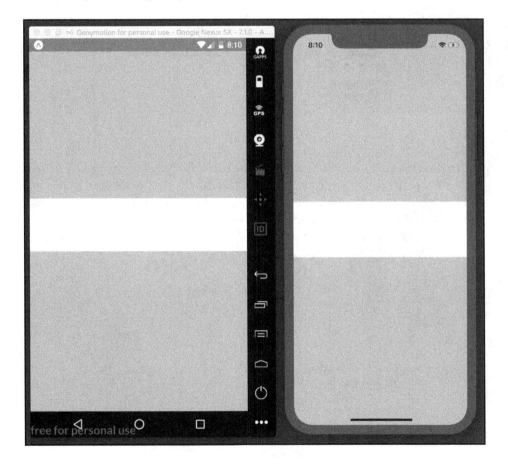

6. Here, we can add a `Text` element to each of the three child `View` elements we created in *step 2*. Note the newly added code has been highlighted:

```
render() {
  return (
    <View style={styles.container}>
      <View style={styles.topSection}>
        <Text style={styles.topSectionText}>
          4  N A M E S
        </Text>
      </View>
      <View style={styles.middleSection}>
        <Text style={styles.middleSectionText}>
          I P S U M
        </Text>
      </View>
      <View style={styles.bottomSection}>
        <Text style={styles.bottomSectionText}>
          C O M
        </Text>
      </View>
    </View>
  );
}
```

7. The text for each section defaults to the top-left corner of that section. We can use flexbox to justify and align each of these elements to the desired positions. All three child `View` elements have the `alignItems` flex property set to `'center'`, which will cause the children of each element to be centered along the *x* axis. `justifyContent` is used on the middle and bottom sections to define how child elements should be justified along the *y* axis:

```
onst styles = StyleSheet.create({
  container: {
    flex: 1,
  },
  topSection: {
    flexGrow: 3,
    backgroundColor: '#5BC2C1',
    alignItems: 'center',
  },
  middleSection: {
    flexGrow: 1,
    backgroundColor: '#FFF',
    justifyContent: 'center',
    alignItems: 'center',
  },
```

```
      bottomSection: {
        flexGrow: 3,
        backgroundColor: '#FD909E',
        alignItems: 'center',
        justifyContent: 'flex-end'
      }
    });
```

8. All that's left to be done is to add basic styles to the `Text` elements to increase
   `fontSize`, `fontWeight`, and the required `margin`:

```
      topSectionText: {
        fontWeight: 'bold',
        marginTop: 50
      },
      middleSectionText: {
        fontSize: 30,
        fontWeight: 'bold'
      },
      bottomSectionText: {
        fontWeight: 'bold',
        marginBottom: 30
      }
```

9. If we open our application in simulators, we should be able to see our completed
   layout:

How it works...

Our application is looking really good, and it was quite easy to accomplish by using flexbox. We created three distinct sections by using `View` elements that take up different fractions of the screen by setting the `flexGrow` properties to 3, 1, and 3, respectively. This causes the top and bottom sections to be of equal vertical size, and the middle section to be one third the size of the top and bottom.

When using flexbox, we have two directions to lay out child content, `row` and `column`:

- `row`: This allows us to arrange the children of the container horizontally.
- `column`: This allows us to arrange the children of the container vertically. This is the default direction in React Native.

When setting `flex: 1` as we did with the container `View` element, we're telling that element to take up all available space. If we were to remove `flex: 1` or set `flex` to 0, we can see the layout collapse in on itself, since the container is no longer flexing into all of the empty space:

Flexbox is great for supporting different screen resolutions as well. Even though different devices may have different resolutions, we can ensure consistent layouts that will look good on any device.

There's more...

There are some differences between how flexbox works in React Native and how it works in CSS. First, the default `flexDirection` property in CSS is `row`, whereas the default `flexDirection` property in React Native is `column`.

The `flex` property also behaves a bit differently in React Native. Instead of setting `flex` to a string value, it can be set to a positive integer, `0`, or `-1`. As the official React Native documentation states:

> *When flex is a positive number, it makes the component flexible and it'll be sized proportional to its flex value. So, a component with flex set to 2 will take twice the space as a component with flex set to 1. When flex is 0, the component is sized according to width and height and is inflexible. When flex is -1, the component is normally sized according width and height. However, if there's not enough space, the component will shrink to its minWidth and minHeight.*

There's a lot more to talk about with flexbox, but for now we've gotten our feet wet. In `Chapter 3`, *Implementing Complex User Interfaces – Part I*, we'll learn more about layouts. we'll learn more about layouts, and we'll create a complex layout that uses more of the available layout properties.

See also

- React Native Layout Props documentation (`https://facebook.github.io/react-native/docs/layout-props.html`)
- React Native Text Style Props documentation (`https://facebook.github.io/react-native/docs/text-style-props.html`)
- Yoga (`https://github.com/facebook/yoga`)—Facebook's Flexbox implementation utilized by React Native
- An excellent Stack Overflow post that covers how React Native flex properties work, with examples—`https://stackoverflow.com/questions/43143258/flex-vs-flexgrow-vs-flexshrink-vs-flexbasis-in-react-native`

Setting up and using navigation

For any application that has more than one view, a navigation system is of paramount importance. The need for navigation is so pervasive in application development that Expo provides two templates when you create a new application: **Blank** or **Tab Navigation**. This recipe is based on a very pared down version of the Tab Navigation app template provided by Expo. We'll still begin the recipe with a Blank app and build our basic Tab Navigation app from scratch to better understand all of the requisite parts. After completing this recipe, I encourage you to start a new app with the Tab Navigation template to see some of the more advanced features we'll be covering in later chapters, including push notifications and stack navigation.

Getting ready

Let's go ahead and create a new blank application named `simple-navigation`. We're also going to need a third-party package for handling our navigation. We'll be using 1.5.9 version of the `react-navigation` package. Using a newer version of this package will not work properly with this code, as the package's API has recently gone through breaking changes.. In the Terminal, navigate to the root of the new project and install this package with the following command:

```
yarn add react-navigation@1.5.9
```

That's all of the setup we need. Let's build!

How to do it...

1. Inside the `App.js` file, let's import our dependencies:

   ```
   import React from 'react';
   import { StyleSheet, View } from 'react-native';
   ```

2. The `App` component for this app will be very simple. We just need an `App` class with a `render` function that renders our app container. We'll also add styles for filling the window and adding a white background:

   ```
   export default class App extends React.Component {
     render() {
       return (
         <View style={styles.container}>
         </View>
   ```

```
    );
  }
}

const styles = StyleSheet.create({
  container: {
    flex: 1,
    backgroundColor: '#fff',
  }
});
```

3. The next step for `App.js` will be to import and use the `MainTabNavigator` component, which is a new component that we'll create in *step 4*:

```
React.Component {
  render() {
    return (
      <View style={styles.container}>
        <MainTabNavigator />
      </View>
    );
  }
}
```

4. We'll need to create a new file for our `MainTabNavigator` component. Let's create a new folder in the root of the project called `navigation`. In this new folder, we'll create `MainTabNavigator.js` for our navigation component.

5. In `MainTabNavigator.js`, we can import all of the dependencies we need for navigation. The dependencies include three screens (`HomeScreen`, `LinksScreen`, and `SettingsScreen`). We'll add these screens in later steps:

```
import React from 'react';
import { Ionicons } from '@expo/vector-icons';
import { TabNavigator, TabBarBottom } from 'react-navigation';

import HomeScreen from '../screens/HomeScreen';
import LinksScreen from '../screens/LinksScreen';
import SettingsScreen from '../screens/SettingsScreen';
```

6. Our navigation component will use the `TabNavigator` method provided by `react-navigation` for defining the routes and navigation for our app. `TabNavigator` takes two parameters: a `RouteConfig` object to define each route and a `TabNavigatorConfig` object to define the options for our `TabNavigator` component:

```
export default TabNavigator({
    // RouteConfig, defined in step 7.
}, {
    // TabNavigatorConfig, defined in steps 8 and 9.
});
```

7. First, we'll define the `RouteConfig` object, which will create a route map for our application. Each key in the `RouteConfig` object serves as the name of the route. We set the screen property for each route to the corresponding screen component we want to be displayed on that route:

```
export default TabNavigator({
  Home: {
    screen: HomeScreen,
  },
  Links: {
    screen: LinksScreen,
  },
  Settings: {
    screen: SettingsScreen,
  },
}, {
  // TabNavigatorConfig, defined in steps 8 and 9.
});
```

8. `TabNavigatorConfig` has a little more to it. We pass the `TabBarBottom` component provided by `react-navigation` to the `tabBarComponent` property to declare what kind of tab bar we want to use (in this case, a tab bar designed for the bottom of the screen). `tabBarPosition` defines whether the bar is on the top or bottom of the screen. `animationEnabled` specifies whether transitions are animated, and `swipeEnabled` declares whether views can be changed via swiping:

```
export default TabNavigator({
    // Route Config, defined in step 7.
}, {
  navigationOptions: ({ navigation }) => ({
    // navigationOptions, defined in step 9.
  }),
```

```
      tabBarComponent: TabBarBottom,
      tabBarPosition: 'bottom',
      animationEnabled: false,
      swipeEnabled: false,
    });
```

9. In the `navigationOptions` property of the `TabNavigatorConfig` object, we'll define dynamic `navigationOptions` for each route by declaring a function that takes the navigation prop for the current route/screen. We can use this function to decide how the tab bar will behave per route/screen, since it's designed to return an object that sets `navigationOptions` for the appropriate screen. We'll use this pattern to define the appearance of the `tabBarIcon` property for each route:

```
      navigationOptions: ({ navigation }) => ({
        tabBarIcon: ({ focused }) => {
          // Defined in step 10
        },
      }),
```

10. The `tabBarIcon` property is set to a function whose parameters are the props for the current route. We'll use the `focused` prop to decide whether to render a colored in icon or an outlined icon, depending on the current route. We get `routeName` from the navigation prop via `navigation.state`, define icons for each of our three routes, and return the rendered icon for the appropriate route. We'll use the `Ionicons` component provided by Expo to create each icon and define the icon's color based on whether the icon's route is `focused`:

```
      navigationOptions: ({ navigation }) => ({
        tabBarIcon: ({ focused }) => {
          const { routeName } = navigation.state;

          let iconName;
          switch (routeName) {
            case 'Home':
              iconName = `ios-information-circle`;
              break;
            case 'Links':
              iconName = `ios-link`;
              break;
            case 'Settings':
              iconName = `ios-options`;
          }
          return (
            <Ionicons name={iconName}
              size={28} style={{marginBottom: -3}}
```

```
        color={focused ? Colors.tabIconSelected :
        Colors.tabIconDefault}
      />
    );
  },
}),
```

11. The last step in setting up `MainTabNavigator` is to create the `Colors` constant used to color each icon:

```
const Colors = {
  tabIconDefault: '#ccc',
  tabIconSelected: '#2f95dc',
}
```

12. Our routing is now complete! All that's left now is to create the three screen components for each of the three routes we imported and defined in `MainTabNavigator.js`. For simplicity's sake, each of the three screens will have identical code, except for background color and identifying text.

13. In the root of the project, we need to create a `screens` folder to house our three screens. In the new folder, we'll need to make `HomeScreen.js`, `LinksScreen.js`, and `SettingsScreen.js`.

14. Let's start by opening the newly created `HomeScreen.js` and adding the necessary dependencies:

```
import React from 'react';
import {
  StyleSheet,
  Text,
  View,
} from 'react-native';
```

15. The `HomeScreen` component itself is quite simple, just a full color page with the word `Home` in the middle of the screen to show which screen we're currently on:

```
export default class HomeScreen extends React.Component {
  render() {
    return (
      <View style={styles.container}>
        <Text style={styles.headline}>
          Home
        </Text>
      </View>
    );
  }
}
```

16. We'll also need to add the styles for our `Home` screen layout:

```
const styles = StyleSheet.create({
  container: {
    flex: 1,
    alignItems: 'center',
    justifyContent: 'center',
    backgroundColor: '#608FA0',
  },
  headline: {
    fontWeight: 'bold',
    fontSize: 30,
    color: 'white',
  }
});
```

17. All that's left now is to repeat *step 14*, *step 15*, and *step 16* for the remaining two screens, along with some minor changes. `LinksScreen.js` should look like `HomeScreen.js` with the following highlighted sections updated:

```
import React from 'react';
import {
  StyleSheet,
  Text,
  View,
} from 'react-native';

export default class LinksScreen extends React.Component {
  render() {
    return (
      <View style={styles.container}>
        <Text style={styles.headline}>
          Links
        </Text>
      </View>
    );
  }
}

const styles = StyleSheet.create({
  container: {
    flex: 1,
    alignItems: 'center',
    justifyContent: 'center',
    backgroundColor: '#F8759D',
  },
  headline: {
    fontWeight: 'bold',
```

```
      fontSize: 30,
      color: 'white',
   }
});
```

18. Similarly, inside `SettingsScreen.js`, we can create the third screen component using the same structure as the previous two screens:

```
import React from 'react';
import {
  StyleSheet,
  Text,
  View,
} from 'react-native';

export default class SettingsScreen extends React.Component {
  render() {
    return (
      <View style={styles.container}>
        <Text style={styles.headline}>
          Settings
        </Text>
      </View>
    );
  }
}

const styles = StyleSheet.create({
  container: {
    flex: 1,
    alignItems: 'center',
    justifyContent: 'center',
    backgroundColor: '#F0642E',
  },
  headline: {
    fontWeight: 'bold',
    fontSize: 30,
    color: 'white',
  }
});
```

19. Our application is complete! When we view our application in the simulator, it should have a tab bar along the bottom of the screen that transitions between our three routes:

How it works...

In this recipe, we covered one of the most common and fundamental navigation patterns in native apps, the tab bar. The React Navigation library is a very robust, feature rich navigation solution and will likely be able to provide your app with any kind of navigation needed. We'll cover more uses of React Navigation in Chapter 3, *Implementing Complex User Interfaces - Part I.*

See also

- React Navigation official documentation (https://reactnavigation.org/)
- Expo's guide on routing and navigation (https://docs.expo.io/versions/ latest/guides/routing-and-navigation.html)

Implementing Complex User Interfaces - Part I

3

In this chapter, we will implement complex user interfaces. We will learn more about using flexbox to create components that work on different screen sizes, how to detect orientation changes, and more.

The chapter will cover the following recipes:

- Creating a reusable button with theme support
- Building a complex layout for tablets using flexbox
- Including custom fonts
- Using font icons

Creating a reusable button with theme support

Reusability is very important when developing software. We should avoid repeating the same thing over and over again, and instead we should create small components that we can reuse as many times as possible.

In this recipe, we will create a `Button` component, and we are also going to define several properties to change its look and feel. While going through this recipe, we will learn how to dynamically apply different styles to a component.

Getting ready

We need to create an empty app. Let's name it `reusable-button`.

How to do it...

1. In the root of our new app, we'll need to create a new `Button` folder for our reusable button-related code. Let's also create `index.js` and `styles.js` in our new `Button` folder.

2. We will start by importing the dependencies for our new component. In the `Button/index.js` file, we will be creating a `Button` component. This means we'll need to import the `Text` and `TouchableOpacity` components. You'll notice we're also importing styles that do not exist yet. We will define these styles in a different file later in this recipe. In the `Button/index.js` file, we should have these imports:

```
import React, { Component } from 'react';

import {
  Text,
  TouchableOpacity,
} from 'react-native';

import {
  Base,
  Default,
  Danger,
  Info,
  Success
} from './styles';
```

3. Now that we have our dependencies imported, let's define the class for this component. We are going to need some properties and two methods. It's also required that we export this component so we can use it elsewhere:

```
export default class Button extends Component {
  getTheme() {
    // Defined in a later step
  }

  render() {
    // Defined in a later step
  }
}
```

4. We need to select the styles to apply to our component based on the given `properties`. For this purpose, we will define the `getTheme` method. This method will check whether any of the `properties` are `true` and will return the appropriate styles. If none are `true`, it will return the `Default` style:

```
getTheme() {
  const { danger, info, success } = this.properties;

  if (info) {
    return Info;
  }

  if (success) {
    return Success;
  }

  if (danger) {
    return Danger;
  }

  return Default;
}
```

5. It's required that all components have a `render` method. Here, we need to return the JSX elements for this component. In this case, we will get the styles for the given `properties` and apply them to the `TouchableOpacity` component. We are also defining a label for the button. Inside this label, we will render the `children` property. If a callback function is received, then it will be executed when the user presses this component:

```
render() {
  const theme = this.getTheme();
  const {
    children,
    onPress,
    style,
    rounded,
  } = this.properties;

  return (
    <TouchableOpacity
      activeOpacity={0.8}
      style={[
        Base.main,
        theme.main,
        rounded ? Base.rounded : null ,
```

```
        style,
      ]}
      onPress={onPress}
    >
      <Text style={[Base.label, theme.label]}>{children}</Text>
    </TouchableOpacity>
  );
}
```

6. We are almost done with our `Button` component. We still need to define our styles, but first let's move over to the `App.js` file in the root of the project. We need to import the dependencies, including the `Button` component we have created.
   We are going to display an alert message when the user clicks the button, therefore, we also need to import the `Alert` component:

```
import React from 'react';
import {
  Alert,
  StyleSheet,
  View
} from 'react-native';
import Button from './Button';
```

7. Once we have all the dependencies, let's define a stateless component that renders a few buttons. The first button will use the default style, and the second button will use the success style, which will add a nice green color to the button's background. The last button will display an alert when it gets pressed. For that, we need to define the callback function that will use the `Alert` component, just setting the title and message:

```
export default class App extends React.Component {
  handleButtonPress() {
    Alert.alert('Alert', 'You clicked this button!');
  }

  render() {
    return(
      <View style={styles.container}>
        <Button style={styles.button}>
          My first button
        </Button>
        <Button success style={styles.button}>
          Success button
        </Button>
        <Button info style={styles.button}>
```

```
        Info button
      </Button>
      <Button danger rounded style={styles.button}
      onPress={this.handleButtonPress}>
        Rounded button
      </Button>
    </View>
  );
}
}
```

8. We are going to add some styles for how the main layout should align and justify each button, along with some margins:

```
const styles = StyleSheet.create({
  container: {
      flex: 1,
      alignItems: 'center',
      justifyContent: 'center',
    },
  button: {
    margin: 10,
  },
});
```

9. If we try to run the app now, we will get some errors. This is because we haven't declared the styles for our button. Let's work on that now. Inside the `Button/styles.js` file, we need to define the base styles. These styles will be applied to every instance of the button. Here, we will define a radius, padding, font color, and all the common styles that we need for this component:

```
import { StyleSheet } from 'react-native';

const Base = StyleSheet.create({
  main: {
    padding: 10,
    borderRadius: 3,
  },
  label: {
    color: '#fff',
  },
  rounded: {
    borderRadius: 20,
  },
});
```

10. Once we have the common styles for our button, we need to define the styles for the Danger, Info, Success, and Default themes. For this, we are going to define different objects for each theme. Inside each theme, we will use the same object but with specific styles for that theme.

    To keep things simple, we are only going to change the backgroundColor, but we do have the option to use as many style properties as we want:

    ```
    const Danger = StyleSheet.create({
      main: {
        backgroundColor: '#e74c3c',
      },
    });

    const Info = StyleSheet.create({
      main: {
        backgroundColor: '#3498db',
      },
    });

    const Success = StyleSheet.create({
      main: {
        backgroundColor: '#1abc9c',
      },
    });

    const Default = StyleSheet.create({
      main: {
        backgroundColor: 'rgba(0 ,0 ,0, 0)',
      },
      label: {
        color: '#333',
      },
    });
    ```

11. Finally, let's export the styles. This step is necessary so that the Button component can import all the styles for each theme:

    ```
    export {
      Base,
      Danger,
      Info,
      Success,
      Default,
    };
    ```

12. If we open the app, we should be able to see our completed layout:

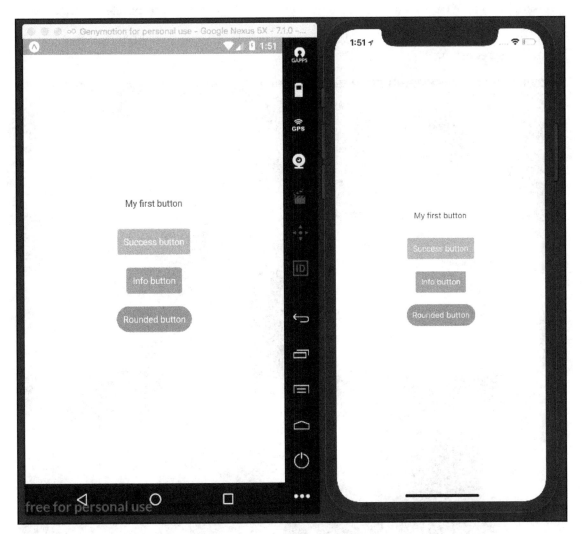

How it works...

In this example, we made use of the TouchableOpacity component. This component allows us to define a nice animation that changes the opacity when the user presses the button.

We can use the `activeOpacity` property to set the opacity value when the button gets pressed. The value can be any number between 0 and 1, where 0 is completely transparent.

If we press the rounded button, we will see a native **Alert** message, as shown in the following screenshot:

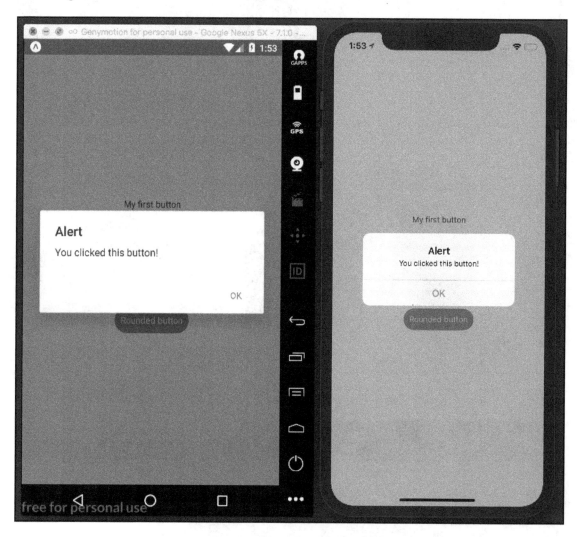

Building a complex layout for tablets using flexbox

Flexbox is really convenient when it comes to creating responsive layouts. React Native uses flexbox as a layout system, and if you are already familiar with these concepts, it will be really easy for you to start creating layouts of any kind.

As discussed in the previous chapter, there are some differences between the way flexbox works in React Native as compared to how it works in CSS. For more information on the differences between React Native and CSS flexbox, please refer to the *How it works...* section of the *Using flexbox to create a layout* recipe in Chapter 2, *Creating a Simple React Native App*.

In this recipe, we will create a layout to display a list of blog posts. Each post will be a small card with an image, an excerpt, and a button to read more. We will use flexbox to arrange the posts on the main container based on screen size. This will allow us to handle the screen rotation by properly aligning the cards in both landscape and portrait.

Getting ready

We are going to need a new app for this recipe. Let's name it tablet-flexbox.

When we create a new app with Expo, there is an app.json that gets created at the base of the project that provides some basic configuration. In this recipe, we are building an app that we want to be sure looks good on a tablet, particularly in landscape mode. When we open app.json, we should see an orientation property set to 'portrait'. This property determines which orientations should be allowed within our app. The orientation property accepts 'portrait' (lock app to portrait mode), 'landscape' (lock app to landscape mode), and 'default' (allow app to adjust screen orientation based on the device's orientation). For our app, we will set the orientation to 'landscape' so that we can support both landscape and portrait layouts.

We'll also be using some images, which need to be hosted remotely for this recipe to properly simulate loading remote data and displaying images with the Image component. I have uploaded these images to the www.imgur.com image hosting service, and referenced these remote images in the data.json file that the recipe uses for its consumable data. If, for any reason these remote images don't load properly for you, they are also in included in the repository for this recipe under the /assets folder. Feel free to upload them to any server or hosting service, and update the image URLs in data.json accordingly. The repository can be found on GitHub at https://github.com/warlyware/react-native-cookbook/tree/master/chapter-3/tablet-flexbox.

How to do it...

1. First, we need to create a Post folder in the root of the project. We need to also create an index.js and a styles.js file in the new Post folder. We will use this Post component to display each post for our app. Finally, we need to add a data.json file to the root of the project, which we will use to define a list of posts.

2. Now we can move on to building the App.js component. First, we need to import the dependencies for this class. We are going to use a ListView component to render the list of posts. We'll also need Text and View components for content containers. We are going to create a custom Post component to render each post on the list, and we will also need to import the data.json file:

```
import React, { Component } from 'react';
import { ListView, StyleSheet, Text, View } from 'react-native';

import Post from './Post';
import data from './data.json';
```

3. Let's create the class for the App component. Here, we will use the data from the .json file to create the dataSource for the list. We will add some actual data to our data.json file in the next step. In the render method, we are going to define a simple top toolbar and the List component. We are going to use the Post component for every record and get the dataSource from the state.

If you have any questions regarding the ListView component, you should take a look at the recipe in Chapter 2, *Creating a Simple React Native App*, where we created a list of orders:

```
const dataSource = new ListView.DataSource({
  rowHasChanged: (r1, r2) => r1 !== r2,
});

export default class App extends Component {
  state = {
    dataSource: dataSouce.cloneWithRows(data.posts),
  };

  render() {
    return (
      <View style={styles.container}>
        <View style={styles.toolbar}>
          <Text style={styles.title}>Latest posts</Text>
        </View>
        <ListView
          dataSource={this.state.dataSource}
          renderRow={post => <Post {...post} />}
          style={styles.list}
          contentContainerStyle={styles.content}
        />
      </View>
    );
  }
}
```

4. Two files are still missing: the `.json` file with the data and the `Post` component. In this step, we will create the data that we are going to use for each post. To make things simple, there is only one record of data in the following code snippet, but the rest of the `POST` object I used in this recipe can be found in the `data.json` file of the code repository for this recipe, located at `https://github.com/warlyware/react-native-cookbook/blob/master/chapter-3/tablet-flexbox/data.json`:

```json
{
  "posts": [
    {
      "title": "The Best Article Ever Written",
      "img": "https://i.imgur.com/mf9daCT.jpg",
      "content": "Lorem ipsum dolor sit amet...",
      "author": "Bob Labla"
    },
    // Add more records here.
  ]
}
```

5. Now that we have some data, we are ready to work on the `Post` component. In this component, we need to display the image, title, and button. Since this component does not need to know about state, we will use a stateless component. The following code uses all the components we learned about in Chapter 2, *Creating a Simple React Native App*. If something is unclear, please review that chapter again.

This component receives the data as a parameter, which we then use for displaying the content in the component. The `Image` component will use the `img` property defined on each object in the `data.json` file to display the remote image:

```javascript
import React from 'react';
import {
  Image,
  Text,
  TouchableOpacity,
  View
} from 'react-native';

import styles from './styles';

const Post = ({ content, img, title }) => (
  <View style={styles.main}>
    <Image
      source={{ uri: img }}
```

```
        style={styles.image}
      />
      <View style={styles.content}>
        <Text style={styles.title}>{title}</Text>
        <Text>{content}</Text>
      </View>
      <TouchableOpacity style={styles.button} activeOpacity={0.8}>
        <Text style={styles.buttonText}>Read more</Text>
      </TouchableOpacity>
    </View>
  );
);

export default Post;
```

6. Once we have defined the component, we also need to define the styles for each post. Let's create an empty `StyleSheet` export so that the `Post` component relying on `styles.js` will properly function:

```
import { StyleSheet } from 'react-native';

const styles = StyleSheet.create({
  // Defined in later steps
});

export default styles;
```

7. If we try to run the app, we should be able to see the data from the `.json` file on the screen. It won't be very pretty though, since, we haven't applied any styles yet.

8. We have everything we need on the screen. Now we are ready to start working on the layout. First, let's add styles for our `Post` container. We'll be setting `width`, `height`, `borderRadius`, and a few others. Let's add them to the `/Post/styles.js` file:

```
const styles = StyleSheet.create({
  main: {
    backgroundColor: '#fff',
    borderRadius: 3,
    height: 340,
    margin: 5,
    width: 240,
  }
});
```

9. By now, we should see small boxes vertically aligned. That's some progress, but we need to add more styles to the image so we can see it onscreen. Let's add an `image` property to the same `styles` const from the last step. The `resizeMode` property will allow us to set how we want to resize the image. In this case, by selecting `cover`, the image will keep the aspect ratio of the original:

```
image: {
  backgroundColor: '#ccc',
  height: 120,
  resizeMode: 'cover',
}
```

10. For the `content` of the post, we want to take up all of the available height on the card, therefore we need to make it flexible and add some padding. We'll also add `overflow: hidden` to the content to avoid overflowing the `View` element. For the `title`, we only need to change the `fontSize` and add a `margin` to the bottom:

```
content: {
  padding: 10,
  overflow: 'hidden',
  flex: 1,
},
title: {
  fontSize: 18,
  marginBottom: 5,
},
```

11. Finally, for the button, we will set the `backgroundColor` to green and the text to white. We also need to add some `padding` and `margin` for spacing:

```
button: {
  backgroundColor: '#1abc9c',
  borderRadius: 3,
  padding: 10,
  margin: 10,
},
buttonText: {
  color: '#fff',
  textAlign: 'center',
}
```

12. If we refresh the simulator, we should see our posts in small cards. Currently, the cards are arranged vertically, but we want to render all of them horizontally. We are going to fix that in the following steps:

Primary styles have been added for all post elements

13. Currently, we can only see the first three items on the list in a column instead of in a row across the screen. Let's return to the App.js file and start adding our styles. We add `flex: 1` to the `container` so that our layout will always fill the screen. We also want to show a toolbar at the top. For that, we just need to define some `padding` and `color` as follows:

```
const styles = StyleSheet.create({
  container: {
    flex: 1,
  },
  toolbar: {
    backgroundColor: '#34495e',
    padding: 10,
    paddingTop: 20,
  },
  title: {
    color: '#fff',
    fontSize: 20,
    textAlign: 'center',
  }
});
```

14. Let's add some basic styles to the `list` as well. Just a nice background color and some padding. We'll also add the `flex` property, which will ensure the list takes all the available height on the screen. We only have two components here: the toolbar and the list. The toolbar is taking about 50 px. If we make the list flexible, it will take all of the remaining available space, which is exactly what we want when rotating the device or when running the app in different screen resolutions:

```
list: {
    backgroundColor: '#f0f3f4',
    flex: 1,
    paddingTop: 5,
    paddingBottom: 5,
}
```

15. If we check the app in the simulator once more, we should be able to see the toolbar and list being laid out as expected:

Styles have been applied to each post to give them a card like appearance

16. We are almost done with this app. All we have left to do is to arrange the cards horizontally. This can be achieved with flexbox in three simple steps:

```
content: {
    flexDirection: 'row',
    flexWrap: 'wrap',
    justifyContent: 'space-around',
},
```

The first step is applying these `content` styles via the `contentContainerStyle` property in the `ListView` component. Internally, the `ListView` component will apply these styles to the content container, which wraps all of the child views. We then set the `flexDirection` to row. This will horizontally align the cards on the list; however, this presents a new problem: we can only see one single row of posts. To fix the problem, we need to wrap the items. We do this by setting the `flexWrap` property to `wrap`, which will automatically move the items that don't fit in the view to the next row. Lastly, we use the `justifyContent` property and set it to `center`, which will center our `ListView` in the middle of our app.

17. We now have a responsive app that looks good on a tablet in landscape mode:

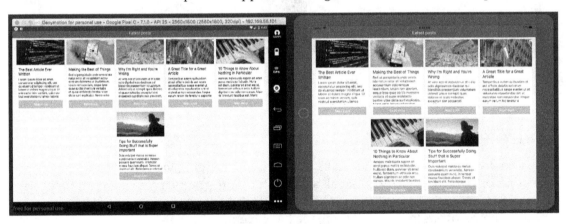

Side-by-side comparison of iPad and Android tablet screenshots in landscape mode

And looks just as good in portrait mode:

Side-by-side comparison of iPad and Android tablet screenshots in portrait mode

There's more...

Expo also provides a `ScreenOrientation` helper for changing the orientation configuration of the app. This helper also allows for more granular orientation settings (such as `ALL_BUT_UPSIDE_DOWN` or `LANDSCAPE_RIGHT`). If your app needs dynamic, granular control over screen orientation, see the `ScreenOrientation` Expo documentation for information: `https://docs.expo.io/versions/v24.0.0/sdk/screen-orientation.html`.

See also

Official documentation on static image resources and the `<Image>` component can be found at `https://facebook.github.io/react-native/docs/images.html`.

Including custom fonts

At some point, we are probably going to want to display text with a custom font family. Until now, we've been using the default font, but we can use any other that we like.

Before Expo, the process of adding custom fonts was more difficult, required working with native code, and needed to be implemented differently in iOS and Android. Luckily, through the use of Expo's font helper library, this has become streamlined and simplified.

In this recipe, we will import a few fonts and then display text using each of the imported font families. We will also use different font styles, such as **bold** and *italic*.

Getting ready

In order to work on this example we need some fonts. You can use whatever fonts you want. I recommend going to Google Fonts (`https://fonts.google.com/`) and downloading your favorites. For this recipe, we will be using the Josefin Sans and Raleway fonts.

Once you have the fonts downloaded, let's create an empty app and name it `custom-fonts`. When we create a blank app with Expo, it creates an `assets` folder in the root of the project for placing all of your assets (images, fonts, and so on), so we'll follow the standard and add our fonts to this folder. Let's create the `/assets/fonts` folder and add our custom font files downloaded from Google Fonts.

When downloading fonts from Google Fonts, you'll get a `.zip` file containing a `.ttf` file for each of the font family variants. We will be using the regular, **bold**, and *italic* variations, so copy the corresponding `.ttf` files for each variant in each family to our `/assets/fonts` folder.

How to do it...

1. With our font files in place, the first step is to open `App.js` and add the imports we'll need:

```
import React from 'react';
import { Text, View, StyleSheet } from 'react-native';
import { Font } from 'expo';
```

2. Next, we'll add a simple component for displaying some text that we want to style with our custom fonts. We'll start with just one `Text` element to display the regular variant of the Roboto font:

```
export default class App extends React.Component {
  render() {
    return (
      <View style={styles.container}>
        <Text style={styles.josefinSans}>
          Hello, Josefin Sans!
        </Text>
      </View>
    );
  }
}
```

3. Let's also add some starter styles for the component we've just created. For now, we'll just increase the font size for our `josefinSans` class styles:

```
const styles = StyleSheet.create({
  container: {
    flex: 1,
    backgroundColor: '#fff',
    alignItems: 'center',
    justifyContent: 'center',
  },
  josefinSans: {
    fontSize: 40,
  }
});
```

4. If we open the app now in our simulator, we will see the **Hello, Josefin Sans!** text displayed in the middle of the screen using the default font:

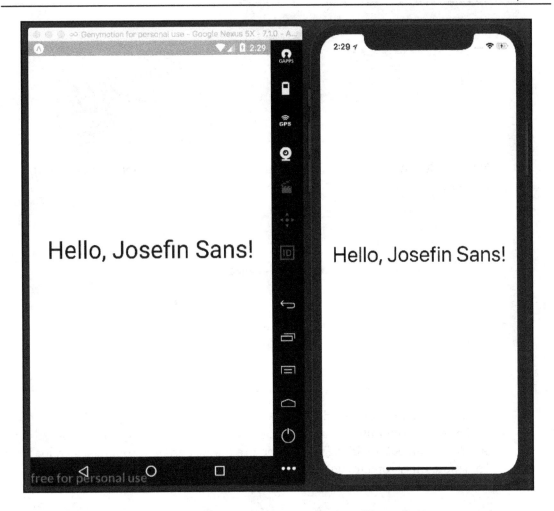

5. Let's load our `JosefinSans-Regular.ttf` font file so that we can style our text with it. We'll use the `componentDidMount` life cycle hook provided by React Native to tell our app when to start loading the font:

```
export default class App extends React.Component {

  componentDidMount() {
    Font.loadAsync({
      'josefin-sans-regular': require('./assets/fonts/JosefinSans-
Regular.ttf'),
    });
  }

  render() {
```

```
      return (
        <View style={styles.container}>
          <Text style={styles.josefinSans}>
            Hello, Josefin Sans!
          </Text>
        </View>
      );
    }
  }
```

6. Next, we'll add the font we're loading to the styles being applied to our `Text` element:

```
const styles = StyleSheet.create({
  // Other styles from step 3
  josefinSans: {
    fontSize: 40,
    fontFamily: 'josefin-sans-regular'
  }
});
```

7. We now have styles, right? Well, not quite. If we look back at our simulators, we'll see that we're getting an error instead:

```
console.error: "fontFamily 'josefin-sans-regular' is not a system
font and has not been loaded through Expo.Font.loadAsync"
```

8. But we did just load fonts via `Expo.Font.loadAsync`! What gives? It turns out we have a race condition on our hands. The `josefinSans` styles we defined for our `Text` element are being applied before the Josefin Sans font has been loaded. To handle this problem, will need to use the component's `state` to keep track of the load status of the font:

```
export default class App extends React.Component {
  state = {
    fontLoaded: false
  };
```

9. Now that our component has a `state`, we can update the state's `fontLoaded` property to `true` once the font is loaded. Using the ES6 feature `async/await` makes this succinct and straightforward. Let's do this in our `componentDidMount` code block:

```
async componentDidMount() {
  await Font.loadAsync({
    'josefin-sans-regular': require('./assets/fonts/JosefinSans-
    Regular.ttf'),
  });
}
```

10. Since we are now awaiting the `Font.loadAsync()` call, we can set the state of `fontLoaded` to `true` once the call is complete:

```
async componentDidMount() {
  await Font.loadAsync({
    'josefin-sans-regular': require('./assets/fonts/JosefinSans-
    Regular.ttf'),
  });

  this.setState({ fontLoaded: true });
}
```

11. All that's left to do is to update our `render` method to only render the `Text` element that depends on the custom font when the `fontLoaded` state property is `true`:

```
<View style={styles.container}>
  {
    this.state.fontLoaded ? (
      <Text style={styles.josefinSans}>
        Hello, Josefin Sans!
      </Text>
    ) : null
  }
</View>
```

12. Now, when we check out our app in the simulators, we should see our custom font being applied:

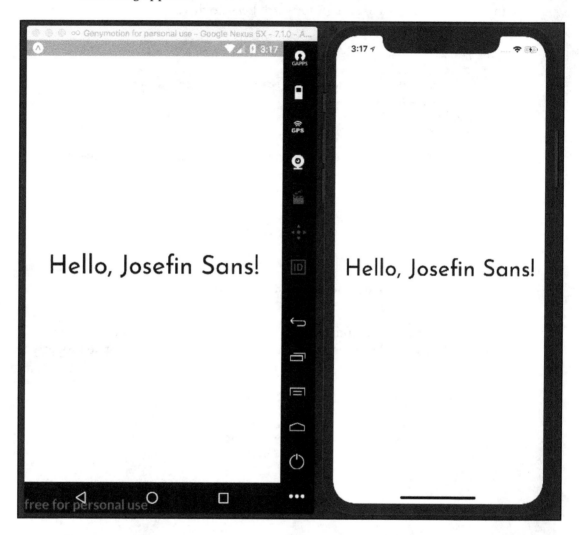

13. Let's load the rest of our fonts so that we can use them in our app as well:

```
await Font.loadAsync({
    'josefin-sans-regular': require('./assets/fonts/JosefinSans-
    Regular.ttf'),
    'josefin-sans-bold': require('./assets/fonts/JosefinSans-
    Bold.ttf'),
    'josefin-sans-italic': require('./assets/fonts/JosefinSans-
```

```
    Italic.ttf'),
    'raleway-regular': require('./assets/fonts/Raleway-
    Regular.ttf'),
    'raleway-bold': require('./assets/fonts/Raleway-Bold.ttf'),
    'raleway-italic': require('./assets/fonts/Raleway-
    Italic.ttf'),
  });
```

14. We'll also need `Text` elements for displaying text in each of our new font families/variants. Note that we'll also need to wrap all our `Text` elements in another `View` element, since JSX expressions require that there be only one parent node. We're also now passing the `style` property an array of styles to apply in order to consolidate the `fontSize` and `padding` styles we'll be applying in the next step:

```
    render() {
      return (
        <View style={styles.container}>
          {
            this.state.fontLoaded ? (
              <View style={styles.container}>
                <Text style={[styles.josefinSans,
                styles.textFormatting]}>
                  Hello, Josefin Sans!
                </Text>
                <Text style={[styles.josefinSansBold,
                styles.textFormatting]}>
                  Hello, Josefin Sans!
                </Text>
                <Text style={[styles.josefinSansItalic,
                styles.textFormatting]}>
                  Hello, Josefin Sans!
                </Text>
                <Text style={[styles.raleway,
    styles.textFormatting]}>
                  Hello, Raleway!
                </Text>
                <Text style={[styles.ralewayBold,
                styles.textFormatting]}>
                  Hello, Raleway!
                </Text>
                <Text style={[styles.ralewayItalic,
                styles.textFormatting]}>
                  Hello, Raleway!
                </Text>
              </View>
            ) : null
```

```
        }
      </View>
    );
  }
```

15. All that's left to apply our custom fonts is to add the new styles to the
    `StyleSheet`:

```
const styles = StyleSheet.create({
  container: {
    flex: 1,
    backgroundColor: '#fff',
    alignItems: 'center',
    justifyContent: 'center',
  },
  josefinSans: {
    fontFamily: 'josefin-sans-regular',
  },
  josefinSansBold: {
    fontFamily: 'josefin-sans-bold',
  },
  josefinSansItalic: {
    fontFamily: 'josefin-sans-italic',
  },
  raleway: {
    fontFamily: 'raleway-regular',
  },
  ralewayBold: {
    fontFamily: 'josefin-sans-bold'
  },
  ralewayItalic: {
    fontFamily: 'josefin-sans-italic',
  },
  textFormatting: {
    fontSize: 40,
    paddingBottom: 20
  }
});
```

16. Now, in our app, we'll see six different text elements, each styled with its own
    custom font:

How it works...

In *step 5* and *step 6*, we used the `componentDidMount` React life cycle hook to tell when our app finishes loading. While it may seem tempting to use `componentWillMount`, this too will throw an error, since `componentWillMount` is not guaranteed to wait for our `Font.loadAsync` to finish. By using `componentDidMount`, we can also assure we are not blocking the initial rendering of the app.

In *step 9*, we used the ES6 feature `async/await`. You're likely familiar with this pattern if you're a web developer, but if you'd like more information, I've included an awesome article from `ponyfoo.com` in the *See also* section at the end of this recipe, which does a great job of explaining how `async/await` works.

In *step 11*, we used a ternary statement to render either our custom font styled `Text` element if loaded, or to render nothing if it's not loaded by returning `null`.

 Fonts loaded through Expo don't currently support the `fontWeight` or `fontStyle` properties—you will need to load those variations of the font and specify them by name, as we have done here with bold and italic.

See also

A great article on `async/await` can be found at `https://ponyfoo.com/articles/understanding-javascript-async-await`.

Using font icons

Icons are an indispensable part of almost any app, particularly in navigation and buttons. Similar to Expo's font helper, covered in the previous chapter, Expo also has an icon helper that makes adding icon fonts much less of a hassle than using vanilla React Native. In this recipe, we'll see how to use the icon helper module with the popular `FontAwesome` and `Ionicons` icon font libraries.

Getting ready

We'll need to make a new project for this recipe. Let's name this project `font-icons`.

How to do it...

1. We'll begin by opening `App.js` and importing the dependencies that we need to build the app:

```
import React from 'react';
import { StyleSheet, Text, View } from 'react-native';
import { FontAwesome, Ionicons } from '@expo/vector-icons';
```

2. Next, we can add the shell of the application, where we will display the icons:

```
export default class App extends React.Component {
  render() {
    return (
      <View style={styles.container}>
      </View>
    );
  }
}
```

3. Inside of the `View` element, let's add two more `View` elements for holding icons from each icon set:

```
export default class App extends React.Component {
  render() {
    return (
      <View style={styles.container}>
        <View style={styles.iconRow}>

        </View>
        <View style={styles.iconRow}>

        </View>
      </View>
    );
  }
}
```

4. Now, let's add the styles for each of our declared elements. As we've seen in previous recipes, the `container` styles fill the screen with `flex: 1` and center the items with `alignItems` and `justifyContent` set to `center`. The `iconRow` property sets the `flexDirection` to `row` so that our icons will be lined up in a row:

```
const styles = StyleSheet.create({
  container: {
    flex: 1,
    backgroundColor: '#fff',
    alignItems: 'center',
    justifyContent: 'center',
  },
  iconRow: {
    flexDirection: 'row',
  },
});
```

5. Now that the basic structure of our app is in place, let's add our icons. In the first row of icons, we'll use four `FontAwesome` components to display four icons from the `FontAwesome` font library. The `name` property determines which icon should be used, the `size` property sets the size of the icon in pixels, and the `color` sets what color the icon should be:

```
<View style={styles.iconRow}>
  <FontAwesome style={styles.iconPadding} name="glass" size={48}
color="green" />
  <FontAwesome style={styles.iconPadding} name="beer" size={48}
color="red" />
  <FontAwesome style={styles.iconPadding} name="music" size={48}
color="blue" />
  <FontAwesome style={styles.iconPadding} name="taxi" size={48}
color="#1CB5AD" />
</View>
```

Just as in CSS, the `color` property can be a color keyword defined in the CSS specification (you can check out the full list in the MDN docs at `https://developer.mozilla.org/en-US/docs/Web/CSS/color_value`), or a hex code for a given color.

6. In the next `View` element, we'll add icons from the `Ionicons` font library. As you can see, the `Ionicons` element takes the same properties as the `FontAwesome` elements used in the previous step:

```
<View style={styles.iconRow}>
  <Ionicons style={styles.iconPadding} name="md-pizza" size={48}
color="orange" />
  <Ionicons style={styles.iconPadding} name="md-tennisball"
size={48} color="maroon" />
  <Ionicons style={styles.iconPadding} name="ios-thunderstorm"
size={48} color="purple" />
  <Ionicons style={styles.iconPadding} name="ios-happy" size={48}
color="#DF7977" />
</View>
```

7. The last step in this recipe is to add the remaining style, `iconPadding`, which just adds some padding to evenly space out each of our icons:

```
const styles = StyleSheet.create({
  container: {
    flex: 1,
    backgroundColor: '#fff',
    alignItems: 'center',
    justifyContent: 'center',
  },
  iconRow: {
    flexDirection: 'row',
  },
  iconPadding: {
    padding: 8,
  }
});
```

8. That's all it takes! When we check out our app, there will be two rows of icons, each row showcasing icons from FontAwesome and Ionicons respectively:

How it works...

The `vector-icons` package that comes with Expo provides access to 11 full icon sets. All you have to do is import the associated component (for example, the `FontAwesome` component for Font Awesome icons) and provide it with the name that corresponds to the icon in the set that you'd like to use. You can find a full, searchable list of all the icons you can use with the `vector-icons` helper library in the `vector-icons` directory, hosted at `https://expo.github.io/vector-icons/`. Simply set the element's `name` property to the icon name listed in the directory, add `size` and `color` properties, and you're done!

As the GitHub README for `vector-icons` states, this library is a compatibility layer created for using the icons provided by the `react-native-vector-icons` package in Expo. You can find this package at `https://github.com/oblador/react-native-vector-icons`. If you are building a React Native app without Expo, you can get the same functionality by using the `react-native-vector-icons` library instead.

See also

A catalog of all of the icons available in the `vector-icons` library can be found at `https://expo.github.io/vector-icons/`.

4
Implementing Complex User Interfaces - Part II

This chapter will cover more recipes on building UIs with React Native. We'll get our first look at linking to other applications and websites, handling a change in device orientation, and how to build a form for collecting user input.

In this chapter, we will cover the following recipes:

- Dealing with universal applications
- Detecting orientation changes
- Using a WebView to embed external websites
- Linking to websites and other applications
- Creating a form component

Dealing with universal applications

One of the benefits of using React Native is its ability to easily create universal applications. We can share a lot of code between phone and tablet applications. The layouts might change, depending on the device, but we can reuse pieces of code for both types of device across layouts.

In this recipe, we will build an app that runs on phones and tablets. The tablet version will include a different layout, but we will reuse the same internal components.

Getting ready

For this recipe, we will show a list of contacts. For now, we will load the data from a `.json` file. We will explore how to load remote data from a **Representational State Transfer (REST)** API in a later chapter.

Let's open the following URL and copy the generated JSON to a file called `data.json` at the root of the project. We will use this data to render the list of contacts. It returns a JSON object of fake user data at `http://api.randomuser.me/?results=20`.

Let's create a new app called `universal-app`.

How to do it...

1. Let's open `App.js` and import the dependencies we'll need in this app, as well as our `data.json` file we created in the previous *Getting ready* section. We'll also import a `Device` utility from `./utils/Device`, which we will build in a later step:

```
import React, { Component } from 'react';
import { StyleSheet, View, Text } from 'react-native';
import Device from './utils/Device';

import data from './data.json';
```

2. Here, we're going to create the main `App` component and its basic layout. This top-level component will decide whether to render the phone or tablet UI. We are only rendering two `Text` elements. The `renderDetail` text should be displayed on tablets only and the `renderMaster` text should be displayed on phones and tablets:

```
export default class App extends Component {
  renderMaster() {
    return (
      <Text>Render on phone and tablets!!</Text>
    );
  }

  renderDetail() {
    if (Device.isTablet()) {
      return (
        <Text>Render on tablets only!!</Text>
      );
```

```
      }
    }

    render() {
      return (
        <View style={styles.content}>
          {this.renderMaster()}
          {this.renderDetail()}
        </View>
      );
    }
  }
```

3. Under the `App` component, we'll add a few basic styles. The styles temporarily include `paddingTop:  40` so that our rendered text is not overlapped by the device's system bar:

```
const styles = StyleSheet.create({
  content: {
    paddingTop: 40,
    flex: 1,
    flexDirection: 'row',
  },
});
```

4. If we try to run our app as it is, it will fail with an error telling us that the `Device` module cannot be found, so let's create it. The purpose of this utility class is to calculate whether the current device is a phone or tablet, based on the screen dimensions. It will have an `isTablet` method and an `isPhone` method. We need to create a `utils` folder in the root of the project and add a `Device.js` for the utility. Now we can add the basic structure of the utility:

```
import { Dimensions, Alert } from 'react-native';

// Tablet portrait dimensions
const tablet = {
  width: 552,
  height: 960,
};

class Device {
  // Added in next steps
}

const device = new Device();
export default device;
```

5. Let's start building out the utility by creating two methods: one to get the dimensions in portrait and the other to get the dimensions in landscape. Depending on the device rotation, the values of width and height will change, which is why we need these two methods to always get the correct values, whether the device is landscape or portrait:

```
class Device {
  getPortraitDimensions() {
    const { width, height } = Dimensions.get("window");

    return {
      width: Math.min(width, height),
      height: Math.max(width, height),
    };
  }

  getLandscapeDimensions() {
    const { width, height } = Dimensions.get("window");

    return {
      width: Math.max(width, height),
      height: Math.min(width, height),
    };
  }
}
```

6. Now let's create the two methods our app will use to determine whether the app is running on a tablet or a phone. To calculate this, we need to get the dimensions in portrait mode and compare them with the dimensions we have defined for a tablet:

```
isPhone() {
  const dimension = this.getPortraitDimensions();
  return dimension.height < tablet.height;
}

isTablet() {
  const dimension = this.getPortraitDimensions();
  return dimension.height >= tablet.height;
}
```

7. Now, if we open the app, we should see two different texts being rendered, depending on whether we're running the app on a phone or a tablet:

8. The utility works as expected! Let's return to working on the `renderMaster` method of the main `App.js`. We want this method to render the list of contacts that live in the `data.json` file. Let's import a new component, which we'll build out in the following steps, and update the `renderMaster` method to use our new component:

```
import UserList from './UserList';

export default class App extends Component {
  renderMaster() {
    return (
      <UserList contacts={data.results} />
    );
  }
```

```
      //...
    }
```

9. Let's create a new `UserList` folder. Inside this folder, we need to create the `index.js` and `styles.js` files for the new component. The first thing we need to do is import the dependencies into the new `index.js`, create the `UserList` class, and export it as the `default`:

```
import React, { Component } from 'react';
import {
  StyleSheet,
  View,
  Text,
  ListView,
  Image,
  TouchableOpacity,
} from 'react-native';
import styles from './styles';

export default class UserList extends Component {
  // Defined in the following steps
}
```

10. We've already covered how to create a list. If you are not clear on how the `ListView` component works, read the *Displaying a list of items* recipe in `Chapter 2, Creating a Simple React Native App*. In the constructor of the class, we will create the `dataSource` and then add it to the `state`:

```
export default class UserList extends Component {
  constructor(properties) {
    super(properties);
    const dataSource = new ListView.DataSource({
      rowHasChanged: (r1, r2) => r1 !== r2
    });

    this.state = {
      dataSource: dataSource.cloneWithRows(properties.contacts),
    };
  }
  //...
}
```

11. The `render` method also follows the same pattern introduced in the `ListView` recipe, *Displaying a list of items*, from `Chapter 2`, *Creating a Simple React Native App*:

```
render() {
 return (
  <View style={styles.main}>
   <Text style={styles.toolbar}>
   My contacts!
   </Text>
   <ListView dataSource={this.state.dataSource}
    renderRow={this.renderContact}
    style={styles.main} />
  </View> );
 }
```

12. As you can see, we need to define the `renderContact` method to render each of the rows. We are using the `TouchableOpacity` component as the main wrapper, which will allow us to use a callback function to perform some actions when a list item is pressed. For now, we are not doing anything when the button is pressed. We will learn more about communicating between components using Redux in `Chapter 9`, *Implementing Redux*:

```
renderContact = (contact) => {
  return (
    <TouchableOpacity style={styles.row}>
      <Image source={{uri: `${contact.picture.large}`}} style=
      {styles.img} />
      <View style={styles.info}>
        <Text style={styles.name}>
          {this.capitalize(contact.name.first)}
          {this.capitalize(contact.name.last)}
        </Text>
        <Text style={styles.phone}>{contact.phone}</Text>
      </View>
    </TouchableOpacity>
  );
}
```

13. We don't have a way to capitalize the texts using styles, so we need to use JavaScript for that. The `capitalize` function is quite simple, and sets the first letter of the given string to uppercase:

```
capitalize(value) {
  return value[0].toUpperCase() + value.substring(1);
}
```

14. We are almost done with this component. All that's left are the `styles`. Let's open the `/UserList/styles.js` file and add styles for the main container and the toolbar:

```
import { StyleSheet } from 'react-native';

export default StyleSheet.create({
  main: {
    flex: 1,
    backgroundColor: '#dde6e9',
  },
  toolbar: {
    backgroundColor: '#2989dd',
    color: '#fff',
    paddingTop: 50,
    padding: 20,
    textAlign: 'center',
    fontSize: 20,
  },
  // Remaining styles added in next step.
});
```

15. Now, for each row, we want to render the image of each contact on the left, and the contact's name and phone number on the right:

```
row: {
  flexDirection: 'row',
  padding: 10,
},
img: {
  width: 70,
  height: 70,
  borderRadius: 35,
},
info: {
  marginLeft: 10,
},
name: {
  color: '#333',
  fontSize: 22,
  fontWeight: 'bold',
},
phone: {
  color: '#aaa',
  fontSize: 16,
},
```

16. Let's switch over to the `App.js` file and remove the `paddingTop` property we used for making text legible in *step 7*; the line to be removed is shown in bold:

```
const styles = StyleSheet.create({
  content: {
    paddingTop: 40,
    flex: 1,
    flexDirection: 'row',
  },
});
```

17. If we try to run our app, we should be able to see a really nice list on the phone as well as the tablet, and the same component on the two different devices:

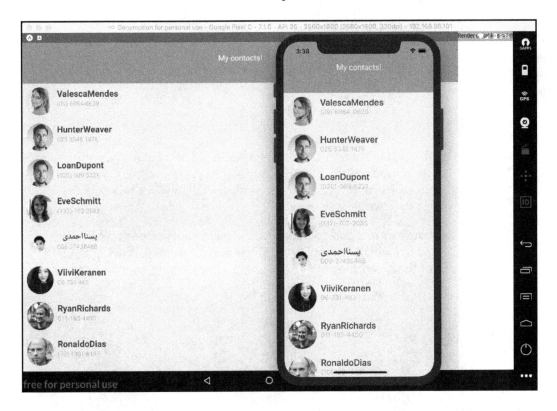

18. We are already displaying two different layouts based on the current device! Now we need to work on the `UserDetail` view, which will show the selected contact. Let's open `App.js`, import the `UserDetail` views, and update the `renderDetail` method, as follows:

```
import UserDetail from './UserDetail';

export default class App extends Component {
  renderMaster() {
    return (
      <UserList contacts={data.results} />
    );
  }

  renderDetail() {
    if (Device.isTablet()) {
      return (
        <UserDetail contact={data.results[0]} />
      );
    }
  }
}
```

 As mentioned earlier, in this recipe, we are not focusing on sending data from one component to another, but instead on rendering a different layout in tablets and phones. Therefore, we will always send the first record to the user details view for this recipe.

19. To make things simple and to make the recipe as short as possible, for the user details view, we will only display a toolbar and some text showing the first and last name of the given record. We are going to use a stateless component here:

```
import React from 'react';
import {
  View,
  Text,
} from 'react-native';
import styles from './styles';

const UserList = ({ contact }) => (
  <View style={styles.main}>
    <Text style={styles.toolbar}>Details should go here!</Text>
    <Text>
      This is the detail view:{contact.name.first}
{contact.name.last}
    </Text>
  </View>
```

```
);

export default UserList;
```

20. Finally, we need to style this component. We want to assign three-quarters of the screen to the details page and one-quarter to the master list. This can be done easily by using flexbox. Since the `UserList` component has a `flex` property of `1`, we can set the `flex` property of `UserDetail` to 3, allowing `UserDetail` to take up 75% of the screen. Here are the styles we'll add to the `/UserDetail/styles.js` file:

```
import { StyleSheet } from 'react-native';

const styles = StyleSheet.create({
  main: {
    flex: 3,
    backgroundColor: '#f0f3f4',
  },
  toolbar: {
    backgroundColor: '#2989dd',
    color: '#fff',
    paddingTop: 50,
    padding: 20,
    textAlign: 'center',
    fontSize: 20,
  },
});

export default styles;
```

21. If we try to run our app again, we will see that on the tablet, it will render a nice layout showing both the list view and the detail view, while on the phone it only shows the list of contacts:

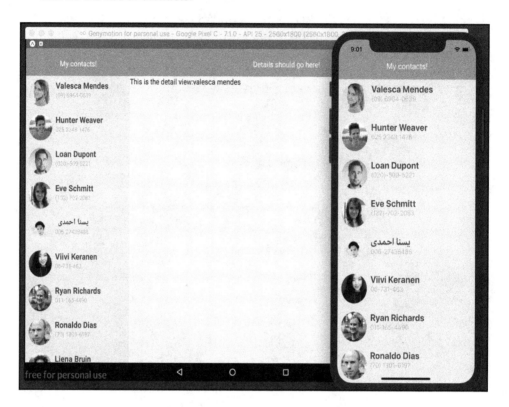

How it works...

In the `Device` utility, we imported a dependency that React Native provides called `Dimension` for getting the dimensions of the current device. We also defined a `tablet` constant in the `Device` utility, which is an object containing the `width` and `height` that is used with `Dimension` to calculate whether the device is a tablet or not. The values of this constant are based on the smallest Android tablet available on the market.

In *step 5*, we got the width and height by calling the `Dimensions.get("window")` method, and then we got the maximum and minimum values depending on the orientation we wanted.

In *step 12*, it's important to note that we used an arrow function to define the `renderContact` method. Using an arrow function keeps the correct binding scope, otherwise, the `this` in the call to `this.capitalize` would be bound to the wrong scope. Check the *See also* section for more information on how both the `this` keyword and arrow functions work.

See also

- A good explanation of ES6 arrow functions from ponyfoo at `https://ponyfoo.com/articles/es6-arrow-functions-in-depth`
- An in-depth look at how `this` works in JavaScript by Kyle Simpson at `https://github.com/getify/You-Dont-Know-JS/blob/master/this%20%26%20object%20prototypes/ch2.md`

Detecting orientation changes

When building complex interfaces, it's very common to render different UI components, based on the device's orientation. This is especially true when dealing with tablets.

In this recipe, we will render a menu based on screen orientation. In landscape, we will render an expanded menu with icons and texts, and in portrait, we will only render the icons.

Getting ready

To support orientation changes, we are going to use Expo's helper utility called `ScreenOrientation`.

We will also use the `FontAwesome` component provided by the Expo package `@expo/vector-icons`. The *Using font icons* recipe in `Chapter 2`, *Creating a Simple React Native App*, describes how to use this component.

Before we get started, let's create a new app called `screen-orientation`. We'll also need to make a tweak to the `app.json` file that Expo creates in the root of the directory. This file has a few basic settings Expo uses when building the app. One of these settings is `orientation`, which is automatically set to `portrait` for every new app. This setting determines the orientations the app allows, and can be set to `portrait`, `landscape`, or `default`. If we change this to `default`, our app will allow both portrait and landscape orientations.

To see these changes take effect, be sure to restart your Expo project.

How to do it...

1. We'll start by opening `App.js` and adding the imports we'll be using:

```
import React from 'react';
import {
  Dimensions,
  StyleSheet,
  Text,
  View
} from 'react-native';
```

2. Next, we'll add the empty `App` class for the component, along with some basic styles:

```
export default class App extends React.Component {

}

const styles = StyleSheet.create({
  container: {
    flex: 1,
    justifyContent: 'center',
    alignItems: 'center',
    backgroundColor: '#fff'
  },
  text: {
    fontSize: 40,
  }
});
```

3. With the shell of our app in place, we can now add the render method. In the render method, you'll notice we've got a View component using the onLayout property, which will fire off whenever the orientation of the device changes. The onLayout will then run this.handleLayoutChange, which we will define in the next step. In the Text element, we simply display the value of orientation on the state object:

```
export default class App extends React.Component {
  render() {
    return (
      <View
        onLayout={() => this.handleLayoutChange}
        style={styles.container}
      >
        <Text style={styles.text}>
          {this.state.orientation}
        </Text>
      </View>
    );
  }
}
```

4. Let's create the handleLayoutChange method of our component, as well as the getOrientation function that the handleLayoutChange method calls. The getOrientation function uses the React Native Dimensions utility to get the width and height of the screen. If $height > width$, we know that the device is in portrait orientation, and if not, then it is in landscape orientation. By updating state, a re-render will be initiated, and the value of this.state.orientation will reflect the orientation:

```
handleLayoutChange() {
  this.getOrientation();
}

getOrientation() {
  const { width, height } = Dimensions.get('window');
  const orientation = height > width ? 'Portrait' : 'Landscape';
  this.setState({
    orientation
  });
}
```

5. If we run the app at this point, we'll get the error **TypeError: null is not an object: (evaluating 'this.state.orientation')**. This happens because the `render` method is attempting to read from the `this.state.orientation` value before it's even been defined. We can easily fix this problem by getting the orientation before `render` runs for the first time, via the React life cycle `componentWillMount` hook:

```
componentWillMount() {
  this.getOrientation();
}
```

6. That's all it takes to get the basic functionality we're looking for! Run the app again and you should see the displayed text reflect the orientation of the device. Rotate the device, and the orientation text should update:

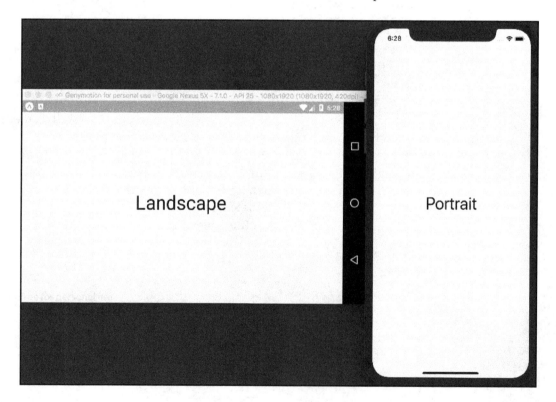

7. Now that the orientation `state` value is updating properly, we can focus on the UI. As mentioned before, we will create a menu that renders the options slightly differently based on the current orientation. Let's import a `Menu` component, which we'll build out in the next steps, and update the `render` method of our `App` component to use the new `Menu` component. Notice that we are now passing `this.state.orientation` to the `orientation` property of the `Menu` component:

```
import Menu from './Menu';

export default class App extends React.Component {

    // ...

    render() {
        return (
            <View
                onLayout={() => {this.handleLayoutChange()}}
                style={styles.container}
            >
                <Menu orientation={this.state.orientation} />
                <View style={styles.main}>
                    <Text>Main Content</Text>
                </View>
            </View>
        );
    }
}
```

8. Let's also update the styles for our `App` component. You can replace the styles from *step 2* with the following code. By setting the `flexDirection` to `row` on the `container` styles, we'll be able to display the two components horizontally:

```
const styles = StyleSheet.create({
    container: {
        flex: 1,
        flexDirection: 'row',
    },
    main: {
        flex: 1,
        backgroundColor: '#ecf0f1',
        justifyContent: 'center',
        alignItems: 'center',
    }
});
```

9. Next, let's build out the `Menu` component. We'll need to create a new `/Menu/index.js` file, which will define the `Menu` class. This component will receive the `orientation` property and decide how to render the menu options based on the `orientation` value. Let's start by importing the dependencies for this class:

```
import React, { Component } from 'react';
import { StyleSheet, View, Text } from 'react-native';
import { FontAwesome } from '@expo/vector-icons';
```

10. Now we can define the `Menu` class. On the `state` object, we will define an array of `options`. These `option` objects will be used to define the icons. As discussed in the *Using font icons* recipe in the previous chapter we can define icons via keywords, as defined in the vector-icon directory, found at `https://expo.github.io/vector-icons/`:

```
export default class Menu extends Component {
  state = {
    options: [
      {title: 'Dashboard', icon: 'dashboard'},
      {title: 'Inbox', icon: 'inbox'},
      {title: 'Graphs', icon: 'pie-chart'},
      {title: 'Search', icon: 'search'},
      {title: 'Settings', icon: 'gear'},
    ],
  };

  // Remainder defined in following steps
}
```

11. The `render` method for this component loops through the array of `options` in the `state` object:

```
render() {
  return (
    <View style={styles.content}>
      {this.state.options.map(this.renderOption)}
    </View>
  );
}
```

12. As you can see, inside the JSX in the last step, there's a call to `renderOption`. In this method, we are going to render the icon and the label for each option. We'll also use the orientation value to toggle showing the label, and to change the icon's size:

```
renderOption = (option, index) => {
    const isLandscape = this.properties.orientation ===
'Landscape';
    const title = isLandscape
        ? <Text style={styles.title}>{option.title}</Text>
        : null;
    const iconSize = isLandscape ? 27 : 35;

    return (
        <View key={index} style={[styles.option, styles.landscape]}>
            <FontAwesome name={option.icon} size={iconSize}
color="#fff" />
            {title}
        </View>
    );
}
```

In the previous code block, notice that we are defining a `key` property. When dynamically creating a new component, we always need to set a `key` property. This property should be unique for each item, since it's used internally by React. In this case, we are using the index of the loop iteration. This way, we can be assured that every item will have a unique `key` value since the data is static. You can read more about it in the official documentation at `https://reactjs.org/docs/lists-and-keys.html`.

13. Finally, we'll define the styles for the menu. First, we will set the `backgroundColor` to dark blue, and then, for each option, we'll change the `flexDirection` to render the icon and label horizontally. The rest of the styles add margins and paddings so that the menu items are nicely spaced apart:

```
const styles = StyleSheet.create({
    content: {
        backgroundColor: '#34495e',
        paddingTop: 50,
    },
    option: {
        flexDirection: 'row',
        paddingBottom: 15,
    },
```

```
        landscape: {
          paddingRight: 30,
          paddingLeft: 30,
        },
        title: {
          color: '#fff',
          fontSize: 16,
          margin: 5,
          marginLeft: 20,
        },
    });
```

14. If we run our application now, it will display the menu UI differently depending on the orientation of the screen. Rotate the device, and the layout will automatically update:

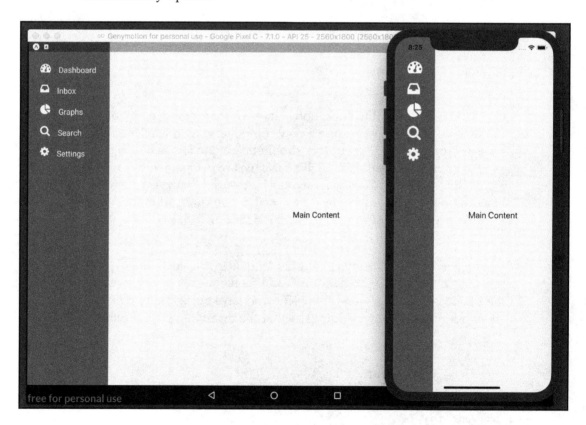

There's more...

In this recipe, we had a look at the `app.json` file that exists as part of every Expo project. There are many useful settings that can be adjusted in this file that affect the build process of the project. You can use this file to adjust orientation lock, define an app icon, and set a splash screen, among many other settings. You can review all of the settings supported by `app.json` in the Expo configuration documentation, hosted at `https://docs.expo.io/versions/latest/guides/configuration.html`.

Expo also provides the `ScreenOrientation` utility, which can be used instead to declare the allowed orientations for your app. Using the utility's main method `ScreenOrientation.allow(orientation)`, will overwrite the corresponding setting in `app.json`. The utility also provides more granular options than the setting in `app.json`, such as `ALL_BUT_UPSIDE_DOWN` and `LANDSCAPE_RIGHT`. For more on this utility, you can read the documentation at `https://docs.expo.io/versions/latest/sdk/screen-orientation.html`.

Using a WebView to embed external websites

For many applications, it's required that external links can be visited and displayed within the app. This can be for showing a third-party website, online help, and the terms and conditions of using your app, among other things.

In this recipe, we will see how to open a WebView by clicking on a button in our app and dynamically setting the URL value. We'll also be using the `react-navigation` package for creating basic stack navigation in this recipe. Please check out the *Setting up and using navigation* recipe in `Chapter 3`, *Implementing Complex User Interfaces – Part I* for a deeper dive into building navigation.

If the needs of your app are better met by loading external websites via the device's browser, see the next recipe, *Linking to websites and other applications*.

Getting ready

We will need to create a new app for our WebView-based recipe. Let's name our new app web-view. We'll also be using react-navigation, so be sure to install this as well. You can use yarn or npm to install the package. In the root of the project, run the following:

```
yarn add react-navigation
```

Alternatively, install them using npm:

```
npm install --save react-navigation
```

How to do it...

1. Let's start by opening the App.js file. In this file, we'll be using the StackNavigator component provided by the react-navigation package. First, let's add the imports we'll be using in this file. HomeScreen is a component we will be building later in this recipe:

```
import React, { Component } from 'react';
import { StackNavigator } from 'react-navigation';

import HomeScreen from './HomeScreen';
```

2. Now that we have our imports, let's use the StackNavigator component to define the first route; we'll be using a Home route with links that should be displayed using the React Native WebView component. The navigationOptions property allows us to define a title to be displayed in the navigation header:

```
const App = StackNavigator({
  Home: {
    screen: HomeScreen,
    navigationOptions: ({ navigation }) => ({
      title: 'Home'
    }),
  },
});

export default App;
```

3. We are now ready to create the `HomeScreen` component. Let's create a new folder in the root of our project, called `HomeScreen`, and add an `index.js` file to the folder. As usual, we can begin with our imports:

```
import React, { Component } from 'react';
import {
  TouchableOpacity,
  View,
  Text,
  SafeAreaView,
} from 'react-native';

import styles from './styles';
```

4. Now we can declare our `HomeScreen` component. Let's also add a `state` object to the component with a `links` array. This array has an object for each link we'll be using in this component. I've provided four `links` for you to use; however, you can edit the `title` and `url` in each `links` array object to any websites you'd like:

```
export default class HomeScreen extends Component {
  state = {
    links: [
      {
        title: 'Smashing Magazine',
        url: 'https://www.smashingmagazine.com/articles/'
      },
      {
        title: 'CSS Tricks',
        url: 'https://css-tricks.com/'
      },
      {
        title: 'Gitconnected Blog',
        url: 'https://medium.com/gitconnected'
      },
      {
        title: 'Hacker News',
        url: 'https://news.ycombinator.com/'
      }
    ],
  };
}
```

5. We're ready to add a `render` function to this component. Here, we are using the `SafeAreaView` for the container element. This works just like a normal `View` element, but also accounts for the notch area on the iPhone X so that no part of our layout is obscured by the device bezels. You'll notice that we are using `map` to map over the `links` array from the previous step, passing each one to the `renderButton` function:

```
render() {
  return (
    <SafeAreaView style={styles.container}>
      <View style={styles.buttonList}>
        {this.state.links.map(this.renderButton)}
      </View>
    </SafeAreaView>
  );
}
```

6. Now that we have defined the `render` method, we'll need to create the `renderButton` method that it's using. This method takes each link as a parameter called `button`, and the `index`, which we'll use as the unique `key` for each element `renderButton` is creating. For more on this point, see the *Tip* in *step 12* of the second recipe in this chapter, *Detecting orientation changes*. The `TouchableOpacity` button element will fire `this.handleButtonPress(button)` when pressed:

```
renderButton = (button, index) => {
  return (
    <TouchableOpacity
      key={index}
      onPress={() => this.handleButtonPress(button)}
      style={styles.button}
    >
      <Text style={styles.text}>{button.title}</Text>
    </TouchableOpacity>
  );
}
```

7. Now we need to create the `handleButtonPress` method used in the previous step. This method uses the `url` and `title` properties from the passed-in `button` parameter. We can then use these in a call to `this.properties.navigation.navigate()`, passing in the name of the route we want to navigate to and the parameters that should be passed along to that route. We have access to a `property` called `navigation` because we are using `StackNavigator`, which we set up in *step 2*:

```
handleButtonPress(button) {
    const { url, title } = button;
    this.properties.navigation.navigate('Browser', { url, title });
}
```

8. The `HomeScreen` component is done, except for the styles. Let's add a `styles.js` file in the `HomeScreen` folder to define these styles:

```
import { StyleSheet } from 'react-native';

const styles = StyleSheet.create({
  container: {
    flex: 1,
    justifyContent: 'center',
    alignItems: 'center',
  },
  buttonList: {
    flex: 1,
    justifyContent: 'center',
  },
  button: {
    margin: 10,
    backgroundColor: '#c0392b',
    borderRadius: 3,
    padding: 10,
    paddingRight: 30,
    paddingLeft: 30,
  },
  text: {
    color: '#fff',
    textAlign: 'center',
  },
});

export default styles;
```

9. Now, if we open the app, we should see the `HomeScreen` component being rendered with our list of four link buttons, and a header with the title **Home** rendered in the native style on each device. Since there is no `Browser` route in our `StackNavigator`, however, the buttons will not actually do anything when pressed:

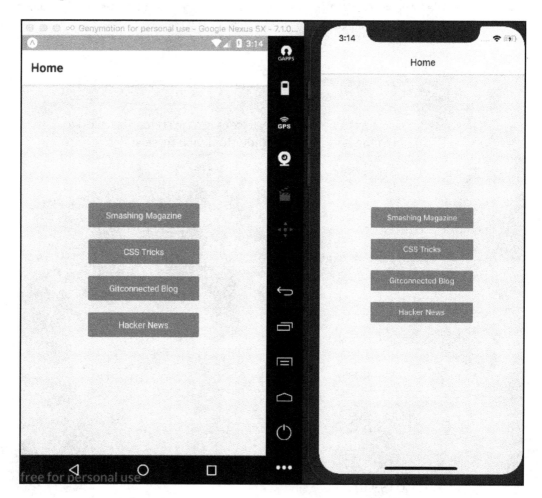

10. Let's return to the `App.js` file and add the `Browser` route. First, we'll need to import the `BrowserScreen` component, which we'll create in the following steps:

```
import BrowserScreen from './BrowserScreen';
```

11. Now that the `BrowserScreen` component has been imported, we can add it to the `StackNavigator` object to create a `Browser` route. In `navigationOptions`, we're defining a dynamic title based on the parameters passed to the route. These parameters are the same as the object we passed into the `navigation.navigate()` call as the second argument in *step 7*:

```
const App = StackNavigator({
  Home: {
    screen: HomeScreen,
    navigationOptions: ({ navigation }) => ({
      title: 'Home'
    }),
  },
  Browser: {
    screen: BrowserScreen,
    navigationOptions: ({ navigation }) => ({
      title: navigation.state.params.title
    }),
  },
});
```

12. We are ready to create the `BrowserScreen` component. Let's create a new folder in the root of the project called `BrowserScreen` with a new `index.js` file inside, then add the imports this component needs:

```
import React, { Component } from 'react';
import { WebView } from 'react-native';
```

13. The `BrowserScreen` component is fairly simple. It consists only of a render method that reads the `params` property from the `navigation.state` property passed in to call to the `this.properties.navigation.navigate` that fires when a button is pressed, as defined in *step 7*. All we need to do is render the `WebView` component and set its `source` property to an object with the `uri` property set to `params.url`:

```
export default class BrowserScreen extends Component {
  render() {
    const { params } = this.properties.navigation.state;

    return(
      <WebView
        source={{uri: params.url}}
      />
    );
  }
}
```

14. Now, if we go back to the app running in the simulator, we can see our WebView in action!

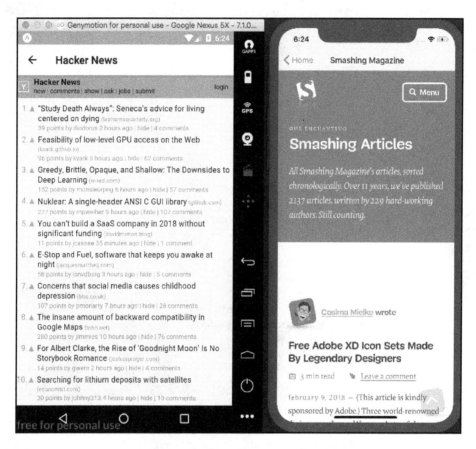

Hacker News and Smashing Magazine visited from our app

How it works...

Using a WebView to open external sites is a great way to allow a user to consume external websites while keeping them in our app. Many applications out there do this, allowing the user to return to the main portion of the app easily.

In *step 6*, we used an arrow function to bind the function in the `onPress` property to the scope of the current class instance, since we are using this function when looping through the array of links.

In *step 7*, whenever a button is pressed, we use the title and URL that are bound to that button, passing them along as parameters as we navigate to the `Browser` screen. The `navigationOptions` in *step 11* use this same title value as the title of the screen. The `navigationOptions` take a function whose first parameter is an object containing `navigation`, which provides the parameters used when navigating. In *step 11*, we structure navigation from this object so that we can set the view's title to `navigation.state.params.title`.

Thanks to the `StackNavigator` component provided by `react-navigation`, we get a header with OS-specific animations, built in with a back button. You can read the `StackNavigation` documentation for more information on this component at `https://reactnavigation.org/docs/stack-navigator.html`.

Step 13 uses the URL passed to the `BrowserScreen` component to render a WebView by using the URL in the WebView's `source` property. You can find a list of all available WebView properties in the official documentation located at `https://facebook.github.io/react-native/docs/webview.html`.

Linking to websites and other applications

We have learned how to use a WebView to render a third-party website as an embedded part of our app. However, sometimes, we might want to use the native browser to open a site, link to other native system applications (such as email, phone, and SMS), or even deep link to a completely separate app.

In this recipe, we will link to an external site via both the native browser and a browser modal within our app, create links to the phone and messaging applications, and create a deep link that will open the Slack app and automatically load the #general channel in the `gitconnected.com` Slack group.

 You will need to run this app on a real device in order to open the links in this app that use the device's system applications, such as email, phone, and SMS links. In my experience, this will not work in the simulator.

Getting ready

Let's create a new app for this recipe. We'll call it `linking-app`.

How to do it...

1. Let's start by opening `App.js` and adding the imports we'll be using:

```
import React from 'react';
import { StyleSheet, Text, View, TouchableOpacity, Platform } from
'react-native';
import { Linking } from 'react-native';
import { WebBrowser } from 'expo';
```

2. Next, let's add both an `App` component and a `state` object. In this app, the `state` object will house all of the links that we'll be using in this recipe in an array called `links`. Notice how the `url` property in each `links` object has a protocol attached to it (`tel`, `mailto`, `sms`, and so on). These protocols are used by the device to properly handle each link:

```
export default class App extends React.Component {
  state = {
    links: [
      {
        title: 'Call Support',
        url: 'tel:+12025550170',
        type: 'phone'
      },
      {
        title: 'Email Support',
        url: 'mailto:support@email.com',
        type: 'email',
      },
      {
        title: 'Text Support',
        url: 'sms:+12025550170',
        type: 'text message',
      },
      {
        title: 'Join us on Slack',
        url: 'slack://channel?team=T5KFMSASF&id=C5K142J57',
        type: 'slack deep link',
      },
      {
        title: 'Visit Site (internal)',
        url: 'https://google.com',
        type: 'internal link'
      },
      {
        title: 'Visit Site (external)',
```

```
        url: 'https://google.com',
        type: 'external link'
      }
    ]
  }
}
```

The phone number used in the **Text Support** and **Call Support** buttons is an unused number at the time of writing, as generated by `https://fakenumber.org/`. This number is likely to still be unused, but this could possibly change. Feel free to use a different fake number for these links, just make sure to keep the protocol in place.

3. Next, let's add the `render` function for our app. The JSX here is simple: we map over the `state.links` array from the previous step, passing each to our `renderButton` function defined in the next step:

```
render() {
  return(
    <View style={styles.container}>
      <View style={styles.buttonList}>
        {this.state.links.map(this.renderButton)}
      </View>
    </View>
  );
}
```

4. Let's build out the `renderButton` method used in the last step. For each link, we create a button with `TouchableOpacity` and set the `onPress` property to execute the `handleButtonPress` and pass it the `button` property:

```
renderButton = (button, index) => {
  return(
    <TouchableOpacity
      key={index}
      onPress={() => this.handleButtonPress(button)}
      style={styles.button}
    >
      <Text style={styles.text}>{button.title}</Text>
    </TouchableOpacity>
  );
}
```

5. Next, we can build out the `handleButtonPress` function. Here, we'll be using the `type` property that we've added to each object in the `links` array. If the type is `'internal link'`, we want to open the URL *within* our app using the Expo `WebBrowser` component's `openBrowserAsync` method, and for everything else, we'll use the React Native `Linking` component's `openURL` method. If there's a problem with the `openURL` call and the URL is using the `slack://` protocol, it means the device does not know how to handle the protocol, probably because the slack app isn't installed. We'll handle this problem with the `handleMissingApp` function, which we'll add in the next step:

```
handleButtonPress(button) {
  if (button.type === 'internal link') {
    WebBrowser.openBrowserAsync(button.url);
  } else {
    Linking.openURL(button.url).catch(({ message }) => {
      if (message.includes('slack://')) {
        this.handleMissingApp();
      }
    });
  }
}
```

6. Now we can create our `handleMissingApp` function. Here, we use the React Native helper `Platform`, which provides information about the platform the app is running on. `Platform.OS` will always return the operating system, which, on phones, should always resolve to either `'ios'` or `'android'`. You can read more about the capabilities of `Platform` in the official documentation at `https://facebook.github.io/react-native/docs/platform-specific-code.html`. If the link to the Slack app does not work as expected, we'll use `Linking.openURL` again; this time, to open the app in the app store appropriate for the device:

```
handleMissingApp() {
  if (Platform.OS === 'ios') {
    Linking.openURL(`https://itunes.apple.com/us/app/id618783545`);
  } else {
    Linking.openURL(
      `https://play.google.com/store/applications/details?id=com.Slack`
    );
  }
}
```

7. Our app doesn't have any styles yet, so let's add some. Nothing fancy here, just aligning the buttons in the center of the screen, coloring and centering text, and providing padding on each button:

```
const styles = StyleSheet.create({
  container: {
    flex: 1,
    backgroundColor: '#fff',
    justifyContent: 'center',
    alignItems: 'center',
  },
  buttonList: {
    flex: 1,
    justifyContent: 'center',
  },
  button: {
    margin: 10,
    backgroundColor: '#c0392b',
    borderRadius: 3,
    padding: 10,
    paddingRight: 30,
    paddingLeft: 30,
  },
  text: {
    color: '#fff',
    textAlign: 'center',
  },
});
```

8. That's all there is to this app. Once we load the app, there should be a column of buttons representing each of our links. The **Call Support** and **Email Support** buttons will not work on the iOS simulator. Run this recipe on a real device to see all of the links working properly.:

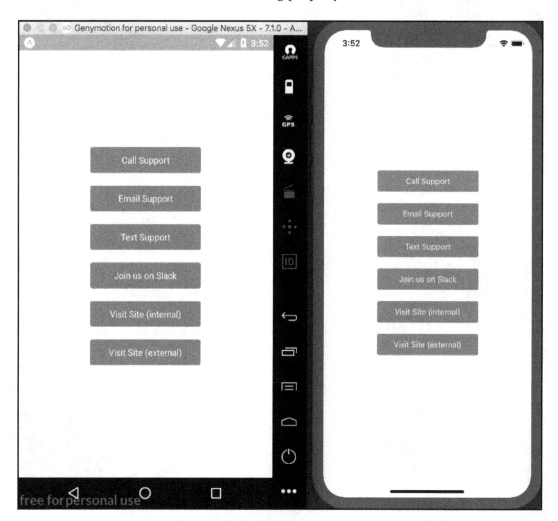

How it works...

In *step 2*, we defined all the links that our app uses. Each link object has a `type` property that we use in the `handleButtonPress` method defined in *step 5*.

This `handleButtonPress` function uses the link's type to determine which one of two strategies will be used. If the link's type is `'internal link'`, we want to open the link with the device browser as a modal that pops up within the app itself. For this purpose, we can use Expo's `WebBrowser` helper, passing the URL to its `openBrowserAsync` method. If the link's type is `'external link'`, we'll open the link with React Native's `Linking` helper. This lets you see the different ways you can open a website from your app.

The `Linking` helper can handle protocols other than HTTP and HTTPS as well. By simply using the proper protocol in the link we pass to `Linking.openURL`, we can open the telephone (`tel:`), messaging (`sms:`), or email (`mailto:`).

`Linking.openURL` can also handle deep links to other applications, as long as the app you want to link to has a protocol for doing so, such as how we open Slack by using the `slack://` protocol. For more information on Slack's deep linking protocol and what you can do with it, visit their documentation at `https://api.slack.com/docs/deep-linking`.

In *step 5*, we `catch` any error caused by calling `Linking.openURL`, check whether the error was caused by the Slack protocol using `message.includes('slack://')`, and if so, we know the Slack app is not installed on the device. In this case, we fire `handleMissingApp`, which opens the app store link for Slack using the appropriate link, as determined by `Platform.OS`.

See also

Official documentation on the `Linking` module can be found at `https://docs.expo.io/versions/latest/guides/linking.html`.

Creating a form component

Most applications require a way to input data, whether it's a simple registration and login form or a more complex component with many input fields and controls.

In this recipe, we will create a form component to handle text inputs. We will collect data using different keyboards, and show an alert message with the resulting information.

Getting ready

We need to create an empty app. Let's name it `user-form`.

How to do it...

1. Let's start by opening `App.js` and adding our imports. The imports include the `UserForm` component that we'll be building out in a later step:

```
import React from 'react';
import {
 Alert,
 StyleSheet,
 ScrollView,
 SafeAreaView,
 Text,
 TextInput,
} from 'react-native';

import UserForm from './UserForm';
```

2. Since this component is going to be very simple, we are going to create a stateless component for our `App`. We will only render a top toolbar inside a `ScrollView` for the `UserForm` component:

```
const App = () => (
  <SafeAreaView style={styles.main}>
    <Text style={styles.toolbar}>Fitness App</Text>
    <ScrollView style={styles.content}>
      <UserForm />
    </ScrollView>
  </SafeAreaView>
);

const styles = StyleSheet.create({
  // Defined in a later step
});

export default App;
```

3. We need to add some styles to these components. We'll add some colors and padding, as well as setting the `main` class to `flex: 1` to fill the remainder of the screen:

```
const styles = StyleSheet.create({
  main: {
    flex: 1,
    backgroundColor: '#ecf0f1',
  },
  toolbar: {
```

```
      backgroundColor: '#1abc9c',
      padding: 20,
      color: '#fff',
      fontSize: 20,
    },
    content: {
      padding: 10,
    },
  });
```

4. We have defined the main `App` component. Now let's get to work on the actual form. Let's create a new directory called `UserForm` in the base of the project and add an `index.js` file. Then, we'll import all the dependencies for this class:

```
import React, { Component } from 'react';
import {
  Alert,
  StyleSheet,
  View,
  Text,
  TextInput,
  TouchableOpacity,
} from 'react-native';
```

5. This is the class that will render the inputs and keep track of the data. We are going to save the data on the `state` object, so we'll start by initializing `state` as an empty object:

```
export default class UserForm extends Component {
  state = {};

  // Defined in a later step
}

const styles = StyleSheet.create({
  // Defined in a later step
});
```

6. In the `render` method, we are going to define the components that we want to display, which in this case are three text inputs and a button. We are going to define a `renderTextfield` method that accepts a configuration object as a parameter. We'll define the `name` of the field, the `placeholder`, and the `keyboard` type that should be used on the input. In addition, we're also calling a `renderButton` method that will render the **Save** button:

```
render() {
  return (
    <View style={styles.panel}>
      <Text style={styles.instructions}>
        Please enter your contact information
      </Text>
      {this.renderTextfield({ name: 'name', placeholder: 'Your
      name' })}
      {this.renderTextfield({ name: 'phone', placeholder: 'Your
      phone number', keyboard: 'phone-pad' })}
      {this.renderTextfield({ name: 'email', placeholder: 'Your
      email address', keyboard: 'email-address'})}
      {this.renderButton()}
    </View>
  );
}
```

7. To render the text fields, we are going to use the `TextInput` component in our `renderTextfield` method. This `TextInput` component is provided by React Native and works on both iOS and Android. The `keyboardType` property allows us to set the keyboard that we want to use. The four available keyboards on both platforms are `default`, `numeric`, `email-address`, and `phone-pad`:

```
renderTextfield(options) {
  return (
    <TextInput
      style={styles.textfield}
      onChangeText={(value) => this.setState({ [options.name]:
      value })}
      placeholder={options.label}
      value={this.state[options.name]}
      keyboardType={options.keyboard || 'default'}
    />
  );
}
```

8. We already know how to render buttons and respond to the `Press` action. If this is unclear, I recommend reading the *Creating a reusable button with theme support* recipe in `Chapter 3`, *Implementing Complex User Interfaces – Part I*:

```
renderButton() {
  return (
    <TouchableOpacity
      onPress={this.handleButtonPress}
      style={styles.button}
    >
      <Text style={styles.buttonText}>Save</Text>
    </TouchableOpacity>
  );
}
```

9. We need to define the `onPressButton` callback. For simplicity, we'll just show an alert with the input data that we have on the `state` object:

```
handleButtonPress = () => {
  const { name, phone, email } = this.state;

  Alert.alert(`User's data`, `Name: ${name}, Phone: ${phone},
  Email: ${email}`);
}
```

10. We are almost done with this recipe! All we need to do is apply some styles – some colors, padding, and margins; nothing fancy really:

```
const styles = StyleSheet.create({
 panel: {
  backgroundColor: '#fff',
  borderRadius: 3,
  padding: 10,
  marginBottom: 20,
 },
 instructions: {
  color: '#bbb',
  fontSize: 16,
  marginTop: 15,
  marginBottom: 10,
 },
 textfield: {
  height: 40,
  marginBottom: 10,
 },
 button: {
  backgroundColor: '#34495e',
```

```
      borderRadius: 3,
      padding: 12,
      flex: 1,
    },
    buttonText: {
      textAlign: 'center',
      color: '#fff',
      fontSize: 16,
    },
  });
```

11. If we run our app, we should be able to see a form that uses native controls on both Android and iOS, as expected:

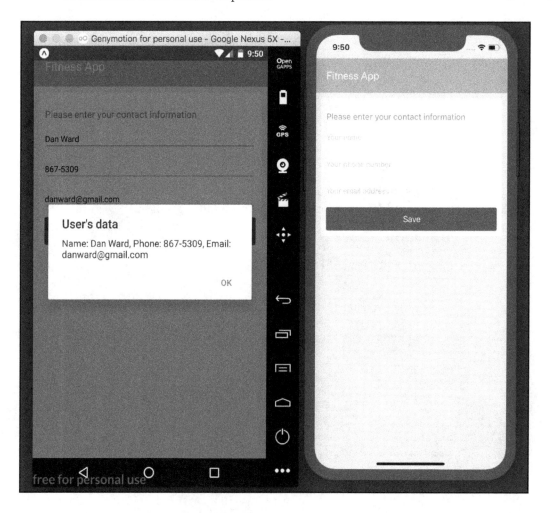

You might not be able to see the keyboard as defined by `keyboardType` when running your app in a simulator. Run the app on a real device to ensure that the `keyboardType` is properly changing the keyboard for each `TextInput`.

How it works...

In *step 8*, we defined the `TextInput` component. In React (and React Native), we can use two types of input: controlled and uncontrolled components. In this recipe, we're using controlled input components, as recommended by the React team.

A controlled component will have a `value` property, and the component will always display the content of the `value` property. This means that we need a way to change the value when the user starts typing into the input. If we don't update that value, then the text in the input won't ever change, even if the user tries to type something.

In order to update the `value`, we can use the `onChangeText` callback and set the new value. In this example, we are using the state to keep track of the data and we are setting a new key on the state with the content of the input.

An uncontrolled component, on the other hand, will not have a `value` property assigned. We can assign an initial value using the `defaultValue` property. Uncontrolled components have their own state, and we can get their value by using an `onChangeText` callback, just as we can with controlled components.

Implementing Complex User Interfaces - Part III

In this chapter, we will cover the following recipes:

- Creating a map app
- Creating an audio player
- Creating an image carousel
- Adding push notifications to your app
- Implementing browser-based authentication

Introduction

In this chapter, we'll cover some of the more advanced features you might need to add to an app. The applications we'll build in this chapter include building a fully functional audio player, map integration, and implementing browser-based authentication so that your app can connect to public APIs for developers.

Creating a map app

Using a mobile device is a portable experience, so it's no surprise that maps are a common part of many iOS and Android applications. Your app may need to tell a user where they are, where they're going, or where other users are in real time.

In this recipe, we'll be making a simple app that uses Google Maps on Android, and Apple's Maps app on iOS, to display a map centered on the user's location. We will be using Expo's `Location` helper library to get the latitude and longitude of the user and will use that data to render the map using Expo's `MapView` component. `MapView` is an Expo ready version of the react-native-maps package created by Airbnb, so you can expect the react-native-maps documentation to apply, which can be found at `https://github.com/react-community/react-native-maps`.

Getting ready

We will need to create a new app for this recipe. Let's call it `map-app`. Since the user pin in this recipe will use a custom icon, we'll also need an image for that. I used the icon **You Are Here** by Maico Amorim, which you can download from `https://thenounproject.com/term/you-are-here/12314/`. Feel free to use any image you'd like to represent the user pin. Save the image to the `assets` folder in the root of the project.

How to do it...

1. We'll start by opening `App.js` and adding our imports:

```
import React from 'react';
import {
  Location,
  Permissions,
  MapView,
  Marker
} from 'expo';
import {
  StyleSheet,
  Text,
  View,
} from 'react-native';
```

2. Next, let's define the `App` class and the initial `state`. In this recipe, `state` will only need to keep track of the user's `location`, which we initialize to `null`:

```
export default class App extends Component {
  state = {
    location: null
  }
  // Defined in following steps
}
```

3. Next, we'll define the `componentDidMount` life cycle hook, which will ask the user to grant permission to access the user's location via the device's geolocation. If the user grants the app permission to use its location, the return object will have a `status` property with the value `'granted'`. If granted, we'll get the user's location with `this.getLocation`, defined in the next step:

```
async componentDidMount() {
  const permission = await
Permissions.askAsync(Permissions.LOCATION);
  if (permission.status === 'granted') {
    this.getLocation();
  }
}
```

4. The `getLocation` function is simple. It grabs the location information from the device's GPS using the `getCurrentPositionAsync` method of the `Location` component, then saves that location information to `state`. That information contains the latitude and longitude of the user, which we'll use when we render the map:

```
async getLocation() {
  let location = await Location.getCurrentPositionAsync({});
  this.setState({
    location
  });
}
```

5. Now, let's use that location information to render our map. First, we'll check that a `location` has been saved on `state`. If so, we'll render the `MapView`, and otherwise render `null`. The only property we need to set to render our map is the `initialRegion` property, which defines the location the map should display when it is first rendered. We'll pass this property on the object with the latitude and longitude saved to `state`, and define a starting zoom level with `latitudeDelta` and `longitudeDelta`:

```
renderMap() {
  return this.state.location ?
    <MapView
      style={styles.map}
      initialRegion={{
        latitude: this.state.location.coords.latitude,
        longitude: this.state.location.coords.longitude,
        latitudeDelta: 0.09,
        longitudeDelta: 0.04,
      }}
```

```
   >
     // Map marker is defined in next step
   </MapView> : null
 }
```

6. Within the `MapView`, we'll need to add a marker at the user's current location. The `Marker` component is part of the `MapView` parent component, so in the JSX we'll define a `MapView.Marker` child element of the `MapView` element. This element takes the user's location, a title, and description for displaying when the icon is tapped, and a custom image via the `image` property:

```
<MapView
  style={styles.map}
  initialRegion={{
    latitude: this.state.location.coords.latitude,
    longitude: this.state.location.coords.longitude,
    latitudeDelta: 0.09,
    longitudeDelta: 0.04,
  }}
>
  <MapView.Marker
    coordinate={this.state.location.coords}
    title={"User Location"}
    description={"You are here!"}
    image={require('./assets/you-are-here.png')}
  />
</MapView> : null
```

7. Now, let's define our `render` function. It simply renders the map within a containing `View` element:

```
render() {
 return (
   <View style={styles.container}>
    {this.renderMap()}
   </View>
 );
}
```

8. Lastly, let's add our styles. We'll set `flex` to `1` on both the container and the map, so that both fill the screen:

```
const styles = StyleSheet.create({
 container: {
  flex: 1,
  backgroundColor: '#fff',
 },
```

```
map: {
  flex: 1
  }
});
```

9. Now, if we open the app, we'll see a map rendered with our custom user icon at the location provided by the device! Unfortunately, Google Maps integration may not work in the Android emulator, so a real device may be needed to test the Android implementation of the app. Check out the *There's more...* section at the end of this recipe for more information. Don't be surprised that the iOS app running on a simulator displays the user's location in San Francisco; this is due to how Xcode location defaults work. Run it on a real iOS device to see it render your location:

How it works...

By making use of the `MapView` component provided by Expo, the implementation of a map in your React Native app is now a much simpler and straightforward process than it once was.

In *step 3*, we made use of the `Permissions` helper library. `Permissions` has a method called `askAsync`, which takes one parameter defining what type of permissions your app would like to request from the user. `Permissions` also has constants for each type of permission you can request from the user. These permission types include `LOCATION`, `NOTIFICATIONS` (which we'll use later in this chapter), `CAMERA`, `AUDIO_RECORDING`, `CONTACTS`, `CAMERA_ROLL`, and `CALENDAR`. Since we need the location in this recipe, we passed in the constant `Permissions.LOCATION`. Once the `askAsync` return promise resolves, the return object will have a `status` property and an `expiration` property. If the user has allowed the requested permission, `status` will be set to the `'granted'` string. If granted, we will fire off our `getLocation` method.

In *step 4*, we defined the function that gets the location from the device's GPS. We call the `getCurrentPositionAsync` method of the `Location` component. This method will return an object with a `coords` property and a `timestamp` property. The `coords` property gives us access to the `latitude` and `longitude`, as well as the `altitude`, `accuracy` (radius of uncertainty for the location, measured in meters), `altitudeAccuracy` (accuracy of the altitude value, in meters (iOS only)), `heading`, and `speed`. Once received, we save the location to `state` so that the `render` function will be called, and our map will be rendered.

In *step 5*, we defined the `renderMap` method to render the map. First, we check whether there is a location, and if there is, we render the `MapView` element. This element only requires us to define the value for one property: `initialRegion`. This property takes an object with four properties: `latitude`, `longitude`, `latitudeDelta`, and `longitudeDelta`. We set the `latitude` and `longitude` equal to those in the `state` object, and provide initial values for `latitudeDelta` and `longitudeDelta`. These last two properties dictate the initial zoom level that the map should be rendered at; the larger this number is, the more zoomed out the map will be. I suggest experimenting with these two values to see how they affect the rendered map.

In *step 6*, we added the marker to the map by adding a `MapView.Marker` element as a child of the `MapView` element. We defined the coordinates by passing the info saved on `state` (`state.location.coords`) to the `coords` property, and set a `title` and `description` for the marker's popup when tapped. We were also able to easily define a custom pin by inlining our custom image with a `require` statement in the `image` property.

There's more...

As mentioned previously, you can read the docs for the react-native-maps project to learn more about the features of this excellent library (`https://github.com/react-community/react-native-maps`). For instance, you can easily customize the appearance of your Google map by using Google Maps Styling Wizard (`https://mapstyle.withgoogle.com/`) to generate a `mapStyle` JSON object, then pass that object to the `MapView` component's `customMapStyle` property. Or, you could add geometric shapes to your map with the `Polygon` and `Circle` components.

Once you're ready to deploy your app, there are a few follow-up steps that you will need to take to take to ensure the map works properly on Android. You can read the details on how deploying to a standalone Android app with a `MapView` component works in the Expo documentation at `https://docs.expo.io/versions/latest/sdk/map-view#deploying-to-a-standalone-app-on-android`.

 There is a known issue that could cause problems when rendering Google Maps within the Android simulator. You can refer to the following GitHub link for more information: `https://github.com/react-native-community/react-native-maps/issues/942`.

Creating an audio player

Audio players are another common interface built into many applications. Whether your app needs to play audio files stored locally on the device or stream audio from a remote location, Expo's `Audio` component comes to the rescue.

In this recipe, we'll be building a full-fledged basic audio player, with play/pause, next track, and previous track functionality. For simplicity, we'll be hardcoding the information for the tracks we'll be using, but in a real-world scenario, you'll likely be working with similar objects to what we're defining: an object with a track title, album name, artist name, and a URL to a remote audio file. I've chosen three random live tracks from the Internet Archive's **Live Music Archive** (`https://archive.org/details/etree`).

Getting ready

We'll need to create a new app for this recipe. Let's call it `audio-player`.

How to do it...

1. Let's start by opening up `App.js` and adding the dependencies we'll need:

```
import React, { Component } from 'react';
import { Audio } from 'expo';
import { Feather } from '@expo/vector-icons';
import {
  StyleSheet,
  Text,
  TouchableOpacity,
  View,
  Dimensions
} from 'react-native';
```

2. An audio player needs audio to play. We'll create a `playlist` array to hold the audio tracks. Each track is represented by an object with a `title`, `artist`, `album`, and `uri`:

```
const playlist = [
  {
    title: 'People Watching',
    artist: 'Keller Williams',
    album: 'Keller Williams Live at The Westcott Theater on
2012-09-22',
    uri:
'https://ia800308.us.archive.org/7/items/kwilliams2012-09-22.at853.
flac16/kwilliams2012-09-22at853.t16.mp3'
  },
  {
    title: 'Hunted By A Freak',
    artist: 'Mogwai',
    album: 'Mogwai Live at Ancienne Belgique on 2017-10-20',
    uri:
'https://ia601509.us.archive.org/17/items/mogwai2017-10-20.brussels
.fm/Mogwai2017-10-20Brussels-07.mp3'
  },
  {
    title: 'Nervous Tic Motion of the Head to the Left',
    artist: 'Andrew Bird',
    album: 'Andrew Bird Live at Rio Theater on 2011-01-28',
    uri:
'https://ia800503.us.archive.org/8/items/andrewbird2011-01-28.early
.dr7.flac16/andrewbird2011-01-28.early.t07.mp3'
  }
];
```

3. Next, we'll define our `App` class and initial `state` object with four properties:

   - `isPlaying` for defining whether the player is playing or paused
   - `playbackInstance` to hold the `Audio` instance
   - `volume` and `currentTrackIndex` for the currently playing track
   - `isBuffering` to display a `Buffering...` message while the track is buffering at the beginning of playback

As shown in following code:

```
export default class App extends Component {
  state = {
    isPlaying: false,
    playbackInstance: null,
    volume: 1.0,
    currentTrackIndex: 0,
    isBuffering: false,
  }

  // Defined in following steps
}
```

4. Let's define the `componentDidMount` life cycle hook next. We'll use this method to configure the `Audio` component via the `setAudioModeAsync` method, passing in an `options` object with a few recommended settings. These will be discussed more in the *How it works...* section at the end of the recipe. After this, we'll load the audio with `loadAudio`, defined in the next step:

```
async componentDidMount() {
  await Audio.setAudioModeAsync({
    allowsRecordingIOS: false,
    playThroughEarpieceAndroid: true,
    interruptionModeIOS: Audio.INTERRUPTION_MODE_IOS_DO_NOT_MIX,
    playsInSilentModeIOS: true,
    shouldDuckAndroid: true,
    interruptionModeAndroid:
    Audio.INTERRUPTION_MODE_ANDROID_DO_NOT_MIX,
  });
  this.loadAudio();
}
```

5. The `loadAudio` function will handle loading the audio for our player. First, we'll create a new instance of `Audio.Sound`. We'll then call the `setOnPlaybackStatusUpdate` method on our new `Audio` instance, passing in a handler that will be called whenever the state of playback within the instance has changed. Finally, we call `loadAsync` on the instance, passing it a source from the `playlist` array, as well as a status object with the volume and a `shouldPlay` property set to the `isPlaying` value of `state`. The third parameter dictates whether we want to wait for the file to finish downloading before it is played, so we pass in `false`:

```
async loadAudio() {
    const playbackInstance = new Audio.Sound();
    const source = {
      uri: playlist[this.state.currentTrackIndex].uri
    }
    const status = {
      shouldPlay: this.state.isPlaying,
      volume: this.state.volume,
    };
    playbackInstance
      .setOnPlaybackStatusUpdate(
        this.onPlaybackStatusUpdate
      );
    await playbackInstance.loadAsync(source, status, false);
    this.setState({
      playbackInstance
    });
  }
```

6. We still need to define the callback for handling status updates. All we need to do in this function is set the value of `isBuffering` on `state` to the `isBuffering` value on the `status` parameter that was passed in from the `setOnPlaybackStatusUpdate` function call:

```
onPlaybackStatusUpdate = (status) => {
  this.setState({
    isBuffering: status.isBuffering
  });
}
```

7. Our app now knows how to load an audio file from the `playlist` array and update `state` with the current buffering status of the loaded audio file, which we'll use later in the `render` function to display a message to the user. All that's left is to add the behavior for the player itself. First, we'll handle the play/pause state. The `handlePlayPause` method checks the value of `this.state.isPlaying` to determine whether the track should be played or paused, and calls the associated method on the `playbackInstance` accordingly. Finally, we need to update the value of `isPlaying` for `state`:

```
handlePlayPause = async () => {
  const { isPlaying, playbackInstance } = this.state;
  isPlaying ? await playbackInstance.pauseAsync() : await
playbackInstance.playAsync();
  this.setState({
    isPlaying: !isPlaying
  });
}
```

8. Next, let's define the function for handling skipping to the previous track. First, we'll clear the current track from the `playbackInstance` by calling `unloadAsync`. We'll update the `currentTrackIndex` value of `state` to either one less than the current value, or 0 if we're at the beginning of the `playlist` array. Then, we'll call `this.loadAudio` to load the proper track:

```
handlePreviousTrack = async () => {
  let { playbackInstance, currentTrackIndex } = this.state;
  if (playbackInstance) {
    await playbackInstance.unloadAsync();
    currentTrackIndex === 0 ? currentTrackIndex = playlist.length
    - 1 : currentTrackIndex -= 1;
    this.setState({
      currentTrackIndex
    });
    this.loadAudio();
  }
}
```

9. Not surprisingly, `handleNextTrack` is the same as the preceding function, but this time we'll either add `1` to the current index, or set the index to `0` if we're at the end of the `playlist` array:

```
handleNextTrack = async () => {
  let { playbackInstance, currentTrackIndex } = this.state;
  if (playbackInstance) {
    await playbackInstance.unloadAsync();
    currentTrackIndex < playlist.length - 1 ? currentTrackIndex
+=
    1 : currentTrackIndex = 0;
    this.setState({
      currentTrackIndex
    });
    this.loadAudio();
  }
}
```

10. It's time to define our `render` function. We will need three basic pieces in our UI: a `'Buffering...'` message when the track is playing but still buffering, a section for displaying information for the current track, and a section to hold the player's controls. The `'Buffering...'` message will only display if both `this.state.isBuffering` and `this.state.isPlaying` are `true`. The song info is rendered via the `renderSongInfo` method, which we'll define in *step 12*:

```
render() {
  return (
    <View style={styles.container}>
      <Text style={[styles.largeText, styles.buffer]}>
        {this.state.isBuffering && this.state.isPlaying ?
        'Buffering...' : null}
      </Text>
      {this.renderSongInfo()}
      <View style={styles.controls}>

        // Defined in next step.

      </View>
    </View>
  );
}
```

11. The player controls are made up of three `TouchableOpacity` button elements, each with a corresponding icon from the Feather icon library. You can find more information on using icons in `Chapter 3`, *Implementing Complex User Interfaces – Part I*. We'll determine whether to display the Play icon or the Pause icon depending on the value of `this.state.isPlaying`:

```
<View style={styles.controls}>
  <TouchableOpacity
    style={styles.control}
    onPress={this.handlePreviousTrack}
  >
    <Feather name="skip-back" size={32} color="#fff"/>
  </TouchableOpacity>
  <TouchableOpacity
    style={styles.control}
    onPress={this.handlePlayPause}
  >
    {this.state.isPlaying ?
      <Feather name="pause" size={32} color="#fff"/> :
      <Feather name="play" size={32} color="#fff"/>
    }
  </TouchableOpacity>
  <TouchableOpacity
    style={styles.control}
    onPress={this.handleNextTrack}
  >
    <Feather name="skip-forward" size={32} color="#fff"/>
  </TouchableOpacity>
</View>
```

12. The `renderSongInfo` method returns basic JSX for displaying the metadata associated with the track currently playing:

```
renderSongInfo() {
  const { playbackInstance, currentTrackIndex } = this.state;
  return playbackInstance ?
  <View style={styles.trackInfo}>
    <Text style={[styles.trackInfoText, styles.largeText]}>
      {playlist[currentTrackIndex].title}
    </Text>
    <Text style={[styles.trackInfoText, styles.smallText]}>
      {playlist[currentTrackIndex].artist}
    </Text>
    <Text style={[styles.trackInfoText, styles.smallText]}>
      {playlist[currentTrackIndex].album}
    </Text>
  </View>
```

```
        : null;
    }
```

13. All that's left to add are the styles. The styles defined here are well-covered ground by now, and don't go beyond centering, colors, font size, and adding padding and margins:

```
const styles = StyleSheet.create({
  container: {
    flex: 1,
    backgroundColor: '#191A1A',
    alignItems: 'center',
    justifyContent: 'center',
  },
  trackInfo: {
    padding: 40,
    backgroundColor: '#191A1A',
  },
  buffer: {
    color: '#fff'
  },
  trackInfoText: {
    textAlign: 'center',
    flexWrap: 'wrap',
    color: '#fff'
  },
  largeText: {
    fontSize: 22
  },
  smallText: {
    fontSize: 16
  },
  control: {
    margin: 20
  },
  controls: {
    flexDirection: 'row'
  }
});
```

14. You can now check out your app in the simulator, and you should have a fully working audio player! Note that audio playback in the Android emulator may be too slow for the playback to work properly, and may sound very choppy. Open the app on a real Android device to hear the track playing properly:

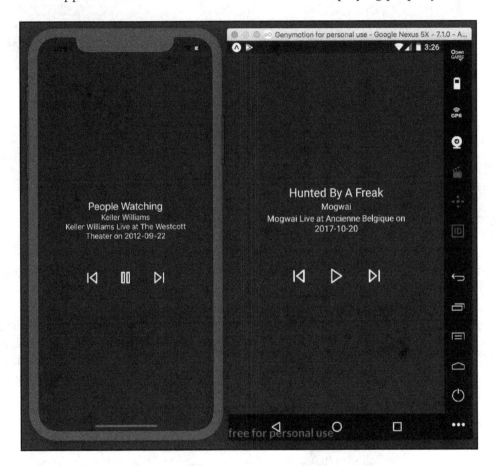

How it works...

In *step 4*, we initialized options on the `Audio` component once the app finished loading via the `componentDidMount` method. The `Audio` component's `setAudioModeAsync` method takes an option object as its only parameter.

Let's review some of the options we used in this recipe:

- `interruptionModeIOS` and `interruptionModeAndroid` set how the audio in your app should interact with the audio from other applications on the device. We used the `Audio` component's `INTERRUPTION_MODE_IOS_DO_NOT_MIX` and `INTERRUPTION_MODE_ANDROID_DO_NOT_MIX` enums, respectively, to declare that our app's audio should interrupt any other applications playing audio.

- `playsInSilentModeIOS` is a Boolean that determines whether your app should play audio when the device is in silent mode.

- `shouldDuckAndroid` is a Boolean that determines whether your app's audio should lower in volume (duck) when audio from another app interrupts your app. While this setting defaults to `true`, I've added it to the recipe so that you're aware that it's an option.

In *step 5*, we defined the `loadAudio` method, which performs the heavy lifting in this recipe. First, we created a new instance of the `Audio.Sound` class and saved it to the `playbackInstance` variable for later use. Next, we set the `source` and `status` variables that will be passed into the `loadAsync` function on the `playbackInstance` for actually loading the audio file. In the `source` object, we set the `uri` property to the corresponding `uri` property on the object in the `playlist` array at the index stored in `this.state.currentTrackIndex`. In the `status` object, we set the volume to the `volume` value saved on `state`, and set `shouldPlay`, a Boolean that determines whether the audio should be playing, initially to `this.state.isPlaying`. And, since we want to stream the remote MP3 file instead of waiting for the entire file to download, we pass `false` the third, `downloadFirst`, parameter.

Before calling the `loadAsync` method, we first called `setOnPlaybackStatusUpdate` of `playbackInstance`, which takes a callback function that should be called when the state of `playbackInstance` has changed. We defined that handler in *step 6*. The handler simply saves the `isBuffering` value from the callback's `status` parameter to the `isBuffering` property of `state`, which will fire a rerender, updating the '**Buffering...**' message in the UI accordingly.

In *step 7*, we defined the `handlePlayPause` function for toggling play and pause functionality in the app. If there's a track playing, `this.state.isPlaying` will be `true`, so we'll call the `pauseAsync` function on the `playbackInstance` otherwise, we'll call `playAsync` to start playing the audio again. Once we've played or paused, we update the value of `isPlaying` on `state`.

In *step 8* and *step 9*, we created the functions that handle skipping to the next and previous tracks. Each of these functions increases or decreases the value of `this.state.currentTrackIndex` as appropriate, so that by the time `this.loadAudio` is called at the bottom of each function, it will load the track associated with the object in the `playlist` array at the new index.

There's more...

The features of our current app are more basic than you'll find in most audio players, but all the tools you need for building a feature-rich audio player are at your disposal. For instance, you could display the current track time in the UI by tapping into the `positionMillis` property on the `status` parameter in the `setOnPlaybackStatusUpdate` callback. Or, you could use a React Native `Slider` component to allow the user to adjust the volume or playback rate. Expo's `Audio` component provides all the building blocks for a great audio player app.

Creating an image carousel

There are all kinds of applications that make use of image carousels. Any time there's a collection of images that you'd like your user to be able to peruse, a carousel is likely among the most effective UI patterns for accomplishing the task.

There are a number of packages in the React Native community for handling the creation of carousels, but in my experience none are more stable or more versatile than react-native-snap-carousel (`https://github.com/archriss/react-native-snap-carousel`). This package provides a great API for customizing the look and behavior of your carousel, and supports Expo app development without the need for ejecting. You can easily change how slides appear as they slide in and out of the carousel frame via the Carousel component's `layout` property, and as of version 3.6, you can even create custom interpolations!

While you are not limited to only displaying images with this package, we'll be building a carousel that just displays images along with a caption to keep the recipe simple. We'll be using the excellent license-free photo site unsplash.com to get random images for displaying in our carousel via the Unsplash Source project hosted at source.unsplash.com. Unsplash Source allows you to easily request random images from Unsplash without needing to access the official API. You can visit the Unsplash Source site for more information on how it works.

Getting ready

We'll need to create a new app for this recipe. Let's call this app carousel.

How to do it...

1. We'll start by opening App.js and importing dependencies:

```
import React, { Component } from 'react';
import {
  SafeAreaView,
  StyleSheet,
  Text,
  View,
  Image,
  TouchableOpacity,
  Picker,
  Dimensions,
} from 'react-native';
import Carousel from 'react-native-snap-carousel';
```

2. Next, let's define the `App` class and the initial `state` object. The `state` has three properties: a Boolean for whether we're currently displaying the carousel or not, a `layoutType` property for setting the layout style of our carousel, and an array of `imageSearchTerms` we'll use later to get images from Unsplash Source. Feel free to change the `imageSearchTerms` array to your heart's content:

```
export default class App extends React.Component {
  state = {
    showCarousel: false,
    layoutType: 'default',
    imageSearchTerms: [
      'Books',
      'Code',
      'Nature',
      'Cats',
    ]
  }

  // Defined in following steps
}
```

3. Let's define the `render` method next. We'll just check the value of `this.state.showCorousel` and either show the carousel or the controls accordingly:

```
render() {
  return (
    <SafeAreaView style={styles.container}>
      {this.state.showCarousel ?
        this.renderCarousel() :
        this.renderControls()
      }
    </SafeAreaView>
  );
}
```

4. Next, let's create the `renderControls` function. This will be the layout the user sees when they first open the app, and consists of a React Native `Picker` for selecting a layout type to use in the carousel and a button for opening the carousel. The `Picker` has three options available: default, tinder, and stack:

```
renderControls = () => {
  return(
    <View style={styles.container}>
      <Picker
        selectedValue={this.state.layoutType}
        style={styles.picker}
        onValueChange={this.updateLayoutType}
      >
        <Picker.Item label="Default" value="default" />
        <Picker.Item label="Tinder" value="tinder" />
        <Picker.Item label="Stack" value="stack" />
      </Picker>
      <TouchableOpacity
        onPress={this.toggleCarousel}
        style={styles.openButton}
      >
        <Text style={styles.openButtonText}>Open Carousel</Text>
      </TouchableOpacity>
    </View>
  )
}
```

5. Let's define the `toggleCarousel` function. This function simply sets the value of `showCarousel` on `state` to its opposite. By defining a toggle function, we can use the same function to both open and close the carousel:

```
toggleCarousel = () => {
  this.setState({
    showCarousel: !this.state.showCarousel
  });
}
```

6. Similarly, the `updateLayoutType` method just updates the `layoutType` on state to the `layoutType` value passed into it from the `Picker` component:

```
updateLayoutType = (layoutType) => {
  this.setState({
    layoutType
  });
}
```

7. The `renderCarousel` function returns the markup for the carousel. It's made up of a button for closing the carousel and the `Carousel` component itself. This component takes a `layout` property, as set by the `Picker`. It also has a `data` property, which takes the data that should be looped over for each carousel slide, and a `renderItem` callback that handles the rendering of each individual slide:

```
renderCarousel = () => {
  return (
   <View style={styles.carouselContainer}>
    <View style={styles.closeButtonContainer}>
     <TouchableOpacity
      onPress={this.toggleCarousel}
      style={styles.button}
     >
      <Text style={styles.label}>x</Text>
     </TouchableOpacity>
    </View>
    <Carousel
     layout={this.state.layoutType}
     data={this.state.imageSearchTerms}
     renderItem={this.renderItem}
     sliderWidth={350}
     itemWidth={350}
    >
    </Carousel>
   </View>
  );
}
```

8. We still need the function that handles the rendering of each slide. This function receives one object parameter containing the next item in the array passed to the `data` property. We'll return an `Image` component that uses the `item` parameter value to get a random item from Unsplash Source that's `350x350` in size. We'll also add a `Text` element to display the type of image being displayed:

```
renderItem = ({item}) => {
  return (
    <View style={styles.slide}>
      <Image
        style={styles.image}
        source={{ uri: `https://source.unsplash.com/350x350/?
        ${item}` }}
      />
      <Text style={styles.label}>{item}</Text>
    </View>
  );
}
```

9. The last thing we'll need is some styles to lay out our UI. The `container` styles apply to the main wrapping `SafeAreaView` element, so we set `justifyContent` to `'space-evenly'` so that the `Picker` and `TouchableOpacity` components fill up the screen. To display the close button in the top-right corner of the screen, we'll apply `flexDirection: 'row'` and `justifyContent: 'flex-end'` to the wrapping element. The rest of the styles are just dimensions, colors, padding, margins, and font size:

```
const styles = StyleSheet.create({
  container: {
    flex: 1,
    flexDirection: 'column',
    backgroundColor: '#fff',
    alignItems: 'center',
    justifyContent: 'space-evenly',
  },
  carouselContainer: {
    flex: 1,
    alignItems: 'center',
    justifyContent: 'center',
    backgroundColor: '#474747'
  },
  closeButtonContainer: {
    width: 350,
    flexDirection: 'row',
    justifyContent: 'flex-end'
  },
```

```
    slide: {
      flex: 1,
      justifyContent: 'center',
      alignItems: 'center',
    },
    image: {
      width:350,
      height: 350,
    },
    label: {
      fontSize: 30,
      padding: 40,
      color: '#fff',
      backgroundColor: '#474747'
    },
    openButton: {
      padding: 10,
      backgroundColor: '#000'
    },
    openButtonText: {
      fontSize: 20,
      padding: 20,
      color: '#fff',
    },
    closeButton: {
      padding: 10
    },
    picker: {
      height: 150,
      width: 100,
      backgroundColor: '#fff'
    }
});
```

10. We've completed our carousel app. It probably won't win any design awards, but it's a working carousel app with smooth, native-feeling behavior:

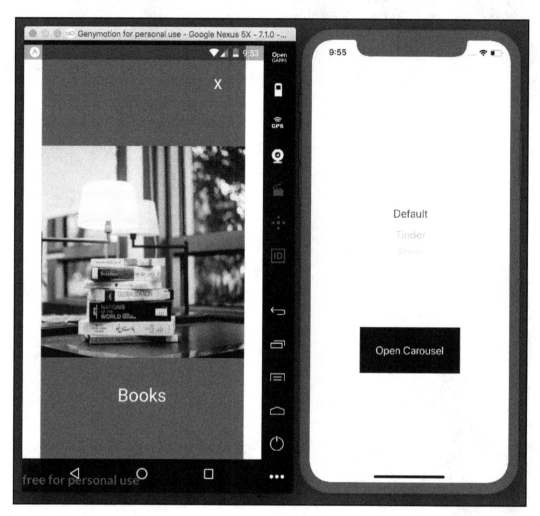

How it works...

In *step* 4, we defined the `renderControls` function, which renders the UI when the app is first launched. This is the first recipe in which we've used the `Picker` component. It's a part of the core React Native library and provides the drop-down type selector used to select options in many applications. The `selectedValue` property is the value tied to whichever item is currently selected in the picker. By setting it to `this.state.layoutType`, we'll default the selection to the `'default'` layout, and keep the values synced when a different `Picker` item is selected. Each item in the picker is represented by a `Picker.Item` component. Its `label` property defines the display text for the item, and the `value` property represents the string value for the item. Since we provided the `onValueChange` property with the `updateLayoutType` function, it will be called whenever a new item is selected, which in turn will update `this.state.layoutType` accordingly.

In *step* 7, we defined the JSX for the carousel. The carousel's `data` and `renderItem` properties are required, and work together to render each slide in the carousel. When the carousel is instantiated, the array passed into the `data` property will be looped over, and the `renderItem` callback function will be called for each item in the area, with that item passed into the `renderItem` as a parameter. We also set the `sliderWidth` and `itemWidth` properties, which are required for horizontal carousels.

In *step* 8, we defined the `renderItem` function that gets called for each entry in the array passed into `data`. We set the source of the returned `Image` component to an Unsplash source URL, which will return a random image of the type requested.

There's more...

There are a few things we could do to improve this recipe. We could make use of the `Image.prefetch()` method to download the first image before opening the carousel, so that the image is ready right away, or add an input to allow the user to select their own image search terms.

The react-native-snap-carousel package provides a great way to build a multimedia carousel for a React Native app. There are a number of features we didn't have the time to cover here, including parallax images and custom pagination. For the adventurous developer, the package provides a way to create custom interpolations, allowing you to make your own layouts beyond the three built-in layouts.

Adding push notifications to your app

Push notifications are a great way to provide a constant feedback loop between the app and the user by continually providing app-specific data that's relevant to the user. Messaging applications send notifications when new messages arrive. Reminder applications display a notification to remind the user of a task at a specific time or location. A podcast app might use notifications to inform the user that a new episode has been published. A shopping app could use notifications to alert the user to check out a limited-time deal.

Push notifications are a proven way to increase user interaction and retention. If your app makes use of time-sensitive or event-based data, push notifications could be a valuable asset. In this recipe, we'll be using Expo's push notification implementation, which simplifies some of the setup that would be required with a vanilla React Native project. If the needs of your app demand a non-Expo project, I would recommend considering the react-native-push-notification package at `https://github.com/zo0r/react-native-push-notification`.

In this recipe, we'll be making a very simplistic messaging app with push notifications. We'll request proper permissions, then register a push notification token to an Express server we'll be building. We'll also render a `TextInput` for the user to enter a message into. When the **Send** button is pressed, the message will be sent to our server, and the server will send a push notification via Expo's push notification server, with the message from the app, to all devices that have registered a token with our Express server.

Thanks to Expo's built-in push notification service, the complicated work of creating a notification for each native device is offloaded to an Expo hosted backend. The Express server we build in this recipe will just pass off JSON objects for each push notification to the Expo backend, and the rest is taken care of. The following diagram from the Expo docs (`https://docs.expo.io/versions/latest/guides/push-notifications`) illustrates the life cycle of a push notification:

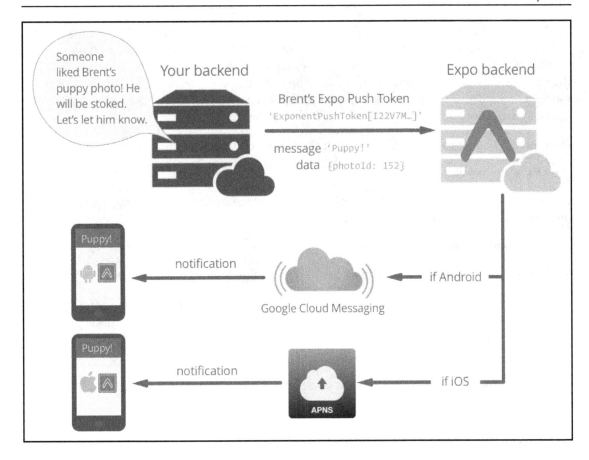

Image source: `https://docs.expo.io/versions/latest/guides/push-notifications/`

While implementing push notifications using Expo is less setup work than it would otherwise be, the requirements of the technology still mean we will need to run a server for handling registrations and sending notifications, which means this recipe will be a little longer than most. Let's get started!

Getting ready

One of the first things we'll need to do in this app is request permission from the device to use push notifications. Unfortunately, push notification permissions do not work properly in emulators, so a real device will be needed to test this app.

We'll also need to be able to access the push notification server from an address outside of the localhost. In a real-world setup, the push notification server would already have a public URL, but in a development environment, the easiest solution is to create a tunnel that exposes the development push notification server to the internet. We'll be using the ngrok tool for this purpose, since it is a mature, robust, and incredibly easy-to-use solution. You can read more about the software at https://ngrok.com.

First, install ngrok globally via npm using the following command:

```
npm i -g ngrok
```

Once it's installed, you can create a tunnel from the internet to a port on your local machine by executing ngrok with the https parameter:

```
ngrok https [port-to-expose]
```

We'll use this command later in the recipe to expose the development server.

Let's create a new app for this recipe. We'll call it push-notifications. We're going to need three extra npm packages for this recipe: express for the push notification server, esm for using ES6 syntax support on the server, and expo-server-sdk for processing push notifications. Install them with yarn:

```
yarn add express esm expo-server-sdk
```

Alternatively, install them using npm:

```
npm install express esm expo-server-sdk --save
```

How to do it...

1. Let's start with building the App. We'll start that by adding the dependencies we need to App.js:

```
import React from 'react';
import {
  StyleSheet,
  Text,
  View,
  TextInput,
  TouchableOpacity
} from 'react-native';
import { Permissions, Notifications } from 'expo';
```

2. We're going to declare two constants for the API endpoints on our server, but the url will be generated by ngrok when we run the server later in the recipe, so we'll update the value of these constants at that point:

```
const PUSH_REGISTRATION_ENDPOINT = 'http://generated-ngrok-
url/token';
const MESSAGE_ENPOINT = 'http://generated-ngrok-url/message';
```

3. Let's create the App component and initialize the state object. We'll need a notification property to hold notifications received by the Notifications listener, which we will define in a later step:

```
export default class App extends React.Component {
  state = {
    notification: null,
    messageText: ''
  }

  // Defined in following steps
}
```

4. Let's define the method that will handle registering the push notification token to the server. We'll ask for notification permission from the user via the askAsync method on the Permissions component. If permission is granted, get the token from the device from the getExpoPushTokenAsync method of the Notifications component:

```
registerForPushNotificationsAsync = async () => {
  const { status } = await
Permissions.askAsync(Permissions.NOTIFICATIONS);
  if (status !== 'granted') {
    return;
  }
  let token = await Notifications.getExpoPushTokenAsync();

  // Defined in following steps
}
```

5. Once we have the appropriate token, we'll send it over to the push notification server for registration. We will then make a POST request to PUSH_REGISTRATION_ENDPOINT, sending a token object and user object in the request body. I've hardcoded the values in the user object, but in a real app this would be the metadata you've stored for the current user:

```
registerForPushNotificationsAsync = async () => {
  // Defined in above step

  fetch(PUSH_REGISTRATION_ENDPOINT, {
    method: 'POST',
    headers: {
      'Accept': 'application/json',
      'Content-Type': 'application/json',
    },
    body: JSON.stringify({
      token: {
        value: token,
      },
      user: {
        username: 'warly',
        name: 'Dan Ward'
      },
    }),
  });

  // Defined in next step
}
```

6. After the token is registered, we'll set up an event listener to listen to any notifications that occur while the app is open and foregrounded. In certain cases, we will need to manually handle displaying the information from an incoming push notification. Check the *How it works...* section at the end of this recipe for more on why this is necessary and how it can be leveraged. We'll define the handler in the next step:

```
registerForPushNotificationsAsync = async () => {
  // Defined in above steps

  this.notificationSubscription =
  Notifications.addListener(this.handleNotification);
}
```

7. Whenever a new notification is received, the `handleNotification` method will be run. We'll just store the new notification passed to this callback on the `state` object for later use in the `render` function:

```
handleNotification = (notification) => {
  this.setState({ notification });
}
```

8. We want our app to ask for permission to use push notifications, and to register the push notification token when the app launches. We'll utilize the `componentDidMount` life cycle hook to run our `registerForPushNotificationsAsync` method:

```
componentDidMount() {
  this.registerForPushNotificationsAsync();
}
```

9. The UI will be very minimal to keep the recipe simple. It's made up of a `TextInput` for the message text, a **Send** button for sending the message, and a `View` for displaying any notifications heard by the notification listener:

```
render() {
  return (
    <View style={styles.container}>
      <TextInput
        value={this.state.messageText}
        onChangeText={this.handleChangeText}
        style={styles.textInput}
      />
      <TouchableOpacity
        style={styles.button}
        onPress={this.sendMessage}
      >
        <Text style={styles.buttonText}>Send</Text>
      </TouchableOpacity>
      {this.state.notification ?
        this.renderNotification()
      : null}
    </View>
  );
}
```

10. The `TextInput` component defined in the previous step is missing the method it needs for its `onChangeText` property. Let's create that method next. It just saves the text input by the user to `this.state.messageText` so it can be used by the `value` property and elsewhere:

```
handleChangeText = (text) => {
  this.setState({ messageText: text });
}
```

11. The `TouchableOpacity` component's `onPress` property calls the `sendMessage` method to send the message text when the user presses the button. In this function, we'll just take the message text and `POST` it to the `MESSAGE_ENDPOINT` on our push notification server. The server will handle things from there. Once the message is sent, we'll clear the `messageText` property on `state`:

```
sendMessage = async () => {
  fetch(MESSAGE_ENPOINT, {
    method: 'POST',
    headers: {
      Accept: 'application/json',
      'Content-Type': 'application/json',
    },
    body: JSON.stringify({
      message: this.state.messageText,
    }),
  });
  this.setState({ messageText: '' });
}
```

12. The last piece we need for the `App` is the styles. These styles are straightforward, and should all look quite familiar by now:

```
const styles = StyleSheet.create({
  container: {
    flex: 1,
    backgroundColor: '#474747',
    alignItems: 'center',
    justifyContent: 'center',
  },
  textInput: {
    height: 50,
    width: 300,
    borderColor: '#f6f6f6',
    borderWidth: 1,
    backgroundColor: '#fff',
    padding: 10
```

```
    },
    button: {
      padding: 10
    },
    buttonText: {
      fontSize: 18,
      color: '#fff'
    },
    label: {
      fontSize: 18
    }
  });
```

13. With the React Native app portion out of the way, let's move on to the server portion. First, we'll create a new `server` folder in the root of the project with an `index.js` file inside of it. Let's start by importing `express` to run the server and `expo-server-sdk` to handle the registration and sending of push notifications. We'll create an Express server app and store it in the `app` const, and a new instance of the Expo server SDK in the `expo` const. We'll also add a `savedPushTokens` array for storing any tokens that are registered with the React Native app, and a `PORT_NUMBER` const for the port we want to run the server on:

```
import express from 'express';
import Expo from 'expo-server-sdk';

const app = express();
const expo = new Expo();

let savedPushTokens = [];
const PORT_NUMBER = 3000;
```

14. Our server will need to expose two endpoints (one for registering tokens, and one for accepting messages from the React Native app), so we'll create two functions that will be executed when these routes are hit. We'll define the `saveToken` function first. It just takes a token, checks whether it's stored in the `savedPushTokens` array, and pushes it to the array if it isn't there already:

```
const saveToken = (token) => {
  if (savedPushTokens.indexOf(token === -1)) {
    savedPushTokens.push(token);
  }
}
```

15. The other function our server needs is a handler for sending push notifications when a message is received from the React Native app. We'll loop over all of the tokens that have been saved to the `savedPushTokens` array and create a message object for each token. Each message object has a title of `Message received!`, which will display in bold on the push notification, and the message text as the body of the notification:

```
const handlePushTokens = (message) => {
  let notifications = [];
  for (let pushToken of savedPushTokens) {
    if (!Expo.isExpoPushToken(pushToken)) {
      console.error(`Push token ${pushToken} is not a valid Expo
push token`);
      continue;
    }
    notifications.push({
      to: pushToken,
      sound: 'default',
      title: 'Message received!',
      body: message,
      data: { message }
    })
  }

  // Defined in following step
}
```

16. Once we have an array of messages, we can send them to Expo's server, which in turn will send the push notification to all registered devices. We'll send the messages array via the expo server's `chunkPushNotifications` and `sendPushNotificationsAsync` methods, and `console.log` the success receipts, or an error, as appropriate to the server console. There's more on how this works in the *How it works...* section at the end of this recipe:

```
const handlePushTokens = (message) => {
  // Defined in previous step

  let chunks = expo.chunkPushNotifications(notifications);

  (async () => {
    for (let chunk of chunks) {
      try {
        let receipts = await
expo.sendPushNotificationsAsync(chunk);
        console.log(receipts);
      } catch (error) {
```

```
        console.error(error);
      }
    }
  })();
}
```

17. Now that we have the functions defined for handling push notifications and messages, let's expose those functions by creating API endpoints. If you're not familiar with Express, it's a powerful and easy-to-use framework for running a web server in Node. You can quickly get up to speed on the basics of routing with the basic routing docs at https://expressjs.com/en/starter/basic-routing.html. We'll be working with JSON data, so the first step will be applying the JSON parser middleware with a call to express.json():

    ```
    app.use(express.json());
    ```

18. Even though we won't really be using the root path (/) of the server, it's good practice to define one. We'll just respond with a message that the server is running:

    ```
    app.get('/', (req, res) => {
       res.send('Push Notification Server Running');
    });
    ```

19. First, let's implement the endpoint for saving a push notification token. When a POST request is sent to the /token endpoint, we'll pass the token value to the saveToken function and return a response stating that the token was received:

    ```
    app.post('/token', (req, res) => {
      saveToken(req.body.token.value);
      console.log(`Received push token, ${req.body.token.value}`);
      res.send(`Received push token, ${req.body.token.value}`);
    });
    ```

20. Likewise, the /message endpoint will take the message from the request body and pass it to the handlePushTokens function for processing. Then, we'll send back a response that the message was received:

    ```
    app.post('/message', (req, res) => {
      handlePushTokens(req.body.message);
      console.log(`Received message, ${req.body.message}`);
      res.send(`Received message, ${req.body.message}`);
    });
    ```

21. The last piece to the server is the call to Express's `listen` method on the server instance, which will start the server:

```
app.listen(PORT_NUMBER, () => {
  console.log('Server Online on Port ${PORT_NUMBER}');
});
```

22. We're going to need a way to start the server, so we'll add a custom script to the `package.json` file called serve. Open the `package.json` file and update it to have a scripts object with a new `serve` script. With this added, we can run the server with yarn via the `yarn run serve` command or with npm via the command `npm run serve`. The `package.json` file should look something like this:

```
{
  "main": "node_modules/expo/AppEntry.js",
  "private": true,
  "dependencies": {
    "esm": "^3.0.28",
    "expo": "^27.0.1",
    "expo-server-sdk": "^2.3.3",
    "express": "^4.16.3",
    "react": "16.3.1",
    "react-native":
"https://github.com/expo/react-native/archive/sdk-27.0.0.tar.gz"
  },
  "scripts": {
    "serve": "node -r esm server/index.js"
  }
}
```

23. We've got all the code in place, let's use it! As mentioned previously, push notification permissions do not work properly on the emulator, so a real device will be needed to test the push notification functionality. First, we'll fire up our newly created server by running the following commands:

```
yarn run serve
npm run serve
```

You should be greeted by the `Server Online` message we defined in the `listen` method call in *step 21*:

24. Next, we'll need to run `ngrok` to expose our server to the internet. Open a new Terminal window and create an `ngrok` tunnel with the following command:

    ngrok http 3000

    You should see the `ngrok` interface in the Terminal. This displays the URLs generated by `ngrok`. In this case, `ngrok` is forwarding my server located at `http://localhost:3000` to the URL `http://ddf558bd.ngrok.io`. Let's copy that URL:

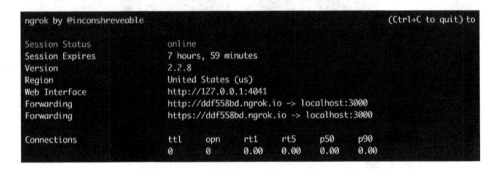

25. You can test that the server is running and accessible from the internet by visiting the generated URL in a browser. Navigating directly to this URL behaves exactly the same as navigating to `http://localhost:3000`, which means the `GET` endpoint we defined in previous step should run. That function returns the **Push Notification Server Running** string, and should display in your browser:

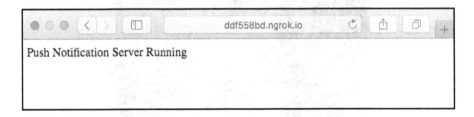

26. Now that we've confirmed that the server is running, let's update the React Native app to use the correct server URL. In *step 2*, we added to constants to hold our API endpoints, but we didn't have the correct URL yet. Let's update these URLs to reflect the tunnel URL generated by ngrok:

```
const PUSH_REGISTRATION_ENDPOINT =
'http://ddf558bd.ngrok.io/token';
const MESSAGE_ENPOINT = 'http://ddf558bd.ngrok.io/message';
```

27. As mentioned previously, you'll need to run this app on a real device for the permissions request to work correctly. As soon as you open the app, you should be prompted by the device, asking if you'd like to allow the app to send notifications:

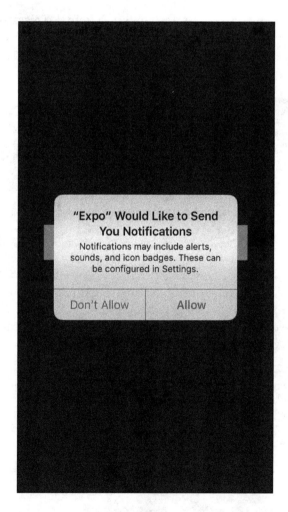

28. As soon as **Allow** is selected, the push notification token will be sent to the server's `/token` endpoint to be saved. This should also print the associated `console.log` statement in the server Terminal with the saved token. In this case, my iPhone's push token is the string `ExponentPushToken[g5sIEbOm2yFdzn5VdSSy9n]`:

```
yarn run v1.5.1
$ node -r esm server/index.js
Server Online on Port 3000
Received push token, ExponentPushToken[g5sIEbOm2yFdzn5VdSSy9n]
```

29. At this point, if you have a second Android or iOS device, go ahead and open the React Native app on that device as well. If not, don't worry. There's another easy way to test that our push notification functionality is working without using a second device.

30. You can use the React Native app's text input to send a message to other registered devices.. If you've got a second device that has registered a token with the server, it should receive a push notification corresponding to the newly sent message. You should also see two new instances of `console.log` in the server: one that displays the received message, and another that displays the `receipts` array received back from the Expo servers. Each receipt object in the array will have a `status` property with the value `'ok'` if the operation was successful:

```
yarn run v1.5.1
$ node -r esm server/index.js
Server Online on Port 3000
Received push token, ExponentPushToken[g5sIEbOm2yFdzn5VdSSy9n]
Received message, This is a message sent from my iPhone!
[ { status: 'ok' } ]
```

31. If you don't have a second device to test on, you can use Expo's push notification tool, hosted at `https://expo.io/dashboard/notifications`. Just copy the `push token` from the server Terminal and paste it into the input labeled **EXPO PUSH TOKEN** (from your app). To emulate a message sent from our React Native app, set **MESSAGE TITLE** to `Message received!`, **MESSAGE BODY** to the message text you'd like to send, and check the **Play Sound** checkbox. If you like, you can also emulate the `data` object by providing a JSON object with a key of `"message"` and a value of your message text, such as `{ "message": "This is a test message." }`. The received message should then look something like this screenshot:

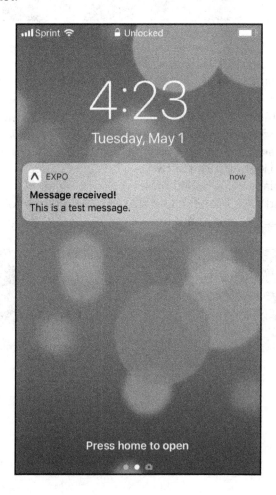

How it works...

The recipe we built here is a little contrived, but the core concepts needed to request permissions, register tokens, accept app data, and send push notifications in response to app data are all there.

In *step 4*, we defined the first part of the registerForPushNotificationsAsync function. We began by asking the user for their permission to send them notifications from our app via the Permissions.askAsync method, passing in the constant for the push notifications permission, Permissions.NOTIFICATIONS. We then saved the status property from the resolved return object, which will have the value 'granted' if the user granted permission. If we don't get permission, we return right away; otherwise, we get the token from Expo's Notifications component by calling getExpoPushTokenAsync. This function returns a token string, which will be in the following format:

    ExponentPushToken[xxxxxxxxxxxxxxxxxxxxx]

In *step 5*, we defined the POST call to the server's registration endpoint (/token). This function sends the token in the request body, which is then saved on the server using the saveToken function defined in *step 14*.

In *step 6*, we created an event listener that will listen for any new incoming push notifications. This is done by calling Notifications.addListener and passing in a callback function to be executed every time a new notification is received. On iOS devices, the system is designed to only produce a push notification if the app sending the push notification isn't open and foregrounded. That means if you try to send your user a push notification while they're currently using your app, they will never receive it.

To overcome this issue, Expo suggests manually displaying the push notification data from within your app. This Notifications.addListener method was created to fulfill this need. When a push notification is received, the callback passed to addListener will be executed and will receive the new notification object as a parameter. In *step 7*, we saved this notification to state so that the UI would be re-rendered accordingly. We only displayed the message text in a Text component in this recipe, but you could also use a modal for a more notification-like presentation.

In *step 11*, we created the sendMessage function, which posts the message text stored on state to the server's /message endpoint. This will execute the handlePushToken server function defined in *step 15*.

In *step 13*, we started working on the server, which utilizes Express and the Expo server SDK. A new server is created with express by calling `express()` directly, as a local const, usually named `app` by convention. We were able to create a new Expo server SDK instance with `new Expo()`, storing it in the `expo` const. We later used the Expo server SDK to send the push notification using `expo`, define routes using `app` in *steps 17* to *step 20*, and initiate the server by calling `app.listen()` in *step 22*.

In *step 14*, we defined the `saveToken` function, which will be executed when the `/token` endpoint is used by the React Native app to register a token. This function saves the incoming token to the `savedPushTokens` array, to be used later when a message arrives from a user. In a real app, this is where you would likely want to save the tokens to a persistent database of some kind, such as SQL, MongoDB, or Firebase Database.

In *step 15*, we started defining the `handlePushTokens` function, which runs when the React Native app uses the `/message` endpoint. The function loops over the `savedPushTokens` array for processing. Each token is checked for validity using the Expo server SDK's `isExpoPushToken` method, which takes in a token and returns `true` if the token is valid. If it's invalid, we log an error to the server console. If it's valid, we push a new notification object onto the local `notifications` array for batch processing in the next step. Each notification object requires a `to` property with the value set to a valid Expo push token. All other properties are optional. The optional properties we set were as follows:

- **Sound**: Can be default to play the default notification sound or `null` for no sound
- **Title**: The title of the push notification, usually displayed in bold
- **Body**: The body of the push notification
- **Data**: A custom data JSON object

In *step 16*, we used the Expo server SDK's `chunkPushNotifications` instance method to create an array of data chunks optimized for sending to Expo's push notification server. We then looped over the chunks, and sent each chunk to Expo's push notification server via the `expo.sendPushNotificationsAsync` method. It returned a promise that resolved to an array of receipts for each push notification. If the process is successful, there will be a `{ status: 'ok' }` object for each notification in the array.

This endpoint's behavior is simpler than a real server would probably be, because most message applications would have a more complicated way of handling a message. At the very least, there would likely be a list of recipients that would dictate which registered devices would in turn receive a particular push notification. The logic was intentionally kept simple to portray the basic flow.

In *step 18*, we defined the first accessible route on our server, the root (/) path. Express provides the get and post helper methods for easily making API endpoints for GET and POST requests respectively. The callback function receives a request object and response object as parameters. All server URLs need to respond to the request; otherwise, the request would time out. The response is sent via the send method on the response object. This route doesn't process any data, so we just returned the string indicating that our server is running.

In *step 19* and *step 20*, we defined POST endpoints for /token and /message, which will execute saveToken and handlePushTokens respectively. We also added console.log statements to each, to log the token and the message to the server Terminal for ease of development.

In *step 21*, we defined the listen method on our Express server, which starts the server. The first parameter is the port number to listen for requests on, and the second parameter is a callback function, usually used to console.log a message to the server Terminal that the server has been started.

In *step 22*, we added a custom script to the package.json file of our project. Any command that can be run in the Terminal can be made a custom npm script by adding a scripts key to the package.json file set to an object whose keys are the name of the custom script, and whose values are the command that should be executed when that custom script is run. In this recipe, we defined a custom scripted named serve that runs the node -r esm server/index.js command. This command runs our server file (server/index.js) with Node, using the esm npm package we installed at the beginning of this recipe. Custom scripts can be executed with npm:

```
npm run [custom-script-name]
```

They can also be executed using yarn:

```
yarn run [custom-script-name]
```

There's more...

Push notifications can be complicated, but thankfully Expo simplifies the process in a number of ways. There's great documentation on Expo's push notification service, which covers the specifics of notification timing, Expo server SDKs in other languages, and how to implement notifications over HTTP/2. I encourage you to read more at https://docs.expo.io/versions/latest/guides/push-notifications.

Implementing browser-based authentication

In the *Logging in with Facebook* recipe in `Chapter 8`, *Working with Application Logic and Data*, we will cover using the Expo `Facebook` component to create a login workflow for providing our app with the user's basic Facebook account information. Expo also provides a `Google` component, which provides similar functionality for getting a user's Google account information. But what do we do if we want to create a login workflow that uses account information from a different site? In this case, Expo provides the `AuthSession` component.

`AuthSession` is built on Expo's `WebBrowser` component, which we've already used in `Chapter 4`, *Implementing Complex User Interfaces – Part II*. The typical login workflow consists of four steps:

1. The user initiates the login process
2. The web browser opens to the login page
3. The authentication provider provides a redirect on successful login
4. The React Native app handles the redirect

In this app, we'll be using the Spotify API to get Spotify account information for our app via user login. Head over to `https://beta.developer.spotify.com/dashboard/applications` to create a new Spotify dev account (if you don't already have one) and a new app. The app can be named whatever you like. Once the app is created with Spotify, you'll see a client ID string displayed in the information for your app. We'll need this ID when building the React Native app.

Getting ready

We will need a new app for this recipe. Let's name the app `browser-based-auth`.

The redirect URI also needs to be whitelisted in the Spotify app we created previously. The redirect should be in the form of `https://auth.expo.io/@YOUR_EXPO_USERNAME/YOUR_APP_SLUG`. Since my Expo username is `warlyware`, and since this React Native app we're building is named `browser-based-auth`, my redirect URI is `https://auth.expo.io/@warlyware/browser-based-auth`. Be sure to add this to the Redirect URIs list in the settings of the Spotify app.

How to do it...

1. We'll start by opening `App.js` and importing the dependencies we will be using:

```
import React, { Component } from 'react';
import { TouchableOpacity, StyleSheet, Text, View } from 'react-
native';
import { AuthSession } from 'expo';
import { FontAwesome } from '@expo/vector-icons';
```

2. Let's also declare the `CLIENT_ID` as a constant to be used later. Copy the client ID for the Spotify app we created previously so that we can save it in the `CLIENT_ID` const:

```
const CLIENT_ID = Your-Spotify-App-Client-ID;
```

3. Let's create the `App` class and the initial `state`. The `userInfo` property will hold the user information we receive back from the Spotify API, and `didError` is a Boolean for tracking whether an error occurred during login:

```
export default class App extends React.Component {
  state = {
    userInfo: null,
    didError: false
  };

  // Defined in following steps
}
```

4. Next, let's define the method that logs the user in to Spotify. The `AuthSession` component's `getRedirectUrl` method provides the redirect URL needed for returning to the React Native app after login, which is the same redirect URI we saved in the Spotify app in the *Getting ready* section of this recipe. We'll then use the redirect URL in the login request, which we'll launch with the `AuthSession.startAsync` method, passing in an options object with the `authUrl` property set to the Spotify endpoint for authorizing user data with an app. There's more information on this URL in the *How it works...* section at the end of this recipe:

```
handleSpotifyLogin = async () => {
  let redirectUrl = AuthSession.getRedirectUrl();
  let results = await AuthSession.startAsync({
    authUrl:
`https://accounts.spotify.com/authorize?client_id=${CLIENT_ID}
    &redirect_uri=${encodeURIComponent(redirectUrl)}
```

```
            &scope=user-read-email&response_type=token`
        });

        // Defined in next step
    };
```

5. We saved the results of hitting the Spotify endpoint for user authentication in the local `results` variable. If the `type` property on the results object returns anything other than `'success'`, then an error occurred, so we'll update the `didError` property of `state` accordingly. Otherwise, we'll hit the `/me` endpoint with the access token we received from authorization to get the user's info, which we'll save to `this.state.userInfo`:

```
    handleSpotifyLogin = async () => {

        if (results.type !== 'success') {
            this.setState({ didError: true });
        } else {
            const userInfo = await
    axios.get(`https://api.spotify.com/v1/me`, {
                headers: {
                    "Authorization": `Bearer ${results.params.access_token}`
                }
            });
            this.setState({ userInfo: userInfo.data });
        }
    };
```

6. Now that the `auth` related methods are defined, let's create the `render` function. We'll use the `FontAwesome` Expo icon library to display the Spotify logo, add a button to allow the user to log in, and add methods for rendering either an error or the user info, depending on the value of `this.state.didError`. We'll also disable the login button once there's data saved on the `userInfo` property of `state`:

```
    render() {
      return (
        <View style={styles.container}>
          <FontAwesome
            name="spotify"
            color="#2FD566"
            size={128}
          />
          <TouchableOpacity
            style={styles.button}
```

```
          onPress={this.handleSpotifyLogin}
          disabled={this.state.userInfo ? true : false}
        >
          <Text style={styles.buttonText}>
            Login with Spotify
          </Text>
        </TouchableOpacity>
        {this.state.didError ?
          this.displayError() :
          this.displayResults()
        }
      </View>
    );
  }
```

7. Next, let's define the JSX for handling errors. The template just displays a generic error message to indicate that the user should try again:

```
displayError = () => {
  return (
    <View style={styles.userInfo}>
      <Text style={styles.errorText}>
        There was an error, please try again.
      </Text>
    </View>
  );
}
```

8. The `displayResults` function will be a `View` component that displays the user's image, username, and email address if there is `userInfo` saved to `state`, otherwise it will prompt the user to log in:

```
displayResults = () => {
  { return this.state.userInfo ? (
    <View style={styles.userInfo}>
      <Image
        style={styles.profileImage}
        source={ {'uri': this.state.userInfo.images[0].url} }
      />
      <View>
        <Text style={styles.userInfoText}>
          Username:
        </Text>
        <Text style={styles.userInfoText}>
          {this.state.userInfo.id}
        </Text>
        <Text style={styles.userInfoText}>
          Email:
```

```
                        </Text>
                        <Text style={styles.userInfoText}>
                          {this.state.userInfo.email}
                        </Text>
                    </View>
                  </View>
                ) : (
                  <View style={styles.userInfo}>
                    <Text style={styles.userInfoText}>
                      Login to Spotify to see user data.
                    </Text>
                  </View>
                )}
        }
```

9. The styles for this recipe are quite simple. It uses a column flex layout, applies the Spotify color scheme of black and green, and adds font sizes and margins:

```
const styles = StyleSheet.create({
  container: {
    flexDirection: 'column',
    backgroundColor: '#000',
    flex: 1,
    alignItems: 'center',
    justifyContent: 'space-evenly',
  },
  button: {
    backgroundColor: '#2FD566',
    padding: 20
  },
  buttonText: {
    color: '#000',
    fontSize: 20
  },
  userInfo: {
    height: 250,
    width: 200,
    alignItems: 'center',
  },
  userInfoText: {
    color: '#fff',
    fontSize: 18
  },
  errorText: {
    color: '#fff',
    fontSize: 18
  },
  profileImage: {
```

```
    height: 64,
    width: 64,
    marginBottom: 32
  }
});
```

10. Now, if we look at the app, we should be able to log in to Spotify, and see the associated image, username, and email address for the account used to log in:

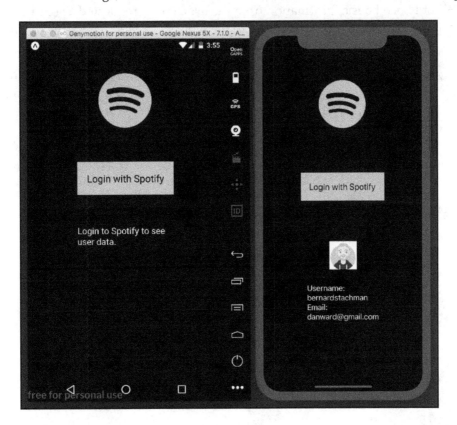

How it works...

In *step 4*, we created the method for handling the Spotify login process. The `AuthSession.startAsync` method just needed an `authUrl`, which was provided by the Spotify Developers documentation. The four pieces required are the `Client-ID`, the redirect URI for handling the response from Spotify, a `scope` parameter indicating the scope of user information the app is requesting, and a `response_type` parameter of `token`. We only need basic information from the user, so we requested a scope type of `user-read-email`. For information on all the scopes available, check the documentation at `https://beta.developer.spotify.com/documentation/general/guides/scopes/`.

In *step 5*, we completed the Spotify login handler. If the login was not successful, we updated `didError` on `state` accordingly. If it was successful, we used that response to access the Spotify API endpoint for getting user data (`https://api.spotify.com/v1/me`). We defined the `Authorization` header of the `GET` request with `Bearer ${results.params.access_token}` to validate the request, as per Spotify's documentation. On the success of this request, we stored the returned user data in the `userInfo` `state` object, which re-rendered the UI and displayed the user's information.

For a deeper dive into Spotify's auth process, you can find the guide at `https://beta.developer.spotify.com/documentation/general/guides/authorization-guide/`.

See also

- Expo Permissions docs: `https://docs.expo.io/versions/latest/sdk/permissions`
- Expo `MapView` docs: `https://docs.expo.io/versions/latest/sdk/map-view`
- Airbnb's React Native Maps package: `https://github.com/react-community/react-native-maps`
- Expo Audio docs: `https://docs.expo.io/versions/latest/sdk/audio`
- React Native Image Prefetch docs: `https://facebook.github.io/react-native/docs/image.html#prefetch`
- React Native Snap Carousel Custom Interpolations docs: `https://github.com/archriss/react-native-snap-carousel/blob/master/doc/CUSTOM_INTERPOLATIONS.md`
- Expo Push Notifications docs: `https://docs.expo.io/versions/latest/guides/push-notifications`
- Express Basic Routing guide: `https://expressjs.com/en/starter/basic-routing.html`
- esm package: `https://github.com/standard-things/esm`
- Expo server SDK for Node: `https://github.com/expo/exponent-server-sdk-node`
- ngrok package: `https://github.com/inconshreveable/ngrok`

6
Adding Basic Animations to Your App

In this chapter, we will cover the following recipes:

- Creating simple animations
- Running multiple animations
- Creating animated notifications
- Expanding and collapsing containers
- Creating a button with a loading animation

Introduction

In order to provide a good user experience, we'll likely want to add some animations to direct the user's attention, to highlight specific actions, or just to add a distinctive touch to our app.

There's an initiative in progress to move all the processing from JavaScript to the native side. At the time of writing (React Native Version 0.58), we can choose to use the native driver to run all these calculations in the native world. Unfortunately, this cannot be used with all animations, particularly those related to layout, such as flexbox properties. Read more about caveats when using native animation in the documentation at `http://facebook.github.io/react-native/docs/animations#caveats`.

All of the recipes in this chapter use the JavaScript implementation. The React Native team has promised to use the same API when moving all of the processing to the native side, so we don't need to worry about breaking changes to the existing API.

Creating simple animations

In this recipe, we will learn the basics of animations. We will use an image to create a simple linear movement from the right to the left of the screen.

Getting ready

In order to go through this recipe, we need to create an empty app. Let's call it `simple-animation`.

We are going to use a PNG image of a cloud for this recipe. You can find the image in the recipe's repository hosted on GitHub at `https://github.com/warlyware/react-native-cookbook/tree/master/chapter-6/simple-animation/assets/images`. Place the image in the `/assets/images` folder for use in the app.

How to do it...

1. Let's begin by opening `App.js` and importing the dependencies for the `App` class. The `Animated` class will be responsible for creating the values for the animation. It provides a few components that are ready to be animated, and it also provides several methods and helpers to run smooth animations.
   The `Easing` class provides several helper methods for both calculating movements (such as `linear` and `quadratic`) and predefined animations (such as `bounce`, `ease`, and `elastic`).
   We are going to use the `Dimensions` class to get the current device size so that we know where to place the element in the initialization of the animation:

```
import React, { Component } from 'react';
import {
  Animated,
  Easing,
  Dimensions,
  StyleSheet,
  View,
} from 'react-native';
```

2. We'll also initialize some constants that we are going to need in our app. In this case, we are going to get the device dimensions, set the size of the image, and `require` our image that will be animated:

```
const { width, height } = Dimensions.get('window');
const cloudImage = require('./assets/images/cloud.png');
const imageHeight = 200;
const imageWidth = 300;
```

3. Now, let's create the `App` component. We are going to use two methods from the component's life cycle system. If you are not familiar with this concept, please review the related React docs (`http://reactjs.cn/react/docs/component-specs.html`). This page also has a really nice tutorial on how life cycle hooks work:

```
export default class App extends Component {
  componentWillMount() {
    // Defined on step 4
  }

  componentDidMount() {
    // Defined on step 7
  }

  startAnimation () {
    // Defined on step 5
  }

  render() {
    // Defined on step 6
  }
}

const styles = StyleSheet.create({
  // Defined on step 8
});
```

4. In order to create an animation, we need to define a standard value to drive the animation. `Animated.Value` is a class that handles the animation values for each frame over time. The first thing we need to do is to create an instance of this class when the component is created. In this case, we are using the `componentWillMount` method, but we can also use the `constructor` or even the default values of a property:

```
componentWillMount() {
    this.animatedValue = new Animated.Value();
}
```

5. Once we have created the animated value, we can define the animation. We are also creating a loop by passing the `start` method of `Animated.timing` an arrow function that executes this `startAnimation` function again. Now, when the image reaches the end of the animation, we will start the same animation again to create an infinitely looping animation:

```
startAnimation() {
    this.animatedValue.setValue(width);
    Animated.timing(
      this.animatedValue,
      {
        toValue: -imageWidth,
        duration: 6000,
        easing: Easing.linear,
        useNativeDriver: true,
      }
    ).start(() => this.startAnimation());
}
```

6. We have our animation in place, but we are currently only calculating the values for each frame over time, not doing anything with those values. The next step is to render the image on the screen and set the property on the styles that we want to animate. In this case, we want to move the element on the *x*-axis; therefore, we should update the `left` property:

```
render() {
  return (
    <View style={styles.background}>
      <Animated.Image
        style={[
          styles.image,
          { left: this.animatedValue },
        ]}
        source={cloudImage}
      />
```

```
            </View>
        );
    }
```

7. If we refresh the simulator, we will see the image on the screen, but it's not being animated yet. In order to fix this, we need to call the `startAnimation` method. We will start the animation once the component is fully rendered, using the `componentDidMount` lifecycle hook:

```
componentDidMount() {
    this.startAnimation();
}
```

8. If we run the app again, we will see how the image is moving at the top of the screen, just like we wanted! As a final step, let's add some basic styles to the app:

```
const styles = StyleSheet.create({
    background: {
        flex: 1,
        backgroundColor: 'cyan',
    },
    image: {
        height: imageHeight,
        position: 'absolute',
        top: height / 3,
        width: imageWidth,
    },
});
```

The output is as shown in the following screenshot:

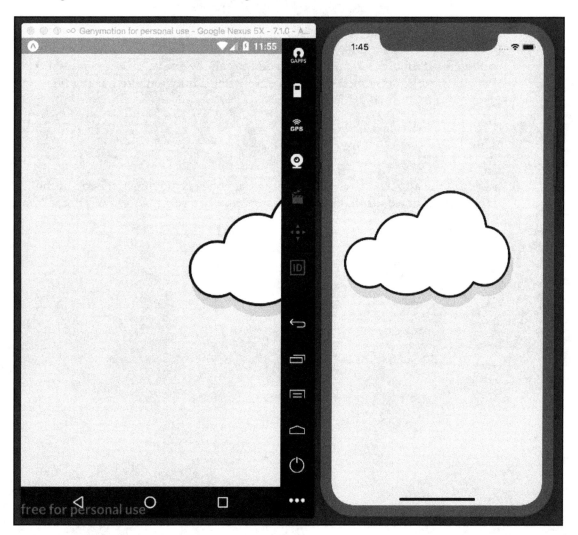

How it works...

In *step 5*, we set the animation values. The first line resets the initial value every time we call this method. For this example, the initial value will be the `width` of the device, which will move the image to the right-hand side of the screen, where we want to start our animation.

Then, we use the `Animated.timing` function to create an animation based on time and take two parameters. For the first parameter, we pass in `animatedValue`, which we created in the `componentWillMount` lifecycle hook in *step 4*. The second parameter is an object with configurations for the animation. In this case, we are going to set the end value to minus the width of the image, which will place the image on the left-hand side of the screen. We complete the animation there.

With the entire configuration in place, the `Animated` class will calculate all the frames required in the 6 seconds allotted to perform a linear animation from right to left (via the `duration` property being set to `6000` milliseconds).

We have another helper provided by React Native that can be paired with `Animated`, called `Easing`. In this case, we are using the `linear` property of the `Easing` helper class. `Easing` provides other common easing methods, such as `elastic` and `bounce`. Take a look at the `Easing` class documentation and try setting different values for the `easing` property to see how each works. You can find the documentation at `https://facebook.github.io/react-native/docs/easing.html`.

Once the animation is configured correctly, we need to run it. We do this by calling the `start` method. This method receives an optional `callback` function parameter that will be executed when the animation is completed. In this case, we are running the same `startAnimation` function recursively. This will create an infinite loop, which is what we want to achieve.

In *step 6*, we are rendering the image. If we want to animate an image, we should always use the `Animate.Image` component. Internally, this component will handle the values of the animation and will set each value for every frame on the native component. This avoids running the render method in the JavaScript layer on every frame, allowing for smoother animations.

Along with the `Image`, we can also animate the `View`, `Text`, and `ScrollView` components. There's support for all four of these components out of the box, but we could also create a new component and add support for animations via `Animated.createAnimatedComponent()`. All four of these components are able to handle style changes. All we have to do is pass `animatedValue` to the property that we want to animate, in this case the `left` property, but we could use any of the available styles on each component.

Running multiple animations

In this recipe, we will learn how to use the same animation values in several elements. This way, we can reuse the same values, along with interpolation, to get different values for the remaining elements.

This animation will be similar to the previous recipe. This time, we will have two clouds: one will be smaller with slower movement, the other larger and faster moving. At the center of the screen, we will have a static airplane. We won't add any animation to the airplane, but the moving clouds will make it appear as though the plane is moving.

Getting ready

Let's start this recipe by creating an empty app called `multiple-animations`.

We are going to use three different images: two clouds and an airplane. You can download the images from the recipe's repository, hosted on GitHub at `https://github.com/warlyware/react-native-cookbook/tree/master/chapter-6/multiple-animations/assets/images`. Make sure to place the images in the `/assets/images` folder.

How to do it...

1. Let's start by opening `App.js` and adding our imports:

```
import React, { Component } from 'react';
import {
  View,
  Animated,
  Image,
  Easing,
  Dimensions,
  StyleSheet,
} from 'react-native';
```

2. Additionally, we need to define some constants and require the images that we are going to use for the animations. Note that we're using the same cloud image as `cloudImage1` and `cloudImage2`, but we will treat them as separate entities in this recipe:

```
const { width, height } = Dimensions.get('window');
const cloudImage1 = require('./assets/images/cloud.png');
const cloudImage2 = require('./assets/images/cloud.png');
```

```
const planeImage = require('./assets/images/plane.gif');
const cloudHeight = 100;
const cloudWidth = 150;
const planeHeight = 60;
const planeWidth = 100;
```

3. In the next step, we are going to create the `animatedValue` instance when the component gets created, then we will start the animation when the component is fully rendered. We are creating an animation that runs in an infinite loop. The initial value will be 1 and the final value will be 0. If you are not clear about this code, make sure to read the first recipe in this chapter:

```
export default class App extends Component {
  componentWillMount() {
    this.animatedValue = new Animated.Value();
  }

  componentDidMount() {
    this.startAnimation();
  }

  startAnimation () {
    this.animatedValue.setValue(1);
    Animated.timing(
      this.animatedValue,
      {
        toValue: 0,
        duration: 6000,
        easing: Easing.linear,
      }
    ).start(() => this.startAnimation());
  }

  render() {
    // Defined in a later step
  }
}

const styles = StyleSheet.create({
  // Defined in a later step
});
```

4. The `render` method in this recipe is going to be quite different from the last. In this recipe, we are going to animate two images using the same `animatedValue`. The animated value will return values from 1 to 0; however, we want to move the clouds from right to left, so we need to set the `left` value on each element. In order to set the correct values, we need to interpolate `animatedValue`. For the smaller cloud, we will set the initial `left` value to the width of the device, but for the bigger cloud, we will set the initial `left` value far away from the right-hand edge of the device. This will make the movement distance bigger, and therefore it will move faster:

```
render() {
  const left1 = this.animatedValue.interpolate({
    inputRange: [0, 1],
    outputRange: [-cloudWidth, width],
  });

  const left2 = this.animatedValue.interpolate({
    inputRange: [0, 1],
    outputRange: [-cloudWidth*5, width + cloudWidth*5],
  });

  // Defined in a later step
}
```

5. Once we have the correct `left` values, we need to define the elements we want to animate. Here, we will set the interpolated value to the `left` styles property:

```
render() {
  // Defined in a later step

  return (
    <View style={styles.background}>
      <Animated.Image
        style={[
          styles.cloud1,
          { left: left1 },
        ]}
        source={cloudImage1}
      />
      <Image
        style={styles.plane}
        source={planeImage}
      />
      <Animated.Image
        style={[
          styles.cloud2,
```

```
                    { left: left2 },
                ]}
                source={cloudImage2}
            />
        </View>
    );
}
```

6. As for the last step, we need to define some styles, just to set the `width` and `height` of each cloud as well as assign styles to the `top`:

```
const styles = StyleSheet.create({
  background: {
    flex: 1,
    backgroundColor: 'cyan',
  },
  cloud1: {
    position: 'absolute',
    width: cloudWidth,
    height: cloudHeight,
    top: height / 3 - cloudWidth / 2,
  },
  cloud2: {
    position: 'absolute',
    width: cloudWidth * 1.5,
    height: cloudHeight * 1.5,
    top: height/2,
  },
  plane: {
    position: 'absolute',
    height: planeHeight,
    width: planeWidth,
    top: height / 2 - planeHeight,
    left: width / 2 - planeWidth,
  }
});
```

7. If we refresh our app, we should see the animation:

How it works...

In *step 4*, we defined the interpolations to get the left value for each cloud. The interpolate method receives an object with two required configurations, inputRange and outputRange.

The `inputRange` configuration receives an array of values. These values should always be ascending values; you could use negative values too, as long as the values are ascending.

`outputRange` should match the number of values defined on `inputRange`. These are the values that we need as a result of the interpolation.

For this recipe, `inputRange` goes from 0 to 1, which are the values of our `animatedValue`. In `outputRange`, we defined the limits of the movement that we need.

Creating animated notifications

In this recipe, we will create a notification component from scratch. When showing the notification, the component will slide in from the top of the screen. After a few seconds, we will automatically hide it by sliding it out.

Getting ready

We are going to create an app. Let's call it `notification-animation`.

How to do it...

1. We'll start by working on the `App` component. First, let's import all the required dependencies:

```
import React, { Component } from 'react';
import {
  Text,
  TouchableOpacity,
  StyleSheet,
  View,
  SafeAreaView,
} from 'react-native';
import Notification from './Notification';
```

2. Once we have all the dependencies imported, we can define the `App` class. In this case, we are going to initialize the `state` with a `notify` property equal to `false`. We are going to use this property to show or hide the notification. By default, the notification will not be shown onscreen. To make things simple, we will define the `message` property in the `state` with the text we want to display:

```
export default class App extends Component {
  state = {
    notify: false,
    message: 'This is a notification!',
  };

  toggleNotification = () => {
    // Defined on later step
  }

  render() {
    // Defined on later step
  }
}

const styles = StyleSheet.create({
    // Defined on later step
});
```

3. Inside the `render` method, we need to show the notification only if the `notify` property is `true`. We can achieve this by using an `if` statement:

```
render() {
  const notify = this.state.notify
    ? <Notification
        autoHide
        message={this.state.message}
        onClose={this.toggleNotification}
      />
    : null;
    // Defined on next step
}
```

4. In the previous step, we only defined the reference to the `Notification` component, but we are not using it yet. Let's define a `return` with all of the JSX needed for this app. To keep things simple, we are only going to define a toolbar, some text, and a button to toggle the state of the notification when pressed:

```
render() {
  // Code from previous step
  return (
    <SafeAreaView>
      <Text style={styles.toolbar}>Main toolbar</Text>
      <View style={styles.content}>
        <Text>
          Lorem ipsum dolor sit amet, consectetur adipiscing
          elit,
          sed do eiusmod tempor incididunt ut labore et
          dolore magna.
        </Text>
        <TouchableOpacity
          onPress={this.toggleNotification}
          style={styles.btn}
        >
          <Text style={styles.text}>Show notification</Text>
        </TouchableOpacity>
        <Text>
          Sed ut perspiciatis unde omnis iste natus error sit
          accusantium doloremque laudantium.
        </Text>
        {notify}
      </View>
    </SafeAreaView>
  );
}
```

5. We also need to define the method that toggles the `notify` property on the `state`, which is very simple:

```
toggleNotification = () => {
  this.setState({
    notify: !this.state.notify,
  });
}
```

6. We are almost done with this class. The only things left are the styles. In this case, we will only add basic styles such as `color`, `padding`, `fontSize`, `backgroundColor`, and `margin`, nothing really special:

```
const styles = StyleSheet.create({
  toolbar: {
    backgroundColor: '#8e44ad',
    color: '#fff',
    fontSize: 22,
    padding: 20,
    textAlign: 'center',
  },
  content: {
    padding: 10,
    overflow: 'hidden',
  },
  btn: {
    margin: 10,
    backgroundColor: '#9b59b6',
    borderRadius: 3,
    padding: 10,
  },
  text: {
    textAlign: 'center',
    color: '#fff',
  },
});
```

7. If we try to run the app, we will see an error that the `./Notification` module couldn't be resolved. Let's fix that by defining the `Notification` component. Let's create a `Notifications` folder, with an `index.js` file inside of it. Then, we can import our dependencies:

```
import React, { Componen } from 'react';
import {
  Animated,
  Easing,
  StyleSheet,
  Text,
} from 'react-native';
```

8. Once we have the dependencies imported, let's define the props and the initial state of our new component. We are going to define something very simple, just a property to receive the message to display, and two `callback` functions to allow the running of some actions when the notification appears on the screen and when it gets closed. We'll also add a property to set the number of milliseconds to display the notification before it autohides:

```
export default class Notification extends Component {
  static defaultProps = {
    delay: 5000,
    onClose: () => {},
    onOpen: () => {},
  };

  state = {
    height: -1000,
  };
}
```

9. It's finally time to work on the animation! We need to start the animation as soon as the component gets rendered. If there's something not clear in the following code, I recommend you take a look at the first and second recipes in this chapter:

```
componentWillMount() {
  this.animatedValue = new Animated.Value();
}

componentDidMount() {
  this.startSlideIn();
}

getAnimation(value, autoHide) {
  const { delay } = this.props;
  return Animated.timing(
    this.animatedValue,
    {
      toValue: value,
      duration: 500,
      easing: Easing.cubic,
      delay: autoHide ? delay : 0,
    }
  );
}
```

10. So far, we've defined a method to get the animation. For the slide-in movement, we need to calculate the values from 0 to 1. Once the animation is complete, we need to run the onOpen callback. If the autoHide property is set to true when the onOpen method is called, we will automatically run the slide-out animation to remove the component:

```
startSlideIn () {
  const { onOpen, autoHide } = this.props;

  this.animatedValue.setValue(0);
  this.getAnimation(1)
    .start(() => {
      onOpen();
      if (autoHide) {
        this.startSlideOut();
      }
    });
}
```

11. Similar to the preceding step, we need a method for the slide-out movement. Here, we need to calculate the values from 1 to 0. We are sending the autoHide value as a parameter to the getAnimation method. This will automatically delay the animation by the amount of milliseconds defined by the delay property (in our case, 5 seconds). After the animation has completed, we need to run the onClose callback function, which will remove the component from the App class:

```
startSlideOut() {
  const { autoHide, onClose } = this.props;

  this.animatedValue.setValue(1);
  this.getAnimation(0, autoHide)
    .start(() => onClose());
}
```

12. Finally, let's add the `render` method. Here, we will get the `message` value provided by `props`. We also need the `height` of the component to move the component to the initial position of the animation; by default, it's –1000 but we will set the correct value at runtime in the next steps. The `animatedValue` goes from 0 to 1 or 1 to 0, depending on whether the notification is opening or closing; therefore, we need to interpolate it to get the actual values. The animation will go from minus the height of the component to 0; this will result in a nice slide in/out animation:

```
render() {
  const { message } = this.props;
  const { height } = this.state;
  const top = this.animatedValue.interpolate({
     inputRange: [0, 1],
     outputRange: [-height, 0],
   });
  // Defined on next step
  }
}
```

13. To keep things as simple as possible, we will return an `Animated.View` with some text. Here, we are setting the `top` style with the interpolation result, meaning we will animate the top style. As mentioned before, we need to calculate the height of the component at runtime. In order to achieve that, we need to use the `onLayout` property of the view. This function will be called every time the layout updates and will send the new dimensions of this component as a parameter:

```
render() {
   // Code from previous step
   return (
    <Animated.View
      onLayout={this.onLayoutChange}
      style={[
        styles.main,
        { top }
      ]}
    >
      <Text style={styles.text}>{message}</Text>
    </Animated.View>
  );
  }
}
```

14. The `onLayoutChange` method will be very simple. We just need to get the new `height` and update the `state`. This method receives an `event`. From this object, we can grab useful information. For our purposes, we will access the data at `nativeEvent.layout` in the `event` object. The `layout` object contains the screen's `width` and `height`, and the *x* and *y* positions on the screen where the `Animated.View` called this function:

```
onLayoutChange = (event) => {
  const {layout: { height } } = event.nativeEvent;
    this.setState({ height });
  }
```

15. For the last step, we will add some styles to the notification component. Since we want this component to animate on top of anything else, we need to set the `position` to `absolute`, and set the `left` and `right` properties to 0. We'll also add some color and padding:

```
const styles = StyleSheet.create({
  main: {
    backgroundColor: 'rgba(0, 0, 0, 0.7)',
    padding: 10,
    position: 'absolute',
    left: 0,
    right: 0,
  },
  text: {
    color: '#fff',
  },
});
```

16. The final app should look something like the following screenshot:

How it works...

In *step 3*, we defined the Notification component. This component receives three parameters: a flag to automatically hide the component after a few seconds, the message that we want to display, and a callback function that will be executed when the notification gets closed.

When the onClose callback gets executed, we will toggle the notify property to remove the Notification instance and clear the memory.

In *step 4*, we defined the JSX to render the components of our app. It's important to render the Notification component after the others so that the component will appear on top of all other components.

In *step 6*, we defined the state of our component. The defaultProps object sets the default values for each property. These values will be applied if no value is assigned to the given property.

We defined the default for each callback as an empty function. This way, we don't have to check whether those props have a value before trying to execute them.

For the initial state, we defined the height property. The actual height value will be calculated at runtime based on the content received in the message property. This means we need to initially render the component far away from the original position. Since there's a short delay when the layout is calculated, we don't want to display the notification at all before it moves to the correct position.

In *step 9*, we created the animation. The getAnimation method receives two parameters: the delay to be applied and the autoHide Boolean, which determines whether the notification automatically closes. We used this method in *step 10* and *step 11*.

In *step 13*, we defined the JSX for this component. The onLayout function is very useful for getting the dimensions of the component when there are updates to the layout. For example, if the device orientation changes, the dimensions will change, in which case we would like to update the initial and final coordinates for the animation.

There's more...

The current implementation works pretty well, but there's a performance problem we should address. Currently, the onLayout method gets executed on every frame of the animation, which means we are updating the state on every frame, which leads to the component re-rendering on every frame! We should avoid this, and only update it once to get the actual height.

To fix this, we could add a simple validation just to update the state if the current value is different than the initial value. This will avoid updating the state on every frame and we won't force the render over and over again:

```
onLayoutChange = (event) => {
  const {layout: { height } } = event.nativeEvent;
  if (this.state.height === -1000) {
    this.setState({ height });
  }
}
```

While this works for our purposes, we could also go further and make sure the height also gets updated when the orientation changes. However, we'll stop here, as this recipe is quite long already.

Expanding and collapsing containers

In this recipe, we will create a custom container element with a title and content. When a user presses the title, the content will collapse or expand. This recipe will allow us to explore the LayoutAnimation API.

Getting ready

Let's start by creating a new app. We'll call it collapsable-containers.

Once we have created the app, let's also create a Panel folder with an index.js file in it for housing our Panel component.

How to do it...

1. Let's start by focusing on the `Panel` component. First, we need to import all the dependencies that we are going to use for this class:

```
import React, { Component } from 'react';
import {
  View,
  LayoutAnimation,
  StyleSheet,
  Text,
  TouchableOpacity,
} from 'react-native';
```

2. Once we have the dependencies, let's declare the `defaultProps` for initializing this component. In this recipe, we only need to initialize the `expanded` property to `false`:

```
export default class Panel extends Component {
  static defaultProps = {
    expanded: false
  };
}

const styles = StyleSheet.create({
  // Defined on later step
});
```

3. We are going to use the `height` property on the `state` object to expand or collapse the container. The first time this component gets created, we need to check the `expanded` property in order to set the correct initial `height`:

```
state = {
  height: this.props.expanded ? null : 0,
};
```

4. Let's render the required JSX elements for this component. We need to get the `height` value from `state` and set it to the content's style view. When pressing the `title` element, we will execute the `toggle` method (defined later) to change the `height` value of the state:

```
render() {
  const { children, style, title } = this.props;
  const { height } = this.state;

  return (
```

```
      <View style={[styles.main, style]}>
        <TouchableOpacity onPress={this.toggle}>
          <Text style={styles.title}>
            {title}
          </Text>
        </TouchableOpacity>
        <View style={{ height }}>
          {children}
        </View>
      </View>
    );
  }
```

5. As mentioned before, the `toggle` method will be executed when the `title` element is pressed. Here, we will toggle the `height` on the `state` and call the animation we want to use when updating the styles on the next render cycle:

```
toggle = () => {
  LayoutAnimation.spring();
  this.setState({
    height: this.state.height === null ? 0 : null,
  })
}
```

6. To complete this component, let's add some simple styles. We need to set the `overflow` to `hidden`, otherwise the content will be shown when the component is collapsed:

```
const styles = StyleSheet.create({
  main: {
    backgroundColor: '#fff',
    borderRadius: 3,
    overflow: 'hidden',
    paddingLeft: 30,
    paddingRight: 30,
  },
  title: {
    fontWeight: 'bold',
    paddingTop: 15,
    paddingBottom: 15,
  }
```

7. Once we have our `Panel` component defined, let's use it on the `App` class. First, we need to require all the dependencies in `App.js`:

```
import React, { Component } from 'react';
import {
  Text,
  StyleSheet,
  View,
  SafeAreaView,
  Platform,
  UIManager
} from 'react-native';
import Panel from './Panel';
```

8. In the previous step, we imported the `Panel` component. We are going to declare three instances of this class in the JSX:

```
export default class App extends Component {
  render() {
    return (
      <SafeAreaView style={[styles.main]}>
        <Text style={styles.toolbar}>Animated containers</Text>
        <View style={styles.content}>
          <Panel
            title={'Container 1'}
            style={styles.panel}
          >
            <Text style={styles.panelText}>
              Temporibus autem quibusdam et aut officiis
              debitis aut rerum necessitatibus saepe
              eveniet ut et voluptates repudiandae sint et
              molestiae non recusandae.
            </Text>
          </Panel>
          <Panel
            title={'Container 2'}
            style={styles.panel}
            >
            <Text style={styles.panelText}>
              Et harum quidem rerum facilis est et expedita
              distinctio. Nam libero tempore,
              cum soluta nobis est eligendi optio cumque.
            </Text>
          </Panel>
          <Panel
            expanded
            title={'Container 3'}
            style={styles.panel}
```

```
        >
          <Text style={styles.panelText}>
            Nullam lobortis eu lorem ut vulputate.
          </Text>
          <Text style={styles.panelText}>
            Donec id elementum orci. Donec fringilla lobortis
            ipsum, vitae commodo urna.
          </Text>
        </Panel>
      </View>
    </SafeAreaView>
  );
}
}
```

9. We are using the React Native `LayoutAnimation` API in this recipe. This API is disabled on Android by default in the current version of React Native. Before the `App` component mounts, we'll use the `Platform` helper with the `UIManager` to enable this feature on Android devices:

```
componentWillMount() {
  if (Platform.OS === 'android') {
    UIManager.setLayoutAnimationEnabledExperimental(true);
  }
}
```

10. Finally, let's add some styles to the toolbar and the main container. We just need some simple styles you're likely used to by now: `padding`, `margin`, and `color`:

```
const styles = StyleSheet.create({
  main: {
    flex: 1,
  },
  toolbar: {
    backgroundColor: '#3498db',
    color: '#fff',
    fontSize: 22,
    padding: 20,
    textAlign: 'center',
  },
  content: {
    padding: 10,
    backgroundColor: '#ecf0f1',
    flex: 1,
  },
  panel: {
    marginBottom: 10,
```

```
      },
    panelText: {
      paddingBottom: 15,
      }
  });
```

11. The final app should look similar to the following screenshots:

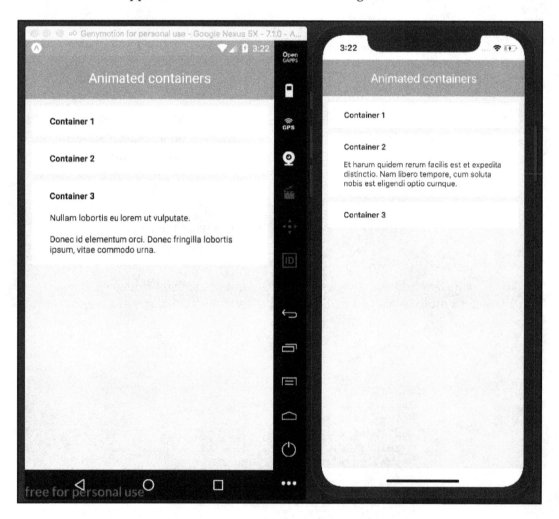

How it works...

In *step 3*, we set the initial `height` of the content. If the `expanded` property was set to `true`, then we should show the content. By setting the `height` value to `null`, the layout system will calculate the `height` based on the content; otherwise, we need to set the value to `0`, which will hide the content when the component is collapsed.

In *step 4*, we defined all the JSX for the `Panel` component. There are a few concepts in this step worth covering. First, the `children` property is passed in from the `props` object, which will contain any elements defined between `<Panel>` and `</Panel>` when this component is used in the `App` class. This is very helpful because, by using this property, we are allowing this component to receive any other components as children.

In this same step, we're also getting the `height` from the `state` object and setting it as the `style` applied to the `View` with the collapsible content. This will update the `height`, causing the component to correspondingly expand or collapse. We also declared the `onPress` callback, which toggles the `height` on the `state` when the title element is pressed.

In *step 7*, we defined the `toggle` method, which toggles the `height` value. Here, we used the `LayoutAnimation` class. By calling the `spring` method, the layout system will animate every change that happens to the layout on the next render. In this case, we are only changing `height`, but we can change any other property we want, such as `opacity`, `position`, or `color`.

The `LayoutAnimation` class contains a couple of predefined animations. In this recipe, we used `spring`, but we could also use `linear` or `easeInEaseOut`, or you could create your own using the `configureNext` method.

If we remove the `LayoutAnimation`, we won't see an animation; the component will expand and collapse by jumping from `0` to total height. But by adding that single line, we're able to easily add a nice, smooth animation. If you need more control over the animation, you'll probably want to use the Animation API instead.

In *step 9*, we checked the OS property on the `Platform` helper, which returned the `'android'` or `'ios'` strings, depending on which device the app is running on. If the app is running on Andriod, we use the `UIManager` helper's `setLayoutAnimationEnabledExperimental` method to enable the `LayoutAnimation` API.

See also

- LayoutAnimation API documentation at https://facebook.github.io/react-native/docs/layoutanimation.html
- A quick intro to React's props.children at https://codeburst.io/a-quick-intro-to-reacts-props-children-cb3d2fce4891

Creating a button with a loading animation

In this recipe, we'll continue working with the LayoutAnimation class. Here, we will create a button, and when the user presses the button, we will show a loading indicator and animate the styles.

Getting ready

To get started, we'll need to create an empty app. Let's call it button-loading-animation.

Let's also create a Button folder with an index.js file in it for our Button component.

How to do it...

1. Let's start with the Button/index.js file. First, we'll import all the dependencies for this component:

```
import React, { Component } from 'react';
import {
  ActivityIndicator,
  LayoutAnimation,
  StyleSheet,
  Text,
  TouchableOpacity,
  View,
} from 'react-native';
```

2. We're going to use only four props for this component: a `label`, a `loading` Boolean to toggle displaying either the loading indicator or the label inside the button, a callback function to be executed when the button is pressed, and custom styles. Here, we'll `init` the `defaultProps` for loading to `false`, and the `handleButtonPress` to an empty function:

```
export default class Button extends Component {
  static defaultProps = {
    loading: false,
    onPress: () => {},
  };
  // Defined on later steps
}
```

3. We'll keep the `render` method of this component as simple as possible. We'll render the label and the activity indicator based on the value of the `loading` property:

```
render() {
  const { loading, style } = this.props;

  return (
    <TouchableOpacity
      style={[
        styles.main,
        style,
        loading ? styles.loading : null,
      ]}
      activeOpacity={0.6}
      onPress={this.handleButtonPress}
    >
      <View>
        {this.renderLabel()}
        {this.renderActivityIndicator()}
      </View>
    </TouchableOpacity>
  );
}
```

4. In order to render the `label`, we need to check whether the `loading` property is `false`. If it is, then we return only a `Text` element with the `label` we received from `props`:

```
renderLabel() {
  const { label, loading } = this.props;
  if(!loading) {
    return (
      <Text style={styles.label}>{label}</Text>
    );
  }
}
```

5. Likewise, the `renderActivityIndicator` indicator should only apply if the value of the `loading` property is `true`. If so, we will return the `ActivityIndicator` component. We'll use the props of `ActivityIndicator` to define a `size` of small and a `color` of white (`#fff`):

```
renderActivityIndicator() {
  if (this.props.loading) {
    return (
      <ActivityIndicator size="small" color="#fff" />
    );
  }
}
```

6. One method is still missing from our class: `handleButtonPress`. We need to inform the parent of this component when the button has been pressed, which can be done by calling the `onPress` callback passed to this component via `props`. We'll also use the `LayoutAnimation` to queue an animation on the next render:

```
handleButtonPress = () => {
  const { loading, onPress } = this.props;

  LayoutAnimation.easeInEaseOut();
  onPress(!loading);
}
```

7. To complete this component, we need to add some styles. We'll define some colors, rounded corners, alignment, padding, and so on. For the `loading` styles, which will be applied when the loading indicator is displayed, we'll update the padding to create a circle around the loading indicator:

```
const styles = StyleSheet.create({
  main: {
    backgroundColor: '#e67e22',
```

```
      borderRadius: 20,
      padding: 10,
      paddingLeft: 50,
      paddingRight: 50,
    },
    label: {
      color: '#fff',
      fontWeight: 'bold',
      textAlign: 'center',
      backgroundColor: 'transparent',
    },
    loading: {
      padding: 10,
      paddingLeft: 10,
      paddingRight: 10,
    },
});
```

8. We are done with the `Button` component. Now, lets's work on the `App` class. Let's start by importing all the dependencies:

```
import React, { Component } from 'react';
import {
  Text,
  StyleSheet,
  View,
  SafeAreaView,
  Platform,
  UIManager
} from 'react-native';
import Button from './Button';
```

9. The `App` class is relatively simple. We will only need to define a `loading` property on the `state` object, which will toggle the `Button`'s animation. We'll also render a `toolbar` and a `Button`:

```
export default class App extends Component {
  state = {
    loading: false,
  };

  // Defined on next step

  handleButtonPress = (loading) => {
    this.setState({ loading });
  }

  render() {
```

```
      const { loading } = this.state;

      return (
        <SafeAreaView style={[styles.main, android]}>
          <Text style={styles.toolbar}>Animated containers</Text>
          <View style={styles.content}>
            <Button
              label="Login"
              loading={loading}
              onPress={this.handleButtonPress}
            />
          </View>
        </SafeAreaView>
      );
    }
  }
```

10. As in the last recipe, we'll need to manually enable the `LayoutAnimation` API on Android devices:

```
componentWillMount() {
  if (Platform.OS === 'android') {
    UIManager.setLayoutAnimationEnabledExperimental(true);
  }
}
```

11. Finally, we'll add some `styles`, just some colors, padding, and alignment for centering the button on the screen:

```
const styles = StyleSheet.create({
  main: {
    flex: 1,
  },
  toolbar: {
    backgroundColor: '#f39c12',
    color: '#fff',
    fontSize: 22,
    padding: 20,
    textAlign: 'center',
  },
  content: {
    padding: 10,
    backgroundColor: '#ecf0f1',
    flex: 1,
    alignItems: 'center',
    justifyContent: 'center',
  },
});
```

12. The final app should look similar to the following screenshot:

How it works...

In *step 3*, we added the `render` method for the `Button` component. Here, we received the `loading` property and, based on that value, we applied the corresponding styles to the `TouchableOpacity` button element. We also used two methods: one for rendering the label and the other for rendering the activity indicator.

In *step 6*, we executed the `onPress` callback. By default, we declared an empty function, so we don't have to check whether the value is present or not.

The parent of this button should be responsible for updating the loading property when the `onPress` callback is called. From this component, we are only responsible for informing the parent when this button has been pressed.

The `LayoutAnimation.eadeInEaseOut` method only queues an animation for the next render phase, which means the animation isn't executed right away. We are responsible for changing the styles that we want to animate. If we don't change any styles, then we won't see any animations.

The `Button` component doesn't know how the `loading` property gets updated. It might be because of a fetch request, a timeout, or any other action. The parent component is responsible for updating the `loading` property. Whenever any changes happen, we apply the new styles to the button and a smooth animation will occur.

In *step 9*, we defined the content of the `App` class. Here, we make use of our `Button` component. When the button is pressed, the `state` of the `loading` property is updated, which will cause the animation to run every time the button is pressed.

Conclusion

In this chapter, we've covered the fundamentals of animating your React Native app. These recipes have been aimed at both providing useful practical code solutions, and also establishing how to use the basic building blocks so that you are better equipped to create animations that fit your app. Hopefully, by now, you should be getting comfortable with the `Animated` and `LayoutAnimation` animation helpers. In `Chapter 7`, *Adding Advanced Animations to Your App*, we will combine the things we've learned here to build out more complex and interesting app-centric UI animations.

Adding Advanced Animations to Your App

7

In this chapter, we'll cover the following recipes:

- Removing items from a list component
- Creating a Facebook reactions widget
- Displaying images in fullscreen

Introduction

In the previous chapter, we covered the basics of using the two main animation helpers in React Native: `Animated` and `LayoutAnimation`. In this chapter, we'll take these concepts further by building out more complicated recipes that exhibit common native UX patterns.

Removing items from a list component

In this recipe, we'll learn how to create list items in a `ListView` with an animated sideways slide. If the user slides the item past a threshold, the item is removed. This is a common pattern in many mobile apps with editable lists. We are also going to see how to use `PanResponder` to handle drag events.

Getting ready

We need to create an empty app. For this recipe, we'll name it `removing-list-items`.

We also need to create a new `ContactList` folder and two files inside it: `index.js` and `ContactItem.js`.

How to do it...

1. Let's start by importing the dependencies for the main `App` class, as follows:

```
import React from 'react';
import {
  Text,
  StyleSheet,
  SafeAreaView,
} from 'react-native';
import ContactList from './ContactList';
```

2. This component will be simple. All we need to render is a `toolbar` and the `ContactList` component that we imported in the previous step, as follows:

```
const App = () => (
  <SafeAreaView style={styles.main}>
    <Text style={styles.toolbar}>Contacts</Text>
    <ContactList style={styles.content} />
  </SafeAreaView>
);

const styles = StyleSheet.create({
  main: {
    flex: 1,
  },
  toolbar: {
    backgroundColor: '#2c3e50',
    color: '#fff',
    fontSize: 22,
    padding: 20,
    textAlign: 'center',
  },
  content: {
    padding: 10,
    flex: 1,
  },
});

export default App;
```

3. This is all we need in order to start working on the actual list. Let's open the file at `ContactList/index.js` and import all of the dependencies, as follows:

```
import React, { Component } from 'react';
import {
  ListView,
```

```
    ScrollView,
} from 'react-native';
import ContactItem from './ContactItem';
```

4. We then need to define some data. In a real-world app, we would fetch the data
   from an API, but to keep things simple and focused only on the drag
   functionality, let's just define the data in this same file:

```
const data = [
    { id: 1, name: 'Jon Snow' },
    { id: 2, name: 'Luke Skywalker' },
    { id: 3, name: 'Bilbo Baggins' },
    { id: 4, name: 'Bob Labla' },
    { id: 5, name: 'Mr. Magoo' },
];
```

5. The `state` for this component will only contain two properties: the data for the
   list and a Boolean value that will be updated when the dragging starts or ends. If
   you are not familiar with how `ListView` works, checkout the *Displaying a list of
   items* recipe in `Chapter 2`, *Creating a Simple React Native App*. Let's define the data
   as follows:

```
export default class ContactList extends Component {
    ds = new ListView.DataSource({
        rowHasChanged: (r1, r2) => r1 !== r2
    });

    state = {
        dataSource: this.ds.cloneWithRows(data),
        swiping: false,
    };
    // Defined in later steps
}
```

6. The `render` method only needs to display the list. In
   the `renderScrollComponent` property, we'll enable scrolling only when the
   user is not swiping an item on the list. If the user is swiping, we want to disable
   vertical scrolling, as follows:

```
render() {
    const { dataSource, swiping } = this.state;

    return (
    <ListView
        key={data}
        enableEmptySections
        dataSource={dataSource}
```

```
            renderScrollComponent={
            (props) => <ScrollView {...props}
    scrollEnabled={!swiping}/>
            }
            renderRow={this.renderItem}
        />
      );
    }
```

7. The `renderItem` method will return each item in the list. Here, we need to send the contact information as a property, along with three callbacks:

```
renderItem = (contact) => (
  <ContactItem
    contact={contact}
    onRemove={this.handleRemoveContact}
    onDragEnd={this.handleToggleSwipe}
    onDragStart={this.handleToggleSwipe}
  />
);
```

8. We need to toggle the value of the swiping property on the `state` object, which will toggle whether vertical scroll on the list is locked or not:

```
handleToggleSwipe = () => {
  this.setState({ swiping: !this.state.swiping });
}
```

9. When removing an item, we need to find the `index` of the given `contact` and then remove it from the original list. After that, we need to update `dataSource` on the state to re-render the list with the resulting data:

```
handleRemoveContact = (contact) => {
  const index = data.findIndex(
    (item) => item.id === contact.id
  );
  data.splice(index, 1);

  this.setState({
      dataSource: this.ds.cloneWithRows(data),
  });
}
```

10. We are done with the list, so now let's focus on the list items. Let's open the `ContactList/ContactItem.js` file and import the dependencies we'll need:

```
import React, { Component } from 'react';
import {
  Animated,
  Easing,
  PanResponder,
  StyleSheet,
  Text,
  TouchableHighlight,
  View,
} from 'react-native';
```

11. We need to define `defaultProps` for this component. The `defaultProps` object will need an empty function for each of the four props being passed into it from the parent `ListView` element. The `onPress` function will execute when the item is pressed, the `onRemove` function will execute when the contact gets removed, and two drag functions will listen for drag events. On `state` , we only need to define an animated value to hold the *x* and *y* coordinates of the dragging, as follows:

```
export default class ContactItem extends Component {
  static defaultProps = {
    onPress: () => {},
    onRemove: () => {},
    onDragEnd: () => {},
    onDragStart: () => {},
  };

  state = {
    pan: new Animated.ValueXY(),
  };
```

12. When the component is created, we need to configure `PanResponder`. We will do this in the `componentWillMount` life cycle hook. `PanResponder` is responsible for handling gestures. It provides a simple API to capture the events generated by the user's finger, as follows:

```
componentWillMount() {
  this.panResponder = PanResponder.create({
    onMoveShouldSetPanResponderCapture: this.handleShouldDrag,
    onPanResponderMove: Animated.event(
      [null, { dx: this.state.pan.x }]
    ),
```

```
        onPanResponderRelease: this.handleReleaseItem,
        onPanResponderTerminate: this.handleReleaseItem,
      });
    }
```

13. Now let's define the actual functions that will get executed for each callback defined in the previous step. We can start with the `handleShouldDrag` method, as follows:

```
handleShouldDrag = (e, gesture) => {
  const { dx } = gesture;
  return Math.abs(dx) > 2;
}
```

14. `handleReleaseItem` is a little bit more complicated. We are going to split this method into two steps. First, we need to figure out whether the current item needs to be removed or not. In order to do that, we need to set a threshold. If the user slides the element beyond our threshold, we'll remove the item, as follows:

```
handleReleaseItem = (e, gesture) => {
  const { onRemove, contact,onDragEnd } = this.props;
  const move = this.rowWidth - Math.abs(gesture.dx);
  let remove = false;
  let config = { // Animation to origin position
    toValue: { x: 0, y: 0 },
    duration: 500,
  };

  if (move < this.threshold) {
    remove = true;
    if (gesture.dx > 0) {
      config = { // Animation to the right
        toValue: { x: this.rowWidth, y: 0 },
        duration: 100,
      };
    } else {
      config = { // Animation to the left
        toValue: { x: -this.rowWidth, y: 0 },
        duration: 100,
      };
    }
  }
  // Remainder in next step
}
```

15. Once we have the configurations for the animation, we are ready to move the item! First, we'll execute the `onDragEnd` callback and, if the item should be removed, we'll run the `onRemove` function, as follows:

```
handleReleaseItem = (e, gesture) => {
  // Code from previous step

  onDragEnd();
  Animated.spring(
    this.state.pan,
    config,
  ).start(() => {
    if (remove) {
      onRemove(contact);
    }
  });
}
```

16. We have the full dragging system in place. Now we need to define the `render` method. We just need to display the contact name within the `TouchableHighlight` element, wrapped inside an `Animated.View`, as follows:

```
render() {
  const { contact, onPress } = this.props;

  return (
    <View style={styles.row} onLayout={this.setThreshold}>
      <Animated.View
        style={[styles.pan, this.state.pan.getLayout()]}
        {...this.panResponder.panHandlers}
      >
        <TouchableHighlight
          style={styles.info}
          onPress={() => onPress(contact)}
          underlayColor="#ecf0f1"
        >
          <Text>{contact.name}</Text>
        </TouchableHighlight>
      </Animated.View>
    </View>
  );
}
```

17. We need one more method on this class, which is fired on layout change via the `View` element's `onLayout` prop. `setThreshold` will get the current `width` of `row` and set `threshold`. In this case, we're setting it to be a third of the width of the screen. These values are required to decide whether to remove the item or not, as follows:

```
setThreshold = (event) => {
  const { layout: { width } } = event.nativeEvent;
  this.threshold = width / 3;
  this.rowWidth = width;
}
```

18. Finally, we'll add some styles to the rows, as follows:

```
const styles = StyleSheet.create({
  row: {
    backgroundColor: '#ecf0f1',
    borderBottomWidth: 1,
    borderColor: '#ecf0f1',
    flexDirection: 'row',
  },
  pan: {
    flex: 1,
  },
  info: {
    backgroundColor: '#fff',
    paddingBottom: 20,
    paddingLeft: 10,
    paddingTop: 20,
  },
});
```

19. The final app should look something like this screenshot:

How it works...

In *step 5*, we defined the `swiping` property on the `state`. This property is just a Boolean that will be set to `true` when the dragging starts and to `false` when it has completed. We need this information in order to lock the vertical scrolling on the list while dragging around the item.

In *step 7*, we defined the content of each row in the list. The onDragStart property receives the handleToggleSwipe method, which will be executed when the dragging starts. We are also going to execute the same method when the dragging is completed.

In the same step, we also send the handleRemoveContact method to each item. As the name suggests, we are going to remove the current item from the list when the user swipes it out.

In *step 11*, we defined defaultProps and state for the item component. In past recipes, we have been creating animations using a single value, but for this case we need to handle the *x* and *y* coordinates, so we'll need an instance of Animated.ValueXY. Internally, this class handles two Animated.Value instances, and therefore the API is almost identical to those we've seen before.

In *step 12*, PanResponder gets created. The gesture system in React Native, like the event system in the browser, handles gestures in two phases when there's a touch event: the capture and the bubble. In our case, we need to use the capture phase to figure out whether the current event is pressing the item or whether it's trying to drag it. onMoveShouldSetPanResponderCapture will capture the event. Then, we need to decide whether we'll drag the item or not by returning true or false.

The onPanResponderMove prop will get the values from the animation on each frame, which will be applied to the pan object in the state. We need to use Animated.event to access the animation values for each frame. In this case, we only need the x value. Later, we'll use this value to run a different animation while returning the element to its original place or removing it from the screen.

The onPanResponderRelease function will be executed when the user releases the item. If, for any other reason, the dragging gets interrupted, onPanResponderTerminate will get executed instead.

In *step 13*, we need to check whether the current event is a simple press or a drag. We can do this by checking the delta on the *x*-axis. If the touch event has been moved more than two pixels, then the user is trying to drag the item, otherwise, they're trying to press the button. We evaluate the difference as an absolute number because the movement could be from left to right or right to left, and we want to accommodate both movements.

In *step 14*, we need to get the distance the item has moved with respect to the width of the device. If this distance is below our threshold we defined in setThreshold, then we need to remove these items. We are defining the config object for each animation, which will otherwise return the item to the original position. But if we need to remove the item, we check the direction and set the configuration accordingly.

In *step 16*, we defined the JSX. We set the styles that we want to animate
on `Animated.View`. In this case, it's the `left` property, but instead of manually creating an
object, we can call the `getLayout` method from our instance of `Animated.ValueXY` that
we stored in `state.pan`, which returns the top and left properties with their existing
values.

In the same step, we also set the event handlers for `Animated.View` by spreading
out `this.panResponder.panHandlers` with a spread operator, which binds the dragging
configuration we defined in the previous steps to `Animated.View`.

We also defined a call to the `onPress` callback from `props`, passing in the
current `contact` information.

See also

You can find the `PanResponder` API documentation at:

`https://facebook.github.io/react-native/docs/panresponder.html`

Creating a Facebook reactions widget

In this recipe, we'll be creating a component that emulates the Facebook reaction widget.
We will have a like button image which, when pressed, will show five icons. The row of
icons will use a staggered slide-in animation while increasing opacity from 0 to 1.

Getting ready

Let's create an empty app called `facebook-widget`.

We are going to need some images to display a fake timeline. A few pictures of your cat
will work, or you can use the cat pictures included in the corresponding repository on
GitHub (`https://github.com/warlyware/react-native-cookbook/tree/master/chapter-7/facebook-widget`). We'll also need five icons to display the five reactions, such as, angry,
laughing, heart, and surprised, which can also be found in the corresponding repository.

To start we'll create two JavaScript files in our empty
app: `Reactions/index.js` and `Reactions/Icon.js`. We need to copy our cat pictures to
an `images/` folder in the root of the app, and the reaction icons should be placed
in `Reactions/images`.

How to do it...

1. We are going to be creating a fake Facebook timeline on the `App` class. Let's start by importing the dependencies, as follows:

```
import React from 'react';
import {
  Dimensions,
  Image,
  Text,
  ScrollView,
  StyleSheet,
  SafeAreaView,
} from 'react-native';
import Reactions from './Reactions';
```

2. We'll need to import some images to render in our timeline. The JSX in this step is very simple: it's just a `toolbar`, a `ScrollView` with two `Image`, and two `Reaction` components, as follows:

```
const image1 = require('./images/01.jpg');
const image2 = require('./images/02.jpg');
const { width } = Dimensions.get('window');

const App = () => (
  <SafeAreaView style={styles.main}>
    <Text style={styles.toolbar}>Reactions</Text>
    <ScrollView style={styles.content}>
      <Image source={image1} style={styles.image}
resizeMode="cover" />
      <Reactions />
      <Image source={image2} style={styles.image}
resizeMode="cover" />
      <Reactions />
    </ScrollView>
  </SafeAreaView>
);

export default App;
```

3. We need to add some basic `styles` for this component, as follows:

```
const styles = StyleSheet.create({
  main: {
    flex: 1,
  },
  toolbar: {
```

```
      backgroundColor: '#3498db',
      color: '#fff',
      fontSize: 22,
      padding: 20,
      textAlign: 'center',
    },
    content: {
      flex: 1,
    },
    image: {
      width,
      height: 300,
    },
});
```

4. We are ready to start working on the `Reactions` component of this recipe. Let's start by importing dependencies, as follows. We will build out the imported `Icon` component in later steps:

```
import React, { Component } from 'react';
import {
  Image,
  Text,
  TouchableOpacity,
  StyleSheet,
  View,
} from 'react-native';
import Icon from './Icon';
```

5. Let's define `defaultProps` and the initial `state` next. We'll also need to require the `like` icon image to display it on screen, as follows:

```
const image = require('./images/like.png');

export default class Reactions extends Component {
  static defaultProps = {
    icons: [
      'like', 'heart', 'angry', 'laughing', 'surprised',
    ],
  };

  state = {
    show: false,
    selected: '',
  };

  // Defined at later steps
}
```

6. Let's define two methods: one that sets the selected value of `state` to the selected `reaction`, and another that toggles the `show` value of `state` to show or hide the row of reactions accordingly, as follows:

```
onSelectReaction = (reaction) => {
  this.setState({
    selected: reaction,
  });
  this.toggleReactions();
}

toggleReactions = () => {
  this.setState({
    show: !this.state.show,
  });
};
```

7. We'll define the `render` method for this component. We are going to display an image, which when pressed, will call the `toggleReactions` method that we defined previously, as follows:

```
render() {
  const { style } = this.props;
  const { selected } = this.state;

  return (
    <View style={[style, styles.container]}>
      <TouchableOpacity onPress={this.toggleReactions}>
        <Image source={image} style={styles.icon} />
      </TouchableOpacity>
      <Text>{selected}</Text>
      {this.renderReactions()}
    </View>
  );
}
```

8. You'll notice in this step that we're calling the `renderReactions` method. Next, we'll render all of the icons that we want to display when the user presses the main reaction button, as follows:

```
renderReactions() {
  const { icons } = this.props;
  if (this.state.show) {
    return (
      <View style={styles.reactions}>
        { icons.map((name, index) => (
          <Icon
```

```
            key={index}
            name={name}
            delay={index * 100}
            index={index}
            onPress={this.onSelectReaction}
          />
        ))
      }
      </View>
    );
  }
}
```

9. We need to set `styles` for this component. We'll set sizes for the reaction icon images and define some padding. The `reactions` container will have a height of 0, since the icons will be floating, and we don't want any extra space added:

```
const styles = StyleSheet.create({
  container: {
    padding: 10,
  },
  icon: {
    width: 30,
    height: 30,
  },
  reactions: {
    flexDirection: 'row',
    height: 0,
  },
});
```

10. The `Icon` component is currently missing, so if we try to run our app at this point, it will fail. Let's build out this component by opening the `Reactions/Icon.js` file and adding the imports for the component, as follows:

```
import React, { Component } from 'react';
import {
  Animated,
  Dimensions,
  Easing,
  Image,
  StyleSheet,
  TouchableOpacity,
  View,
} from 'react-native';
```

11. Let's define the icons we'll be using. We are going to use an object for the icons so that we can easily retrieve each image by its key name, as follows:

```
const icons = {
  angry: require('./images/angry.png'),
  heart: require('./images/heart.png'),
  laughing: require('./images/laughing.png'),
  like: require('./images/like.png'),
  surprised: require('./images/surprised.png'),
};
```

12. Now we should define `defaultProps` for this component. We don't need to define an initial state:

```
export default class Icon extends Component {
  static defaultProps = {
    delay: 0,
    onPress: () => {},
  };


}
```

13. The icons should appear on screen via an animation, so we'll need to create and run the animation when the component is mounted, as follows:

```
componentWillMount() {
  this.animatedValue = new Animated.Value(0);
}

componentDidMount() {
  const { delay } = this.props;

  Animated.timing(
    this.animatedValue,
    {
      toValue: 1,
      duration: 200,
      easing: Easing.elastic(1),
      delay,
    }
  ).start();
}
```

14. When the icon is pressed, we need to execute the `onPress` callback to inform the parent that a reaction was selected. We will send the name of the reaction as a parameter, as follows:

```
onPressIcon = () => {
  const { onPress, name } = this.props;
  onPress(name);
}
```

15. The last piece of the puzzle is the `render` method, where we'll define the JSX for this component, as follows:

```
render() {
  const { name, index, onPress } = this.props;
  const left = index * 50;
  const top = this.animatedValue.interpolate({
    inputRange: [0, 1],
    outputRange: [10, -95],
  });
  const opacity = this.animatedValue;

  return (
    <Animated.View
      style={[
        styles.icon,
        { top, left, opacity },
      ]}
    >
      <TouchableOpacity onPress={this.onPressIcon}>
        <Image source={icons[name]} style={styles.image} />
      </TouchableOpacity>
    </Animated.View>
  );
}
```

16. As the final step, we'll add styles for each `icon`. We need the icons to float, so we'll set `position` to `absolute` and `width` and `height` to 40 pixels. After this change, we should be able to run our app:

```
icon: {
  position: 'absolute',
},
image: {
  width: 40,
  height: 40,
},
});
```

17. The final app should look something like this screenshot:

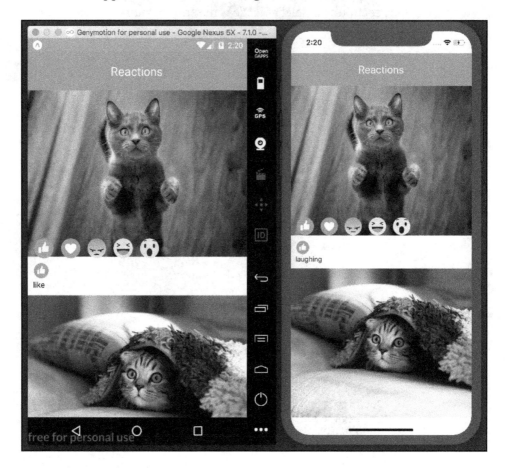

How it works...

In *step 2*, we defined the `Reactions` component in the timeline. For now, we are not focusing on handling data, but rather on displaying the UI. Therefore, we are not sending any callback via `Reactions` props to get the selected value.

In *step 5*, we defined `defaultProps` and the initial `state`.

We have two properties in the state:

- The `show` prop is a Boolean. We use it to toggle the reactions icons when the user presses the main button. When `false`, we hide the reactions, and when `true`, we run the animation to show each icon.
- `selected` contains the current selection. Every time a new reaction gets selected, we are going to update this prop.

In *step 8*, we render the icons. Here, we need to send the name of the icon to every instance created. We also send a `delay` of 100 milliseconds for each icon, which will create a nice stagger animation. The `onPress` prop receives the `onSelectReaction` method defined in *step 6*, which sets the selected reaction on `state`.

In *step 13*, we create the animation. First, we define the `animatedValue` variable using the `Animated.Value` helper, which, as mentioned in previous recipes, is the class responsible for holding the value for each frame in the animation. As soon as the component is mounted, we run the animation. The animations progress from 0 to 1, with a duration of 200 milliseconds and using an elastic easing function, and we delay the animation based on the received `delay` prop.

In *step 15*, we defined the JSX for the `Icon` component. Here we animate the `top` and `opacity` properties. For the `top` property, we need to interpolate the values from `animatedValue`, so that the icon moves 95 pixels up from its original position. The required values for the `opacity` property are from 0 to 1, and since we don't need to interpolate anything to accomplish this, we can use `animatedValue` directly.

The `left` value is calculated based on the `index`: we just move the icon 50 pixels to the left of the previous icon, which will avoid rendering the icons all in the sample place.

Displaying images in fullscreen

In this recipe, we'll create a timeline of images. When the user presses any of the images, it will fullscreen the image with a black background.

We will use an opacity animation for the background, and we'll slide the image in from its original position.

Getting ready

Let's create an empty app called `photo-viewer`.

In addition, we'll also create `PostContainer/index.js` for showing each image in the timeline, and `PhotoViewer/index.js` for showing the selected image in fullscreen.

You can either use the images included in this recipe's repository hosted on GitHub (`https://github.com/warlyware/react-native-cookbook/tree/master/chapter-7/photo-viewer`), or use a few photos of your own. Place them in an `images` folder in the root of the project.

How to do it...

1. We are going to display a timeline with images in the `App` class. Let's import all of the dependencies, including the two other components we'll build out in later steps, as follows:

```
import React, { Component } from 'react';
import {
  Dimensions,
  Image,
  Text,
  ScrollView,
  StyleSheet,
  SafeAreaView,
} from 'react-native';
import PostContainer from './PostContainer';
import PhotoViewer from './PhotoViewer';
```

2. In this step, we'll define the data that we are going to render. It's just a simple array of objects containing `title` and `image`, as follows:

```
const image1 = require('./images/01.jpg');
const image2 = require('./images/02.jpg');
const image3 = require('./images/03.jpg');
const image4 = require('./images/04.jpg');

const timeline = [
  { title: 'Enjoying the fireworks', image: image1 },
  { title: 'Climbing the Mount Fuji', image: image2 },
  { title: 'Check my last picture', image: image3 },
  { title: 'Sakuras are beautiful!', image: image4 },
];
```

3. Now we need to declare the initial `state` of this component. We will update the `selected` and `position` properties when any of the images gets pressed, as follows:

```
export default class App extends Component {
  state = {
    selected: null,
    position: null,
  };
  // Defined in following steps
}
```

4. In order to update `state`, we are going to declare two methods: one to set the value of the image that has been pressed and another to remove those values when the viewer gets closed:

```
showImage = (selected, position) => {
  this.setState({
    selected,
    position,
  });
}

closeViewer = () => {
  this.setState({
    selected: null,
    position: null,
  });
}
```

5. Now we are ready to work on the `render` method. Here we'll need to render each image inside `ScrollView` so the list will be scrollable, as follows:

```
render() {
  return (
    <SafeAreaView style={styles.main}>
      <Text style={styles.toolbar}>Timeline</Text>
      <ScrollView style={styles.content}>
      {
        timeline.map((post, index) =>
          <PostContainer key={index} post={post}
          onPress={this.showImage} />
        )
      }
      </ScrollView>
      {this.renderViewer()}
    </SafeAreaView>
```

```
    );
  }
```

6. In the previous step, we are calling the `renderViewer` method. Here we'll show the viewer component only if there's a post `selected` in the state. We are also sending the initial position to start the animation and a callback to close the viewer, as follows:

```
renderViewer() {
  const { selected, position } = this.state;

  if (selected) {
    return (
      <PhotoViewer
        post={selected}
        position={position}
        onClose={this.closeViewer}
      />
    );
  }
}
```

7. The styles for this component are very simple, only some colors and padding, as follows:

```
const styles = StyleSheet.create({
  main: {
    backgroundColor: '#ecf0f1',
    flex: 1,
  },
  toolbar: {
    backgroundColor: '#2c3e50',
    color: '#fff',
    fontSize: 22,
    padding: 20,
    textAlign: 'center',
  },
  content: {
    flex: 1,
  },
});
```

8. The timeline is complete, but if we try to run our app, it will fail. Let's work on the `PostContainer` component. We'll start by importing the dependencies, as follows:

```
import React, { Component } from 'react';
import {
  Dimensions,
  Image,
  Text,
  TouchableOpacity,
  StyleSheet,
  View,
} from 'react-native';
```

9. We only need two `props` for this component. The `post` prop will receive the image data, `title` and `image`, and the `onPress` prop is a callback that we'll execute when the image gets pressed, as follows:

```
const { width } = Dimensions.get('window');

export default class PostContainer extends Component {
  static defaultProps = {
    onPress: () => {},
  };
  // Defined on following steps
}
```

10. This component will be inside of `ScrollView`. This means its position will be changing when the user starts scrolling the content. When pressing the image, we need to get the current position on the screen and send this information to the parent component, as follows:

```
onPressImage = (event) => {
  const { onPress, post } = this.props;
  this.refs.main.measure((fx, fy, width, height, pageX, pageY) =>
{
    onPress(post, {
      width,
      height,
      pageX,
      pageY,
    });
  });
}
```

11. It's time to define the JSX for this component. To keep things simple, we are only going to render `image` and `title`:

```
render() {
  const { post: { image, title } } = this.props;

  return (
    <View style={styles.main} ref="main">
      <TouchableOpacity
        onPress={this.onPressImage}
        activeOpacity={0.9}
        >
        <Image
          source={image}
          style={styles.image}
          resizeMode="cover"
        />
      </TouchableOpacity>
      <Text style={styles.title}>{title}</Text>
    </View>
  );
}
```

12. As always, we need to define some styles for this component. We are going to add some colors and padding, as follows:

```
const styles = StyleSheet.create({
  main: {
    backgroundColor: '#fff',
    marginBottom: 30,
    paddingBottom: 10,
  },
  content: {
    flex: 1,
  },
  image: {
    width,
    height: 300,
  },
  title: {
    margin: 10,
    color: '#ccc',
  }
});
```

13. If we run the app now, we should be able to see the timeline, however if we press any of the images, an error will be thrown. We need to define the viewer, so let's open the `PhotoViewer/index.js` file and import the dependencies:

```
import React, { Component } from 'react';
import {
  Animated,
  Dimensions,
  Easing,
  Text,
  TouchableOpacity,
  StyleSheet,
} from 'react-native';
```

14. Let's define `props` for this component. In order to center the image on the screen, we need to know the `height` of the current device:

```
const { width, height } = Dimensions.get('window');

export default class PhotoViewer extends Component {
  static defaultProps = {
    onClose: () => {},
  };
  // Defined on following steps
}
```

15. We want to run two animations when showing this component, so we'll need to initialize and run the animation after the component is mounted. The animation is simple: it just goes from `0` to `1` in `400` milliseconds with some easing applied, as follows:

```
componentWillMount() {
  this.animatedValue = new Animated.Value(0);
}

componentDidMount() {
  Animated.timing(
    this.animatedValue,
    {
      toValue: 1,
      duration: 400,
      easing: Easing.in,
    }
  ).start();
}
```

16. When the user presses the close button, we need to execute the `onClose` callback to inform the parent that this component needs to be removed, as follows:

```
onPressBtn = () => {
  this.props.onClose();
}
```

17. We are going to split the `render` method into two steps. First, we need to interpolate the values for the animations, as follows:

```
render() {
  const { post: { image, title }, position } = this.props;
  const top = this.animatedValue.interpolate({
    inputRange: [0, 1],
    outputRange: [position.pageY, height/2 - position.height/2],
  });
  const opacity = this.animatedValue;
  // Defined on next step
}
```

18. We only need to define three elements: `Animated.View` to animate the background, `Animated.Image` to display the image, and a close button. We are setting the `opacity` style to the main view, which will animate the image background from transparent to black. The image will slide in at the same time, creating a nice effect:

```
// Defined on previous step
render() {
  return (
    <Animated.View
      style={[
        styles.main,
        { opacity },
      ]}
    >
      <Animated.Image
        source={image}
        style={[
          styles.image,
          { top, opacity }
        ]}
      />
      <TouchableOpacity style={styles.closeBtn}
        onPress={this.onPressBtn}
      >
        <Text style={styles.closeBtnText}>X</Text>
      </TouchableOpacity>
```

```
        </Animated.View>
      );
    }
```

19. We are almost done! The last step in this recipe is to define the styles. We need to set the position of the main container to absolute so that the image is on top of everything else. We'll also move the close button to the top-right of the screen, as follows:

```
const styles = StyleSheet.create({
  main: {
    backgroundColor: '#000',
    bottom: 0,
    left: 0,
    position: 'absolute',
    right: 0,
    top: 0,
  },
  image: {
    width,
    height: 300,
  },
  closeBtn: {
    position: 'absolute',
    top: 50,
    right: 20,
  },
  closeBtnText: {
    fontSize: 20,
    color: '#fff',
    fontWeight: 'bold',
  },
});
```

20. The final app should look similar to the following screenshot:

How it works...

In *step 4*, we defined two properties on state: selected and position.
The selected property holds the image data for the pressed image, which can be any of
the timeline objects defined in *step 3*. The position property will hold the current *y*-
coordinate on the screen, which is used later to animate the image from its original position
to the center of the screen.

In *step 5*, we map over the timeline array to render each post. We used
the PostContainer element for each post, sending the post information and using
the onPress callback to set the pressed image.

In *step 10*, we need the current position of the image. To achieve this, we use
the measure method from the component we want to get the information from. This
method receives a callback function and retrieves, among other properties, width, height,
and the current position on the screen.

We are using a reference to access the component, declared in the JSX on the next step.

In *step 11*, we declared the JSX for the component. In the main wrapper container, we set
the ref property, which is used to get the current position of the image. Whenever we want
to access a component on any of the methods of the current class, we use a reference. We
can create references by simply setting the ref property and assigning a name to any
component.

In *step 18*, we interpolate the animation values to get the correct top value for each frame.
The output of that interpolation will start from the current position of the image and
progress to the middle of the screen. This way, depending on whether the values
are negative or positive, the animation will run from bottom to top, or the other way
around.

We don't need to interpolate opacity, since the current animated value already goes
from 0 to 1.

See also

An in depth explanation of Refs and the DOM can be found at the following link:

https://reactjs.org/docs/refs-and-the-dom.html.

Working with Application Logic and Data

8

In this chapter, we will cover the following recipes:

- Storing and retrieving data locally
- Retrieving data from a remote API
- Sending data to a remote API
- Establishing real-time communication with WebSockets
- Integrating persistent database functionality with Realm
- Masking the application upon network connection loss
- Synchronizing locally persisted data with a remote API

Introduction

One of the most important aspects of developing any application is handling data. This data may come locally from the user, may be served by a remote server that exposes an API, or, as with most business applications, may be some combination of both. You may be wondering what strategies are best for dealing with data, or how to even accomplish simple tasks such as making an HTTP request. Luckily, React Native makes your life that much simpler by providing mechanisms for easily dealing with data from all different sources.

The open source community has taken things a step further and provided some excellent modules that can be used with React Native. In this chapter, we will discuss how to work with data in all aspects, and how it integrates into our React Native applications.

Storing and retrieving data locally

When developing a mobile app, we need to consider the network challenges that need to be overcome. A well-designed app should allow the user to continue using the app when there is no internet connection. This requires the app to save data locally on the device when there's no internet connection, and to also sync that data with the server when the network is available again.

Another challenge to overcome is network connectivity, which might be slow or limited. To improve the performance of our app, we should save critical data on the local device to avoid putting stress on our server API.

In this recipe, we will learn about a basic and effective strategy for saving and retrieving data locally from the device. We will create a simple app with a text input and two buttons, one to save the content of the field and one to load the existing content. We will use the `AsyncStorage` class to achieve our goal.

Getting ready

We need to create an empty app named `local-data-storage`.

How to do it...

1. We'll begin with the `App` component. Let's start by importing all of the dependencies:

```
import React, { Component } from 'react';
import {
  Alert,
  AsyncStorage,
  StyleSheet,
  Text,
  TextInput,
  TouchableOpacity,
  View,
} from 'react-native';
```

2. Now, let's create the `App` class. We are going to create a `key` constant so that we can set the name of the key we will use to save the content. On the `state`, we'll have two properties: one to keep the value from the text input component, and another to load and display the currently stored value:

```
const key = '@MyApp:key';

export default class App extends Component {
  state = {
    text: '',
    storedValue: '',
  };
  //Defined in later steps
}
```

3. When the component mounts, we want to load the existing stored value if it exists. We'll display the content once the app loads, so we'll need to read the local value in the `componentWillMount` life cycle method:

```
componentWillMount() {
  this.onLoad();
}
```

4. The `onLoad` function loads the current content from the local storage. Like `localStorage` in the browser, it's as easy as using the key we defined when saving the data:

```
onLoad = async () => {
  try {
    const storedValue = await AsyncStorage.getItem(key);
    this.setState({ storedValue });
  } catch (error) {
    Alert.alert('Error', 'There was an error while loading the
    data');
  }
}
```

5. Saving the data is straightforward as well. We'll declare a key to save any data we want to associate with that key, via the `setItem` method of `AsyncStorage`:

```
onSave = async () => {
  const { text } = this.state;

  try {
    await AsyncStorage.setItem(key, text);
    Alert.alert('Saved', 'Successfully saved on device');
  } catch (error) {
```

```
      Alert.alert('Error', 'There was an error while saving the
      data');
    }
  }
```

6. Next, we need a function for saving the value from the input text to the `state`. When the value of the input changes, we will get the new value and save it to the `state`:

```
onChange = (text) => {
  this.setState({ text });
}
```

7. Our UI will be simple: just a `Text` element to render the saved content, a `TextInput` component to allow the user to enter a new value, and two buttons. One button will call the `onLoad` function to load the current saved value, and the other will save the value from the text input:

```
render() {
  const { storedValue, text } = this.state;

  return (
    <View style={styles.container}>
      <Text style={styles.preview}>{storedValue}</Text>
      <View>
        <TextInput
          style={styles.input}
          onChangeText={this.onChange}
          value={text}
          placeholder="Type something here..."
        />
        <TouchableOpacity onPress={this.onSave} style=
        {styles.button}>
          <Text>Save locally</Text>
        </TouchableOpacity>
        <TouchableOpacity onPress={this.onLoad} style=
        {styles.button}>
          <Text>Load data</Text>
        </TouchableOpacity>
      </View>
    </View>
  );
}
```

8. Finally, let's add some styles. This will be simple colors, paddings, margins, and a layout, as covered in Chapter 2, *Creating a Simple React Native App*:

```
const styles = StyleSheet.create({
  container: {
    flex: 1,
    justifyContent: 'center',
    alignItems: 'center',
    backgroundColor: '#fff',
  },
  preview: {
    backgroundColor: '#bdc3c7',
    width: 300,
    height: 80,
    padding: 10,
    borderRadius: 5,
    color: '#333',
    marginBottom: 50,
  },
  input: {
    backgroundColor: '#ecf0f1',
    borderRadius: 3,
    width: 300,
    height: 40,
    padding: 5,
  },
  button: {
    backgroundColor: '#f39c12',
    padding: 10,
    borderRadius: 3,
    marginTop: 10,
  },
});
```

9. The final app should look similar to the following screenshot:

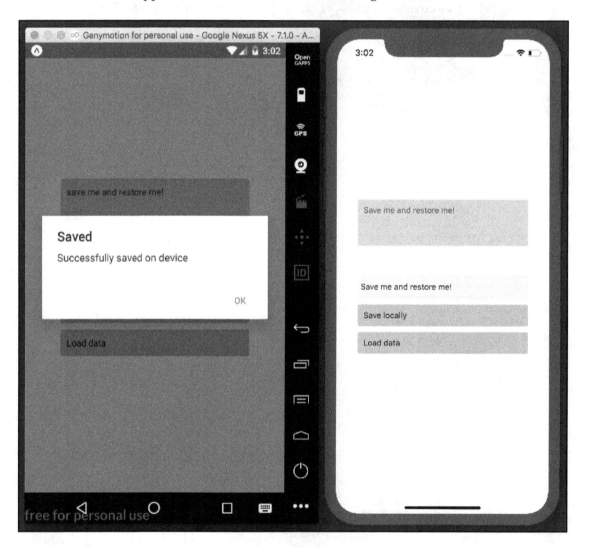

How it works...

The AsyncStorage class allows us to easily save data on the local device. On iOS, this is accomplished by using dictionaries on text files. On Android, it will use RocksDB or SQLite, depending on what's available.

It's not recommended to save sensitive information using this method, as the data is not encrypted.

In *step 4*, we loaded the current saved data. The `AsyncStorage` API contains a `getItem` method. This method receives the key we want to retrieve as a parameter. We are using the `await/async` syntax here since this call is asynchronous. After we get the value, we just set it to `state`; this way, we will be able to render the data on the view.

In *step 7*, we saved the text from the `state`. Using the `setItem` method, we can set a new `key` with any value we want. This call is asynchronous, therefore we used the `await/async` syntax.

See also

A great article on how `async/await` in JavaScript works, available at `https://ponyfoo.com/articles/understanding-javascript-async-await`.

Retrieving data from a remote API

In the previous chapters we used data from a JSON file or directly defined in the source code. While that worked for our previous recipes, it's rarely very helpful in real-world applications.

In this recipe, we will learn how to request data from an API. We will make a `GET` request from an API to get a JSON response. For now, however, we are only going to display the JSON in a text element. We'll be using the Fake Online REST API for Testing and Prototyping, hosted at `http://jsonplaceholder.typicode.com` and powered by the excellent development test API software, JSON Server (`https://github.com/typicode/json-server`).

We will keep this app simple so that we can focus on data management. We will have a text component that will display the response from the API and also add a button that requests the data when pressed.

Getting ready

We need to create an empty app. Let's name this one `remote-api`.

How to do it...

1. Let's start by importing our dependencies into the `App.js` file:

```
import React, { Component } from 'react';
import {
  StyleSheet,
  Text,
  TextInput,
  TouchableOpacity,
  View
} from 'react-native';
```

2. We are going to define a `results` property on the `state`. This property will hold the response from the API. We'll need to update the view once we get the response:

```
export default class App extends Component {
  state = {
    results: '',
  };
  // Defined later
}

const styles = StyleSheet.create({
  // Defined later
});
```

3. We'll send the request when the button is pressed. Next, let's create a method to handle that request:

```
onLoad = async () => {
  this.setState({ results: 'Loading, please wait...' });
  const response = await
fetch('http://jsonplaceholder.typicode.com/users', {
    method: 'GET',
  });
  const results = await response.text();
  this.setState({ results });
}
```

4. In the `render` method, we'll display the response, which will be read from the `state`. We will use a `TextInput` to display the API data. Via properties, we'll declare editing as disabled and support multiline functionality. The button will call the `onLoad` function that we created in the previous step:

```
render() {
  const { results } = this.state;

  return (
    <View style={styles.container}>
      <View>
        <TextInput
          style={styles.preview}
          value={results}
          placeholder="Results..."
          editable={false}
          multiline
        />
        <TouchableOpacity onPress={this.onLoad} style=
        {styles.btn}>
          <Text>Load data</Text>
        </TouchableOpacity>
      </View>
    </View>
  );
}
```

5. Finally, we'll add some styles. Again, this will just be the layout, colors, margins, and padding:

```
const styles = StyleSheet.create({
  container: {
    flex: 1,
    justifyContent: 'center',
    alignItems: 'center',
    backgroundColor: '#fff',
  },
  preview: {
    backgroundColor: '#bdc3c7',
    width: 300,
    height: 400,
    padding: 10,
    borderRadius: 5,
    color: '#333',
    marginBottom: 50,
  },
  btn: {
```

```
        backgroundColor: '#3498db',
        padding: 10,
        borderRadius: 3,
        marginTop: 10,
      },
    });
```

6. The final app should look similar to the following screenshot:

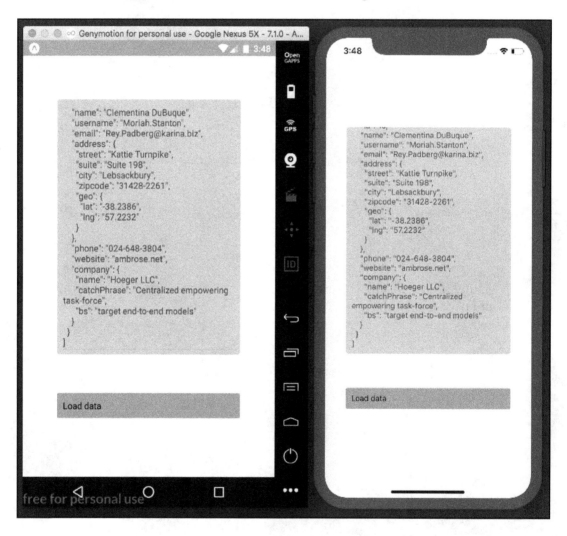

How it works...

In *step 4*, we sent the request to the API. We use the `fetch` method to make the request. The first parameter is a string with the URL of the endpoint, while the second parameter is a configuration object. For this request, the only option we need to define is the `request` method to `GET`, but we can also use this object to define headers, cookies, parameters, and many other things.

We are also using `async/await` syntax to wait on the response and finally set it on the `state`. If you prefer, you could, of course, use promises for this purpose instead.

Also, note how we are using an arrow function here to properly handle the scope. This will automatically set the correct scope when this method is assigned to the `onPress` callback.

Sending data to a remote API

In the previous recipe, we covered how to get data from an API using `fetch`. In this recipe, we will learn how to `POST` data to the same API. This app will emulate creating a forum post, and the request for the post will have `title`, `body`, and `user` parameters.

Getting ready

Before going through this recipe, we need to create a new empty app named `remote-api-post`.

In this recipe, we will also be using the very popular `axios` package for handling our API requests. You can install it via the Terminal with `yarn`:

```
yarn add axios
```

Alternatively, you can use npm:

```
npm install axios --save
```

How to do it...

1. First, we'll need to open the `App.js` file and import the dependencies we'll be using:

```
import React, { Component } from 'react';
import axios from 'axios';
import {
  Alert,
  ScrollView,
  StyleSheet,
  Text,
  TextInput,
  TouchableOpacity,
  SafeAreaView,
} from 'react-native';
```

2. We'll define the `App` class with a `state` object that has three properties. The `title` and `body` properties will be used for making the request, and `results` will hold the API's response:

```
const endpoint = 'http://jsonplaceholder.typicode.com/posts';

export default class App extends Component {
  state = {
    results: '',
    title: '',
    body: '',
  };

  const styles = StyleSheet.create({
    // Defined later
  });
}
```

3. After saving a new post, we will request all of the posts from the API. We are going to define an `onLoad` method to fetch the new data. This code works just the same as the `onLoad` method in the previous recipe, but this time, we'll be using the `axios` package to create the request:

```
onLoad = async () => {
  this.setState({ results: 'Loading, please wait...' });
  const response = await axios.get(endpoint);
  const results = JSON.stringify(response);
  this.setState({ results });
}
```

4. Let's work on saving the new data. First, we need to get the values from the
   `state`. We could also run some validations here to make sure that the `title`
   and `body` are not empty. On the `POST` request, we need to define the content type
   of the request, which, in this case, will be JSON. We will hard code the `userId`
   property to `1`. In a real app, we would have probably gotten this value from a
   previous API request. After the request has completed, we get the JSON
   response, which, if successful, will fire the `onLoad` method that we defined
   previously:

```
onSave = async () => {
  const { title, body } = this.state;
  try {
    const response = await axios.post(endpoint, {
      headers: {
        'Content-Type': 'application/json;charset=UTF-8',
      },
      params: {
        userId: 1,
        title,
        body
      }
    });
    const results = JSON.stringify(response);
    Alert.alert('Success', 'Post successfully saved');
    this.onLoad();
  } catch (error) {
    Alert.alert('Error', `There was an error while saving the
    post: ${error}`);
  }
}
```

5. The save functionality is complete. Next, we need methods for saving the `title`
   and `body` to the `state`. These methods will be executed as the user types in the
   input text, keeping track of the values on the `state` object:

```
onTitleChange = (title) => this.setState({ title });
onPostChange = (body) => this.setState({ body });
```

6. We have everything we need for the functionality, so let's add the UI. The `render` method will display a toolbar, two input texts, and a Save button for calling the `onSave` method that we defined in *step 4*:

```
render() {
  const { results, title, body } = this.state;

  return (
    <SafeAreaView style={styles.container}>
      <Text style={styles.toolbar}>Add a new post</Text>
      <ScrollView style={styles.content}>
        <TextInput
          style={styles.input}
          onChangeText={this.onTitleChange}
          value={title}
          placeholder="Title"
        />
        <TextInput
          style={styles.input}
          onChangeText={this.onPostChange}
          value={body}
          placeholder="Post body..."
        />
        <TouchableOpacity onPress={this.onSave} style=
        {styles.button}>
          <Text>Save</Text>
        </TouchableOpacity>
        <TextInput
          style={styles.preview}
          value={results}
          placeholder="Results..."
          editable={false}
          multiline
        />
      </ScrollView>
    </SafeAreaView>
  );
}
```

7. Finally, let's add the styles to define the layout, color, padding, and margins:

```
const styles = StyleSheet.create({
  container: {
    flex: 1,
    backgroundColor: '#fff',
  },
  toolbar: {
    backgroundColor: '#3498db',
    color: '#fff',
    textAlign: 'center',
    padding: 25,
    fontSize: 20,
  },
  content: {
    flex: 1,
    padding: 10,
  },
  preview: {
    backgroundColor: '#bdc3c7',
    flex: 1,
    height: 500,
  },
  input: {
    backgroundColor: '#ecf0f1',
    borderRadius: 3,
    height: 40,
    padding: 5,
    marginBottom: 10,
    flex: 1,
  },
  button: {
    backgroundColor: '#3498db',
    padding: 10,
    borderRadius: 3,
    marginBottom: 30,
  },
});
```

8. The final app should look similar to the following screenshot:

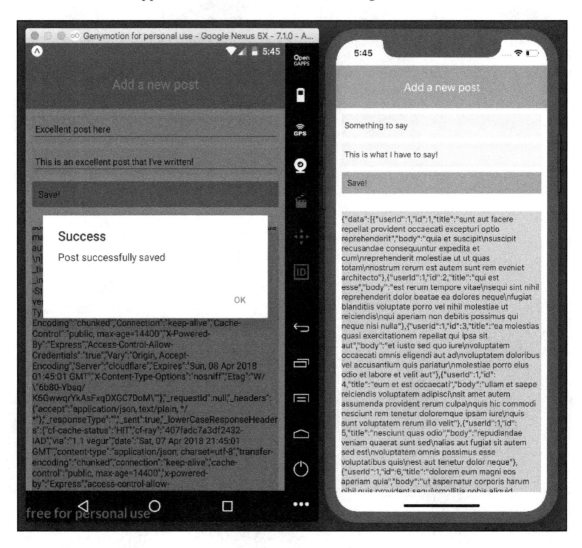

How it works...

In *step 2*, we defined three properties on the `state`. The `results` property will contain the response from the server API, which we later use to display the value in the UI.

We used the `title` and `body` properties to hold the values from the input text components so that the user can create a new post. Those values will then be sent to the API when pressing the **Save** button.

In *step 6*, we declared the elements on the UI. We used two inputs for post data and the **Save** button, which calls the `onSave` method when pressed. Finally, we used input text to display the result.

Establishing real-time communication with WebSockets

In this recipe, we will integrate WebSockets in a React Native application. We are going to use the *Hello World* of WebSockets applications, that is, a simple chat app. This app will allow users to send and receive messages.

Getting ready

To support WebSockets on React Native, we will need to run a server to handle all connected clients. The server should be able to broadcast a message when it receives a message from any of the connected clients.

We'll start with a new, empty React Native app. We'll name it `web-sockets`. In the root of the project, let's add a `server` folder with an `index.js` file inside of it. If you don't already have it, you'll need Node to run the server. You can get Node.js from `https://nodejs.org/` or by using the Node Version Manager (`https://github.com/creationix/nvm`).

We'll be using the excellent WebSocket package, `ws`. You can add the package via the Terminal with `yarn`:

```
yarn add ws
```

Alternatively, you can use `npm`:

```
npm install --save ws
```

Once you've got the package installed, add the following code to the /server/index.js file. Once this server is running, it will listen for incoming connections via server.on('connection') and incoming messages via socket.on('message'). For more information on how ws works, you can check out the documentation at https:// github.com/websockets/ws:

```
const port = 3001;
const WebSocketServer = require('ws').Server;
const server = new WebSocketServer({ port });

server.on('connection', (socket) => {
  socket.on('message', (message) => {
    console.log('received: %s', message);

    server.clients.forEach(client => {
      if (client !== socket) {
        client.send(message);
      }
    });
  });
});

console.log(`Web Socket Server running on port ${port}`);
```

Once the server code is in place, you can start up the server using Node by running the following command in the Terminal at the root of the project:

```
node server/index.js
```

Leave the server running so that, once we've built the React Native app, we can use the server to communicate between clients.

How to do it...

1. First, let's create the App.js file and import all the dependencies we'll be using:

```
import React, { Component } from 'react';
import {
  Dimensions,
  ScrollView,
  StyleSheet,
  Text,
  TextInput,
  SafeAreaView,
  View,
```

```
        Platform
    } from 'react-native';
```

2. On the `state` object, we'll declare a `history` property. This property will be an array for holding all of the messages that have been sent back and forth between users:

```
export default class App extends Component {
  state = {
    history: [],
  };
    // Defined in later steps
}

const styles = StyleSheet.create({
  // Defined in later steps
});
```

3. Now, we need to integrate WebSockets into our app by connecting to the server and setting up the callback functions for receiving messages, errors, and when the connection is opened or closed. We will do this when the component has been created, by using the `componentWillMount` life cycle hook:

```
componentWillMount() {
  const localhost = Platform.OS === 'android' ? '10.0.3.2' :
  'localhost';

  this.ws = new WebSocket(`ws://${localhost}:3001`);
  this.ws.onopen = this.onOpenConnection;
  this.ws.onmessage = this.onMessageReceived;
  this.ws.onerror = this.onError;
  this.ws.onclose = this.onCloseConnection;
}
```

4. Let's define the callbacks for opened/closed connections and for handling received errors. We are just going to log the actions, but this is where we could show an alert message when the connection is closed, or display an error message when an error is thrown by the server:

```
onOpenConnection = () => {
  console.log('Open!');
}

onError = (event) => {
  console.log('onerror', event.message);
}
```

```
onCloseConnection = (event) => {
  console.log('onclose', event.code, event.reason);
}
```

5. When receiving a new message from the server, we need to add it to the `history` property on the `state` so that we can render the new content as soon as it arrives:

```
onMessageReceived = (event) => {
  this.setState({
    history: [
      ...this.state.history,
      { isSentByMe: false, messageText: event.data },
    ],
  });
}
```

6. Now, on to sending the message. We need to define a method that will get executed when the user presses the *Return* key on the keyboard. We need to do two things at this point: add the new message to `history`, and then send the message through the socket:

```
onSendMessage = () => {
  const { text } = this.state;

  this.setState({
    text: '',
    history: [
      ...this.state.history,
      { isSentByMe: true, messageText: text },
    ],
  });
  this.ws.send(text);
}
```

7. In the previous step, we got the `text` property from the `state`. We need to keep track of the value whenever the user types something into the input, so we'll need a function for listening to keystrokes and saving the value to `state`:

```
onChangeText = (text) => {
  this.setState({ text });
}
```

8. We have all of the functionality in place, so let's work on the UI. In the `render` method, we'll add a toolbar, a scroll view to render all of the messages in `history`, and a text input to allow the user to send a new message:

```
render() {
  const { history, text } = this.state;

  return (
    <SafeAreaView style={[styles.container, android]}>
      <Text style={styles.toolbar}>Simple Chat</Text>
      <ScrollView style={styles.content}>
        { history.map(this.renderMessage) }
      </ScrollView>
      <View style={styles.inputContainer}>
        <TextInput
          style={styles.input}
          value={text}
          onChangeText={this.onChangeText}
          onSubmitEditing={this.onSendMessage}
        />
      </View>
    </SafeAreaView>
  );
}
```

9. To render the messages from `history`, we'll loop through the `history` array and render each message via the `renderMessage` method. We'll need to check whether the current message belongs to the user on this device so that we can apply the appropriate styles:

```
renderMessage(item, index){
  const sender = item.isSentByMe ? styles.me : styles.friend;

  return (
    <View style={[styles.msg, sender]} key={index}>
      <Text>{item.msg}</Text>
    </View>
  );
}
```

10. Finally, let's work on the styles! Let's add styles to the toolbar, the `history` component, and the text input. We need to set the `history` container as flexible, since we want it to take up all of the available vertical space:

```
const styles = StyleSheet.create({
  container: {
    backgroundColor: '#ecf0f1',
    flex: 1,
  },
  toolbar: {
    backgroundColor: '#34495e',
    color: '#fff',
    fontSize: 20,
    padding: 25,
    textAlign: 'center',
  },
  content: {
    flex: 1,
  },
  inputContainer: {
    backgroundColor: '#bdc3c7',
    padding: 5,
  },
  input: {
    height: 40,
    backgroundColor: '#fff',
  },
  // Defined in next step
});
```

11. Now, on to the styles for each message. We are going to create a common styles object called `msg` for all messages, then styles for messages from the user on the device, and finally, styles for messages from others, changing the color and alignment accordingly:

```
msg: {
  margin: 5,
  padding: 10,
  borderRadius: 10,
},
me: {
  alignSelf: 'flex-start',
  backgroundColor: '#1abc9c',
  marginRight: 100,
},
friend: {
  alignSelf: 'flex-end',
```

```
        backgroundColor: '#fff',
        marginLeft: 100,
    }
```

12. The final app should look similar to the following screenshot:

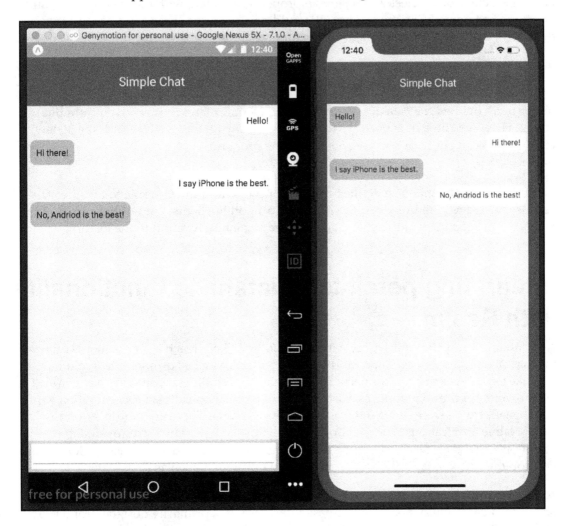

How it works...

In *step 2*, we declared the `state` object with a `history` array for keeping track of messages. The `history` property will hold objects representing all of the messages being exchanged between clients. Each object will have two properties: a string with the message text, and a Boolean flag to determine the sender. We could add more data here, such as the name of the user, a URL of the avatar image, or anything else we might need.

In *step 3*, we connected to the socket provided by the WebSocket server and set up callbacks for handling socket events. We specified the server address as well as the port.

In *step 5*, we defined the callback to execute when a new message is received from the server. Here, we add a new object to the `history` array on the `state` every time a new message is received. Each message object has the properties `isSentByMe` and `messageText`.

In *step 6*, we sent the message to the server. We need to add the message to the history because the server will broadcast the message to all other clients, but not the author of the message. To keep track of this message, we need to manually add it to the history.

Integrating persistent database functionality with Realm

As your application becomes more complex, you will likely reach a point where you need to store data on the device. This could be business data, such as user lists, to avoid having to make expensive network connections to a Remote API. Maybe you don't have an API at all and your application works as a self-sufficient entity. Regardless of the situation, you may benefit from leveraging a database to store your data. There are multiple options for React Native applications. The first option is `AsyncStorage`, which we covered in the *Storing and retrieving data locally* recipe in this chapter. You could also consider SQLite, or you could write an adapter to an OS-specific data provider, such as Core Data.

Another excellent option is using a mobile database, such as Realm. Realm is an extremely fast, thread-safe, transactional, object-based database. It is primarily designed for use by mobile devices, with a straightforward JavaScript API. It supports other features, such as encryption, complex querying, UI bindings, and more. You can read all about it at `https://realm.io/products/realm-mobile-database/`.

In this recipe, we will walk through using Realm in React Native. We will create a simple database and perform basic operations, such as inserting, updating, and deleting records. We will then display these records in the UI.

Getting ready

Let's create a new empty React Native app named `realm-db`.

Installing Realm requires running the following command:

```
react-native link
```

Because of this, we will be working on an app that is ejected from Expo. This means that you could create this app with the following command:

```
react-native init
```

Alternatively, you could create a new Expo app with the following command:

```
expo init
```

Then, you can eject the app that was created with Expo via the following command:

```
expo eject
```

Once you've created a React Native app, be sure to install the CocoaPods dependencies via the `ios` directory by using `cd` inside the new app and running the following:

```
pod install
```

Refer to `Chapter 10`, *App Workflow and Third-party Plugins*, for a in-depth explanation of how CocoaPods works, and how ejected (or pure React Native) applications differ from Expo React Native applications.

In the *Sending data to a remote API* recipe, we handled our AJAX calls with the `axios` package. In this recipe, we will be using the native JavaScript `fetch` method for AJAX calls. Either method works just as well, and having exposure to both will hopefully allow you to decide which you prefer for your projects.

Once you've taken care of creating an ejected app, install Realm with `yarn`:

```
yarn add realm
```

Alternatively, you can use npm:

```
npm install --save realm
```

With the package installed, you can link the native packages with the following code:

```
react-native link realm
```

How to do it...

1. First, let's open App.js and import the dependencies we'll be using:

```
import React, { Component } from 'react';
import {
  StyleSheet,
  Text,
  View,
  TouchableOpacity
} from 'react-native';
import Realm from 'realm';
```

2. Next, we need to instantiate our Realm database, which we'll do in the componentWillMount method. We'll keep a reference to it by using the realm class variable:

```
export default class App extends Component {
  realm;
  componentWillMount() {
    const realm = this.realm = new Realm({
      schema: [
        {
          name: 'User',
          properties: {
            firstName: 'string',
            lastName: 'string',
            email: 'string'
          }
        }
      ]
    });
  }
  // Defined in later steps.
}
```

3. To create the `User` entries, we will use the random user generator API provided by `randomuser.me`. Let's create a method with the `getRandomUser` function. This will `fetch` this data:

```
getRandomUser() {
  return fetch('https://randomuser.me/api/')
    .then(response => response.json());
}
```

4. We'll also need a method for creating users in our app. The `createUser` method will use the function we defined previously to get a random user, before saving it to our realm database with the `realm.write` method and the `realm.create` method:

```
createUser = () => {
  const realm = this.realm;

  this.getRandomUser().then((response) => {
    const user = response.results[0];
    const userName = user.name;
    realm.write(() => {
      realm.create('User', {
        firstName: userName.first,
        lastName: userName.last,
        email: user.email
      });
      this.setState({users:realm.objects('User')});
    });
  });
}
```

5. Since we're interacting with a database, we should also add a function for updating a `User` in the database. `updateUser` will, for simplicity, take the first record in the collection and change its information:

```
updateUser = () => {
  const realm = this.realm;
  const users = realm.objects('User');

  realm.write(() => {
    if(users.length) {
      let firstUser = users.slice(0,1)[0];
      firstUser.firstName = 'Bob';
      firstUser.lastName = 'Cookbook';
      firstUser.email = 'react.native@cookbook.com';
      this.setState(users);
    }
```

```
      });
   }
```

6. Finally, let's add a way to delete our users. We'll add a `deleteUsers` method for removing all users. This is achieved by calling `realm.write` with a callback function that executes `realm.deleteAll`:

```
deleteUsers = () => {
  const realm = this.realm;
  realm.write(() => {
    realm.deleteAll();
    this.setState({users:realm.objects('User')});
  });
}
```

7. Let's build our UI. We will render a list of `User` objects and a button for each of our `create`, `update`, and `delete` methods:

```
render() {
  const realm = this.realm;
  return (
    <View style={styles.container}>
      <Text style={styles.welcome}>
        Welcome to Realm DB Test!
      </Text>
      <View style={styles.buttonContainer}>
        <TouchableOpacity style={styles.button}
        onPress={this.createUser}>
         <Text style={styles.buttontext}>Add User</Text>
        </TouchableOpacity>
         <TouchableOpacity style={styles.button}
          onPress={this.updateUser}>
          <Text>Update First User</Text>
         </TouchableOpacity>
         <TouchableOpacity style={styles.button}
          onPress={this.deleteUsers}>
          <Text>Remove All Users</Text>
         </TouchableOpacity>
      </View>
      <View style={styles.container}>
      <Text style={styles.welcome}>Users:</Text>
      {this.state.users.map((user, idx) => {
        return <Text key={idx}>{user.firstName} {user.lastName}
        {user.email}</Text>;
      })}
      </View>
    </View>
```

```
    );
  }
```

8. Once we run the app on either platform, our three buttons for interacting with the database should display over the live data that's saved in our Realm database:

How it works...

The Realm database is built in C++ and its core is known as the **Realm Object Store**. There are products that encapsulate this object store for each major platform (Java, Objective-C, Swift, Xamarin, and React Native). The React Native implementation is a JavaScript adapter for Realm. From the React Native side, we do not need to worry about the implementation details. Instead, we get a clean API for persisting and retrieving data. The *step 4* to *step 6* demonstrate using some basic Realm methods. If you want to see more of what you can do with the API, check out the documentation for this, which can be found at `https://realm.io/docs/react-native/latest/api/`.

Masking the application upon network connection loss

An internet connection is not always available, especially when people are moving around a city, on the train, or hiking in the mountains. A good user experience will inform the user when their connection to the internet has been lost.

In this recipe, we will create an app that shows a message when network connection is lost.

Getting ready

We need to create an empty app. Let's name it `network-loss`.

How to do it...

1. Let's start by importing the necessary dependencies into `App.js`:

```
import React, { Component } from 'react';
import {
  SafeAreaView,
  NetInfo,
  StyleSheet,
  Text,
  View,
  Platform
} from 'react-native';
```

2. Next, we'll define the `App` class and a `state` object for storing the connectivity status. The `online` Boolean will be `true` if connected, and the `offline` Boolean will be `true` if it isn't:

```
export default class App extends Component {
  state = {
    online: null,
    offline: null,
  };

  // Defined in later steps
}
```

3. After the component has been created, we need to get the initial network status. We are going to use the `NetInfo` class's `getConnectionInfo` method to get the current status, and we'll also set up a callback that's going to be executed when the status changes:

```
componentWillMount() {
  NetInfo.getConnectionInfo().then((connectionInfo) => {
    this.onConnectivityChange(connectionInfo);
  });
  NetInfo.addEventListener('connectionChange',
  this.onConnectivityChange);
}
```

4. When the component is about to be destroyed, we need to remove the listener via the `componentWillUnmount` life cycle:

```
componentWillUnmount() {
  NetInfo.removeEventListener('connectionChange',
  this.onConnectivityChange);
}
```

5. Let's add the callback that gets executed when the network status changes. It just checks whether the current network type is `none`, and sets the `state` accordingly:

```
onConnectivityChange = connectionInfo => {
  this.setState({
    online: connectionInfo.type !== 'none',
    offline: connectionInfo.type === 'none',
  });
}
```

6. Now, we know when the network is on or off, but we still need a UI for displaying information. Let's render a toolbar with some dummy text as the content:

```
render() {
  return (
    <SafeAreaView style={styles.container}>
      <Text style={styles.toolbar}>My Awesome App</Text>
      <Text style={styles.text}>Lorem...</Text>
      <Text style={styles.text}>Lorem ipsum...</Text>
      {this.renderMask()}
    </SafeAreaView>
  );
}
```

7. As you can see from the previous step, there's a `renderMask` function. This function will return a modal when the network is offline, and nothing if it's online:

```
renderMask() {
  if (this.state.offline) {
    return (
      <View style={styles.mask}>
        <View style={styles.msg}>
          <Text style={styles.alert}>Seems like you do not have
            network connection anymore.</Text>
          <Text style={styles.alert}>You can still continue
            using the app, with limited content.</Text>
        </View>
      </View>
    );
  }
}
```

8. Finally, let's add the styles for our app. We'll start with the toolbar and content:

```
const styles = StyleSheet.create({
  container: {
    flex: 1,
    backgroundColor: '#F5FCFF',
  },
  toolbar: {
    backgroundColor: '#3498db',
    padding: 15,
    fontSize: 20,
    color: '#fff',
    textAlign: 'center',
```

```
      },
      text: {
        padding: 10,
      },
      // Defined in next step
    }
```

9. For the disconnection message, we will render a dark mask on top of all content, and a container with the text at the center of the screen. For the `mask`, we need to set the position to `absolute`, and then set the `top`, `bottom`, `right`, and `left` to `0`. We'll also add opacity to the mask's background color, and justify and align the content to the center:

```
    const styles = StyleSheet.create({
      // Defined in previous step
      mask: {
        alignItems: 'center',
        backgroundColor: 'rgba(0, 0, 0, 0.5)',
        bottom: 0,
        justifyContent: 'center',
        left: 0,
        position: 'absolute',
        top: 0,
        right: 0,
      },
      msg: {
        backgroundColor: '#ecf0f1',
        borderRadius: 10,
        height: 200,
        justifyContent: 'center',
        padding: 10,
        width: 300,
      },
      alert: {
        fontSize: 20,
        textAlign: 'center',
        margin: 5,
      }
    });
```

10. To see the mask displayed in the emulators, the emulated device must be disconnected from the internet. For the iOS simulator, simply disconnect your Mac's Wi-Fi or unplug the Ethernet to disconnect the simulator from the internet. On the Android emulator, you can disable the Wi-Fi connection of the phone via the toolbar:

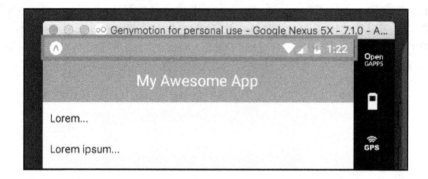

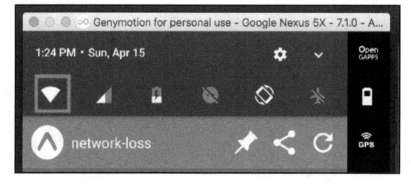

11. Once the device has been disconnected from the internet, the mask should display accordingly:

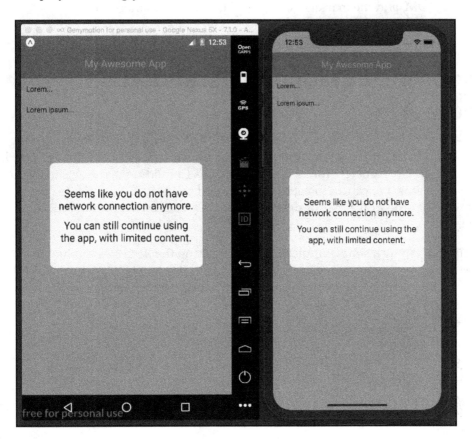

How it works...

In *step 2*, we created the initial state object with two properties: online will be true when a network connection is available, and offline will be true when it's not available.

In *step 3*, we retrieved the initial network status and set up a listener to check when the status changes. The network type returned by NetInfo will be either wifi, cellular, unknown, or none. Android also has the extra options of bluetooth, ethernet, and WiMAX (for WiMAX connections). You can read the documentation to see all of the available values: https://facebook.github.io/react-native/docs/netinfo.html.

In *step 5*, we defined the method that will execute whenever the network status changes, and set the `state` values of `online` and `offline` accordingly. Updating the state re-renders the DOM, and the mask is displayed if there is no connection.

Synchronizing locally persisted data with a remote API

When using a mobile app, network connectivity is something that is often taken for granted. But what happens when your app needs to make an API call, and the user has just lost connectivity? Fortunately for us, React Native has a module that reacts to the network connectivity status. We can architect our application in a way that supports the loss of connectivity by synchronizing our data automatically as soon as the network connection is restored.

This recipe will show a simple implementation of using the `NetInfo` module to control whether or not our application will make an API call. If connectivity is lost, we will keep a reference of the pending request and complete it when the network access is restored. We will be using `http://jsonplaceholder.typicode.com` again to make a `POST` request to a live server.

Getting ready

For this recipe, we will use an empty React Native application named `syncing-data`.

How to do it...

1. We'll start this recipe by importing our dependencies into `App.js`:

```
import React from 'react';
import {
  StyleSheet,
  Text,
  View,
  NetInfo,
  TouchableOpacity
} from 'react-native';
```

2. We'll need to add the `pendingSync` class variable, which we'll use for storing a pending request when there is no network connection available. We'll also create the `state` object with properties for tracking whether the app is connected (`isConnected`), the status of a sync (`syncStatus`), and the response from the server after our `POST` request is made (`serverResponse`):

```
export default class App extends React.Component {
  pendingSync;

  state = {
    isConnected: null,
    syncStatus: null,
    serverResponse: null
  }

  // Defined in later steps
}
```

3. In the `componentWillMount` life cycle hook, we'll get the status of the network connection via the `NetInfo.isConnected.fetch` method, setting the state's `isConnected` property with the response. We'll also add an event listener to the `connectionChange` event for keeping track of changes to the connection:

```
componentWillMount() {
  NetInfo.isConnected.fetch().then(isConnected => {
    this.setState({isConnected});
  });
  NetInfo.isConnected.addEventListener('connectionChange',
  this.onConnectionChange);
}
```

4. Next, let's implement the callback that will be executed by the event listener we defined in the previous step. In this method, we update the `isConnected` property of `state`. Then, if the `pendingSync` class variable is defined, it means we've got a cached `POST` request, so we'll submit that request and update the state accordingly:

```
onConnectionChange = (isConnected) => {
  this.setState({isConnected});
  if (this.pendingSync) {
    this.setState({syncStatus : 'Syncing'});
    this.submitData(this.pendingSync).then(() => {
      this.setState({syncStatus : 'Sync Complete'});
    });
  }
}
```

5. Next, we need to implement a function that will actually make the API call when there is an active network connection:

```
submitData(requestBody) {
  return fetch('http://jsonplaceholder.typicode.com/posts', {
    method : 'POST',
    body : JSON.stringify(requestBody)
  }).then((response) => {
    return response.text();
  }).then((responseText) => {
    this.setState({
      serverResponse : responseText
    });
  });
}
```

6. The last thing we need to do before we can work on our UI is add a function for handling the onPress event on the **Submit Data** button we will be rendering. This will either perform the call immediately or be saved in this.pendingSync if there is no network connection:

```
onSubmitPress = () => {
  const requestBody = {
    title: 'foo',
    body: 'bar',
    userId: 1
  };
  if (this.state.isConnected) {
    this.submitData(requestBody);
  } else {
    this.pendingSync = requestBody;
    this.setState({syncStatus : 'Pending'});
  }
}
```

7. Now, we can build out our UI, which will render the **Submit Data** button and show the current connection status, sync status, and most recent response from the API:

```
render() {
  const {
    isConnected,
    syncStatus,
    serverResponse
  } = this.state;
  return (
    <View style={styles.container}>
```

```
<TouchableOpacity onPress={this.onSubmitPress}>
  <View style={styles.button}>
    <Text style={styles.buttonText}>Submit Data</Text>
  </View>
</TouchableOpacity>
<Text style={styles.status}>
  Connection Status: {isConnected ? 'Connected' :
  'Disconnected'}
</Text>
<Text style={styles.status}>
  Sync Status: {syncStatus}
</Text>
<Text style={styles.status}>
  Server Response: {serverResponse}
</Text>
    </View>
  );
}
```

8. You can disable the network connection in the simulator in the same way as described in *step 10* of the previous recipe:

How it works...

This recipe leverages the `NetInfo` module to control when an AJAX request should be made.

In *step 6*, we defined the method that's executed when the **Submit Data** button is pressed. If there is no connectivity, we save the request body into the `pendingSync` class variable.

In *step 3*, we defined the `componentWillMount` life cycle hook. Here, two `NetInfo` method calls retrieve the current network connection status and attach an event listener to the change event.

In *step 4*, we defined the function that will be executed whenever the network connection has changed, which informs the state's `isConnected` Boolean property appropriately. If the device is connected, we also check to see whether there is a pending API call, and complete the request if it exists.

This recipe could also be expanded on to support a queue system of pending calls, which would allow multiple AJAX requests to be delayed until an internet connection was re-established.

Logging in with Facebook

Facebook is the largest social media platform in existence, with well over 1 billion users worldwide. This means that there's a good chance that your users will have a Facebook account. Your app can register and link with their account, allowing you to use their Facebook credentials as a login for your app. Depending on the requested permissions, this will also allow you to access data such as user information, and pictures, and even give you the ability to access shared content. You can read more about the available permission options from the Facebook docs at `https://developers.facebook.com/docs/facebook-login/permissions#reference-public_profile`.

In this recipe, we will cover a basic method for logging into Facebook via an app to get a session token. We'll then use that token to access the basic `/me` endpoint provided by Facebook's Graph API, which will give us the user's name and ID. For more complex interactions with the Facebook Graph API, you can look at the documentation, which can be found at `https://developers.facebook.com/docs/graph-api/using-graph-api`.

To keep this recipe simple, we will be building an Expo app that uses the `Expo.Facebook.logInWithReadPermissionsAsync` method to do the heavy lifting of logging into Facebook, which will also allow us to bypass much of the setup that's otherwise necessary for such an app. If you wish to interact with Facebook without using Expo, you will likely want to use the React Native Facebook SDK, which requires a lot more steps. You can find the SDK at `https://github.com/facebook/react-native-fbsdk`.

Getting ready

For this recipe, we'll create a new app called `facebook-login`. You will need to have an active Facebook account to test its functionality.

A Facebook Developer account is also necessary for this recipe. Head over to `https://developers.facebook.com` to sign up if you don't have one. Once you are logged in, you can use the dashboard to create a new app. Make note of the app ID once it's been created, as we'll need it for the recipe.

How to do it...

1. Let's start by opening the `App.js` file and adding our imports:

```
import React from 'react';
import {
  StyleSheet,
  Text,
  View,
  TouchableOpacity,
  Alert
} from 'react-native';
import Expo from 'expo';
```

2. Next, we'll declare the `App` class and add the `state` object. The `state` will keep track of whether the user is logged in with the `loggedIn` Boolean, and will save the retrieved user data from Facebook in an object called `facebookUserInfo`:

```
export default class App extends React.Component {
  state = {
    loggedIn: false,
    facebookUserInfo: {}
  }
  // Defined in later steps
}
```

3. Next, let's define the `logIn` method of our class. This will be the method that's called when the **Login** button is pressed. This method uses the `logInWithReadPermissionsAsync` Expo helper class of the `Facebook` method to prompt the user with a Facebook login screen. Replace the first parameter, labeled `APP_ID` in the following code, with your App's ID:

```
logIn = async () => {
  const { type, token } = await
  Facebook.logInWithReadPermissionsAsync(APP_ID, {
    permissions: ['public_profile'],
  });

  // Defined in next step
}
```

4. In the second half of the `logIn` method, if the request is successful, we'll make a call to the Facebook Graph API using the token that was received from logging in to request the logged-in user's information. Once the response resolves, we set the state accordingly:

```
logIn = async () => {
  //Defined in step above

  if (type === 'success') {
    const response = await fetch(`https://graph.facebook.com/me?
    access_token=${token}`);
    const facebookUserInfo = await response.json();
    this.setState({
      facebookUserInfo,
      loggedIn: true
    });
  }
}
```

5. We'll also need a simple `render` function. We'll display a **Login** button for logging in, as well as `Text` elements that will display user information once the login has completed successfully:

```
render() {
  return (
    <View style={styles.container}>
      <Text style={styles.headerText}>Login via Facebook</Text>
      <TouchableOpacity
        onPress={this.logIn}
        style={styles.button}
      >
```

```
        <Text style={styles.buttonText}>Login</Text>
      </TouchableOpacity>

      {this.renderFacebookUserInfo()}
    </View>
  );
}
```

6. As you can see in the preceding `render` function, we're calling `this.renderFacebookUserInfo` to render user information. This method simply checks whether the user in logged in via `this.state.loggedIn`. If they are, we'll display the user's information. If not, we'll return `null` to display nothing:

```
renderFacebookUserInfo = () => {
  return this.state.loggedIn ? (
    <View style={styles.facebookUserInfo}>
      <Text style={styles.facebookUserInfoLabel}>Name:</Text>
      <Text style={styles.facebookUserInfoText}>
      {this.state.facebookUserInfo.name}</Text>
      <Text style={styles.facebookUserInfoLabel}>User ID:</Text>
      <Text style={styles.facebookUserInfoText}>
      {this.state.facebookUserInfo.id}</Text>
    </View>
  ) : null;
}
```

7. Finally, we'll add styles to complete the layout, setting padding, margins, color, and font sizes:

```
const styles = StyleSheet.create({
  container: {
    flex: 1,
    backgroundColor: '#fff',
    alignItems: 'center',
    justifyContent: 'center',
  },
  button: {
    marginTop: 30,
    padding: 10,
    backgroundColor: '#3B5998'
  },
  buttonText: {
    color: '#fff',
    fontSize: 30
  },
  headerText: {
```

```
        fontSize: 30
      },
      facebookUserInfo: {
        paddingTop: 30
      },
      facebookUserInfoText: {
        fontSize: 24
      },
      facebookUserInfoLabel: {
        fontSize: 20,
        marginTop: 10,
        color: '#474747'
      }
    });
```

8. Now, if we run the app, we'll see our **Login** button, a login modal when the **Login** button is pressed, and the user's information, which will be displayed once the user has successfully logged in:

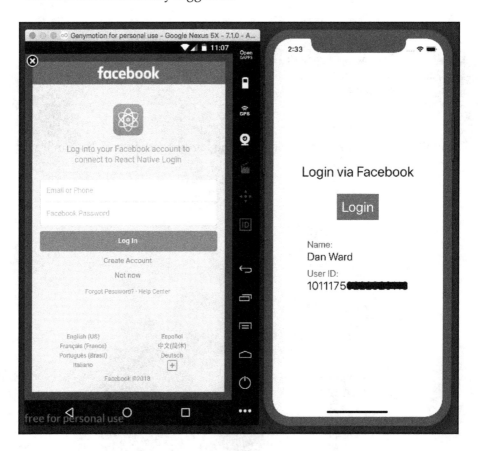

How it works...

Interacting with Facebook in our React Native app is made much easier than it otherwise would be, via Expo's `Facebook` helper library.

In *step 5*, we created the `logIn` function, which uses `Facebook.logInWithReadPermissionsAsync` to make the login request to Facebook. It takes two parameters: an `appID` and an options object. In our case, we're only setting the permissions option. The permissions option takes an array of strings for each type of permission requested, but for our purpose, we only use the most basic permission, `'public_profile'`.

In *step 6*, we completed the `logIn` function. It makes a call to Facebook's Graph API endpoint, `/me`, upon successful login, using the token provided by the data that's returned from `logInWithReadPermissionsAsync`. The user's information and the login status are saved to state, which will trigger a re-render and display the user's data on the screen.

This recipe intentionally only makes a call to one simple API endpoint. You could use the return data from this endpoint to populate user data in your app. Alternatively, you could use the same token that was received from logging in to perform any actions provided by the Graph API. To see what kind of data is at your disposal via the API, you can view the reference docs at `https://developers.facebook.com/docs/graph-api/reference`.

Implementing Redux

9

In this chapter, we'll go step by step through the process of adding Redux to our app. We'll cover the following recipes:

- Installing Redux and preparing our project
- Defining actions
- Defining reducers
- Setting up the store
- Communicating with a remote API
- Connecting the store to the views
- Storing offline content using Redux
- Showing network connectivity status

Introduction

At some point during the development of most applications, we'll need a better way to handle the state of the overall app. This will ease sharing data across components and provide a more robust architecture for scaling our app in the future.

In order to get a better understanding of Redux, the structure of this chapter will differ from previous chapters, since we'll be creating one app through all of these recipes. Each recipe in this chapter will depend on the last recipe.

We will be building a simple app for displaying user posts, and we'll use a `ListView` component to display the data returned from the API. We'll be using the excellent mock data API we've used before located at `https://jsonplaceholder.typicode.com`.

Installing Redux and preparing our project

In this recipe, we'll install Redux in an empty application, and we'll define the basic folder structure of our app.

Getting started

We'll need a new empty app for this recipe. Let's call it `redux-app`.

We'll also need two dependencies: `redux` for handling state management and `react-redux` for gluing together Redux and React Native. You can install them from the command line with yarn:

```
yarn add redux react-redux
```

Or you can use `npm`:

```
npm install --save redux react-redux
```

How to do it...

1. As part of this recipe, we'll build out the folder structure that the app will use. Let's add a `components` folder with an `Album` folder inside of it to hold the photo album component. We'll also need a `redux` folder to hold all of our Redux code.
2. Inside the `redux` folder, let's add an `index.js` file for Redux initialization. We also need a `photos` directory, with an `actions.js` file and a `reducer.js` file.
3. For now, the `App.js` file will only contain an `Album` component, which we'll define later:

```jsx
import React, { Component } from 'react';
import { StyleSheet, SafeAreaView } from 'react-native';

import Album from './components/Album';

const App = () => (
  <SafeAreaView style={styles.container}>
    <Album />
  </SafeAreaView>
);
```

```
const styles = StyleSheet.create({
  container: {
    flex: 1,
  },
});

export default App;
```

How it works...

In *Getting started*, we installed the `redux` and `react-redux` libraries. The `react-redux` library contains the necessary bindings to integrate Redux with React. Redux is not exclusively designed to work with React. You can use Redux with any other JavaScript libraries out there. By using `react-redux`, we'll be able to seamlessly integrate Redux into our React Native application.

In *step 2*, we created the main folders we'll use for our app:

- The `components` folder will contain our app components. In this case, we're only adding one `Album` component to keep this recipe simple.
- The `redux` folder will contain all of the Redux related code (initialization, actions, and reducers).

In a medium to large app, you will probably want to separate your React Native components further. The React community standard is to split the app's components into three separate types:

- `Components`: The community calls them presentational components. In simple terms, these are the kind of components that are not aware of any business logic or Redux actions. These components only receive data via props and should be reusable on any other project. A button or panel would be a perfect example of a presentational component.
- `Containers`: These are components that directly receive data from Redux and are able to call actions. In here, we'll define components such as a header that displays the logged in user. Usually, these components internally use presentational components.
- `Pages/Views`: These are the main modules in the app that use containers and presentational components.

For more information on structuring your Redux powered components, I recommend the excellent article, *Structure your React-Redux project for scalability and maintainability,* at the following link:

```
https://levelup.gitconnected.com/structure-your-react-redux-project-for-
scalability-and-maintainability-618ad82e32b7
```

We will also need to create a `redux/photos` folder. In this folder, we'll create the following:

- The `actions.js` file, which will contain all of the actions the app can perform. We will talk more about actions on the next recipe.
- The `reducer.js` file, which will contain all the code managing the data in the Redux store. We will dig deeper into this subject in later recipes.

Defining actions

An action is a payload of information that sends data to the store. Using these actions is the *only* way components can request or send data to the Redux store, which serves as the global state object for the entire app. An action is just a plain JavaScript object. We'll be defining functions that return these actions. A function that returns an action is called an action creator.

In this recipe, we'll create the actions to load the initial images for the gallery. During this recipe, we'll be adding hardcoded data, but later on, we'll request this data from an API to create a more realistic scenario.

Getting ready

Let's continue working on the code from the previous recipe. Make sure to follow those steps in order to have Redux installed and build out the folder structure that we'll use for this project.

How to do it...

1. We'll need to define types for each the action. Open the
   `redux/photos/actions.js` file. Action types are defined as constants that can
   later be referenced in actions and reducers, as follows:

```
export const FETCH_PHOTOS = 'FETCH_PHOTOS';
```

2. Now let's create our first action creator. Every action needs a `type` property to
   define it, and actions will often have a `payload` property of data to pass along
   with the action. In this recipe, we're hardcoding a mock API response made up of
   an array of two photo objects, as follows:

```
export const fetchPhotos = () => {
  return {
    type: FETCH_PHOTOS,
    payload: {
      "photos": [
        {
          "albumId": 2,
          "title": "dolore esse a in eos sed",
          "url": "http://placehold.it/600/f783bd",
          "thumbnailUrl": "http://placehold.it/150/d83ea2",
          "id": 2
        },
        {
          "albumId": 2,
          "title": "dolore esse a in eos sed",
          "url": "http://placehold.it/600/8e6eef",
          "thumbnailUrl": "http://placehold.it/150/bf6d2a",
          "id": 3
        }
      ]
    }
  }
}
```

3. We will need an action creator for each action we want the app to be able to
   execute, and we want this app to be able to add and remove images. First, let's
   add the `addBookmark` action creator, as follows:

```
export const ADD_PHOTO = 'ADD_PHOTO';
export const addPhoto = (photo) => {
  return {
    type: ADD_PHOTO,
    payload: photo
```

```
    };
  }
```

4. Likewise, we'll need another action creator for removing photos:

```
export const REMOVE_PHOTO = 'REMOVE_PHOTO';
export const removePhoto = (photo) => {
  return {
    type: REMOVE_PHOTO,
    payload: photo
  };
}
```

How it works...

In *step 1*, we defined the action's type to indicate what it does, which in this case is fetch images. We use a constant since it will be used in multiple places, including action creators, reducers, and tests.

In *step 2*, we declared an action creator. Actions are simple JavaScript objects that define an event that happens in our app that will affect the state of the app. We use actions to interact with data that lives in the Redux store.

There's only one single requirement: each action must have a `type` property. In addition, an action will often include a `payload` property that holds data relevant to the action. In this case, we are using an array of photo objects.

 An action is valid as long as the `type` property is defined. If we want to send anything else, it is a common convention to use the `payload` property as popularized by the flux pattern. However, the name property isn't inherently special. We could name this `params` or `data` and the behavior would remain the same.

There's more...

Currently, we have defined the action creators, which are simple functions that return actions. In order to use them, we need to use the `dispatch` method provided by the Redux `store`. We will learn more about the store in later recipes.

Defining reducers

At this point, we have created a few actions for our app. As discussed earlier, actions define that something should happened, but we haven't created anything for putting the action into motion. That's where reducers come in. Reducers are functions that define how an action should affect the data in the Redux `store`. All accessing of data in the `store` happens in a reducer.

Reducers receive two parameters: `state` and `action`. The `state` parameter represents the global state of the app, and the `action` parameter is the action object being used by the reducer. Reducers return a new `state` parameter reflecting the changes that are associated with a given `action` parameter. In this recipe, we'll introduce a reducer for fetching the photos by using the actions we defined in the previous recipe.

Getting ready

This recipe depends on the previous recipe, *Defining actions*. Be sure to start from the beginning of this chapter to avoid any problems or confusion.

How to do it...

1. Let's start by opening the `photos/reducer.js` file and importing all of the action types we defined in the previous recipe, as follows:

```
import {
  FETCH_PHOTOS,
  ADD_PHOTO,
  REMOVE_PHOTO
} from './actions';
```

2. We'll define an initial state object for the state in this reducer. It has a `photos` property initialized to an empty array for the currently loaded photos, as follows:

```
const initialState = () => return {
 photos: []
};
```

3. We can now define the `reducer` function. It'll receive two parameters, the current state and the action that has been dispatched, as follows:

```
export default (state = initialState, action) => {
  // Defined in next steps
}
```

React Native components can also have a `state` object, but that is an entirely separate `state` from that which Redux uses. In this context, `state` refers to the global state stored in the Redux `store`.

4. State is immutable, so instead of manipulating state, inside the reducer function, we need to return a new state for the current action, as follows:

```
export default (state = initialState, action) => {
  switch (action.type) {
    case FETCH_PHOTOS:
      return {
        ...state,
        photos: [...action.payload],
      };
    // Defined in next steps
}
```

5. In order to add a new bookmark to the array, all we need to do is get the payload of the action and include it in the new array. We can use the spread operator to spread the current photos array on `state`, then add `action.payload` to the new array, as follows:

```
case ADD_PHOTO:
  return {
    ...state,
    photos: [...state.photos, action.payload],
  };
```

6. If we want to remove an item from the array, we can use the filter method, as follows:

```
case REMOVE_PHOTO:
  return {
    ...state,
    photos: state.photos.filter(photo => {
      return photo.id !== action.payload.id
    })
  };
```

7. The final step is to combine all of the reducers that we have. In a larger app, you will likely have reason to break your reducers into separate files. Since we're only using one reducer, this step is technically optional, but it illustrates how multiple reducers can be combined together with Redux's `combineReducers` helper. Let's use it in the `redux/index.js` file, which we'll also use to initiate the Redux store in the next recipe, as follows:

```
import { combineReducers } from 'redux';
import photos from './photos/reducers';
const reducers = combineReducers({
  photos,
});
```

How it works...

In *step 1*, we imported all of the action types that we declared in the previous recipe. We use these types to determine what action should be taken and how `action.payload` should affect the Redux state.

In *step 2*, we defined the initial state of the `reducer` function. For now, we only need an empty array for our photos, but we could add other properties to the state, such as Boolean properties of `isLoading` and `didError` to track loading and error states. These can, in turn, be used to update the UI during and in response to `async` actions.

In *step 3*, we defined the `reducer` function, which receives two parameters: the current state and the action that is being dispatched. We set the initial state to `initialState` if we are not provided with one. This way, we can ensure that the photos array exists at all times within the app, which will help in avoiding errors in cases where actions get dispatched that don't affect the Redux state.

In *step 4*, we defined an action for fetching photos. Remember that state is never directly manipulated. If the action's type matches the case, a new state object is created by combining the current `state.photos` array with the incoming photos on `action.payload`.

The `reducer` function should be pure. This means there shouldn't be side effects on any of the input values. Mutating the state or the action is bad practice and should always be avoided. A mutation can lead to inconsistent data or not triggering a render correctly. Also, in order to prevent side effects, we should avoid executing any AJAX requests inside the reducer.

In *step 5,* we created the action for adding a new element to the photos array, but instead of using `Array.push`, we are returning a new array and appended the incoming element to the last position to avoid mutating the original array on the state.

In *step 6,* we added an action for removing the bookmark from the state. The easiest way to do this is by using the `filter` method so we can ignore the element with the ID that was received on the action's payload.

In *step 7,* we use the `combineReducers` function to merge all of the reducers into a single global state object that will be saved in the store. This function will call each reducer with the key in the state that corresponds to that reducer; this function is exactly the same as the following:

```
import photosReducer from './photos/reducer';

const reducers = function(state, action) {
  return {
    photos: photosReducer(state.photos, action),
  };
}
```

The photos reducer has only been called on the part of the state that cares about photos. This will help you avoid managing all state data in a single reducer.

Setting up the Redux store

The Redux store is responsible for updating the information that is calculated on the state inside reducers. It is a single global object, which can be accessed via the store's `getState` method.

In this recipe, we'll tie together the actions and the reducer we created in previous recipes. We will use the existing actions to affect data that lives in the store. We will also learn how to log changes on the state by subscribing to the store changes. This recipe serves more as a proof of concept of how actions, reducers, and the store work together. We'll dive deeper into how Redux is more commonly used within apps later in this chapter.

How to do it...

1. Let's open the `redux/index.js` file and import the `createStore` function from `redux`, as follows:

```
import { combineReducers, createStore } from 'redux';
```

2. Creating the store is extremely simple; all we need to do is call the function imported in *step 1* and send the reducers as the first parameter, as follows:

```
const store = createStore(reducers);
export default store;
```

3. That's it! We've set up the store, so now let's dispatch some actions. The next steps in this recipe will be removed from the final project since they're for testing our setup. Let's start by importing the action creators we would like to dispatch:

```
import {
  loadPhotos,
  addPhotos,
  removePhotos,
} from './photos/actions';
```

4. Before dispatching any actions, let's subscribe to the store, which will allow us to listen to any changes that occur in the store. For our current purposes, we only need to `console.log` the result of `store.getState()`, as follows:

```
const unsubscribe = store.subscribe(() => {
  console.log(store.getState());
});
```

5. Let's dispatch some actions and see the resulting state in the **Developer** console:

```
store.dispatch(loadPhotos());
```

6. In order to add a new bookmark, we need to dispatch the `addBookmark` action creator with the photos object as the parameter:

```
store.dispatch(addPhoto({
  "albumId": 2,
  "title": "dolore esse a in eos sed",
  "url": `http://placehold.it/600/`,
  "thumbnailUrl": `http://placehold.it/150/`
}));
```

7. To remove an item, we pass along the `id` of the photo we want to remove to the action creator, since this is what the reducer is using to find the item that should be deleted:

```
store.dispatch(removePhoto({ id: 1 }));
```

8. After executing all of these actions, we can stop listening to changes on the store by running the unsubscribe function we created in *step 4* when we subscribed to the store, as follows:

```
unsubscribe();
```

9. We need to import the `redux/index.js` file into the `App.js` file, which will run all of the code in this recipe so we can see the related `console.log` messages in the **Developer** console:

```
import store from './redux';
```

How it works...

In *step 3*, we imported the action creators we created in the earlier recipe, *Defining actions*. Even though we don't yet have a UI, we can use the Redux store and observe the changes as they happen. All it takes is calling an action creator and then dispatching the resulting action.

In *step 5*, we called the `dispatch` method from the `store` instance. `dispatch` takes an action, which is created by the `loadBookmarks` action creator. The reducer will be called in turn, which will set the new photos on the state.

Once we have our UI in place, we'll dispatch the actions in a similar fashion from our components, which will update the state, ultimately triggering a re-render of the component, displaying the new data.

Communicating with a remote API

We are currently loading the bookmarks from hardcoded data in the action. In a real app, we're much more likely to be getting data back from an API. In this recipe, we'll use a Redux middleware to help with the process of fetching data from an API.

Getting ready

In this recipe, we'll be using `axios` to make all AJAX requests. Install it with `npm`:

```
npm install --save axios
```

Or you can install it with `yarn`:

```
yarn add axios
```

For this recipe, we'll be using the Redux middleware, `redux-promise-middleware`. Install the package with `npm`:

```
npm install --save redux-promise-middleware
```

Or you can install it with `yarn`:

```
yarn add redux-promise-middleware
```

This middleware will create and automatically dispatch three related actions for each AJAX request made in our app: one when a request begins, one when a request succeeds, and one for when a request fails. Using this middleware, we are able to define an action creator that returns an action object with a *promise* for a payload. In our case, we'll be creating the `async` action, `FETCH_PHOTOS`, whose payload is an API request. The middleware will create and dispatch an action of the `FETCH_PHOTOS_PENDING` type. When the request resolves, the middleware will create and dispatch either an action of the `FETCH_PHOTOS_FULFILLED` type with the resolved data as the `payload` if the request was successful or an action of the `FETCH_PHOTOS_REJECTED` type with the error as a `payload` if the request failed.

How to do it...

1. Let's start by adding the new middleware to our Redux store. In the `redux/index.js` file, let's add the Redux method, `applyMiddleware`. We'll also add the new middleware we just installed, as follows:

```
import { combineReducers, createStore, applyMiddleware } from
'redux';
import promiseMiddleware from 'redux-promise-middleware';
```

2. In the call to `createStore` that we defined previously, we can pass in `applyMiddleware` as the second parameter. `applyMiddleware` takes one parameter, which is the middleware we want to use, `promiseMiddleware`:

```
const store = createStore(reducers,
applyMiddleware(promiseMiddleware()));
```

Unlike some other popular Redux middleware solutions such as `redux-thunk`, `promiseMiddleware` must be invoked when it is passed to `applyMiddleware`. It is a function that returns the middleware.

3. We're going to be making real API requests in our actions now, so we need to import `axios` into `redux/photos/actions`. We'll also add the API's base URL. We are using the same dummy data API we used in previous chapters, hosted at `http://jsonplaceholder.typicode.com`, as follows:

```
import axios from 'axios';
const API_URL='http://jsonplaceholder.typicode.com';
```

4. Next, we'll update our action creators. We'll first update the types we need for handling AJAX requests, as follows:

```
export const FETCH_PHOTOS = 'FETCH_PHOTOS';
export const FETCH_PHOTOS_PENDING = 'FETCH_PHOTOS_PENDING';
export const FETCH_PHOTOS_FULFILLED = 'FETCH_PHOTOS_FULFILLED';
export const FETCH_PHOTOS_REJECTED = 'FETCH_PHOTOS_REJECTED';
```

5. Instead of returning dummy data as `payload` for this action, we'll return a `GET` request. Since this is a `Promise`, it will trigger our new middleware. Also, notice how the action's type is `FETCH_PHOTOS`. This will cause the middleware to automatically create `FETCH_PHOTOS_PENDING`, `FETCH_PHOTOS_FULFILLED` with a `payload` of resolved data when successful, and `FETCH_PHOTOS_REJECTED` with a `payload` of the error that occurred, as follows:

```
export const fetchPhotos = () => {
  return {
    type: FETCH_PHOTOS,
    payload: axios.get(`${API_URL}/photos?_page=1&_limit=20`)
  }
}
```

6. Just like the `FETCH_PHOTOS` action, we'll be making use of the same middleware provided types for the `ADD_PHOTO` action, as follows:

```
export const ADD_PHOTO = 'ADD_PHOTO';
export const ADD_PHOTO_PENDING = 'ADD_PHOTO_PENDING';
export const ADD_PHOTO_FULFILLED = 'ADD_PHOTO_FULFILLED';
export const ADD_PHOTO_REJECTED = 'ADD_PHOTO_REJECTED';
```

7. The action creator itself will no longer just return the passed in photo as the `payload`, but instead will pass a `POST` request promise for adding the image via the API, as follows:

```
export const addPhoto = (photo) => {
  return {
    type: ADD_PHOTO,
    payload: axios.post(`${API_URL}/photos`, photo)
  };
}
```

8. We can follow the same pattern to convert the `REMOVE_PHOTO` action into an AJAX request that uses the API to *delete* a photo. Like the other two action creators for `ADD_PHOTO` and `FETCH_PHOTOS`, we'll define the action types for each action, then return the delete `axios` request as the action's `payload`. Since we'll need `photoId` in the reducer when we remove the image object from the Redux store, we also pass that along as an object on the action's `meta` property, as follows:

```
export const REMOVE_PHOTO = 'REMOVE_PHOTO';
export const REMOVE_PHOTO_PENDING = 'REMOVE_PHOTO_PENDING';
export const REMOVE_PHOTO_FULFILLED = 'REMOVE_PHOTO_FULFILLED';
export const REMOVE_PHOTO_REJECTED = 'REMOVE_PHOTO_REJECTED';
export const removePhoto = (photoId) => {
  console.log(`${API_URL}/photos/${photoId}`);
  return {
    type: REMOVE_PHOTO,
    payload: axios.delete(`${API_URL}/photos/${photoId}`),
    meta: { photoId }
  };
}
```

9. We also need to revisit our reducers to adjust the expected payload. In `redux/reducers.js`, we'll start by importing all of the action types we'll be using, and we'll update `initialState`. For reasons that will be apparent in the next recipe, let's rename the array of photos on the `state` object to `loadedPhotos`, as follows:

```
import {
  FETCH_PHOTOS_FULFILLED,
  ADD_PHOTO_FULFILLED,
  REMOVE_PHOTO_FULFILLED,
} from './actions';

const initialState = {
  loadedPhotos: []
};
```

10. In the reducer itself, update each case to take the FULFILLED variation of the base action: FETCH_PHOTOS becomes FETCH_PHOTOS_FULFILLED, ADD_PHOTOS becomes ADD_PHOTOS_FULFILLED, and REMOVE_PHOTOS becomes REMOVE_PHOTOS_FULFILLED. We'll also update all of the references to the photos array of `state` from `photos` to `loadedPhotos`. When using `axios`, all response objects will contain a `data` parameter that holds the actual data received from the API, which means we'll also need to update all references of `action.payload` to `action.payload.data`. And in the REMOVE_PHOTO_FULFILLED reducer, we can no longer find `photoId` at `action.payload.id`, which is why we passed `photoId` on the action's `meta` property in *step 8*, therefore `action.payload.id` becomes `action.meta.photoId`, as follows:

```
export default (state = initialState, action) => {
  switch (action.type) {
    case FETCH_PHOTOS_FULFILLED:
      return {
        ...state,
        loadedPhotos: [...action.payload.data],
      };
    case ADD_PHOTO_FULFILLED:
      return {
        ...state,
        loadedPhotos: [action.payload.data, ...state.loadedPhotos],
      };
    case REMOVE_PHOTO_FULFILLED:
      return {
        ...state,
        loadedPhotos: state.loadedPhotos.filter(photo => {
```

```
                    return photo.id !== action.meta.photoId
                })
            };
        default:
            return state;
    }
}
```

How it works...

In *step 2*, we applied the middleware that was installed in the *Getting started* section. As mentioned before, this middleware will allow us to make just one action creator for AJAX actions that automatically creates individual action creators for the PENDING, FULFILLED, and REJECTED request states.

In *step 5*, we defined the fetchPhotos action creator. You'll recall from the previous recipes that actions are plain JavaScript objects. Since we defined a Promise on the action's payload property, redux-promise-middleware will intercept this action and automatically create the three associated actions for the three possible request states.

In *step 7* and *step 8*, we defined the addPhoto action creator and the removePhoto action creator which, just like fetchPhotos, have an AJAX request as the action payload.

By utilizing this middleware, we are able to avoid repeating the same boilerplate over and over for making different AJAX requests.

In this recipe, we only handled the success conditions of the AJAX requests made in the app. It would be wise in a real app to also handle the error states represented with actions types ending in _REJECTED. This will be a great place to handle an error by saving it to the Redux store, so that the view can display error information when it occurs.

Connecting the store to the view

So far, we have set up the state, we have included middleware, and we've defined actions, action creators, and reducers for interacting with a remote API. However, we are not able to show any of this data on the screen. In this recipe, we'll enable our component to access the store that we have created.

Getting ready

This recipe depends on all of the previous ones, so make sure to follow each recipe preceding this one.

In the first recipe of this chapter, we installed the `react-redux` library along with our other dependencies. In this recipe, we are finally going to make use of it.

We'll also be using a third-party library for generating random color hexes, which we'll use to request colored images from the placeholder image service at `https://placehold.it/`. Before we begin, install `randomcolor` with `npm`:

```
npm install --save randomcolor
```

Or you can install it with `yarn`:

```
yarn add randomcolor
```

How to do it...

1. Let's start by wiring the Redux store to the React Native app in `App.js`. We'll start with the imports, importing `Provider` from `react-redux` and the store we created earlier. We'll also import the `Album` component we'll be defining shortly, as follows:

```
import React, { Component } from 'react';
import { StyleSheet, SafeAreaView } from 'react-native';
import { Provider } from 'react-redux';
import store from './redux';

import Album from './components/Album';
```

2. It's the job of the `Provider` to connect our Redux store to the React Native app so that the app's components can communicate with the store. `Provider` should be used to wrap the entire app, and since this app lives in the `Album` component, we'll wrap the `Album` component with the `Provider` component. `Provider` takes a `store` prop, where we'll pass in our Redux store. The app and the store are wired:

```
const App = () => (
  <Provider store={store}>
    <Album />
  </Provider>
);

export default App;
```

3. Let's turn to the `Album` component. The component will live at `components/Album/index.js`. We'll start with the imports. We'll import the `randomcolor` package for generating random color hexes, as mentioned in the *Getting started* section. We'll also import `connect` from `react-redux`, and the action creators we defined in previous recipes. `connect` will wire our app to the Redux store, and we can then use the action creators to affect the store's state, as follows:

```
import React, { Component } from 'react';
import {
  StyleSheet,
  Text,
  View,
  SafeAreaView,
  ScrollView,
  Image,
  TouchableOpacity
} from 'react-native';
import randomColor from 'randomcolor';
import { connect } from 'react-redux';
import {
  fetchPhotos,
  addPhoto,
  removePhoto
} from '../../redux/photos/actions';
```

4. Let's create the `Album` class, however, instead of directly exporting `Album` as the `default` export, we'll use `connect` to wire `Album` to the store. Note that `connect` is called with two sets of parentheses and that the component is passed into the second set, as follows:

```
class Album extends Component {

}

export default connect()(Album);
```

5. The first set of parentheses in a call to `connect` takes two function parameters: `mapStateToProps` and `mapDispatchToProps`. We'll define `mapStateToProps` first, which takes `state` as a parameter. This `state` is our global Redux state object containing all of our data. The function returns an object of the pieces of `state` that we want to use in our component. In our case, we just need the `loadedPhotos` property from the `photos` reducer. By setting this value to `photos` in the return object, we can expect `this.props.photos` to be the value stored in `state.photos.loadedPhotos`. And it will change automatically when the Redux store is updated:

```
class Album extends Component {

}

const mapStateToProps = (state) => {
  return {
    photos: state.photos.loadedPhotos
  }
}

export default connect(mapStateToProps)(Album);
```

6. Similarly, the `mapDispatchToProps` function will map our action creators to the component's props as well. The function receives the Redux method, `dispatch`, which is used to execute an action creator. We'll map the execution of each action creator to a key of the same name, so that `this.props.fetchPhotos()` will execute `dispatch(fetchPhotos())`, and so on, as follows:

```
class Album extends Component {

}

const mapStateToProps = (state) => {
  return {
```

```
      photos: state.photos.loadedPhotos
    }
  }

  const mapDispatchToProps = (dispatch) => {
    return {
      fetchPhotos: () => dispatch(fetchPhotos()),
      addPhoto: (photo) => dispatch(addPhoto(photo)),
      removePhoto: (id) => dispatch(removePhoto(id))
    }
  }

export default connect(mapStateToProps, mapDispatchToProps)(Album);
```

7. Now that we've got our Redux store wired to our component, let's create the component itself. We can make use of the `componentDidMount` life cycle hook to fetch our photos, as follows:

```
class Album extends Component {
  componentDidMount() {
    this.props.fetchPhotos();
  }
  // Defined on later steps
}
```

8. We will also need a method for adding photos. Here, we'll use the `randomcolor` package (imported as `randomColor` by convention) to create an image with the `placehold.it` service. The generated color string comes back with a hash prefixing the hex value, which the request to the image service doesn't want, so we can simply remove it with a `replace` call. To add the photo, we just call the `addPhoto` function mapped to `props`, passing in the new `photo` object, as follows:

```
addPhoto = () => {
  const photo = {
    "albumId": 2,
    "title": "dolore esse a in eos sed",
    "url": `http://placehold.it/600/${randomColor().replace('#',
      '')}`,
    "thumbnailUrl":
`http://placehold.it/150/${randomColor().replace('#', '')}`
  };
  this.props.addPhoto(photo);
}
```

9. We will also need a `removePhoto` function. All this function needs to do is call the `removePhoto` function that has been mapped to `props`, passing in the ID of the photo to be removed, as follows:

```
removePhoto = (id) => {
  this.props.removePhoto(id);
}
```

10. The template for the app will need a `TouchableOpacity` button for adding photos, a `ScrollView` for holding all of the images in a scrollable list, and all of our images. Each `Image` component will also be wrapped in a `TouchableOpacity` component for calling the `removePhoto` method when an image is pressed, as follows:

```
render() {
  return (
    <SafeAreaView style={styles.container}>
      <Text style={styles.toolbar}>Album</Text>
      <ScrollView>
        <View style={styles.imageContainer}>
          <TouchableOpacity style={styles.button} onPress=
          {this.addPhoto}>
            <Text style={styles.buttonText}>Add Photo</Text>
          </TouchableOpacity>
          {this.props.photos ? this.props.photos.map((photo) => {
            return(
              <TouchableOpacity onPress={() =>
              this.removePhoto(photo.id)} key={Math.random()}>
                <Image style={styles.image}
                  source={{ uri: photo.url }}
                />
              </TouchableOpacity>
            );
          }) : null}
        </View>
      </ScrollView>
    </SafeAreaView>
  );
}
```

11. Finally, we'll add styles so that the app has a layout, as follows. There's nothing here we haven't covered many times before:

```
const styles = StyleSheet.create({
  container: {
    backgroundColor: '#ecf0f1',
    flex: 1,
  },
  toolbar: {
    backgroundColor: '#3498db',
    color: '#fff',
    fontSize: 20,
    textAlign: 'center',
    padding: 20,
  },
  imageContainer: {
    flex: 1,
    flexDirection: 'column',
    justifyContent: 'center',
    alignItems: 'center',
  },
  image: {
    height: 300,
    width: 300
  },
  button: {
    margin: 10,
    padding: 20,
    backgroundColor: '#3498db'
  },
  buttonText: {
    fontSize: 18,
    color: '#fff'
  }
});
```

12. The app is complete! Clicking on the **Add Photo** button will add a new photo to the beginning of the list of images, and pressing an image will remove it. Note, since we are using a dummy data API, the POST and DELETE requests will return proper responses for the given action. However, no data is actually added or deleted to the database. This means that the image list will reset if the app is refreshed, and that you can expect errors if you attempt to delete any photos you've just added with the **Add Photo** button. Feel free to connect this app to a real API and database to see the expected results:

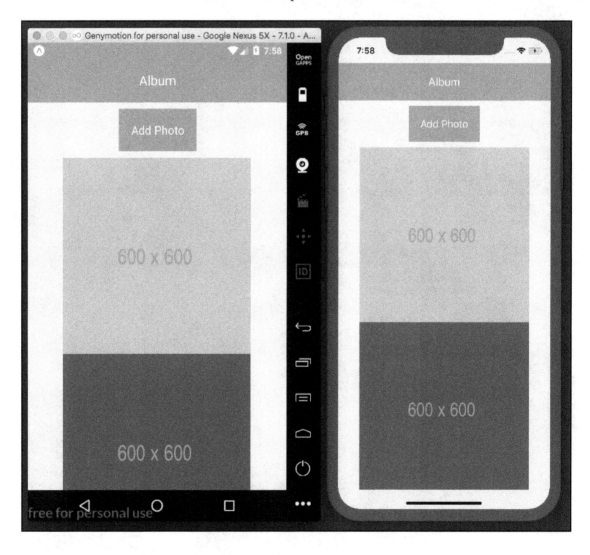

How it works...

In *step 4*, we used the `connect` method provided by `react-redux` to empower the `Album` component with a connection to the Redux store we've been working on this entire chapter. The call to `connect` returns a function that is immediately executed via the second set of parentheses. By passing the `Album` component into this returning function, `connect` glues the component and the store together.

In *step 5*, we defined the `mapStateToProps` function. The first parameter in this function is `state` from the Redux store, which is injected into the function by `connect`. Whatever keys are defined in the object returned from `mapStateToProps` will be properties on the component's `props`. The value of these props will be subscribed to `state` in the Redux store, so that any change affecting these pieces of `state` will be automatically updated within the component.

While `mapStateToProps` will map `state` in the Redux store to the component props, `mapDispatchToProps` will map the *action creators* to the component props. In *step 6*, we defined this function. It has the special Redux method, `dispatch`, injected into it for calling action creators that live in the store. `mapDispatchToProps` returns an object, mapping the `dispatch` calls for actions to the components props at the specified keys.

In *step 7*, we created the `componentDidMount` method. All the component needs to do to get the photos it needs while mounting is to call the action creator mapped to `this.props.fetchPhotos`. That's all! The `fetchPhotos` action creator will be dispatched. The `fetchPhoto` action returned from the action creator will be processed by the `redux-promise-middleware` we applied in a previous recipe since the `payload` property of this action has a Promise stored on it in the form of an `axios` AJAX request. The middleware will intercept the action, process the request, and send a new action to the reducers with the resolved data on the `payload` property. If it was a successful request, the action with the `FETCH_PHOTOS_FULFILLED` type will be dispatched with the resolved data, and if not, the `FETCH_PHOTOS_REJECTED` action will be dispatched with the error as `payload`. On success, the case in the reducer for handling `FETCH_PHOTOS_FULFILLED` will execute, `loadedPhotos` will be updated in the store, and in turn, `this.props.photos` will also be updated. Updating the component props will trigger a re-render, and the new data will be displayed on the screen.

In *step 8* and *step 9*, we followed the same pattern to define `addPhoto` and `removePhoto`, which call the action creators of the same name. The action produced by the action creators are handled by the middleware, the proper reducer handles the resulting action, and if the `state` in the Redux store changes, all subscribed props will be automatically updated!

Storing offline content using Redux

Redux is an excellent tool for keeping track of an app's state while it it's running. But what if we have data that we need to store without using an API? For instance, we could save the state of a component so that when a user closes and reopens the app, the previous state of that component can be restored, allowing us to persist a piece of an app's persistent across sessions. Redux data persistence could also be useful for caching information to avoid calling the API more than necessary. You can refer to the *Masking the application upon network connection loss* recipe in Chapter 8, *Working with Application Logic and Data*, for more information on how to detect and handle network connectivity status.

Getting ready

This recipe depends on the previous ones, so make sure to follow along with all of the previous recipes. In this recipe, we'll be using the redux-persist package to persist the data in our app's Redux store. Install it with npm:

```
npm install --save redux-persist
```

Or you can install it with yarn:

```
yarn add redux-persist
```

How to do it...

1. Let's start by adding the dependencies we'll need in redux/index.js. The storage method we're importing from redux-persist here will use React Native's AsyncStorage method to store Redux data between sessions, as follows:

```
import { persistStore, persistReducer } from 'redux-persist'
import storage from 'redux-persist/lib/storage';
```

2. We'll be using a simple config object for configuring our redux-persist instance. config requires a key property for the key used to store the data with AsyncStore and a storage property that takes the storage instance, as follows:

```
const persistConfig = {
  key: 'root',
  storage
}
```

3. We'll use the `persistReducer` method we imported in *step 1*. This method takes the `config` object we created in *step 2* as the first argument and our reducers as the second:

```
const reducers = combineReducers({
  photos,
});
```

const persistedReducer = persistReducer(persistConfig, reducers);

4. Now let's update our store to use the new `persistedReducer` method. Also note how we no longer export `store` as the default export, since we'll need two exports from this file:

```
export const store = createStore(persistedReducer,
applyMiddleware(promiseMiddleware()));
```

5. The second export we need from this file is `persistor`. `persistor` will work to persist the Redux store between sessions. We can create `persistor` by calling the `persistStore` method and passing in `store`, as follows:

```
export const persistor = persistStore(store);
```

6. Now that we've got both `store` and `persistor` as exports from `redux/index.js`, we're ready to apply them in `App.js`. We'll start by importing them, and we'll import the `PersistGate` component from `redux-persist`. `PersistGate` will ensure that our cached Redux store is loaded before any components are loaded:

```
import { PersistGate } from 'redux-persist/integration/react'
import { store, persistor } from './redux';
```

7. Let's update the `App` component to use `PersistGate`. The component takes two props: the imported `persistor` prop and a `loading` prop. We'll be passing `null` to the `loading` prop, but if we had a loading indicator component, we could pass this in, and `PersistGate` would display this loading indicator as data is restored, as follows:

```
const App = () => (
  <Provider store={store}>
    <PersistGate loading={null} persistor={persistor}>
      <Album />
    </PersistGate>
  </Provider>
);
```

8. In order to test the persistence of our Redux store, let's adjust the `componentDidMount` method in the `Album` component. We'll delay the call to `fetchPhotos` for two seconds, so that we can see the saved data before it is fetched again from the API, as follows:

```
componentDidMount() {
  setTimeout(() => {
    this.props.fetchPhotos();
  }, 2000);
}
```

Depending on what kind of data you're persisting, this kind of functionality could be applied to a number of situations, including persisting user data and app state, even after the app's been closed. It can also be used to improve the offline experience of an app, caching API requests if they can't be made right away and providing users with data filled views.

How it works...

In *step 2*, we created the config object for configuring `redux-persist`. The object is only required to have the `key` and `store` properties, but also supports quite a few others. You can see all of the options this config takes via the type definition hosted here: `https://github.com/rt2zz/redux-persist/blob/master/src/types.js#L13-L27`.

In *step 7*, we used the `PersistGate` component, which is how the documentation recommends delaying rendering until restoring persisted data is complete. If we have a loading indicator component, we can pass it to the `loading` prop for being displayed while data is restored.

10
App Workflow and Third-Party Plugins

This chapter works a bit differently, so we will first look into it before we go ahead and cover the following recipes:

- React Native development tools
- Planning your app and choosing your workflow
- Using NativeBase for cross-platform UI components
- Using glamorous-native for styling UI components
- Using react-native-spinkit for adding animated loading indicators
- Using react-native-side-menu for adding side navigation menus
- Using react-native-modalbox for adding modals

How this chapter works

In this chapter, we'll be taking a closer look at how each method of bootstrapping a new React Native app works, and how we can integrate third-party packages that may or may not be Expo friendly. In previous chapters, the focus has been entirely on building functional pieces of a React Native app. In this chapter, many of these recipes will therefore also serve a secondary purpose of illustrating how different packages can be implemented using different workflows.

In most of the recipes in this chapter, we will begin with a pure React Native project initialized with the React Native CLI command, which is done as follows:

```
react-native init
```

When creating a new React Native app, you'll need to choose the right tooling for initializing your app. Generally speaking, the tools you use for bootstrapping and developing your React Native app will either focus on streamlining the development process and purposefully obfuscating native code from you for the sake of ease and mental overhead, or keep your development process flexible by providing access to all native code and allowing the use of more third-party plugins.

There are two methods for initializing and developing your app: Expo and the React Native CLI. Until recently, there was a distinct third method, using **Create React Native App (CRNA)**. CRNA has since been merged with the Expo project, and only continues to exist as a separate entity to provide backwards compatibility.

Expo falls into the first category of tools, providing a more robust and developer-friendly development workflow at the cost of some flexibility. Apps bootstrapped with Expo also have access to a multitude of useful features provided by the Expo SDK, such as `BarcodeScanner`, `MapView`, `ImagePicker`, and so many more.

Initialize an app with the React Native CLI, via the following command:

```
react-native init
```

This provides flexibility at the cost of ease of development.

```
react-native init
```

It is said to be a pure React Native app, since none of the native code is hidden away from the developer.

As a rule of thumb, a pure React Native app will be required if using third-party packages whose setup requires running the following command:

```
react-native link
```

So what do you do when you are halfway through building an app with Expo, only to find out that a package integral to your app's requirements is not supported by an Expo development workflow? Luckily, Expo has a method for turning an Expo project into a pure React Native app, just as if it had been created with the following command:

```
expo eject
```

When a project is ejected, all of the Native code is unpacked into `ios` and `android` folders, and the `App.js` file is split into `App.js` and `index.js`, exposing the code that mounts the root React Native component.

But what if your Expo app depends on features provided by the Expo SDK? After all, much of the value of developing with Expo comes from the excellent features the SDK provides, including `AuthSession`, `Permissions`, `WebBrowser`, and others.

That's where ExpoKit comes into play. When you choose to eject from a project, you're given the option of including ExpoKit as part of the ejected project. Including ExpoKit will ensure that all of the Expo dependencies being used in your app will continue to work, and also give you the ability to continue using all the features of the Expo SDK, even after the app has been ejected.

For a deeper understanding of the eject processes, you can read the Expo documentation at `https://docs.expo.io/versions/latest/expokit/eject`.

React Native development tools

As with any development tools, there is going to be a trade-off between flexibility and ease of use. I encourage you start by using Expo for your React Native development workflow, unless you're sure you'll need access to the native code.

Expo

This was taken from the `expo.io` site:

> *"Expo is a free and open source toolchain built around React Native to help you build native iOS and Android projects using JavaScript and React."*

Expo is becoming an ecosystem of its own, and is made up of five interconnected tools:

- **Expo CLI**: The command-line interface for Expo.
  We've been using the Expo CLI to create, build, and serve apps. A list of all the commands supported by the CLI can be found in the official documentation at the following link:

  `https://docs.expo.io/versions/latest/workflow/expo-cli`

- **Expo developer tools**: This is a browser-based tool that automatically runs whenever an Expo app is started from the Terminal via the `expo start` command. It provides active logs for your in-development app, and quick access to running the app locally and sharing the app with other developers.
- **Expo Client**: An app for Android and iOS. This app allows you to run your React Native project within the Expo app on the device, without the need for installing it. This allows developers to hot reload on a real device, or share development code with anyone else without the need for installing it.
- **Expo Snack**: Hosted at `https://snack.expo.io`, this web app allows you to work on a React Native app in the browser, with a live preview of the code you're working on. If you've ever used CodePen or JSFiddle, Snack is the same concept applied to React Native applications.
- **Expo SDK**: This is the SDK that houses a wonderful collection of JavaScript APIs that provide Native functionality not found in the base React Native package, including working with the device's accelerometer, camera, notifications, geolocation, and many others. This SDK comes baked in with every new project created with Expo.

These tools together make up the Expo workflow. With the Expo CLI, you can create and build new applications with Expo SDK support baked in. The CLI also provides a simple way to serve your in-development app by automatically pushing your code to Amazon S3 and generating a URL for the project. From there, the CLI generates a QR code linked to the hosted code. Open the Expo Client app on your iPhone or Android device, scan the QR code, and BOOM there's your app, equipped with hot reload! And since the app is hosted on Amazon S3, you can even share the in-development app with other developers in real time.

React Native CLI

The original bootstrapping method for creating a new React Native app using the command is as follows:

```
react-native init
```

This is provided by the React Native CLI. You'll likely only be using this method of bootstrapping a new app if you're sure you'll need access to the native layer of the app.

In the React Native community, an app created with this method is said to be a pure React Native app, since all of the development and Native code files are exposed to the developer. While this provides the most freedom, it also forces the developer to maintain the native code. If you're a JavaScript developer that's jumped onto the React Native bandwagon because you intend on writing native applications solely with JavaScript, having to maintain the native code in a React Native project is probably the biggest disadvantage of this method.

On the other hand, you'll have access to more third-party plugins when working on an app that's been bootstrapped this process.

Get direct access to the native portion of the code base. You'll also be able to sidestep a few of the limitations in Expo currently, particularly the inability to use background audio or background GPS services.

CocoaPods

Once you begin working with apps that have components that use native code, you're going to be using CocoaPods in your development as well. CocoaPods is a dependency manager for Swift and Objective-C Cocoa projects. It works nearly the same as npm, but manages open source dependencies for native iOS code instead of JavaScript code.

We won't be using CocoaPods much in this book, but React Native makes use of CocoaPods for some of its iOS integration, so having a basic understanding of the manager can be helpful. Just as the `package.json` file houses all of the packages for a JavaScript project managed with npm, CocoaPods uses a `Podfile` for listing a project's iOS dependencies. Likewise, these dependencies can be installed using the command:

```
pod install
```

Ruby is required for CocoaPods to run. Run the command at the command line to verify Ruby is already installed:

```
ruby -v
```

If not, it can be installed with Homebrew with the command:

```
brew install ruby
```

Once Ruby has been installed, CocoaPods can be installed via the command:

```
sudo gem install cocoapods
```

If you encounter any issues while installing, you can read the official CocoaPods *Getting Started* guide at `https://guides.cocoapods.org/using/getting-started.html`.

Planning your app and choosing your workflow

When trying to choose which development workflow best fits your app's needs, here are a few things you should consider:

- Will I need access to the native portion of the code base?
- Will I need any third-party packages in my app that are not supported by Expo, that is require running the command react-native link?
- Will my app need to play audio while it is not in the foreground?
- Will my app need location services while it is not in the foreground?
- Am I comfortable working, at least nominally, in Xcode and Android Studio?

In my experience, Expo usually serves as the best starting place. It provides a lot of benefits to the development process, and gives you an escape hatch in the eject process if your app grows beyond the original requirements. I would recommend only starting development with the React Native CLI if you're sure your app needs something that cannot be provided by an Expo app, or if you're sure you will need to work on the native code.

I also recommend browsing the Native Directory hosted at `http://native.directory`. This site has a very large catalog of the third-party packages available for React Native development. Each package listed on the site has an estimated stability, popularity, and links to documentation. Arguably the best feature of the Native Directory, however, is the ability to filter packages by what kind of device/development they support, including iOS, Android, Expo, and web. This will help you narrow down your package choices and better indicate which workflow should be adopted for a given app.

How to do it...

We'll begin with the React Native CLI setup of our app, which will create a new pure React Native app, giving us access to all of the Native code, but also requiring that Xcode and Android Studio are installed.

 You may recall from `Chapter 1`, *Setting Up Your Environment*, that some of these steps have already been covered in detail. There is no need to reinstall anything listed here that was described there as well.

1. First, we'll install all the dependencies needed for working with a pure React Native app, starting with the Homebrew (`https://brew.sh/`) package manager for macOS. As stated on the project's home page, Homebrew can be easily installed from the Terminal via the following command:

   ```
   /usr/bin/ruby -e "$(curl -fsSL
   https://raw.githubusercontent.com/Homebrew/install/master/install)"
   ```

2. Once Homebrew is installed, it can be used to install the dependencies needed for React Native development: Node.js and `nodemon`. If you're a JavaScript developer, you've likely already got Node.js installed. You can check it's installed via the following command:

   `node -v`

   This command will list the version of Node.js that's installed, if any. Note that you will need Node.js version 8 or higher for React Native development. If Node.js is not already installed, you can install it with Hombrew via the following command:

   `brew install node`

3. We also need the `nodemon` package, which React Native uses behind the scenes to enable things like live reload during development. Install `nodemon` with Homebrew via the following command:

   `brew install watchman`

4. We'll also of course need the React Native CLI for running the commands that bootstrap the React Native app. This can be installed globally with `npm` via the following command:

   `npm install -g react-native-cli`

5. With the CLI installed, all it takes to create a new pure React Native app is the following:

```
react-native init name-of-project
```

This will create a new project in a new `name-of-project` directory. This project has all Native code exposed, and requires Xcode for running the iOS app and Android Studio for running the Android app. Luckily, installing Xcode for supporting iOS React Native development is a simple process. The first step is to download Xcode from the App Store and install it. The second step is to install the Xcode command-line tools. To do this, open Xcode, choose **Preferences...** from the Xcode menu, open the **Locations** panel, and install the most recent version from the **Command Line Tools** dropdown:

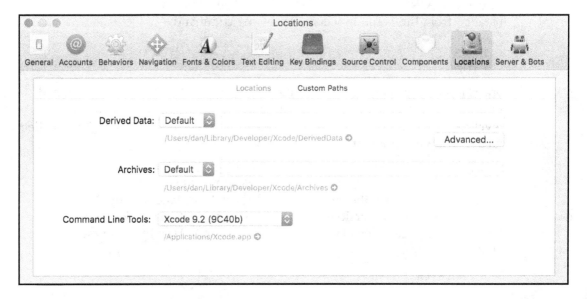

6. Unfortunately, setting up Android Studio for supporting Android React Native development is not as cut and dry, and requires some very specific steps for installing it. Since this process is particularly involved, and since there is some likelihood that the process will have changed by the time you read this chapter, I recommend referring to the official documentation for in-depth, up-to-date instructions on installing all Android development dependencies. These instructions are hosted at the following URL:

```
https://facebook.github.io/react-native/docs/getting-started.html#java
-development-kit
```

7. Now that all dependencies have been installed, we're able to run our pure React Native project via the command line. The iOS app can be executed via the following:

```
react-native run-ios
```

And the Andriod app can be started with this:

```
react-native run-android
```

Be sure you are already running the Android emulator before trying to open your Android app. These commands should start up your app on the associated emulator for the correct platform, install the new app, and run the app within the emulator. If you have any trouble with either of these commands not behaving as expected, you might be able to find an answer in the React Native troubleshooting docs, hosted here:

```
https://facebook.github.io/react-native/docs/troubleshooting.
html#content
```

Expo CLI setup

The Expo CLI can be installed using the Terminal with npm via the following command:

```
npm install -g expo-cli
```

The Expo CLI can be used to do all the great things the Expo GUI client can do. For all the commands that can be run with the CLI, check out the docs here:

```
https://docs.expo.io/versions/latest/workflow/expo-cli
```

Using NativeBase for cross-platform UI components

Similar to Bootstrap on the web, NativeBase is a collection of React Native components for improving the efficiency of React Native app development. The components cover a wide range of use cases for building out UI in Native applications, including ActionSheets, Badges, Cards, Drawers, and grid layouts.

NativeBase is a library that supports both pure React Native applications (those created with the React Native CLI via `react-native init`) and Expo powered applications. Instructions for installing NativeBase into one type of project or another is outlined in the *Getting Started* section of the NativeBase documentation, hosted here:

```
https://github.com/GeekyAnts/NativeBase#4-getting-started
```

Since this is the case, we'll take this opportunity to outline both scenarios in the *Getting ready* section of this recipe.

Getting ready

Whichever method of bootstrapping you use for this recipe, we'll be keeping the *How to do it...* section of the recipe as consistent as possible. One difference that we'll need to take into account is the project naming convention of each app creation method. Pure React Native applications are named in Pascal case (MyCoolApp) and Expo applications are named in kebab case (my-cool-app). If you're creating a pure React Native app, you can use the app name `NativeBase`, and if you're using Expo you can name it `native-base`.

Using a pure React Native app (React Native CLI)

Assuming you've followed the introduction to this chapter, you should already have the React Native CLI installed globally. If not, go ahead and do so now with `npm`:

```
npm install -g react-native-cli
```

To create a new pure React app with the CLI, we'll use the following command:

```
react-native init NativeBase
```

This creates a new pure React Native app in a folder called `NativeBase` in the current directory. The next step is to install the required peer dependencies. Let's `cd` into the new `NativeBase` directory and install the `native-base` package using `npm`:

```
npm install native-base --save
```

Alternatively, you can use `yarn`:

```
yarn add native-base
```

Finally, we will install the Native dependencies with the following command:

```
react-native link
```

If we open up the project in an IDE and look at the folder structure of this pure React Native app, we'll see a few slight differences from the Expo applications we've become accustomed to at this point. First, the repository has an `ios` and an `android` folder, each containing Native code for the respective platform. There's also an `index.js` file at the root of the project that is not included in an app bootstrapped with Expo. In an app made with Expo, this file would be obscured away, just like the `ios` and `android` folders, as follows:

```
import { AppRegistry } from 'react-native';
import App from './App';

AppRegistry.registerComponent('NativeBase', () => App);
```

This simply serves as the bootstrapping process of your React Native app at runtime. `AppRegistry` is imported from the `react-native` packages, the main `App` component is imported from the `App.js` file at the root of the directory, and the `AppRegistry` method `registerComponent` is called with two parameters: the name of our app (`NativeBase`), and an anonymous function that returns the `App` component. For more information on `AppRegistry`, you can find the documentation here:

`https://facebook.github.io/react-native/docs/appregistry.html`

One other minor difference is the existence of two sets of development instructions in the `App.js` boilerplate code, displaying the appropriate dev instructions through the use of the `Platform` component.

Remember to stop and think whenever you see a third-party React Native package whose installation instructions include running the following command:

```
react-native link
```

It is usually safe to assume it is not compatible with an Expo app unless explicitly stated otherwise. In the case of NativeBase, we have an option to use either setup, so let's cover getting started with our other option next, bootstrapping with Expo.

Using an Expo app

Setting up Native Base in an app created with Expo is as simple as installing the required dependencies with `npm` or `yarn`. First, we can create the app using the Expo CLI on the command line:

```
expo init native-base
```

Once the app is created, we can `cd` into it and install the dependencies for NativeBase with `npm`:

```
npm install native-base @expo/vector-icons --save
```

Alternatively, you can use `yarn`:

```
yarn add native-base @expo/vector-icons
```

When using NativeBase with Expo, the NativeBase documentation recommends loading fonts asynchronously with the `Expo.Font.loadAsync` method in the `componentWillMount` method in the `App.js` component. We'll cover how to do this in the appropriate step in the *How to do it...* section of this recipe. You can start up the app from the CLI with the following command:

```
expo start
```

How to do it...

1. We'll start by adding the imports we'll be using in the `App` component in `App.js`. While this app won't have much functionality, we will be using a number of components from NativeBase to see how they can help improve your workflow, as follows:

```
import React, { Component } from 'react';
import { View, Text, StyleSheet } from 'react-native'
import {
  Spinner,
  Button,
  Body,
  Title,
  Container,
  Header,
  Fab,
  Icon,
} from 'native-base';
```

2. Next, let's declare the `App` class and define a starting `state` object. We'll be adding a FAB section to show how NativeBase lets you easily add fly-out menu buttons to your app. We will track whether this menu should be displayed or not with the `fabActive` Boolean. We'll also use the `loading` Boolean later in the `render` method, as follows:

```
export default class App extends Component {
  state = {
    loading: true
    fabActive: false
  }
  // Defined on following steps
}
```

3. You may recall from the *Getting ready* section of the recipe, if you're developing an app with Expo, NativeBase suggests loading the fonts used by NativeBase via the `Expo.Font.loadAsync` function. In the `componentWillMount` method, we'll initialize and await the loading of `require` fonts, then set the `loading` property on `state` to `false`. The `loading` property will be referenced in the `render` method to determine whether the app has finished loading, as follows:

```
// Other import statements
import { Font, AppLoaded } from 'expo';

export default class App extends Component {
  state = {
    fabActive: false
  }

  async componentWillMount() {
    await Font.loadAsync({
      'Roboto': require('native-base/Fonts/Roboto.ttf'),
      'Roboto_medium': require('native-base/Fonts/Roboto_medium.ttf'),
      'Ionicons': require('@expo/vector-icons/fonts/Ionicons.ttf'),
    });
    this.setState({ loading: false });
  }
  // Defined on following steps
}
```

4. Since this app is mostly UI, we're ready to start building the `render` function. To make sure fonts are loaded before we use them, we return the App placeholder Expo component, `AppLoading`, if the `loading` property of `state` is true, otherwise we'll render the App UI. `AppLoading` will instruct the app to continue displaying the app's splash screen until the component is removed.

> If you chose to start this recipe with a pure React Native project, you won't have access to Expo components. You can simply return an empty `View` instead of `AppLoading` in this case.

5. We'll start with the `Container` component, along with the `Header`, `Body`, and `Title` helper components. This will act as the container for the page, displaying a header at the top of the page with the title **Header Title!**

```
render() {
  if (this.state.loading) {
    return <AppLoading />;
  } else {
    return (
      <Container>
        <Header>
          <Body>
            <Title>Header Title!</Title>
          </Body>
        </Header>
      </Container>
    );
  }
}
```

At this point, the app should look similar to the following screenshot:

6. In the following code, the `Header` will have a few more UI elements from NativeBase. The `Spinner` component allows for easily displaying a loading spinner with the desired color passed in as a prop. The `Button` component provides buttons with more built-in customizability when compared with the vanilla `TouchableOpacity` component. Here, we're using the `block` prop to spread the buttons across their container, and an `info` and `success` prop on each to apply their respective default blue and green background colors:

```
<Container>
  <Header>
    <Body>
      <Title>Header Title!</Title>
    </Body>
  </Header>
  <View style={styles.view}>
    <Spinner color='green' style={styles.spinner} />
    <Button block info
      onPress={() => { console.log('button 1 pressed') }}
    >
      <Text style={styles.buttonText}>Click Me! </Text>
    </Button>
    <Button block success
      onPress={() => { console.log('button 2 pressed') }}
    >
      <Text style={styles.buttonText}>No Click Me!</Text>
    </Button>
    {this.renderFab()}
  </View>
</Container>
```

7. The preceding render function also refers to a `renderFab` method we have not yet defined. This makes use of the `Icon` and `Fab` components. NativeBase uses the same `vector-icons` package as Expo under the hood (defaulting to Ionicon fonts if no `type` prop is provided), which was covered in the *Using Font icons* recipe in Chapter 3, *Implementing Complex User Interfaces – Part I*, so please refer to that recipe for more information:

```
renderFab = () => {
  return (
    <Fab active={this.state.fabActive}
      direction="up"
      style={styles.fab}
      position="bottomRight"
      onPress={() => this.setState({ fabActive:
      !this.state.fabActive })}>
      <Icon name="share" />
```

```
          <Button style={styles.facebookButton}
            onPress={() => { console.log('facebook button pressed')
    }}
          >
            <Icon name="logo-facebook" />
          </Button>
          <Button style={styles.twitterButton}
            onPress={() => { console.log('twitter button pressed')}}
          >
            <Icon name="logo-twitter" />
          </Button>
        </Fab>
      );
    }
```

8. Let's round this recipe out with a few styles to align things within the `View` and apply colors to our layout, as follows:

```
const styles = StyleSheet.create({
  view: {
    flex: 1,
    backgroundColor: '#fff',
    alignItems: 'center',
    justifyContent: 'center',
    paddingBottom: 40
  },
  buttonText: {
    color: '#fff'
  },
  fab: {
    backgroundColor: '#007AFF'
  },
  twitterButton: {
    backgroundColor: '#1DA1F2'
  },
  facebookButton: {
    backgroundColor: '#3B5998'
  },
  spinner: {
    marginBottom: 180
  }
});
```

9. Looking back at the completed app, there's now a nice spread of UI that is cross-platform and easy to use:

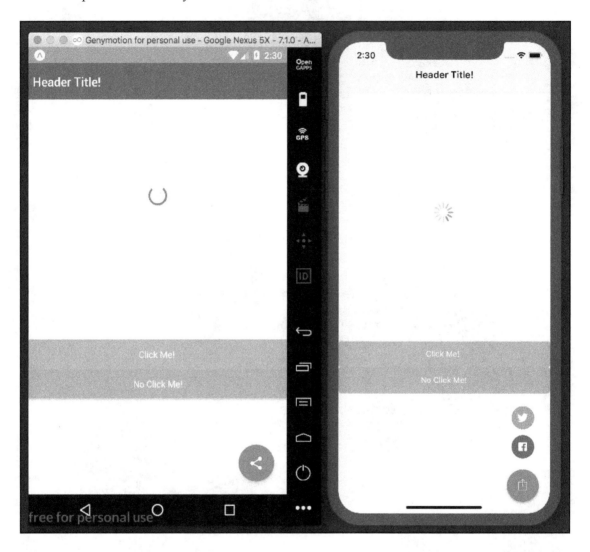

How it works...

While the more complicated portion of this recipe was the set-up of the app itself, we had a quick review of a few of the components provided by NativeBase that might be able to help you develop your next app more efficiently. If you prefer to work in a widget-based system similar to what Bootstrap (`https://getbootstrap.com/`) or Semantic-UI (`https://semantic-ui.com/`) provide on the web platform, be sure to give NativeBase a spin. For more information on all of the components that NativeBase offers and how to use them, you can find the official documentation at `http://docs.nativebase.io/Components.html`.

Using glamorous-native for styling UI components

As a JavaScript developer, you're likely familiar with CSS on the web and how it's used to style web pages and web applications. More recently, a technique called CSS-in-JS has came along in web development, which uses the power of JavaScript to adapt CSS for a more modular, component-based styling approach. One of the main benefits of CSS-in-JS tools is their ability to produce styles that are scoped to a given element, instead of the default cascading behavior of vanilla JavaScript. Scoped CSS allows a developer to apply styles in a more predictable and modular way. This in turn increases usability in larger organizations and makes packaging and publishing styled components easier. If you'd like to learn more about how CSS-in-JS works or where CSS-in-JS comes from conceptually, I've written an article on the topic on the gitconnected Medium blog called *A Brief History of CSS-in-JS: How We Got Here and Where We're Going*, hosted at:

`https://levelup.gitconnected.com/a-brief-history-of-css-in-js-how-we-got-here-and-where-were-going-ea6261c19f04`.

The `StyleSheet` component that comes packaged with React Native is an implementation of CSS-in-JS. One of the most popular implementations of CSS-in-JS on the web is `glamorous`, a library created by the venerable Kent C. Dodds. This library inspired the excellent React Native styling library `glamorous-native`, which we will be using in this recipe.

Getting ready

We'll need to create a new app for this recipe. This package does not require running the following command during setup:

```
react-native link
```

So, should work just fine with an Expo app. Let's name the recipe `glamorous-app`.

We will also need to install the glamorous-app package. This can be installed with `npm`:

```
npm install --save glamorous-native
```

Or, we can use `yarn`:

```
yarn add glamorous-native
```

How to do it...

1. Let's start by importing all the dependencies we'll need in `App.js`, as follows:

   ```
   import React from 'react';
   import glamorous from 'glamorous-native';
   ```

2. Our app will need a containing `View` element to hold all of the other components displayed in the app. Instead of styling this element with an object passed to the `StyleSheet` component, like we've been doing in all previous recipes, we'll use `glamorous` by passing a style object to the `view` method, which returns a styled `View` component that we store in a `const` called `Container` for later use, as follows:

   ```
   const Container = glamorous.view({
     flex: 1,
     justifyContent: 'center',
     alignItems: 'center',
     backgroundColor: '#fff',
   });
   ```

3. Similarly, we'll add three styled `Text` components using `glamorous.text`. By doing this, we have three more styled and explicitly named components ready to be used in `render`, as follows:

```
const Headline = glamorous.text({
  fontSize: 30,
  paddingBottom: 8
});

const SubHeading = glamorous.text({
  fontSize: 26,
  paddingBottom: 8
});

const ButtonText = glamorous.text({
  fontSize: 18,
  color: 'white'
});
```

4. We'll also make a reusable `Button` component with the `glamorous.touchableHighlight` method. This method shows how `glamorous` components can also be created with multiple style declarations of different types. The second parameter passed to `touchableHighlight` in this case is a function that updates the `backgroundColor` style depending on the `props` defined on the element, as follows:

```
const Button = glamorous.touchableHighlight(
  { padding: 10 },
  props => ({backgroundColor: props.warning ? 'red' : 'blue'})
);
```

5. We can also create components styled inline, thanks to the special versions of React Native components `glamorous` ships with. We will use an `Image` component, but instead of importing it from `react-native`, we use the `Image` component from the imported `glamorous` package, as follows:

```
const { Image } = glamorous;
```

6. Now, we are ready to declare the `App` component. `App` will only need a `render` function for rendering all our newly styled components, as follows:

```
export default class App extends React.Component {
  render() {
    // Defined in following steps.
  }
}
```

7. Let's begin building out the render function by adding the `Container` component we created in *step 2*. The improvement in code readability is already apparent. The `Container` is explicitly named and needs no other attributes or properties to declare styles, as follows:

```
render() {
  return (
    <Container>
      // Defined on following steps
    </Container>
  );
}
```

8. Let's add the `Image` component that we pulled from the imported `glamorous` library in *step 5*. Notice how we are able to declare style properties such as `height`, `width`, and `borderRadius` as props directly on the component, unlike the vanilla `Image` component:

```
<Container>
  <Image
    height={250}
    width={250}
    borderRadius={20}
    source={{ uri: 'http://placehold.it/250/3B5998' }}
  />
  // Defined on following steps
</Container>
```

9. Now, we'll add the `Headline` and `Subheading` components we created in *step 3*. Just like the `Container` component, these two components read much more clearly than one `View` and two `Text` elements ever could:

```
<Container>
  <Image
    height={250}
    width={250}
    borderRadius={20}
    source={{ uri: 'http://placehold.it/250/3B5998' }}
  />
  <Headline>I am a headline</Headline>
  <SubHeading>I am a subheading</SubHeading>
  // Defined in following steps
<Container>
```

10. Finally, we'll add the `Button` component we created in *step 4*, and the `ButtonText` component we created in *step 3*. Both buttons have an `onPress` method like any `TouchableOpacity` or `TouchableHighlight` component would, but the second `Button` also has a `warning` prop, causing it to have a red background instead of blue:

```
<Button
  onPress={() => console.log('Thanks for clicking me!')}
>
  <ButtonText>
    Click Me!
  </ButtonText>
</Button>
<Button
  warning
  onPress={() => console.log(`You shouldn't have clicked me!`)}
>
  <ButtonText>
    Don't Click Me!
  </ButtonText>
</Button>
```

11. All of our `glamorous` components have been added to the `render` method. If you run the app, you should be greeted by a fully styled UI.

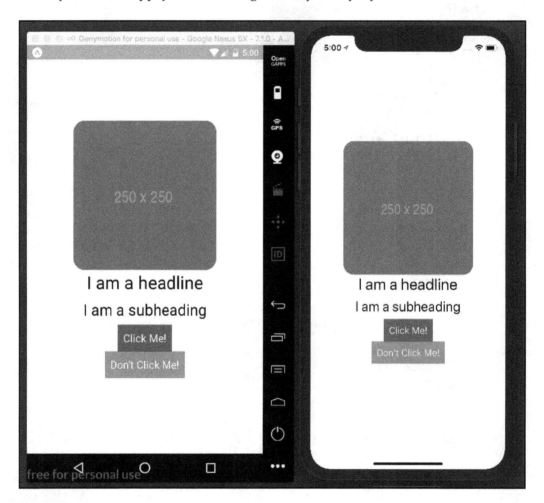

How it works...

In *step 2* and *step 3*, we created styled `View` and `Text` components by using the corresponding `glamorous` method and passing in an object containing all the styles that should be applied to that particular component.

In *step 4*, we created a reusable Button styled component by applying the same method used for creating the View and Text components in previous steps. The way styles are declared in this component is different, however, and shows off the versatility glamorous-native has when processing styles. You can pass any number of style collections as parameters to a glamorous component constructor and they will all be applied. This includes dynamic styles, which usually take the form of using props defined on the component to apply different styles. In *step 10*, we used our Button element. If the prop warning is present, as it is on the first Button in render, the backgroundColor will be red. Otherwise, it will be blue. This provides a very nice system for applying simple and reusable theming across multiple types of components.

In *step 5*, we pulled the Image component from the glamorous library to use in place of the React Native Image component. This special version of the component behaves the same as its React Native counterpart, along with the benefit of being able to apply styles directly to the element itself. In *step 8*, where we used that component, we were able to apply height, width, and borderRadius styles without ever having to use the style prop.

Using react-native-spinkit for adding animated loading indicators

No matter what kind of app you are building, there's a very good chance your app will need to wait on data of one kind or another, whether it be loading assets or waiting on a response from an AJAX request. When this situation arises, you'll probably also want a way for your app to indicate to the user that some required piece of data is still loading. One easy-to-use solution to this problem is using react-native-spinkit. This package provides 15 (four of which are iOS-only) professional looking, easy-to-use loading indicators for displaying while data is loading in your app.

This package requires the following command to be run:

```
react-native link
```

So, it is probably safe to assume that it will not work with an Expo app (unless that app is subsequently ejected). This will provide us with another recipe that depends on a pure React Native workflow.

Getting started

Now that we've established that this recipe will be built in pure React Native, we can begin by initializing a new app from the command line named SpinKitApp as follows:

```
react-native init SpinKitApp
```

This command will begin the scaffolding process. Once it has completed, cd into the new SpinKitApp directory and add react-native spinkit with npm:

```
npm install react-native-spinkit@latest --save
```

Or use yarn:

```
yarn add react-native-spinkit@latest
```

With the library installed, we must link it before it can be used with the command:

```
react-native link
```

At this point, the app is bootstrapped and the dependencies have been installed. The app can then be run in the iOS or Android simulators via this:

```
react-native run-ios
```

Or, use this:

```
react-native run-android
```

 When launching a pure React Native project in the iOS simulator, if you wish to specify a device, you can pass the simulator argument set to a string value for the desired device. For example, react-native run-ios --simulator="iPhone X" will launch the app in a simulated iPhone X.

When launching a pure React Native project in an Android emulator via the command line, you must open the Android emulator you intend to use before running this command.

We'll also be making use of the randomcolor library again in this recipe. Install it with npm:

```
npm install randomcolor --save
```

Or use `yarn`:

```
yarn add randomcolor
```

How to do it...

1. We'll start by adding the dependencies to the `App.js` file in the root of the project, as follows:

```
import React, { Component } from 'react';
import {
  StyleSheet,
  View,
  TouchableOpacity,
  Text
} from 'react-native';
import Spinner from 'react-native-spinkit';
import randomColor from 'randomcolor';
```

2. We're going to be setting up the app in this recipe to cycle through all of the loading spinner types provided by `react-native-spinkit`. To do this, let's create an array with strings for each possible type of spinner. Since the last four types are not fully supported in Android, they will all appear as the same `Plane` spinner on Android, as follows:

```
const types = [
  'Bounce',
  'Wave',
  'WanderingCubes',
  'Pulse',
  'ChasingDots',
  'ThreeBounce',
  'Circle',
  '9CubeGrid',
  'FadingCircleAlt',
  'FadingCircle',
  'CircleFlip',
  'WordPress',
  'Arc',
  'ArcAlt'
];
```

3. Now, we can begin building the `App` component. We will need a `state` object with four properties: an `isVisible` property to track whether the spinner should be displayed, a `type` property for holding the current spinner type, a `typeIndex` for keeping our place in the `types` array, and a color. We'll initialize color to a random hex code by simply calling `randomColor()`, as follows:

```
export default class App extends Component {
  state = {
    isVisible: true,
    typeIndex: 0,
    type: types[0],
    color: randomColor()
  }
}
```

4. We'll need a function for changing the properties of the `Spinner` component, which we will define later in the `render` method. This function simply increases the `typeIndex` by one, or sets it back to `0` if the end of the array has been reached, then updates `state` accordingly, as follows:

```
changeSpinner = () => {
  const { typeIndex } = this.state;
  let nextType = typeIndex === types.length - 1 ? 0 : typeIndex +
  1;
  this.setState({
    color: randomColor(),
    typeIndex: nextType,
    type: types[nextType]
  });
}
```

5. The `render` method will be made up of the `Spinner` component, wrapped in a `TouchableOpacity` component for changing the type and color of `Spinner`. We will also add a `Text` component for displaying the current `Spinner` type, as follows:

```
render() {
  return (
    <View style={styles.container}>
      <TouchableOpacity onPress={this.changeSpinner}>
        <Spinner
          isVisible={this.state.isVisible}
          size={120}
          type={this.state.type}
          color={this.state.color}
        />
      </TouchableOpacity>
      <Text style={styles.text}>{this.state.type}</Text>
    </View>
  );
}
```

6. Finally, let's add a few styles to the center content and increase the font size of the `Text` element via the `text` class, as follows:

```
const styles = StyleSheet.create({
  container: {
    flex: 1,
    justifyContent: 'center',
    alignItems: 'center',
    backgroundColor: '#fff',
  },
  text: {
    paddingTop: 40,
    fontSize: 25
  }
});
```

7. With the recipe complete, we should see a loader that changes on press. Thanks to `react-native-spinkit`, this is all it takes to add slick loading indicators to our React Native applications!

How it works...

In *step 5*, we defined the app's `render` method, where we made use of the `Spinner` component. The `Spinner` component has four optional props:

- `isVisible`: A Boolean that determines whether the component should be displayed. Default: `true`
- `color`: A hex code to determine the spinner's color. Default: `#000000`
- `size`: Determines what size the spinner should be, in pixels. Default: `37`
- `type`: A string that determines the type of spinner to use. Default: `Plane`

Since the `isVisible` prop on the `Spinner` component is set to the value of `isVisible` on the `state` object, we can simply toggle this property to `true` whenever a long running process begins (such as waiting on the response from an AJAX request), and set it back to `false` when the operation completes.

There's more...

Even though the app we've created in this recipe is fairly simple, it has illustrated both how `react-native-spinkit` can be implemented, and how using third-party packages that require the `react-native link` command works in practice. There are all kinds of third-party packages available to use in your next React Native app, thanks to the hard work of countless open source contributors. Being equipped to utilize any third-party package that suits your app's needs, no matter what requirements those package have, will be a vital tool in planning and developing React Native projects.

Using react-native-side-menu for adding side navigation menus

Side menus are a common UX pattern for displaying options, controls, app settings, navigation, and other secondary information in mobile applications. The `react-native-side-menu` third-party package provides an excellent, straightforward way to implement side menus in a React Native app. In this recipe, we will be building an app that has a side menu housing buttons that change the background.

Getting ready

Setting up the `react-native-side-menu` package does not require the command:

```
react-native link
```

So feel free to create this app with Expo or as a pure React Native app. We need to create a new app for this recipe, and for project naming purposes we'll assume this app is being built with Expo and name it `side-menu-app`. If you're using pure React Native, you can name it `SideMenuApp`.

We will also need to install `react-native-side-menu` into our project with `npm`:

```
npm install react-native-side-menu --save
```

Or, use `yarn`:

```
yarn add react-native-side-menu
```

How to do it...

1. Let's start this recipe by adding all the imports we'll need in the `App.js` file in the root of the project. One of these imports is a `Menu` component, which we'll create in a later step:

```
import React from 'react';
import { StyleSheet, Text, View, TouchableOpacity } from 'react-native';
import SideMenu from 'react-native-side-menu';
import Menu from './components/Menu';
```

2. Next, let's define the `App` class and the initial `state`. `state` only needs two properties in this app: an `isOpen` Boolean to keep track of when the side menu should be open, and a `selectedBackgroundColor` property whose value is a string representing the currently selected background color, as follows:

```
export default class App extends React.Component {
  state = {
    isOpen: false,
    selectedBackgroundColor: 'green'
  }
  // Defined in following steps
}
```

3. Our app will need a method for changing the `selectedBackgroundColor` property on `state`. This method takes a `color` string as a parameter, and sets that color to `selectedBackgroundColor`. It will also set `state.isOpen` to `false` so that the side menu closes when a color is selected from the menu, as follows:

```
changeBackgroundColor = color => {
  this.setState({
    isOpen: false,
    selectedBackgroundColor: color,
  });
}
```

4. We're ready to define the `render` method `App`. First, let's set up the `Menu` component so it can be used by `SideMenu` in the next step. We still haven't created the `Menu` component, but we'll be using an `onColorSelected` property to pass along the `changeBackgroundColor` method, as follows:

```
render() {
  const menu = <Menu onColorSelected={this.changeBackgroundColor}
/>;

  // Defined in next step
}
```

5. The rendered UI consists of four pieces. The first is a `View` component, which has a `style` property tied to `state.selectedBackgroundColor`. This `View` component holds a single `TouchableOpacity` button component, which opens the side menu whenever it's pressed. The `SideMenu` component has a required `menu` prop, which takes the component that will act as the side menu itself, and so we'll pass the `Menu` component to this property, as follows:

```
render() {
  const menu = <Menu onColorSelected={this.changeBackgroundColor}
/>;

  return (
    <SideMenu
      menu={menu}
      isOpen={this.state.isOpen}
      onChange={(isOpen) => this.setState({ isOpen })}
    >
      <View style={[
        styles.container,
        { backgroundColor: this.state.selectedBackgroundColor }
```

```
            ]}>
              <TouchableOpacity
                style={styles.button}
                onPress={() => this.setState({ isOpen: true })}
              >
                <Text style={styles.buttonText}>Open Menu</Text>
              </TouchableOpacity>
            </View>
          </SideMenu>
        );
    }
```

6. As the final touch for this component, let's add basic styles to center the layout, and apply colors and font sizes, as follows:

```
const styles = StyleSheet.create({
  container: {
    flex: 1,
    alignItems: 'center',
    justifyContent: 'center',
  },
  button: {
    backgroundColor: 'black',
    padding: 20,
    borderRadius: 10
  },
  buttonText: {
    color: 'white',
    fontSize: 25
  }
});
```

7. It's time to create the `Menu` component. Let's create a `component` folder with a `Menu.js` file inside. We'll start with the component imports. As we've done in previous recipes, we'll also use `Dimensions` to store the dimensions of the app window in a variable for applying styles, as follows:

```
import React from 'react';
import {
  Dimensions,
  StyleSheet,
  View,
  Text,
  TouchableOpacity
} from 'react-native';

const window = Dimensions.get('window');
```

8. The `Menu` component needs only to be a presentational component, since it has no state or need for life cycle hooks. The component will receive `onColorSelected` as a property, which we'll make use of in the next step, as follows:

```
const Menu = ({ onColorSelected }) => {
  return (
    // Defined on next step
  );
}

export default Menu;
```

9. The body of the `Menu` component is simply a list of `TouchableOpacity` buttons that, when pressed, call `onColorSelected`, passing in the corresponding color, as follows:

```
<View style={styles.menu}>
  <Text style={styles.heading}>Select a Color</Text>
  <TouchableOpacity onPress={() => onColorSelected('green')}>
    <Text style={styles.item}>
      Green
    </Text>
  </TouchableOpacity>
  <TouchableOpacity onPress={() => onColorSelected('blue')}>
    <Text style={styles.item}>
      Blue
    </Text>
  </TouchableOpacity>
  <TouchableOpacity onPress={() => onColorSelected('orange')}>
    <Text style={styles.item}>
      Orange
    </Text>
  </TouchableOpacity>
  <TouchableOpacity onPress={() => onColorSelected('pink')}>
    <Text style={styles.item}>
      Pink
    </Text>
  </TouchableOpacity>
  <TouchableOpacity onPress={() => onColorSelected('cyan')}>
    <Text style={styles.item}>
      Cyan
    </Text>
  </TouchableOpacity>
  <TouchableOpacity onPress={() => onColorSelected('yellow')}>
    <Text style={styles.item}>
      Yellow
```

```
        </Text>
      </TouchableOpacity>
      <TouchableOpacity onPress={() => onColorSelected('purple')}>
        <Text style={styles.item}>
          Purple
        </Text>
      </TouchableOpacity>
    </View>
```

10. Let's add a few styles to layout the Menu component, apply colors, and apply font sizes. Note that we're also using the window variable we defined in *step 7* to set the height and width of the component equal to that of the screen, as follows:

```
const styles = StyleSheet.create({
  menu: {
    flex: 1,
    width: window.width,
    height: window.height,
    backgroundColor: '#3C3C3C',
    justifyContent: 'center',
    padding: 20,
  },
  heading: {
    fontSize: 22,
    color: '#f6f6f6',
    fontWeight: 'bold',
    paddingBottom: 20
  },
  item: {
    fontSize: 25,
    paddingTop: 10,
    color: '#f6f6f6'
  }
});
```

11. Our app is complete! When the **Open Menu** button is pressed, a smoothly animated side menu will slide out from the left, displaying a list of colors for the user to choose from. When a color is selected from the list, the background color of the app changes and the menu slides back to closed:

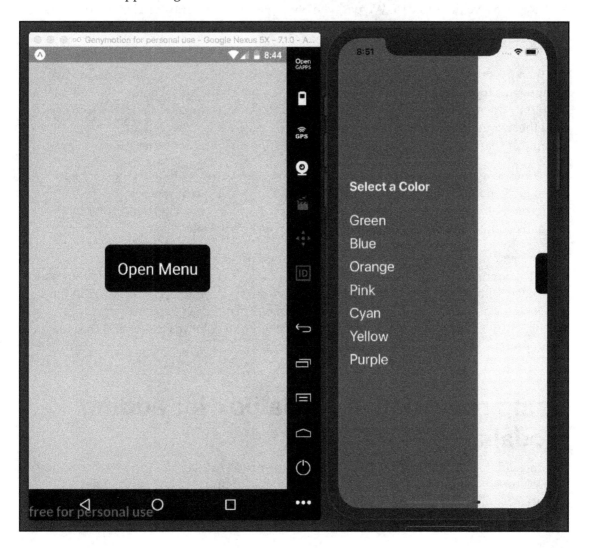

How it works...

In *step 4*, we created the `render` function for the main `App` component. We stored the `Menu` component in a `menu` variable so that it can be legibly passed to the `menu` property of `SideMenu`, as we did in *step 5*. We pass the `changeBackgroundColor` class method via the `onColorSelected` prop on our `Menu` component so that we can use it to properly update `state` in the `App` component.

We then pass the `Menu` component to `SideMenu` as the `menu` prop, which wires the two components together. The second props is `isOpen`, which dictates whether the side menu should be open. The third prop, `onChange`, takes a callback function that's executed every time the menu is opened or closed. The `onChange` callback is provided an `isOpen` parameter that we used to update the value of `isOpen` on `state` so that it stays in sync.

The containing `View` element has a `style` prop set to an array with both the `container` styles defined in *step 6* and an object with the `backgroundColor` key set to `selectedBackgroundColor` on `state`. This will cause the background color of the `View` component to change to this value whenever it updates.

In *step 8* and *step 9*, we built out the `render` method of the `Menu` component. Each `TouchableOpacity` button is wired to call `onColorSelected`, passing in the color associated with the pressed button. This in turn runs `changeBackgroundColor` in the parent `App` class, which updates `state.selectedBackgroundColor` on setting `state.isOpen` to `false`, causing the background color to change and the side menu to close.

Using react-native-modalbox for adding modals

Another common piece of many mobile UIs is the modal. Modals are the perfect solution for isolating data in a meaningful way, alerting a user of updated info, displaying a required action that blocks other user interactions (like a login screen), and so much more.

We will be making use of the third-party package `react-native-modalbox`. This package provides an easy-to-understand and versatile API for creating modals, with options including the following:

- `position`: Top, bottom, center
- `entry`: Direction modal enters from—top or bottom?
- `backdropColor`
- `backdropOpacity`

For all of the available options, refer to the documentation at:

`https://github.com/maxs15/react-native-modalbox`

Getting ready

We will need a new app for this recipe. The `react-native-modalbox` package is Expo friendly, so we can create this app with Expo. We'll name this app `modal-app`. If using a pure React Native project, a name such as `ModalApp` will work, to match naming conventions.

We will also need the third-party package. It can be installed with `npm`:

```
npm install react-native-modalbox --save
```

Or, use `yarn`:

```
yarn add react-native-modalbox
```

How to do it...

1. Let's start by opening the `App.js` file in the root of the project and add the imports, as follows:

```
import React from 'react';
import Modal from 'react-native-modalbox';
import {
  Text,
  StyleSheet,
  View,
  TouchableOpacity
} from 'react-native';
```

2. Next, we will define and export the `App` component, as well as the initial `state` object, as follows. For this app, we'll only need an `isOpen` Boolean for keeping track of whether one of our modals should be opened or closed:

```
export default class App extends Component {
  state = {
    isOpen: false
  };
  // Defined on following steps
}
```

3. Let's skip ahead to building out the `render` method next. The template is made up of two `TouchableOpacity` button components that when pressed, open their respective modal. We'll be defining those two modals in the following steps. These buttons will call two methods for rendering each `Modal` of the two modal components, as follows:

```
render = () => {
  return (
    <View style={styles.container}>
      <TouchableOpacity
        onPress={this.openModal1}
        style={styles.button}
      >
        <Text style={styles.buttonText}>
          Open Modal 1
        </Text>
      </TouchableOpacity>
      <TouchableOpacity
        onPress={this.openModal2}
        style={styles.button}
      >
        <Text style={styles.buttonText}>
          Open Modal 2
        </Text>
      </TouchableOpacity>
      {this.renderModal1()}
      {this.renderModal2()}
    </View>
  );
}
```

4. Now, we're ready to define the `renderModal1` method. The `Modal` component needs a `ref` prop to be assigned a string, which will be used to refer to the `Modal` when we want to open or close it, as follows:

```
renderModal1 = () => {
  return(
    <Modal
      style={[styles.modal, styles.modal1]}
      ref={'modal1'}
      onClosed={this.onClose}
      onOpened={this.onOpen}
    >
      <Text style={styles.modalText}>
        Hello from Modal 1
      </Text>
    </Modal>
  )
}
```

5. Let's add the `openModal1` method next. This is the method that is called by `onPress` on the first `TouchableOpacity` component we added in the `render` method in *step 3*. By passing the `modal1` string to the `ref` prop on the `Modal` component we defined in *step 4*, we're able to access the modal as `this.refs.modal1`. Calling the `open` method on this ref opens the modal. More on this in the *How it works...* section at the end of this recipe. Add the `openModal1` method as follows:

```
openModal1 = () => {
  this.refs.modal1.open();
}
```

6. The `Modal` we defined in *step 4* also has `onClosed` and `onOpened` props, which each take a callback that's executed when the modal is closed or opened, respectively. Let's define the callbacks for these props next. In this recipe, we'll just be firing a `console.log` as a proof of concept, as follows:

```
onClose = () => {
  console.log('modal is closed');
}

onOpen = () => {
  console.log('modal is open');
}
```

7. We're ready to define the second modal. This `Modal` component's `ref` prop will be set to the string `modal2`, and we'll add two other optional props we didn't use on the other modal. The first is `position`, which can be set to `top`, `bottom`, or `center` (default). The `isOpen` prop provides a secondary way of opening and closing a modal via a Boolean. The content of the modal has a `TouchableOpacity` with an **OK** button that, when pressed, will set the `isOpen` Boolean on the `state` object to `false`, closing the modal, as follows:

```
renderModal2 = () => {
    return(
      <Modal
        style={[styles.modal, styles.modal2]}
        ref={'modal2'}
        position={'bottom'}
        onClosed={this.onCloseModal2}
        isOpen={this.state.isOpen}
      >
        <Text style={styles.modalText}>
          Hello from Modal 2
        </Text>
        <TouchableOpacity
          onPress={() => this.setState({isOpen: false})}
          style={styles.button}
        >
          <Text style={styles.buttonText}>
            OK
          </Text>
        </TouchableOpacity>
      </Modal>
    )
}
```

8. Since we're using the `state` Boolean `isOpen` to manipulate the state of the modal, the `openModal2` method will illustrate an alternative method for opening and closing the modal. By setting `isOpen` on `state` to `true`, the second modal will open, as follows:

```
openModal2 = () => {
  this.setState({ isOpen: true });
}
```

9. You might have also noticed that the second modal, defined in *step 7*, has a different `onClosed` callback. If the user presses the **OK** button, the `isOpen` value on `state` will be successfully updated to `false`, but if they dismiss the modal by touching the backdrop, it will not. Adding the `onCloseModal2` method guarantees that the `isOpen` value of the `state` is properly kept in sync no matter how the user dismisses the modal, as follows:

```
onCloseModal2 = () => {
  this.setState({ isOpen: false });
}
```

10. The last step in this recipe is applying styles. We'll have a `modal` class for shared modal styles, `modal1` and `modal2` classes for styles unique to each modal, and classes for applying colors, padding, and margin to buttons and text, as follows:

```
const styles = StyleSheet.create({
  container: {
    backgroundColor: '#f6f6f6',
    justifyContent: 'center',
    alignItems: 'center',
    flex: 1
  },
  modal: {
    width: 300,
    justifyContent: 'center',
    alignItems: 'center'
  },
  modal1: {
    height: 200,
    backgroundColor: "#4AC9B0"
  },
  modal2: {
    height: 300,
    backgroundColor: "#6CCEFF"
  },
  modalText: {
    fontSize: 25,
    padding: 10,
    color: '#474747'
  },
  button: {
    backgroundColor: '#000',
    padding: 16,
    borderRadius: 10,
    marginTop: 20
  },
  buttonText: {
```

```
            fontSize: 30,
            color: '#fff'
        }
    });
```

11. This recipe is complete, and we now have an app with two basic modals, displayed on button press, and living in harmony in the same component:

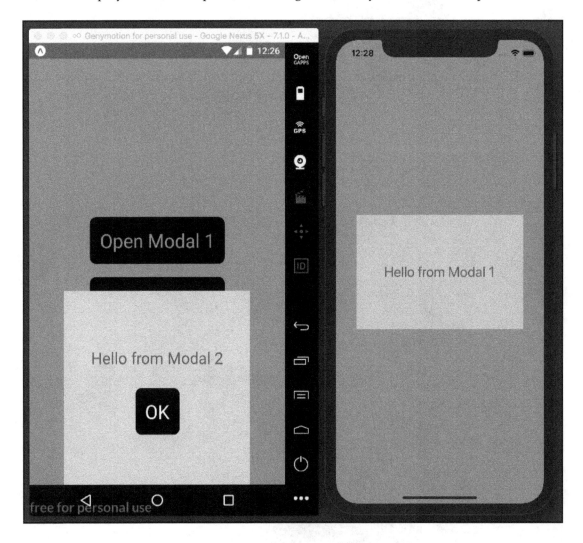

How it works...

In *step 4*, we defined the first `Modal` component. We defined the `onClosed` and `onOpened` props, passing the `onClose` and `onOpen` class methods to these props. Whenever this `Modal` component is opened, `this.onOpen` will fire, and `this.onClose` will execute when the `Modal` is closed. While we didn't do anything exciting with these methods in this recipe, these hooks could serve as the perfect opportunity for logging user actions related to the modal. Or if the modal houses a form, `onOpen` could be used to pre-populate some form inputs with data, and `onClose` could save the form data to the `state` object for use as the modal is closed.

In *step 5*, we defined the method that the first `TouchableOpacity` button component executes when pressed: `openModal1`. In this method, we made use of the `Modal` component's ref. Refs are a core feature of React itself, and provide a place on the component instance for storing DOM nodes and/or React elements that are created in the component's render method. Just as React (and React Native) components have both state and props (`this.state`, and `this.props` in a class component), they can also have refs (which live on `this.ref`). For more on how refs in React work, check the documentation at:

```
https://reactjs.org/docs/refs-and-the-dom.html
```

Since we set the `ref` prop on the first `Modal` to the string `modal1`, we're able to access this same component in the `openModal1` method with the reference `this.ref.modal1`. Since `Modal` has an `open` and a `close` method, calling `this.ref.modal1.open()` opens the `Modal` with a `ref` of `modal1`.

This is not the only way to open and close a `Modal` component, as illustrated with the second modal we defined in *step 7*. Since this component has an `isOpen` prop, the modal can be opened or closed by changing the Boolean value being passed to the prop. By setting `isOpen` to be the `isOpen` value of the state, we can use the **OK** button in this modal to close the modal from within, by setting `isOpen` to false on `state`. In *step 8*, we defined the `openModal2` method, which also illustrates opening the second modal by changing the value of `isOpen` on `state`.

In *step 9*, we defined a separate `isClosed` callback for keeping the `isOpen` value of `state` in sync in case the user dismisses the modal by pressing the backdrop instead of the modal's **OK** button. An alternative strategy would have been to disable the user's ability to dismiss the modal via pressing the backdrop, by adding the `backdropPressToClose` property to the `Modal` component and setting it to `false`.

There are a number of other optional props provided by the `react-native-modalbox` package that can make modal creation easier. We used `position` in this recipe to declare that the second modal be placed at the bottom of the screen, and you can view all other available props for `Modal` in the documentation at:

`https://github.com/maxs15/react-native-modalbox`

 The `react-native-modalbox` library supports multiple modals in a single component; however, attempting to use the `isOpen` prop on more than one of these modals will cause all of those modals to open at once, which is unlikely to be the desired behavior.

Adding Native Functionality - Part I

11

In this chapter, we'll cover the following recipes:

- Exposing custom iOS modules
- Rendering custom iOS view components
- Exposing custom Android modules
- Rendering custom Android view components

Introduction

One of the core principles in React Native development is writing JavaScript to build truly native mobile applications. To accomplish this, many native APIs and UI components are exposed through an abstraction layer and are accessed through the React Native bridge. While the React Native and Expo teams continue to improve and expand on the already impressive APIs that currently exist, through the native APIs we can access functionality that isn't available otherwise, such as vibration, contacts, and native alerts and toasts.

By exposing the native view components, we're able to leverage all of the rendering performance the device has to offer, as we're not going through a WebView as in a hybrid app. This gives a native look and feel that adapts to the platform the user is running the app on. With React Native, we're already able to render many native view components including maps, lists, input fields, toolbars, and pickers.

While React Native comes with many built-in native modules and view components, we're sometimes in a position where we need some custom functionality leveraging the native application layer that isn't provided out of the box. Fortunately, there's an extremely rich open source community supporting React Native that not only contributes to the library itself, but also publishes libraries that export some common native modules and view components. If you can't find a first- or third-party library to accomplish what you need, you can always build it yourself.

In this chapter, we'll cover recipes that go over exposing custom native functionality, whether it's an API or view component, on both platforms.

There will be a lot of generated code in the native portions of the code we'll be using in these recipes. The code blocks provided throughout this chapter will, like in previous chapters, continue to display all of the code used in a particular step, whether it's added by us or generated, unless stated otherwise. This is intended to ease the burden of understanding the context of a piece of code, and facilitates the discussion of these pieces of generated code when further explanation is warranted.

Exposing custom iOS modules

As you begin developing more interesting and complex React Native applications, you could possibly reach a point where executing certain code would be only possible (or significantly improved) in the native layer. This allows for executing data processing that's faster in the native layer when compared with JavaScript, and for accessing certain native functionality that isn't otherwise exposed, such as file I/O, or leveraging existing native code from other applications or libraries in your React Native app.

This recipe will walk you through the process of executing some native Objective-C or Swift code and communicating with the JavaScript layer. We'll build a native `HelloManager` module that will greet our user with a message. We'll also show how to execute native Objective-C and Swift code, taking in arguments, and showing several ways of communicating back with the UI (or JavaScript) layer.

Getting ready

For this recipe, we'll need a new empty, pure React Native application. Let's call it `NativeModuleApp`.

In this recipe, we'll also make use of the `react-native-button` library. This library will allow us to work with a `Button` component that's more sophisticated than the React Native counterparts. It can be installed with `npm`:

```
npm install react-native-button --save
```

Or it can be installed using `yarn`:

```
yarn add react-native-button
```

How to do it...

1. We'll start by opening the iOS Project in Xcode. The project file has an `.xcodeproj` file extension and is located in the `ios/` directory in the root of the project. In our case, the file will be called `NativeModuleApp.xcodeproj`.

2. We need to make a new file by selecting and right-clicking on the group/folder that matches the project name, then clicking on **New File...** as shown in the following:

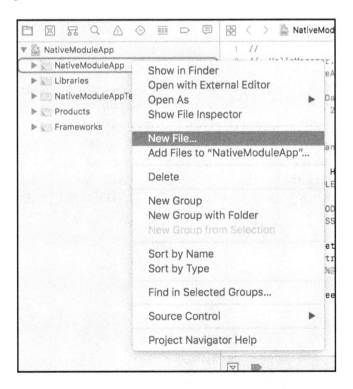

3. We'll be making a Cocoa class, so select **Cocoa Class** and click **Next**.

4. We'll use `HelloManager` for the **Class** name and set the **Subclass of**
to **NSObject**, and the **Language** as **Objective-C** as shown in the following:

5. After clicking **Next**, we'll be prompted to choose the directory for the new class.
We want to save it to the `NativeModuleApp` directory.

6. Creating this new Cocoa class has added two new files to the project: a header
file (`HelloManager.h`) and an implementation file (`HelloManager.m`).

7. Inside the header file (`HelloManager.h`), you should see some generated code
implementing the new `HelloManager` protocol. We need to import the
React `RCTBridgeModule` library as well. The file should ultimately look like this:

```
#import <Foundation/Foundation.h>
#import <React/RCTBridgeModule.h>

@interface HelloManager : NSObject <RCTBridgeModule>

@end
```

8. The implementation file (`HelloManager.m`) houses the functionality of our module. In order for our React Native app to be able to access this module from the JavaScript layer, we need to register it with the React Bridge. This is done by adding `RCT_EXPORT_MODULE()` after the `@implementation` tag. Also note that the header file should already be imported into this file as well:

```
#import "HelloManager.h"

@implementation HelloManager
RCT_EXPORT_MODULE();

@end
```

9. We need to add the function we'll be exporting to the React Native app. We'll create a `greetUser` method that will take two arguments, `name` and `isAdmin`. These arguments will be used to create a greeting message using string concatenation and then send it back to the JavaScript layer via `callback`:

```
#import "HelloManager.h"

@implementation HelloManager
RCT_EXPORT_MODULE();

RCT_EXPORT_METHOD(
  greetUser: (NSString *)name isAdmin:(BOOL *)isAdmin callback:
(RCTResponseSenderBlock) callback
) {
  NSString *greeting =
    [NSString stringWithFormat:
      @"Welcome %@, you %@ an administrator.", name, isAdmin ?
@"are" : @"are not"];

  callback(@[greeting]);
}

@end
```

10. We're ready to switch over to the JavaScript layer, which will have a UI that will invoke the native `HelloManager` `greetUser` method we've just created, then display its output. Fortunately, the React Native bridge does all of the heavy lifting for us and leaves us with a simple-to-use JavaScript object that mimics the `NativeModules` API. In this example, we'll be using `TextInput` and `Switch` to provide `name` and the `isAdmin` value for the native modules method. Let's start with out imports in `App.js`:

```
import React, { Component } from 'react';
import {
  StyleSheet,
  Text,
  View,
  NativeModules,
  TextInput,
  Switch
} from 'react-native';
import Button from 'react-native-button';
```

11. We can use the `NativeModules` component we imported to get the `HelloManager` protocol we created from the native layer:

```
const HelloManager = NativeModules.HelloManager;
```

12. Let's create the `App` component and define the initial `state` object. We'll add a `greetingMessage` property for saving the message received from the native module, `userName` for storing the entered user name, and an `isAdmin` Boolean for representing whether the user is an administrator:

```
export default class App extends Component {
  state = {
    greetingMessage: null,
    userName: null,
    isAdmin: false
  }
  // Defined on following steps
}
```

13. We're ready to start building the `render` method. First, we'll need a `TextInput` component for getting a user name from the user, and a `Switch` component for toggling the `isAdmin` state:

```
render() {
  return (
    <View style={styles.container}>
      <Text style={styles.label}>
        Enter User Name
      </Text>
      <TextInput
        ref="userName"
        autoCorrect={false}
        style={styles.inputField}
        placeholder="User Name"
        onChangeText={(text) => this.setState({ userName: text })
      }
      />
      <Text style={styles.label}>
        Admin
      </Text>
      <Switch style={styles.radio}
        value={this.state.isAdmin}
        onValueChange={(value) =>
          this.setState({ isAdmin: value })
        }
      />

      // Continued below
    </View>
  );
}
```

14. The UI will also need `Button` for submitting the callback to the native module and a `Text` component for displaying the message returned from the native module:

```
render() {
  return (
    // Defined above.
    <Button
      disabled={!this.state.userName}
      style={[
        styles.buttonStyle,
        !this.state.userName ? styles.disabled : null
      ]}
      onPress={this.greetUser}
```

```
        >
          Greet (callback)
        </Button>
        <Text style={styles.label}>
          Response:
        </Text>
        <Text style={styles.message}>
          {this.state.greetingMessage}
        </Text>
      </View>
    );
  }
```

15. With the UI rendering the necessary components, we're ready to wire up the `onPress` handler of `Button` to a call to the native layer. This function passes the `displayResults` class method as the third parameter, which is the callback to be used by the native `greetUser` function. We'll define `displayResults` in the next step:

```
greetUser = () => {
  HelloManager.greetUser(
    this.state.userName,
    this.state.isAdmin,
    this.displayResults
  );
}
```

16. `displayResults` will need to do two things: `blur` the `TextInput` using the `refs` associated with the component and set `greetingMessage` on `state` to the `results` returned from the native module:

```
displayResults = (results) => {
  this.refs.userName.blur();
  this.setState({ greetingMessage: results });
}
```

17. The last step is adding the styles to the layout and styling the app:

```
const styles = StyleSheet.create({
  container: {
    flex: 1,
    justifyContent: 'center',
    alignItems: 'center',
    backgroundColor: '#F5FCFF',
  },
  inputField:{
    padding: 20,
    fontSize: 30
  },
  label: {
    fontSize: 18,
    marginTop: 18,
    textAlign: 'center',
  },
  radio: {
    marginBottom: 20
  },
  buttonStyle: {
    padding: 20,
    backgroundColor: '#1DA1F2',
    color: '#fff',
    fontSize: 18
  },
  message: {
    fontSize: 22,
    marginLeft: 50,
    marginRight: 50,
  },
  disabled: {
    backgroundColor: '#3C3C3C'
  }
});
```

18. We now have a working React Native app that's able to communicate directly with the native iOS layer:

How it works...

The app we built in this recipe will serve as the foundation for many of the following recipes in this chapter. It's also the method Facebook uses to implement many bundled React Native APIs.

There are several important concepts to keep in mind going forward. Any native module class we want to use in the JavaScript layer has to extend `RCTBridgeModule`, as it contains functionality for registering our class onto the React Native bridge. We register our class with the `RCT_EXPORT_MODULE` method call, which registers methods on the module once the module has been registered. Registering the module along with its respective methods and properties is what allows us to interface with the native layer from the JavaScript layer.

The `greetUser` method is executed when the button is pressed. This function in turn makes a call to `HelloManager.greetUser`, passing the `userName` and `isAdmin` properties from `state` and the `displayResults` function as a callback. `displayResults` sets the new `greetingMessage` on `state`, causing the UI to be refreshed and the message to be displayed.

See also

- An explanation of how React Native applications boot up: `https://levelup.gitconnected.com/wait-what-happens-when-my-react-native-application-starts-an-in-depth-look-inside-react-native-5f306ef3250f`
- A deep dive into how React Native events actually work: `https://levelup.gitconnected.com/react-native-events-in-gory-details-what-happens-on-the-way-to-listeners-2cee6c55940c`

Rendering custom iOS view components

While it's very important to leverage the devices processing power in executing code on the native layer in our React Native application, it's equally important to leverage its rendering power to show native UI components. React Native can render any UI component that's an implementation of `UIView` inside an application. These components can be lists, form fields, tables, graphics, and so on.

For this recipe, we'll create a React Native application titled `NativeUIComponent`.

In this recipe, we'll take a native `UIButton` and expose it as a React Native view component. You'll be able to set the button label and attach a handler for when it's pressed.

How to do it...

1. Let's start by opening the iOS project in Xcode. The project file is located in the `ios/` directory of the project and should be called `NativeUIComponent.xcodeproj`.

2. Select and right-click on the group that matches your project name and click on **New File...**:

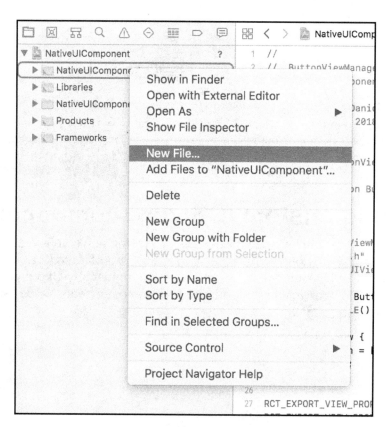

3. We'll be making a Cocoa class, so select **Cocoa Class** and click **Next**.
4. We'll be creating a button, so let's name the **Class** Button and set the **Subclass of** to **UIView** and the **Language** as **Objective-C**:

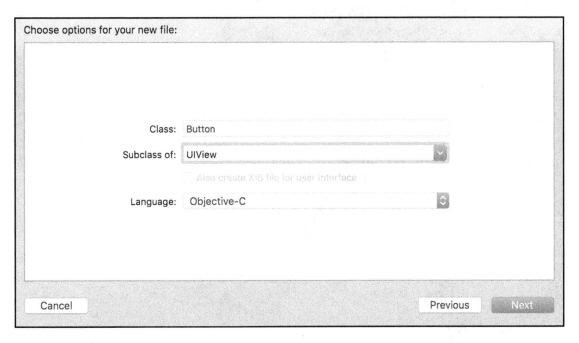

5. After clicking **Next**, we'll be prompted to choose the directory for the new class. We want to save it to the NativeUIComponent directory to create the class.

6. We're also going to need a ButtonViewManager class as well. You can repeat steps 2 to 5 with ButtonViewManager as the class name and RCTViewManager as the subclass.

7. First, we're going to implement our Button UI class. In the header (Button.h) file, we'll import RCTComponent.h from React and add an onTap property to wire up our tap event:

```
#import <UIKit/UIKit.h>
#import "React/RCTComponent.h"

@interface Button : UIView

@property (nonatomic, copy) RCTBubblingEventBlock onTap;

@end
```

8. Let's work on the implementation file (`Button.m`). We'll start by creating references for our `UIButton` instance and the string that will hold the button label:

```
#import "Button.h"
#import "React/UIView+React.h"

@implementation Button {
  UIButton *_button;
  NSString *_buttonText;
}

// Defined in following steps
```

9. The bridge will look for a setter for the `buttonText` property. This is where we'll set the `UIButton` instance title field:

```
-(void) setButtonText:(NSString *)buttonText {
  NSLog(@"Set text %@", buttonText);
  _buttonText = buttonText;
  if(_button) {
    [_button setTitle:
     buttonText forState:UIControlStateNormal];
    [_button sizeToFit];
  }
}
```

10. Our `Button` will accept an `onTap` event handler from the React Native app. We need to wire this to our `UIButton` instance through an action selector:

```
- (IBAction)onButtonTap:(id)sender {
  self.onTap(@{});
}
```

11. We need to instantiate the `UIButton` and place it inside a React `Subview`. We'll call this method `layoutSubviews`:

```
-(void) layoutSubviews {
  [super layoutSubviews];
  if( _button == nil) {
    _button =
    [UIButton buttonWithType:UIButtonTypeRoundedRect];
    [_button addTarget:self action:@selector(onButtonTap:)
     forControlEvents:UIControlEventTouchUpInside];
    [_button setTitle:
     _buttonText forState:UIControlStateNormal];
    [_button sizeToFit];
```

```
        [self insertSubview:_button atIndex:0];
    }
}
```

12. Let's import the React `RCTViewManager` in the `ButtonViewManager.h` header
    file:

    ```
    #import "React/RCTViewManager.h"

    @interface ButtonViewManager : RCTViewManager

    @end
    ```

13. Now we need to implement our `ButtonViewManager`, which will interface with
    our React Native application. Let's work on the implementation file
    (`ButtonViewManager.m`) to make this happen. We use
    `RCT_EXPORT_VIEW_PROPERTY` to pass along the `buttonText` property
    and `onTap` method to the React Native layer:

    ```
    #import "ButtonViewManager.h"
    #import "Button.h"
    #import "React/UIView+React.h"

    @implementation ButtonViewManager
    RCT_EXPORT_MODULE()

    - (UIView *)view {
      Button *button = [[Button alloc] init];
      return button;
    }

    RCT_EXPORT_VIEW_PROPERTY(buttonText, NSString);
    RCT_EXPORT_VIEW_PROPERTY(onTap, RCTBubblingEventBlock);

    @end
    ```

14. We are ready to switch over to the React Native layer. We're going to need a
    custom `Button` component, so let's create a new `components` folder in the root
    of the project with a new `Button.js` file inside of it. We'll also need to import
    the `requireNativeComponent` component from React Native for interfacing
    with our native UI component:

    ```
    import React, { Component } from 'react';
    import {
      StyleSheet,
      Text,
    ```

```
      View
    } from 'react-native';
    import Button from './components/Button';
```

15. The `Button` component will grab the native `Button` module we created earlier via the `requireNativeComponent` React Native helper. The call takes a string to be used as the component's name in the React Native layer as the first parameter, and the second takes the `Button` component in the file, effectively wiring the two together:

```
export default class Button extends Component {
  render() {
    return <ButtonView {...this.properties} />;
  }
}

const ButtonView = requireNativeComponent('ButtonView', Button);
```

16. We're ready to build out the main `App` component in the `App.js` file in the root of the project. We'll start with the imports, which will include the `Button` component we created in the last two steps:

```
import React, { Component } from 'react';
import {
  StyleSheet,
  Text,
  View
} from 'react-native';
import Button from './components/Button';
```

17. Let's define the `App` component and the initial `state` object. The `count` property will keep track of the number of times the `Button` component has been pressed:

```
export default class App extends Component {
  state = {
   count: 0
  }
  // Defined on following steps
 }
```

18. We're ready to define the `render` method, which will just consist of the `Button` component, along with a `Text` element for displaying the current button press count:

```
render() {
  return (
    <View style={styles.container}>
      <Button buttonText="Click Me!"
      onTap={this.handleButtonTap}
      style={styles.button}
    />
      <Text>Button Pressed Count: {this.state.count}</Text>
    </View>
  );
}
```

19. You may recall that the `Button` component we created has an `onTap` property, which takes a callback function. In this case we'll just use this function to increase the counter that lives on `state`:

```
handleButtonTap = () => {
  this.setState({
    count: this.state.count + 1
  });
}
```

20. Let's wrap up this recipe with a few basic styles:

```
const styles = StyleSheet.create({
  container: {
    flex: 1,
    justifyContent: 'center',
    alignItems: 'center',
    backgroundColor: '#F5FCFF',
  },
  button: {
    height: 40,
    width: 80
  }
});
```

21. The app is complete! When the button is pressed, the function passed to `onTap` will be executed, increasing the counter by one:

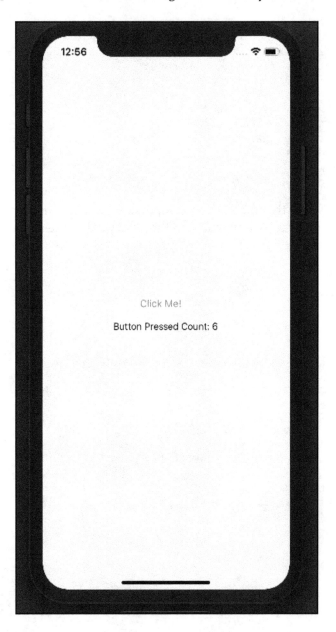

How it works...

In this recipe, we exposed a basic native UI component. This is the same method by which all of the UI components built into React Native (for example, `Slider`, `Picker`, and `ListView`) were created.

 The most important requirement in creating UI components is that your `ViewManager` extends `RCTViewManager` and returns an instance of `UIView`. In our case, we're wrapping `UIButton` with a React-specific `UIView` extension, which improves our ability to layout and style the component.

The next important factor is sending properties and reacting to component events. In step 13, we used the `RCT_EXPORT_VIEW_PROPERTY` method provided by React Native to register the `buttonText` and `onTap` view properties that will come from the JavaScript layer to the `Button` component. That `Button` component is then created and returned to be used in the JavaScript layer:

```
- (UIView *)view {
  Button *button = [[Button alloc] init];
  return button;
}
```

Exposing custom Android modules

Often, you'll find the need for React Native applications to interface with native iOS and Android code. Having discussed integrating native iOS modules, now it's time to cover the equivalent recipes in Android.

This recipe will take us through writing our first Android native module. We're going to create a `HelloManager` native module with a `greetUser` method that takes `name` and an `isAdmin` Boolean as arguments, which will return a greeting message that we'll display in the UI.

Getting ready

For this recipe, we'll need to create another pure React Native app. Let's name this project `NativeModuleApp` as well.

We'll also be making use of the `react-native-button` library again, which can be installed with `npm`:

```
npm install react-native-button --save
```

Alternatively, it can be installed using `yarn`:

```
yarn add react-native-button
```

How to do it...

1. We'll start by opening the new project's Android code in Android Studio. From the Android Studio welcome screen, you can select **Open an existing Android Studio project**, then select the `android` directory inside of the project folder.

2. Once the project has loaded, let's open the project explorer (that is, the directory tree) on the left side of Android Studio and expand the package structure to find the Java source files, which should live in `app/java/com.nativemoduleapp`. The folder should already have two `.java` files in it, `MainActivity` and `MainApplication`:

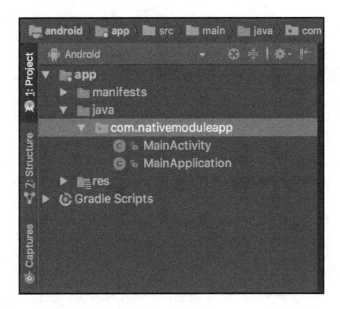

3. Right-click on the **com.nativemoduleapp** package, select **New** | **Java Class**, and name the class `HelloManager`. Also, be sure to set the **Kind** field to **Class**:

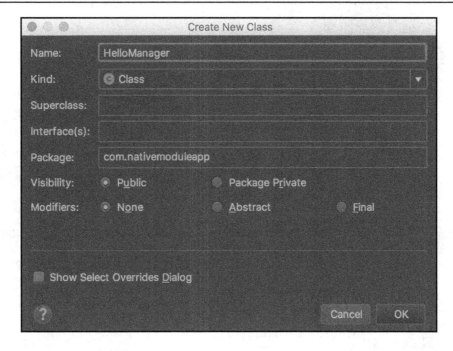

4. We'll also need a `HelloPackage` class in the same directory. You can repeat steps 2 and 3 to create this class, simply applying the new name and keeping the **Kind** field set to **Class**.

5. Let's start by implementing our `HelloManager` native module. We'll start with the `package` name and the dependencies we'll need in this file:

```
package com.nativemoduleapp;

import com.facebook.react.bridge.Callback;
import com.facebook.react.bridge.ReactApplicationContext;
import com.facebook.react.bridge.ReactContextBaseJavaModule;
import com.facebook.react.bridge.ReactMethod;
```

6. `ReactContextBaseJavaModule` is the base class for all React Native modules, so we'll be creating the `HelloManager` class as a subclass of it. We also need to define a `getName` method, which is used for registering native modules with the React Native bridge. This is one difference from the iOS native module implementations, as those are defined via class name:

```
public class HelloManager extends ReactContextBaseJavaModule {
  public HelloManager(ReactApplicationContext reactContext) {
    super(reactContext);
  }
```

```
        @Override
        public String getName() {
          return "HelloManager";
        }
      }
```

7. Now that we've set up our `HelloManager` native module, it's time to add the `greetUser` method to it, which will expect as arguments `name`, `isAdmin`, and the callback that will be executed to send the message to the React Native layer:

```
public class HelloManager extends ReactContextBaseJavaModule {
  // Defined in previous steps

  @ReactMethod
  public void greetUser(String name, Boolean isAdmin, Callback
callback) {
      System.out.println("User Name: " + name + ", Administrator: " +
(isAdmin ? "Yes" : "No"));
      String greeting = "Welcome " + name + ", you " + (isAdmin ?
"are" : "are not") + " an administrator";

      callback.invoke(greeting);
  }
}
```

8. Another step that's unique to Android is having to register the native module with the application, which is a two-step process. The first step is to add our `HelloManager` module to the `HelloPackage` class we created earlier. We'll start with the dependencies for `HelloPackage.java`:

```
package com.nativemoduleapp;

import com.facebook.react.ReactPackage;
import com.facebook.react.bridge.NativeModule;
import com.facebook.react.bridge.ReactApplicationContext;
import com.facebook.react.uimanager.ViewManager;

import java.util.ArrayList;
import java.util.Collections;
import java.util.List;
```

9. The implementation of `HelloPackage` simply follows the pattern provided by the official documentation (`https://facebook.github.io/react-native/docs/native-modules-android.html`). The most important piece here is the call to `modules.add`, where a new instance of `HelloManager` is passed in with `reactContext` as its parameter:

```java
public class HelloPackage implements ReactPackage {

  @Override
  public List<ViewManager>
createViewManagers(ReactApplicationContext reactContext) {
    return Collections.emptyList();
  }

  @Override
  public List<NativeModule>
createNativeModules(ReactApplicationContext reactContext) {
    List<NativeModule> modules = new ArrayList<>();
    modules.add(new HelloManager(reactContext));

    return modules;
  }
}
```

10. The second step in registering the native module with the React Native app is to add `HelloPackage` to the `MainApplication` module. Most of the code here is generated by the React Native bootstrapping process. The `getPackages` method needs to be updated to take both `new MainReactPackage()` and `new HelloPackage()` as arguments passed to `Arrays.asList`:

```java
package com.nativemoduleapp;

import android.app.Application;

import com.facebook.react.ReactApplication;
import com.facebook.react.ReactNativeHost;
import com.facebook.react.ReactPackage;
import com.facebook.react.shell.MainReactPackage;
import com.facebook.soloader.SoLoader;

import java.util.Arrays;
import java.util.List;

public class MainApplication extends Application implements
ReactApplication {
```

```
    private final ReactNativeHost mReactNativeHost = new
ReactNativeHost(this) {
    @Override
    public boolean getUseDeveloperSupport() {
        return BuildConfig.DEBUG;
    }

    @Override
    protected List<ReactPackage> getPackages() {
      return Arrays.asList(
        new MainReactPackage(),
        new HelloPackage()
      );
    }

    @Override
    protected String getJSMainModuleName() {
      return "index";
    }
  };

  @Override
  public ReactNativeHost getReactNativeHost() {
    return mReactNativeHost;
  }

  @Override
  public void onCreate() {
    super.onCreate();
    SoLoader.init(this, /* native exopackage */ false);
  }
}
```

11. We're all done on the Java portion of this recipe. We need to build our UI, which will invoke the native `HelloManager` `greetUser` method and display its output. In this example, we'll be using `TextInput` and `Switch` to provide `name` and the `isAdmin` value for the native module method. This is the same functionality as we implemented on iOS in the *Exposing custom iOS modules* recipe. Let's get to building out `App.js`, starting with the dependencies we'll need:

```
import React, { Component } from 'react';
import {
  StyleSheet,
  Text,
  View,
  NativeModules,
```

```
    TextInput,
    Switch,
    DeviceEventEmitter
} from 'react-native';
import Button from 'react-native-button';
```

12. We need to make a reference to the `HelloManager` object that lives on the imported `NativeModules` component:

```
const { HelloManager } = NativeModules;
```

13. Let's create the `App` class and the initial `state`:

```
export default class App extends Component {
  state = {
    userName: null,
    greetingMessage: null,
    isAdmin: false
  }
}
```

14. We're ready to define the component's `render` function. This piece of code will not be described in great detail, as it's basically the same `render` function defined in the *Exposing custom iOS modules* recipe at the beginning of this chapter:

```
render() {
  return (
    <View style={styles.container}>
      <Text style={styles.label}>
        Enter User Name
      </Text>
      <TextInput
        ref="userName"
        autoCorrect={false}
        style={styles.inputField}
        placeholder="User Name"
        onChangeText={(text) => this.setState({ userName: text })
        }
      />
      <Text style={styles.label}>
        Admin
      </Text>
      <Switch
        style={styles.radio}
        onValueChange={
          value => this.setState({ isAdmin: value })
        }
        value={this.state.isAdmin}
```

```
      />
      <Button
        disabled={!this.state.userName}
        style={[
          styles.buttonStyle,
          !this.state.userName ? styles.disabled : null
        ]}
        onPress={this.greetUser}
      >
        Greet
      </Button>
      <Text style={styles.label}>
        Response:
      </Text>
      <Text style={styles.message}>
        {this.state.greetingMessage}
      </Text>
    </View>
  );
}
```

15. With the UI rendering the necessary components, we now need to wire up the `onPress` handler of `Button` to make the native call via `HelloManager.greetUser`:

```
updateGreetingMessage = (result) => {
  this.setState({
    greetingMessage: result
  });
}

greetUser = () => {
  this.refs.userName.blur();
  HelloManager.greetUser(
    this.state.userName,
    this.state.isAdmin,
    this.updateGreetingMessage
  );
}
```

16. We'll add styles to layout and style the app. Again, these are the same styles as used in the *Exposing custom iOS modules* recipe at the beginning of this chapter:

```
const styles = StyleSheet.create({
  container: {
    flex: 1,
    justifyContent: 'center',
    alignItems: 'center',
    backgroundColor: '#F5FCFF',
  },
  inputField:{
    padding: 20,
    fontSize: 30,
    width: 200
  },
  label: {
    fontSize: 18,
    marginTop: 18,
    textAlign: 'center',
  },
  radio: {
    marginBottom: 20
  },
  buttonStyle: {
    padding: 20,
    backgroundColor: '#1DA1F2',
    color: '#fff',
    fontSize: 18
  },
  message: {
    fontSize: 22,
    marginLeft: 50,
    marginRight: 50,
  },
  disabled: {
    backgroundColor: '#3C3C3C'
  }
});
```

17. The final app should look similar to the following screenshot:

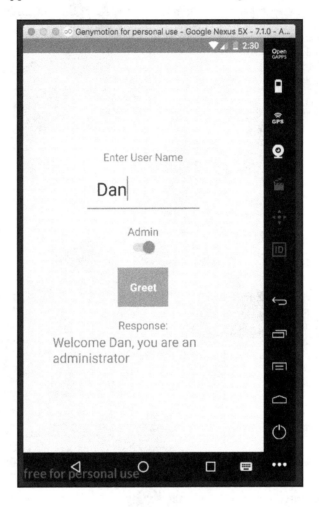

How it works...

This recipe covers the foundation for much of what we'll be doing with adding native Android modules in future recipes. All native module classes need to extend `ReactContextBaseJavaModule`, implement the constructor, and define the `getName` method. All methods that should be exposed to the React Native layer need to have the `@ReactMethod` annotation. Creating a React Native Android native module has more overhead as compared with iOS, since you have to also wrap your module in a class that implements `ReactPackage` (in this recipe, that's the `HelloPackage` module), and register the package with the React Native project. This is done in steps 7 and 8.

In the JavaScript portion of the recipe, the `greetUser` function is executed when the user presses the `Button` component. This, in turn, makes a call to `HelloManager.greetUser`, passing along the `userName` and `isAdmin` properties from `state` and the `updateGreetingMessage` method as a callback. The `updateGreetingMessage` sets the new `greetingMessage` on `state`, causing a refresh of the UI and the message to be displayed.

Rendering custom Android view components

One reason React Native has gained so much popularity so far is its ability to render truly native UI components. With native UI components on Android, we're able to leverage not only the GPU rendering power, but we also get the native look and feel of native components, including native fonts, colors, and animations. Web and hybrid applications on Android use CSS polyfills to simulate a native animation but, in React Native, we can get the real thing.

We'll need a new pure React Native app for this recipe. Let's name it `NativeUIComponent`. In this recipe, we'll take a native `Button` and expose it as a React Native view component.

How to do it...

1. Let's start by opening the Android project in Android Studio. In the Android Studio welcome screen, select **Open an existing Android Studio project** and open the `android` directory of the project.

2. Open the project explorer and expand the package structure until you can see the Java source files (for example, `app/java/com.nativeuicomponent`):

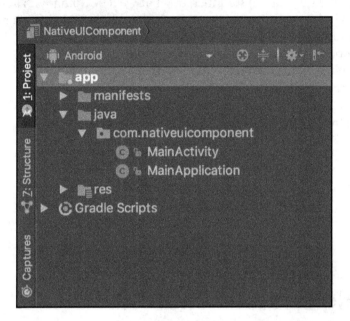

3. Right-click on the package and select **New** | **Java Class**. Use `ButtonViewManager` for the class name and set the **Kind** field to **Class**.

4. Use the same method to also create a `ButtonPackage` class.

5. Let's begin implementing our `ButtonViewManager` class, which must be a subclass of `SimpleViewManager<View>`. We'll start with the imports and define the class itself:

```
package com.nativeuicomponent;

import android.view.View;
import android.widget.Button;

import com.facebook.react.bridge.Arguments;
import com.facebook.react.bridge.ReactContext;
import com.facebook.react.bridge.WritableMap;
import com.facebook.react.uimanager.SimpleViewManager;
import com.facebook.react.uimanager.ThemedReactContext;
import com.facebook.react.uimanager.annotations.ReactProp;
import com.facebook.react.uimanager.events.RCTEventEmitter;

public class ButtonViewManager extends SimpleViewManager<Button>
```

```
implements View.OnClickListener {
  // Defined on following steps
}
```

The file class name `ButtonViewManager` follows the Android naming convention of adding the suffix `ViewManager` to any `View` component.

6. Let's start the class definition with the `getName` method that returns the string name we're assigning the component, which in this case is `ButtonView`:

```
public class ButtonViewManager extends SimpleViewManager<Button>
implements View.OnClickListener{
  @Override
  public String getName() {
    return "ButtonView";
  }

  // Defined on following steps.
}
```

7. The `createViewInstance` method is required for defining how React should initialize the module:

```
@Override
protected Button createViewInstance(ThemedReactContext
reactContext) {
   Button button = new Button(reactContext);
   button.setOnClickListener(this);
   return button;
}
```

8. `setButtonText` will be used from the properties on the React Native element to set the text on the button:

```
@ReactProp(name = "buttonText")
public void setButtonText(Button button, String buttonText) {
  button.setText(buttonText);
}
```

9. The `onClick` method defines what will happen when the button is pressed. This method uses `RCTEventEmitter` to handle receiving events from the React Native layer:

```
@Override
public void onClick(View v) {
```

```
        WritableMap map = Arguments.createMap();
        ReactContext reactContext = (ReactContext) v.getContext();
    reactContext.getJSModule(RCTEventEmitter.class).receiveEvent(v.getI
    d(), "topChange", map);
      }
```

10. Just like in the last recipe, we need to add ButtonViewManager to
    ButtonPackage; however, this time, we're defining it as ViewManager and not
    NativeModule:

```
package com.nativeuicomponent;

import com.facebook.react.ReactPackage;
import com.facebook.react.bridge.NativeModule;
import com.facebook.react.bridge.ReactApplicationContext;
import com.facebook.react.uimanager.ViewManager;

import java.util.Arrays;
import java.util.Collections;
import java.util.List;

public class ButtonPackage implements ReactPackage {
  @Override
  public List<ViewManager>
createViewManagers(ReactApplicationContext reactContext) {
    return Arrays.<ViewManager>asList(new ButtonViewManager());
  }

  @Override
  public List<NativeModule>
createNativeModules(ReactApplicationContext reactContext) {
    return Collections.emptyList();
  }
}
```

11. The last step in the Java layer is adding ButtonPackage
    to MainApplication. MainApplication.java already has quite a bit of
    boilerplate code in it, and we'll only need to change the getPackages method:

```
@Override
protected List<ReactPackage> getPackages() {
  return Arrays.<ReactPackage>asList(
    new MainReactPackage(),
    new ButtonPackage()
  );
}
```

12. Switching over to the JavaScript layer, let's build out our React Native app. First, let's create a new `Button` component in `components/Button.js` in the project's root directory. This is where the native button will live inside the React Native layer of the app. The `render` method uses the native button as `ButtonView`, which we'll define in the next step:

```
import React, { Component } from 'react';
import { requireNativeComponent, View } from 'react-native';

export default class Button extends Component {
  onChange = (event) => {
    if (this.properties.onTap) {
      this.properties.onTap(event.nativeEvent.message);
    }
  }

  render() {
    return (
      <ButtonView
        {...this.properties}
        onChange={this.onChange}
      />
    );
  }
}
```

13. We can create the native button as a React Native component with the `requireNativeComponent` helper, which takes three parameters: the string `ButtonView` to define the components name, the `Button` component defined in the previous step, and the options object. There's more information on this object in the *How it works...* section at the end of this recipe:

```
const ButtonView = requireNativeComponent(
  'ButtonView',
  Button, {
    nativeOnly: {
      onChange: true
    }
  }
);
```

14. We're ready to define the `App` class. Let's start with dependencies, including the `Button` component created previously:

```
import React, { Component } from 'react';
import {
```

```
      StyleSheet,
      Text,
      View
    } from 'react-native';

    import Button from './components/Button';
```

15. The `App` component in this recipe is essentially the same as the *Rendering custom iOS view components* recipe earlier in this chapter. The custom `onTap` property is fired when the `Button` component is pressed, adding 1 to the `count` property on `state`:

```
    export default class App extends Component {
      state = {
        count: 0
      }

      onButtonTap = () => {
        this.setState({
          count : this.state.count + 1
        });
      }

      render() {
        return (
          <View style={styles.container}>
            <Button buttonText="Press Me!"
              onTap={this.onButtonTap}
              style={styles.button}
            />
            <Text>
              Button Pressed Count: {this.state.count}
            </Text>
          </View>
        );
      }
    }
```

16. Let's add a few styles to layout and size the app's UI:

```
    const styles = StyleSheet.create({
      container: {
        flex: 1,
        justifyContent: 'center',
        alignItems: 'center',
        backgroundColor: '#F5FCFF',
      },
      button: {
```

```
        height: 40,
        width: 150
    }
});
```

17. The final app should look similar to the following screenshot:

How it works...

When defining a native view, as we did with the `ButtonViewManager` class, it must extend `SimpleViewManager` and render a type that extends `View`. In our recipe, we rendered a `Button` view, and we used the `@ReactProp` annotation for defining properties. When we need to communicate back to the JavaScript layer, we fire an event from the native component, which we implemented in *step 9* of this recipe.

In *step 12*, we created an `onChange` listener, which will execute the event handler passed in from the Android layer (`event.nativeEvent.message`).

Regarding the use of the `nativeOnly` option on *step 13*, from the React Native documents:

> Sometimes you'll have some special properties that you need to expose for the native component, but don't actually want them as part of the API for the associated React component. For example, `Switch` has a custom `onChange` handler for the raw native event, and exposes an `onValueChange` handler property that is invoked with just the Boolean value, rather than the raw event. Since you don't want these native only properties to be part of the API, you don't want to put them in `propTypes`, but if you don't, you'll get an error. The solution is simply to call them out via the `nativeOnly` option.

Adding Native Functionality - Part II

12

In this chapter, we will cover the following recipes:

- Reacting to changes in application state
- Copying and pasting content
- Authenticating via touch ID or fingerprint sensor
- Hiding application content when multitasking
- Background processing on iOS
- Background processing on Android
- Playing audio files on iOS
- Playing audio files on Android

Introduction

In this chapter, we will continue with more recipes that touch on different aspects of writing React Native apps that interact with native iOS and Android code. We will cover example apps that leverage built-in and community created modules. The recipes cover a range of topics, from rendering a basic button to creating a multithreaded process that does not block the main application thread.

Reacting to changes in application state

The average mobile device user has several apps that they use on a regular basis. Ideally, along with the other social media apps, games, media players, and more, users will also be using your React Native app. Any specific user may spend a short time in each application because he or she multitasks. What if we wanted to react to when the user leaves our app and re-enters? We could use this as a chance to sync data with the server, or to tell the user that we're happy to see them return, or to politely ask for a rating on the app store.

This recipe will cover the basics of reacting to changes in the state of the application, which is to say reacting to when the app is in the foreground (active), background, or inactive.

For this recipe, let's create a new pure React Native app titled `AppStateApp`.

How to do it...

1. Fortunately, React Native provides support for listening to changes to the state of the app through the `AppState` module. Let's begin building out the app by adding dependencies to the `App.js` file, as follows:

```
import React, { Component } from 'react';
import {
  AppState,
  StyleSheet,
  Text,
  View
} from 'react-native';
```

2. In the recipe, we're going to keep track of the previous state to see where the user came from. If it's their first time entering the app, we will welcome them, and if they're returning, we will welcome them back instead. To do so, we need to keep a reference to the previous and current app states. We'll use instance variables `previousAppState` and `currentAppStates` instead of using state for this purpose, simply to avoid potential naming confusion. We'll use `state` to hold the status message to the user, as follows:

```
export default class App extends Component {
  previousAppState = null;
  currentAppState = 'active';
  state = {
    statusMessage: 'Welcome!'
  }
  // Defined on following steps
}
```

3. When the component mounts, we'll use the `AppState` component to add an event listener to the `change` event. Whenever the app's state changes (for example, when the app is backgrounded), the `change` event will be fired, whereupon we'll fire our `handleAppStateChange` handler, defined in the next step, as follows:

```
componentWillMount() {
  AppState.addEventListener('change', this.handleAppStateChange);
}
```

4. The `handleAppStateChange` method will receive the `appState` as a parameter, which we can expect to be one of three strings: `inactive` if the app is unloaded from memory, `background` if the app is in memory and backgrounded, and `active` if the app is foregrounded. We'll use a `switch` statement to update the `statusMessage` on `state` accordingly:

```
handleAppStateChange = (appState) => {
  let statusMessage;

  this.previousAppState = this.currentAppState;
  this.currentAppState = appState;
  switch(appState) {
    case 'inactive':
      statusMessage = "Good Bye.";
      break;
    case 'background':
      statusMessage = "App Is Hidden...";
      break;
```

```
      case 'active':
        statusMessage = 'Welcome Back!'
        break;
  }
  this.setState({ statusMessage });
}
```

5. The `render` method is very basic in this recipe, since it only needs to display the status message to the user, as follows:

```
render() {
    return (
      <View style={styles.container}>
        <Text style={styles.welcome}>
          {this.state.statusMessage}
        </Text>
      </View>
    );
}
```

6. The styles for this app are basic, adding font size, color, and margin, as follows:

```
const styles = StyleSheet.create({
  container: {
    flex: 1,
    justifyContent: 'center',
    alignItems: 'center',
    backgroundColor: '#fff',
  },
  welcome: {
    fontSize: 40,
    textAlign: 'center',
    margin: 10,
  },
  instructions: {
    textAlign: 'center',
    color: '#333333',
    marginBottom: 5,
  },
});
```

7. The completed app should now display the appropriate status message depending on the state of the app on a given device.

How it works...

In this recipe, we made use of the built-in `AppState` module. The module listens to the `Activity` events on Android, and on iOS it uses `NSNotificationCenter` to register a listener on various `UIApplication` events. Note that both platforms support the `active` and `background` states; however, the `inactive` state is an iOS only concept. Android does not explicitly support the `inactive` state due to its multitasking implementation, so only toggles apps between `background` and `active` states. To achieve the equivalent of the iOS inactive state on Android, see the *Hiding application content when multitasking* recipe later in this chapter.

Copying and pasting content

One of the most used features in both desktop and mobile operating systems is the clipboard for copying and pasting content. A common scenario on mobile is filling forms with lengthy text, such as long email addresses or passwords. Instead of typing it with a few typos, it would be easier to just open your contacts application and copy the email from there and paste it into your `TextInput` field.

This recipe will show a basic example on both Android and iOS of how we can copy and paste text inside our React Native application. In our sample app, we will have both a static `Text` view and a `TextInput` field that you can use to copy its contents to the clipboard. Also, there will be a button that outputs the contents of the clipboard to the view.

Getting ready

For this recipe, we'll create a pure React Native application titled `CopyPasteApp`.

In this recipe, we will be using `react-native-button` again. Install it with `npm`:

```
npm install react-native-button
```

Alternatively, we can use `yarn`:

```
yarn add react-native-button
```

How to do it...

1. Let's start off by creating a `ClipboardText` component that both uses a `Text` component to display text and provides the ability to copy its contents to the clipboard via long press. Let's create a `component` folder in the root of the project, and a `ClipboardText.js` file inside of it. We'll start by importing dependencies, as follows:

```
import React, { Component } from 'react';
import {
  StyleSheet,
  Text,
  View,
  Clipboard,
  TextInput
} from 'react-native';
import Button from 'react-native-button';
```

2. Next we'll define the `App` class and the initial `state`. We will use the `clipboardContent` property on `state` for storing text being pasted from the clipboard into the UI, as follows:

```
export default class App extends Component {
  state = {
    clipboardContent: null
  }
  // Defined in following steps
}
```

3. The UI will have one `Text` component whose text will by copyable via long press. Let's define the `copyToClipboard` method. We'll grab the input via its `ref` (which we'll define later), and access the component's text via its `props.children` property. Once the text has been stored in a local variable, we simply pass it to the `setString` method of `Clipboard` to copy the text to the clipboard, as follows:

```
copyToClipboard = () => {
  const sourceText = this.refs.sourceText.props.children;
  Clipboard.setString(sourceText);
}
```

4. Similarly, we'll also need a method that will paste text into the app's UI from the clipboard. This method will use the `getString` method of `Clipboard`, and save the returned string to the `clipboardContent` property of `state`, re-rendering the app's UI to reflect the pasted text, as follows:

```
getClipboardContent = async () => {
  const clipboardContent = await Clipboard.getString();
  this.setState({
    clipboardContent
  });
}
```

5. The `render` method will be made up of two sections: the first is made of things to copy, and the second is a way for pasting text from the clipboard into the UI. Let's start with the first section, which consists of a `Text` input whose `onLongPress` prop is wired to the `copyToClipboard` method we created in *step 3*, and a text input for normal native copy/pasting:

```
render() {
  return (
    <View style={styles.container}>
      <Text style={styles.instructions}>
        Tap and Hold the next line to copy it to the Clipboard:
      </Text>
      <Text
        ref="sourceText"
        onLongPress={this.copyToClipboard}
      >
        React Native Cookbook
      </Text>
      <Text style={styles.instructions}>
        Input some text into the TextInput below and Cut/Copy as
        you normally would:
      </Text>
      <TextInput style={styles.textInput} />

      // Defined on next step
    </View>
  );
}
```

6. The second portion of the UI consists of a `Text` component for displaying the current value saved in `clipboardContent` on `state`, and a button that will paste from the clipboard using the `getClipboardContent` method we defined in *step 4*:

```
render() {
  return (
    <View style={styles.container}>
      // Defined in previous step
      <View style={styles.row}>
        <Text style={styles.rowText}>
          Clipboard Contents:
        </Text>
      </View>
      <View style={styles.row}>
        <Text style={styles.content}>
          {this.state.clipboardContent}
        </Text>
      </View>
      <Button
        containerStyle={styles.buttonContainer}
        style={styles.buttonStyle}
        onPress={this.getClipboardContent}
      >
          Paste Clipboard
      </Button>
    </View>
  );
}
```

The final app should look similar to the following screenshot:

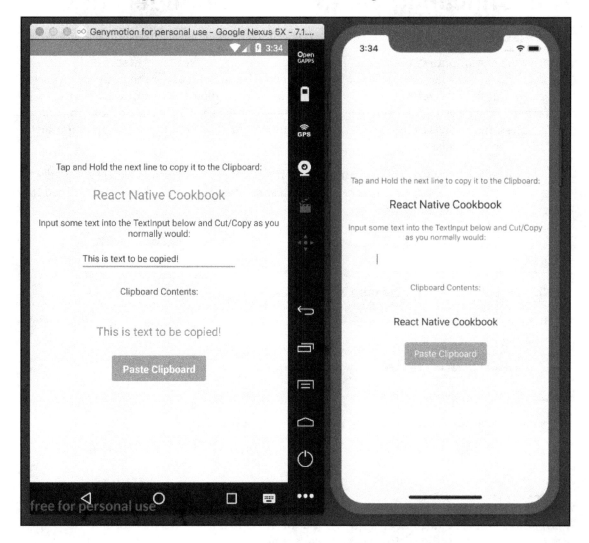

How it works...

In this recipe, we built a simple copy and paste application by using the `Clipboard` API provided by React Native. The `Clipboard` module currently only supports content of type `String`, even though the devices can copy more complicated data. This module makes using the clipboard as easy as calling the methods `setString` and `getString`.

Authenticating via touch ID or fingerprint sensor

Security is a paramount concern in software, especially when there is any sort of authentication. Breaches and leaked passwords have become a part of the daily news cycle, and companies of all sizes are wising up to the need for implementing added security measures in their apps. One such measure in mobile devices is biometric authentication, which uses fingerprint scanning or face recognition technology to provide supplementary identification methods.

This recipe covers how to add fingerprint scanning and face recognition security. Thanks to the `react-native-touch-id` library, this process has been simplified and streamlined in React Native app development.

Getting ready

For this recipe we'll need a new pure React Native app. Let's call it `BiometricAuth`.

We'll be using the `react-native-button` and `react-native-touch-id` libraries. Install them with `npm`:

```
npm install react-native-button react-native-touch-id --save
```

Alternatively, we can use `yarn`:

```
yarn add react-native-button react-native-touch-id
```

Once installed, `react-native-touch-id` will need to be linked, so be sure to follow up with:

```
react-native link
```

Permissions will also need to be adjusted manually. For Android permissions, locate the `AndroidManifest.xml` file in the project, which should be at `BiometricAuth/android/app/src/main/AndroidManifest.xml`. Along with the other permissions in this file, you'll need to add the following:

```
<uses-permission android:name="android.permission.USE_FINGERPRINT" />
```

For iOS permissions, you'll need to update the `Info.plist` file in a text editor. The `Info.plist` can be found at `BiometricAuth/ios/BiometricAuth/Info.plist`. Along with all the other entries, add the following:

```
<key>NSFaceIDUsageDescription</key>
<string>Enabling Face ID allows you quick and secure access to your
account.</string>
```

How to do it...

1. Let's start by adding dependencies to the `App.js` file, as follows:

```
import React, { Component } from 'react';
import {
  StyleSheet,
  Text,
  View
} from 'react-native';
import Button from 'react-native-button';
import TouchID from 'react-native-touch-id';
```

2. Next we'll define that `App` class and the initial `state`. We'll keep track of the authentication status on the `authStatus` property of `state`, as follows:

```
export default class App extends Component {
  state = {
    authStatus: null
  }
  // Defined in following steps
}
```

3. Let's define the `authenticate` method, which will be fired on button press, and will initiate authentication on the device. We can initiate authentication by executing the `TouchID` component's `authenticate` method. This method's first parameter is an optional string explaining the reason for the request, as follows:

```
authenticate = () => {
  TouchID.authenticate('Access secret information!')
    .then(this.handleAuthSuccess)
    .catch(this.handleAuthFailure);
}
```

4. This method fires the `handleAuthSuccess` method on success. Let's define it now. This method simply updates the `authStatus` property of `state` to the string `Authenticated`, as follows:

```
handleAuthSuccess = () => {
  this.setState({
    authStatus : 'Authenticated'
  });
}
```

5. Similarly, if authentication fails, the `handleAuthFailure` function will be called, which will update the same `state.authStatus` to the string `Not Authenticated`, as follows:

```
handleAuthFailure = () => {
  this.setState({
    authStatus : 'Not Authenticated'
  });
}
```

6. The `render` method will need a button to initiate the authentication request, and two `Text` components: one for a label, and one to display the authentication status, as follows:

```
render() {
  return (
    <View style={styles.container}>
      <Button
        containerStyle={styles.buttonContainer}
        style={styles.button}
        onPress={this.authenticate}>
          Authenticate
      </Button>
      <Text style={styles.label}>Authentication Status</Text>
      <Text style={styles.welcome}>{this.state.authStatus}</Text>
    </View>
  );
}
```

7. Finally, we'll add styles to color, size, and layout the UI, as follows:

```
const styles = StyleSheet.create({
  container: {
    flex: 1,
    justifyContent: 'center',
    alignItems: 'center',
    backgroundColor: '#fff',
  },
  welcome: {
    fontSize: 20,
    textAlign: 'center',
    margin: 10,
  },
  label: {
    textAlign: 'center',
    color: '#333333',
    marginBottom: 5,
  },
  buttonContainer: {
    width: 150,
    padding: 10,
    margin: 5,
    height: 40,
    overflow: 'hidden',
    backgroundColor: '#FF5722'
  },
  button: {
    fontSize: 16,
    color: 'white'
  }
});
```

How it works...

This recipe has illustrated how simple it is to incorporate native fingerprint and facial recognition security into a React Native app. The call to `TouchID.authenticate` also takes a second, optional options object parameter with three properties: `title` for the title of the confirmation dialog (Android only), `color` for the color of the dialog (Android only), and a `fallbackLabel` for editing the default **Show Password** label (iOS only).

Hiding application content when multitasking

Keeping the theme of application security going, we have to be wary sometimes of unwanted eyes and hands touching our devices and potentially getting access to our applications. In order to protect the user from prying eyes while looking at sensitive information, we can mask our application when the application is hidden, but still active. Once the user returns to the application, we would simply remove the mask and the user can continue using the app as normal. A good use case for this would be in a banking or password app that hides sensitive information when the app is not in the foreground.

This recipe will show you how to render an image to mask your application and remove it once the application returns to the foreground or active state. We will cover both iOS and Android; however, the implementation varies in its entirety. For iOS, we employ a pure Objective-C implementation for optimal performance. For Android, we're going to have to make some modifications to the `MainActivity` in order to send an event to our JavaScript layer that the application has lost focus. We will handle the rendering of the image mask there.

Getting ready

We're going to need an image handy to use as the mask when the app is not foregrounded. I chose to use an iPhone wallpaper, which you can find at:

```
http://www.hdiphone7wallpapers.com/2016/09/white-squares-iphone-7-and-7-plus-
wallpapers.html
```

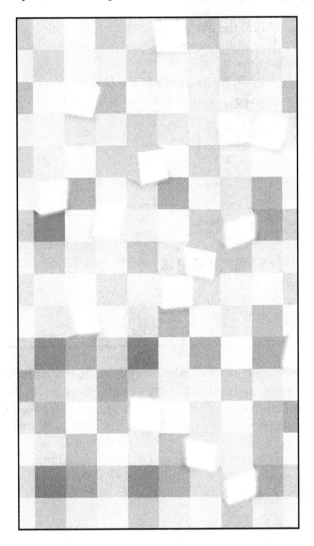

You can of course use whatever image you'd like. In this recipe, the image file will be named hidden.jpg, so rename your image accordingly.

We'll need a new pure React Native app. Let's call it HiddenContentApp.

How to do it...

1. Let's begin by adding the mask image to the iOS portion of the app. We'll need to open the `ios` folder of the project in Xcode, located in the `ios/` directory of the new React Native app.

2. We can add the `hidden.jpg` image to the project by dragging and dropping the image into the `Images.xcassets` folder of the project in Xcode, as shown in this screenshot:

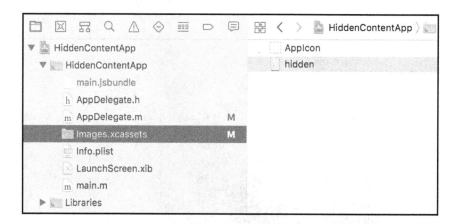

3. Next we'll add a new implementation and two methods to the `AppDelegate.m` file. The entirety of the file can be found as follows, including generated code. The code we're adding is marked in bold for clarity. We're extending the `applicationWillResignActive` method, which will fire whenever a given app changes from being foregrounded, to add an `imageView` with the `hidden.jpg` as its image. Similarly, we also need to extend the opposite method, `applicationDidBecomeActive`, to remove the image when the app is re-foregrounded:

```
#import "AppDelegate.h"

#import <React/RCTBundleURLProvider.h>
#import <React/RCTRootView.h>

@implementation AppDelegate {
  UIImageView *imageView;
}

- (BOOL)application:(UIApplication *)application
didFinishLaunchingWithOptions:(NSDictionary *)launchOptions
```

```
{
  NSURL *jsCodeLocation;

  jsCodeLocation = [[RCTBundleURLProvider sharedSettings]
jsBundleURLForBundleRoot:@"index" fallbackResource:nil];

  RCTRootView *rootView = [[RCTRootView alloc]
initWithBundleURL:jsCodeLocation
moduleName:@"HiddenContentApp"
initialProperties:nil
launchOptions:launchOptions];
  rootView.backgroundColor = [[UIColor alloc] initWithRed:1.0f
green:1.0f blue:1.0f alpha:1];

  self.window = [[UIWindow alloc] initWithFrame:[UIScreen
mainScreen].bounds];
  UIViewController *rootViewController = [UIViewController new];
  rootViewController.view = rootView;
  self.window.rootViewController = rootViewController;
  [self.window makeKeyAndVisible];
  return YES;
}

- (void)applicationWillResignActive:(UIApplication *)application {
  imageView = [[UIImageView alloc] initWithFrame:[self.window
frame]];
  [imageView setImage:[UIImage imageNamed:@"hidden.jpg"]];
  [self.window addSubview:imageView];
}

- (void)applicationDidBecomeActive:(UIApplication *)application {
  if(imageView != nil) {
    [imageView removeFromSuperview];
    imageView = nil;
  }
}

@end
```

4. With the previous three steps, all of the work required for displaying the mask in the iOS app is complete. Let's move on to the Android portion by opening the Android portion of the project in Android Studio. In Android Studio, select **Open an existing Android Studio project** and open the android directory of the project.

5. The only native code we'll need to update in the Android project lives in `MainActivity.java`, located here:

We'll need to add one method, as well as the three imports from React that the method uses. Again, the complete `MainActivity.java` file is below, with added code marked in bold. We're defining an `onWindowFocusChanged` method that extends the base method's functionality. The base `onWindowFocusChanged` Android method is fired whenever a given app's focus has changed, passing with it a `hasFocus` Boolean representing whether the app has focus or not. Our extension will effectively pass that `hasFocus` Boolean from the parent method down to the React Native layer via an event we're naming `focusChange`, as follows:

```
package com.hiddencontentapp;

import com.facebook.react.ReactActivity;
import com.facebook.react.bridge.Arguments;
import com.facebook.react.bridge.WritableMap;
import com.facebook.react.modules.core.DeviceEventManagerModule;

public class MainActivity extends ReactActivity {

  /**
   * Returns the name of the main component registered from JavaScript.
   * This is used to schedule rendering of the component.
   */
  @Override
  protected String getMainComponentName() {
    return "HiddenContentApp";
  }

  @Override
  public void onWindowFocusChanged(boolean hasFocus) {
    super.onWindowFocusChanged(hasFocus);
    if
(getReactNativeHost().getReactInstanceManager().getCurrentReactContext(
```

```
) != null) {
    WritableMap params = Arguments.createMap();
    params.putBoolean("appHasFocus", hasFocus);

    getReactNativeHost().getReactInstanceManager()
      .getCurrentReactContext()
.getJSModule(DeviceEventManagerModule.RCTDeviceEventEmitter.class)
      .emit("focusChange", params);
  }
 }
}
```

6. To use the `hidden.jpg` mask image in Android, we'll need to also add it to the React Native project. Let's create a new `assets` folder in the root of the React Native project, and add the `hidden.jpg` image file to the new folder.

7. With the native pieces in place, we're ready to turn to the JavaScript portion of the app. Let's add the imports we'll be using to `App.js`, as follows:

```
import React, {Component} from 'react';
import {
  StyleSheet,
  Text,
  View,
  DeviceEventEmitter,
  Image
} from 'react-native';
```

8. Next, let's create the `App` class and the initial `state`. The `state` will only need a `showMask` Boolean, which will dictate if the mask should be displayed, as follows:

```
export default class App extends Component {
  state = {
    showMask: null
  }
  // Defined in following steps
}
```

9. When the component mounts, we want to register an event listener to listen to events emitted from the native Android layer using the `DeviceEventEmitter`'s `addListener` method, passing the string `focusChange` as the name of the event to listen for as the first parameter, and a callback to execute as the second parameter. As you may recall, `focusChange` is the name we assigned the event in `MainActivity.java` in the `onWindowFocusChange` method in *step 5*. Register the event listener as follows:

```
componentWillMount() {
  this.subscription = DeviceEventEmitter.addListener(
    'focusChange',
    this.onFocusChange
  );
}
```

10. In this step we will save the event listener to the class member `this.subscription`. This will allow for the event listener to be cleaned up once the component is unmounted. We achieve this by simply calling the `remove` method on `this.subscription` when the component unmounts, via the `componentWillUnmount` life cycle hook, as follows:

```
componentWillUnmount() {
  this.subscription.remove();
}
```

11. Let's define the `onFocusChange` handler used in *step 9*. The method receives a `params` object with an `appHasFocus` Boolean that's been passed from the native layer via the `onWindowFocusChanged` method defined in *step 5*. By setting the `showMask` Boolean on `state` to the inverse of the `appHasFocus` Boolean, we can use that in the `render` function to toggle displaying the `hidden.jpg` image, as follows:

```
onFocusChange = (params) => {
  this.setState({showMask: !params.appHasFocus})
}
```

12. The `render` method's main content is not important in this recipe, but we can use it to apply the `hidden.jpg` mask image when the `showMask` property on state is `true`, as follows:

```
render() {
  if(this.state.showMask) {
    return (<Image source={require('./assets/hidden.jpg')} />);
```

```
  }
  return (
    <View style={styles.container}>
      <Text style={styles.welcome}>Welcome to React
Native!</Text>
    </View>
  );
}
```

13. The app is complete. Once the app is loaded, you should be able to go to the app selection view (double pressing home on iOS, or the square button on Android) and see the mask image applied to the app when it is not foregrounded. Note that Android emulators may not properly apply the mask as expected, so this feature might require an Android device for testing:

How it works...

In this recipe we've seen an example of having to use two separate approaches for accomplishing the same task. For iOS, we handled displaying the image mask exclusively in the native layer, without any need for the React Native layer. For Android, we used React Native to handle the image masking.

In *step 3* we extended two Objective-C methods: `applicationWillResignActive`, which fires when an app changes from being foregrounded, and `applicationDidBecomeActive`, which fires when the app is foregrounded. For each event, we simply toggle an `imageView` that displays the `hidden.jpg` image store in the `Images.xcassettes` folder in the Xcode project.

In *step 5* we used the React class `RCTDeviceEventEmitter` from the `DeviceEventManagerModule` to emit an event named `focusChange`, passing along a `params` object with the `appHasFocus` boolean to the React Native layer, as follows:

```
getReactNativeHost().getReactInstanceManager()
  .getCurrentReactContext()
  .getJSModule(DeviceEventManagerModule.RCTDeviceEventEmitter.class)
  .emit("focusChange", params);
}
```

In *step 9* we defined the `componentWillMount` life cycle hook, which sets up an event listener for this `focusChange` event that will be emitted from the native Android layer, firing the `onFocusChange` method, which will update the value of `state`'s `showMask` value based on the native `appHasFocus` value, triggering a rerender, displaying the mask as appropriate.

Background processing on iOS

Over the last several years, processing power in mobile devices has increased considerably. Users are demanding richer experiences and one method of achieving improved performance on modern mobile devices is via multithreading. Most mobile devices today are powered by multicore processors, and their operating systems now offer developers easy abstractions for executing code in the background, without interfering with the performance of the app's UI.

This recipe will cover both the use of iOS's **Grand Central Dispatch (GCD)** to execute asynchronous background processing on a new thread, and communicating back to the React Native layer when the processing is complete.

Getting ready

For this recipe, we'll need a new pure React Native application. Let's name it MultiThreadingApp.

We'll also be using the react-native-button library. Install it with npm:

```
npm install react-native-button --save
```

Alternatively, we can use yarn:

```
yarn add react-native-button --save
```

How to do it...

1. We'll start by opening the iOS Project in Xcode, located in the ios directory of the new React Native app.
2. Let's add a new Cocoa class file named BackgroundTaskManager of subclass NSObject. Refer to the *Exposing Custom iOS Modules* recipe in this chapter for more details on doing this in Xcode.
3. Next, lets wire the new module to the React RCTBrideModule in the new module's header file, BackgroundTaskManager.h. The code to be added is marked in bold in the following snippet:

```
#import <Foundation/Foundation.h>
#import <dispatch/dispatch.h>
#import "RCTBridgeModule.h"

@interface BackgroundTaskManager : NSObject <RCTBridgeModule> {
  dispatch_queue_t backgroundQueue;
}

@end
```

4. We'll implement the native module in the BackgroundTaskManager.m file. Again, the new code we're adding is marked in bold in the following snippet:

```
#import "BackgroundTaskManager.h"
#import "RCTBridge.h"
#import "RCTEventDispatcher.h"

@implementation BackgroundTaskManager

@synthesize bridge = _bridge;
```

```
RCT_EXPORT_MODULE();

RCT_EXPORT_METHOD(loadInBackground) {
  backgroundQueue =
dispatch_queue_create("com.moduscreate.bgqueue", NULL);
  dispatch_async(backgroundQueue, ^{
    NSLog(@"processing background");
    [self.bridge.eventDispatcher
sendAppEventWithName:@"backgroundProgress" body:@{@"status":
@"Loading"}];
    [NSThread sleepForTimeInterval:5];
    NSLog(@"slept");
    dispatch_async(dispatch_get_main_queue(), ^{
      NSLog(@"Done processing; main thread");
      [self.bridge.eventDispatcher
sendAppEventWithName:@"backgroundProgress" body:@{@"status":
@"Done"}];
    });
  });
}

@end
```

5. Let's turn to the JavaScript layer next. We'll start by adding dependencies to the App.js file. As part of the dependencies, we will also need to import the BackgroundTaskManager native module that we defined in *step 3* and *step 4*, as follows:

```
import React, { Component } from 'react';
import {
  StyleSheet,
  Text,
  View,
  NativeModules,
  NativeAppEventEmitter
} from 'react-native';
import Button from 'react-native-button';

const BackgroundTaskManager = NativeModules.BackgroundTaskManager;
```

6. Let's define the App class, with an initial state of backgroundTaskStatus set to the string Not Started, and a doNothingCount property initialized to 0, as follows:

```
export default class App extends Component {
  state = {
    backgroundTaskStatus: 'Not Started',
```

```
        counter: 0
    }
    // Defined in following steps
}
```

7. We'll need to listen to the `backgroundProcess` event that will be emitted from the native iOS layer from the custom module we created in *step 3* and *step 4*. Let's set up an event listener using the `NativeAppEventEmitter` React Native component, which sets the `backgroundTaskStatus` property of `state` to the value of `status` on the event object received from the native event, as follows:

```
componentWillMount = () => {
  this.subscription = NativeAppEventEmitter.addListener(
    'backgroundProgress',
    event => this.setState({ backgroundTaskStatus: event.status
})
  );
}
```

8. When the component unmounts, we need to remove the event listener from the previous step, as follows:

```
componentWillUnmount = () => {
  this.subscription.remove();
}
```

9. The UI will have two buttons that will each need a method to call when pressed. The `runBackgroundTask` will run the `loadInBackground` method that we defined and exported from the native iOS layer on the `BackgroundTaskManager` custom native module. The `increaseCounter` button will simply increase the `counter` property on `state` by 1, serving to show how the main thread is not blocked, as follows:

```
runBackgroundTask = () => {
  BackgroundTaskManager.loadInBackground();
}

increaseCounter = () => {
  this.setState({
    counter: this.state.counter + 1
  });
}
```

10. The UI of the app will consist of two buttons to show the `Button` components, and a `Text` component for displaying the values saved on `state`. The **Run Task** button will execute the `runBackgroundTask` method to kick off a background process, and `this.state.backgroundTaskStatus` will update to display a new status for the process. For the five seconds that the background process is running, pressing the **Increase Counter** button will still increase the counter by 1, demonstrating that the background process is non-blocking, as shown in the following snippet:

```
render() {
  return (
    <View style={styles.container}>
      <Button
        containerStyle={styles.buttonContainer}
        style={styles.buttonStyle}
        onPress={this.runBackgroundTask}>
          Run Task
      </Button>
      <Text style={styles.instructions}>
        Background Task Status:
      </Text>
      <Text style={styles.welcome}>
        {this.state.backgroundTaskStatus}
      </Text>
      <Text style={styles.instructions}>
        Pressing "Increase Conter" button shows that the task is
        not blocking the main thread
      </Text>
      <Button
        containerStyle={[
          styles.buttonContainer,
          styles.altButtonContainer
        ]}
        style={styles.buttonStyle}
        onPress={this.increaseCounter}
      >
          Increase Counter
      </Button>
      <Text style={styles.instructions}>
        Current Count:
      </Text>
      <Text style={styles.welcome}>
        {this.state.counter}
      </Text>
    </View>
  );
}
```

11. As a final step, let's layout and style the app with the styles block, as follows:

```
const styles = StyleSheet.create({
  container: {
    flex: 1,
    justifyContent: 'center',
    alignItems: 'center',
    backgroundColor: '#F5FCFF',
  },
  welcome: {
    fontSize: 20,
    textAlign: 'center',
    margin: 10,
  },
  instructions: {
    textAlign: 'center',
    color: '#333333',
    marginBottom: 5,
    marginLeft: 20,
    marginRight: 20
  },
  buttonContainer: {
    width: 150,
    padding: 10,
    margin: 5,
    height: 40,
    overflow: 'hidden',
    borderRadius: 4,
    backgroundColor: '#FF5722'
  },
  altButtonContainer : {
    backgroundColor : '#CDDC39',
    marginTop : 30
  },
  buttonStyle: {
    fontSize: 16,
    color: 'white'
  }
});
```

How it works...

In this recipe, we created a native module similar to the module covered in the *Exposing custom iOS modules* recipe from earlier in this chapter. We defined the native module to perform arbitrary execution in the background of the React Native app. In this recipe the background process is made up of the following three steps:

1. Spawn a new thread.
2. Sleep for five seconds on the new thread.
3. After the five second sleep (simulating the end of a running background process), an event is dispatched from the iOS layer to the React Native layer, letting it know that the process has been completed. This is accomplished via the OS's GCD API.

The purpose of the UI in this app is to exhibit that multithreading has been achieved. If the background process was executed in the React Native layer, due to JavaScript's single-threaded nature, the app would have locked up for five seconds while that process was running. When you press a button, the bridge is invoked, whereupon messages can be posted to the native layer. If the native thread is currently busy sleeping, then we cannot process this message. By offloading that processing to a new thread, both can be executed at the same time.

Background processing on Android

In this recipe we'll be building out an Android equivalent to the previous recipe. This recipe will also use the native Android layer to create a new process, keep that process running by sleeping for five seconds, and allow user interaction via the button to exhibit that the app's main processing thread is not blocked.

While the end result will be very much the same, spawning a new process in an Android project is handled a bit differently from iOS. This recipe will make use of the native `AsyncTask` function, specialized for handling short-running background processes, to allow execution in the React Native layer without blocking the main thread.

Getting ready

For this recipe we'll need to create a new pure React Native app. Let's name it `MultiThreadingApp`.

We will also be using the `react-native-button` library. Install it with `npm`:

```
npm install react-native-button --save
```

Alternatively, we can use `yarn`:

```
yarn add react-native-button
```

How to do it...

1. Let's start by opening the Android project in Android Studio. In Android Studio, select **Open an existing Android Studio project** and open the `android` directory of the new project.

2. We'll need two new Java classes: `BackgroundTaskManager` and `BackgroundTaskPackage`.

3. Now that both classes have been created, let's open `BackgroundTaskManager.java` and begin implementing the native module that will wrap an `AsyncTask` operation, starting with imports and defining the class. Furthermore, like any other native Android module, we'll need to define the `getName` method, used to provide React Native with a name for the module, as follows:

```java
package com.multithreadingapp;

import android.os.AsyncTask;

import com.facebook.react.bridge.Arguments;
import com.facebook.react.bridge.ReactApplicationContext;
import com.facebook.react.bridge.ReactContextBaseJavaModule;
import com.facebook.react.bridge.ReactMethod;
import com.facebook.react.bridge.WritableMap;
import com.facebook.react.modules.core.DeviceEventManagerModule;

public class BackgroundTaskManager extends
ReactContextBaseJavaModule {
  public BackgroundTaskManager(ReactApplicationContext
reactApplicationContext) {
    super(reactApplicationContext);
```

```
  }

  @Override
  public String getName() {
    return "BackgroundTaskManager";
  }

  // Defined in following steps
}
```

4. In order to execute an `AsyncTask`, it needs to be subclassed by a private class. We'll need to add a new private inner `BackgroundLoadTask` subclass for this. Before we define it, let's first add a `loadInBackground` method that will ultimately be exported to the React Native layer. This method simply creates a new instance of `BackgroundLoadTask` and calls its `execute` method, as follows:

```
public class BackgroundTaskManager extends
ReactContextBaseJavaModule {
 // Defined in previous step
  @ReactMethod
  public void loadInBackground() {
    BackgroundLoadTask backgroundLoadTask = new
BackgroundLoadTask();
    backgroundLoadTask.execute();
  }
}
```

5. The `BackgroundLoadTask` subclass will also be using a helper function for sending events back and forth across the React Native bridge to communicate the status of the background process. The `sendEvent` method takes an `eventName` and `params` as arguments, then uses React Native's `RCTDeviceEventEmitter` class to `emit` the event, as follows:

```
public class BackgroundTaskManager extends
ReactContextBaseJavaModule {
  // Defined in steps above

  private void sendEvent(String eventName, WritableMap params) {
  getReactApplicationContext().getJSModule(DeviceEventManagerModule.R
CTDeviceEventEmitter.class).emit(eventName, params);
  }
}
```

6. Now let's move on to defining the `BackgroundLoadTask` subclass, which extends `AsyncTask`. The subclass will be made up of three methods: `doInBackground` for spinning up a new thread and sleeping it for five minutes, `onProgressUpdate` for sending a `"Loading"` status to the React Native layer, and `onPostExecute` for sending a `"Done"` status when the background task has completed, as follows:

```java
public class BackgroundTaskManager extends
ReactContextBaseJavaModule {
  // Defined in above steps

  private class BackgroundLoadTask extends AsyncTask<String,
String, String> {
    @Override
    protected String doInBackground(String... params) {
      publishProgress("Loading");
      try {
        Thread.sleep(5000);
      } catch (Exception e) {
        e.printStackTrace();
      }
      return "Done";
    }

    @Override
    protected void onProgressUpdate(String... values) {
      WritableMap params = Arguments.createMap();
      params.putString("status", "Loading");
      sendEvent("backgroundProgress", params);
    }

    @Override
    protected void onPostExecute(String s) {
      WritableMap params = Arguments.createMap();
      params.putString("status", "Done");
      sendEvent("backgroundProgress", params);
    }
  }
}
```

7. Since the only difference between the iOS implementation and the Android implementation lives in the native layer of the recipe, you can follow *step 5* to *step 11* of the previous recipe to implement the JavaScript portion of the app.

8. The final app should behave and look (aside from differences in devices) the same as the app in the previous recipe:

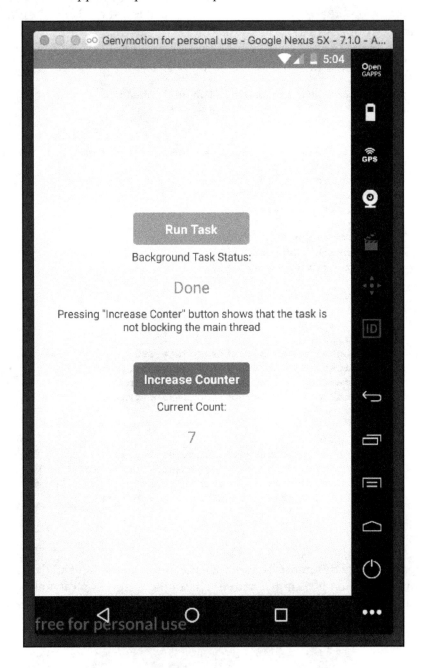

How it works...

In this recipe, we mimicked the functionality we created in the *Background processing on iOS* recipe on Android. We created an Android native module with a method which, when invoked, performs arbitrary execution in the background (sleep for five seconds). When the process is complete, it emits an event to the React Native layer, whereupon we update the app UI to reflect the status of the background process. Android has multiple options for performing multithreaded operations natively. In this recipe, we used `AsyncTask`, since it is geared towards short-running (several seconds) processes, it is relatively simple to implement, and the operating system manages thread creation and resource allocation for us. You can read more about `AsyncTask` in the official documentation at:

```
https://developer.android.com/reference/android/os/AsyncTask
```

Playing audio files on iOS

In the chapter *Implementing Complex User Interfaces – Part III*, we covered building out a relatively sophisticated little audio player in the *Creating an Audio Player* recipe using the `Audio` component provided by the Expo SDK. One of the shortcoming of Expo's `Audio` component, however, is that it cannot be used to play audio when the app is backgrounded. Using the native layer is currently the only way to achieve this.

In this recipe, we will create a native module to show the iOS MediaPicker and then select a music file to play. The selected file will play through the native iOS media player, which allows audio to be played when the app is backgrounded, and allows the user to control the audio via the native iOS control center.

Getting ready

For this recipe, we'll need to create a new pure React Native app. Let's call it `AudioPlayerApp`.

We'll also be using the `react-native-button` library, which can be installed with `npm`:

```
npm install react-native-button --save
```

Alternatively, we can use `yarn`:

```
yarn add react-native-button
```

This is a recipe that should only be expected to work on a real device. You'll also want to make sure you have music synced to the iOS device and available in the media library.

How to do it...

1. Let's start by opening the iOS Project in Xcode located in the `ios` directory of the new React Native app.
2. Next, we'll create a new Objective-C Cocoa class called `MediaManager`.
3. In the `MediaManager` header (`.h`) file, we need to import `MPMediaPickerController` and `MPMusicPlayerController`, along with the React Native bridge (`RCTBridgeModule`), as follows:

```objc
#import <Foundation/Foundation.h>
#import <MediaPlayer/MediaPlayer.h>

#import <React/RCTBridgeModule.h>
#import <React/RCTEventDispatcher.h>

@interface MediaManager : NSObject<RCTBridgeModule,
MPMediaPickerControllerDelegate>

@property (nonatomic, retain) MPMediaPickerController *mediaPicker;
@property (nonatomic, retain) MPMusicPlayerController *musicPlayer;

@end
```

4. First, we are going to need to work on adding the native `MediaPicker` in the `MediaManager` implementation (`MediaManager.m`). The first methods will be for showing and hiding the `MediaPicker`: `showMediaPicker` and `hideMediaPicker`, as follows:

```objc
#import "MediaManager.h"
#import "AppDelegate.h"

@implementation MediaManager
RCT_EXPORT_MODULE();

@synthesize bridge = _bridge;
@synthesize musicPlayer;
```

```
#pragma mark private-methods

-(void)showMediaPicker {
  if(self.mediaPicker == nil) {
    self.mediaPicker = [[MPMediaPickerController alloc]
initWithMediaTypes:MPMediaTypeAnyAudio];
    [self.mediaPicker setDelegate:self];
    [self.mediaPicker setAllowsPickingMultipleItems:NO];
    [self.mediaPicker setShowsCloudItems:NO];
    self.mediaPicker.prompt = @"Select song";
  }
  AppDelegate *delegate = (AppDelegate *)[[UIApplication
sharedApplication] delegate];
  [delegate.window.rootViewController
presentViewController:self.mediaPicker animated:YES
completion:nil];
}

void hideMediaPicker() {
  AppDelegate *delegate = (AppDelegate *)[[UIApplication
sharedApplication] delegate];
  [delegate.window.rootViewController
dismissViewControllerAnimated:YES completion:nil];
}

// Defined on following steps

@end
```

5. Next, we'll implement the two actions that
   the `mediaPicker` needs: `didPickMediaItems` for picking a media item,
   and `mediaPickerDidCancel` for cancelling the action, as follows:

```
-(void) mediaPicker:(MPMediaPickerController *)mediaPicker
didPickMediaItems:(MPMediaItemCollection *)mediaItemCollection {
  MPMediaItem *mediaItem = mediaItemCollection.items[0];
  NSURL *assetURL = [mediaItem
valueForProperty:MPMediaItemPropertyAssetURL];
  [self.bridge.eventDispatcher sendAppEventWithName:@"SongPlaying"
                                              body:[mediaItem
valueForProperty:MPMediaItemPropertyTitle]];
  if(musicPlayer == nil) {
    musicPlayer = [MPMusicPlayerController systemMusicPlayer];
  }
  [musicPlayer setQueueWithItemCollection:mediaItemCollection];
  [musicPlayer play];
  hideMediaPicker();
}
```

```
-(void) mediaPickerDidCancel:(MPMediaPickerController *)mediaPicker
{
   hideMediaPicker();
}
```

6. Next, we're going to need to expose our `MediaManager` to the React Native bridge and create a method that will be invoked to show the `MediaPicker`, as follows:

```
RCT_EXPORT_MODULE();
RCT_EXPORT_METHOD(showSongs) {
   [self showMediaPicker];
}
```

7. We're ready to move on to the JavaScript portion. Let's start by adding dependencies to `App.js`. We also need to import the `MediaManager` native module we created in *step 3* to *step 6* using the `NativeModules` component, as follows:

```
import React, { Component } from 'react';
import {
   StyleSheet,
   Text,
   View,
   NativeModules,
   NativeAppEventEmitter
} from 'react-native';
import Button from 'react-native-button';
const MediaManager = NativeModules.MediaManager;
```

8. Let's define the `App` class and the initial `state`. The `currentSong` property will hold the track info for the currently playing song, as passed from the native layer, as follows:

```
export default class App extends Component {
   state = {
      currentSong: null
   }

   // Defined on following steps
}
```

9. When the component mounts, we'll subscribe to the `SongPlaying` event that will be emitted from the native layer when a song begins playing. We'll save the event listener to a local `subscription` class variable so that we can clean it up with the `remove` method when the component unmounts, as follows:

```
componentWillMount() {
  this.subscription = NativeAppEventEmitter.addListener(
    'SongPlaying',
    this.updateCurrentlyPlaying
  );
}

componentWillUnmount = () => {
  this.subscription.remove();
}
```

10. We'll also need a method for updating the `currentSong` value on `state`, and a method for calling the `showSongs` method on the native `MediaManager` module we defined in *step 3* to *step 6*, as follows:

```
updateCurrentlyPlaying = (currentSong) => {
  this.setState({ currentSong });
}

showSongs() {
  MediaManager.showSongs();
}
```

11. The `render` method will be made up of a `Button` component for executing the `showSongs` method when pressed, and `Text` components for displaying the info for the song that's currently playing, as follows:

```
render() {
  return (
    <View style={styles.container}>
      <Button
        containerStyle={styles.buttonContainer}
        style={styles.buttonStyle}
        onPress={this.showSongs}>
          Pick Song
      </Button>
      <Text style={styles.instructions}>Song Playing:</Text>
      <Text
style={styles.welcome}>{this.state.currentSong}</Text>
    </View>
  );
}
```

12. Finally, we'll add our styles for laying out and styling the app, as follows:

```
const styles = StyleSheet.create({
  container: {
    flex: 1,
    justifyContent: 'center',
    alignItems: 'center',
    backgroundColor: '#F5FCFF',
  },
  welcome: {
    fontSize: 20,
    textAlign: 'center',
    margin: 10,
  },
  instructions: {
    textAlign: 'center',
    color: '#333333',
    marginBottom: 5,
  },
  buttonContainer: {
    width: 150,
    padding: 10,
    margin: 5,
    height: 40,
    overflow: 'hidden',
    borderRadius: 4,
    backgroundColor: '#3B5998'
  },
  buttonStyle: {
    fontSize: 16,
    color: '#fff'
  }
});
```

How it works...

In this recipe we covered how to use the Media Player in iOS by wrapping its functionality in a native module. The media player framework allows us to access the native iPod library, and play audio files from the library on the device using the same functionality as the native iOS Music app.

Playing audio files on Android

A benefit that Google likes to claim that Android has over iOS is flexibility in dealing with file storage. Android devices support external SD cards that can be filled with media files and do not need a proprietary method of adding multimedia as iOS does.

In this recipe, we will use Android's native `MediaPicker`, which is started from an intent. We will then be able to pick a song and have it play through our application.

Getting ready

For this recipe, we'll create a React Native application titled `AudioPlayer`.

In this recipe, we will use the `react-native-button` library. To install it, run the following command in the terminal from your project root directory:

```
$ npm install react-native-button --save
```

Make sure you have music files available in your `Music/` directory on your Android device or emulator.

How to do it...

1. Let's start by opening the Android project using Android Studio. In Android Studio, select **Open an existing Android Studio project** and open the `android` directory of the project.

2. We'll need two new Java classes for this recipe: `MediaManager` and `MediaPackage`.

3. Our `MediaManager` will use intents to show the `mediaPicker`, `MediaPlayer` to play music, and `MediaMetadataRetriever` to parse metadata information from the audio file to send back to the JavaScript layer. Let's start by importing all of the dependencies we'll need in the `MediaManager.java` file, as follows:

   ```
   import android.app.Activity;
   import android.content.Intent;
   import android.media.AudioManager;
   import android.media.MediaMetadataRetriever;
   import android.media.MediaPlayer;
   import android.net.Uri;
   import android.provider.MediaStore;
   ```

```
import com.facebook.react.bridge.ActivityEventListener;
import com.facebook.react.bridge.Arguments;
import com.facebook.react.bridge.ReactApplicationContext;
import com.facebook.react.bridge.ReactContextBaseJavaModule;
import com.facebook.react.bridge.ReactMethod;
import com.facebook.react.bridge.WritableMap;
import com.facebook.react.modules.core.DeviceEventManagerModule;
```

4. `showSongs`, `getName`, `playSong`, `mediaPlayer`, `onActivityResult`, `mediaMetadataRetreiver`, **and** `SongPlaying` **should be in code formatting.** Replace with:

```
public class MediaManager extends ReactContextBaseJavaModule
implements ActivityEventListener {
  private MediaPlayer mediaPlayer = null;
  private MediaMetadataRetriever mediaMetadataRetriever = null;

  public MediaManager(ReactApplicationContext
reactApplicationContext) {
    super(reactApplicationContext);
    reactApplicationContext.addActivityEventListener(this);
  }

  @Override
  public String getName() {
    return "MediaManager";
  }

  @Override
  public void onCatalystInstanceDestroy() {
    super.onCatalystInstanceDestroy();
    mediaPlayer.stop();
    mediaPlayer.release();
    mediaPlayer = null;
  }

  @ReactMethod
  public void showSongs() {
    Activity activity = getCurrentActivity();
    Intent intent = new Intent(Intent.ACTION_PICK,
MediaStore.Audio.Media.EXTERNAL_CONTENT_URI);
    activity.startActivityForResult(intent, 10);
  }

  @Override
  public void onActivityResult(Activity activity, int requestCode,
int resultCode, Intent data) {
    if (data != null) {
```

```
        playSong(data.getData());
      }
    }

    @Override
    public void onNewIntent(Intent intent) {
    }

    private void playSong(Uri uri) {
      try {
        if (mediaPlayer != null) {
          mediaPlayer.stop();
          mediaPlayer.reset();
        } else {
          mediaMetadataRetriever = new MediaMetadataRetriever();
          mediaPlayer = new MediaPlayer();
          mediaPlayer.setAudioStreamType(AudioManager.STREAM_MUSIC);
        }

        mediaPlayer.setDataSource(getReactApplicationContext(), uri);

        mediaPlayer.prepare();
        mediaPlayer.start();

mediaMetadataRetriever.setDataSource(getReactApplicationContext(),
uri);
        String artist =
mediaMetadataRetriever.extractMetadata(MediaMetadataRetriever.METAD
ATA_KEY_ARTIST);
        String songTitle =
mediaMetadataRetriever.extractMetadata(MediaMetadataRetriever.METAD
ATA_KEY_TITLE);

        WritableMap params = Arguments.createMap();
        params.putString("songPlaying", artist + " - " + songTitle);

        getReactApplicationContext()
.getJSModule(DeviceEventManagerModule.RCTDeviceEventEmitter.class)
          .emit("SongPlaying", params);
      } catch (Exception ex) {
        ex.printStackTrace();
      }
    }
  }
```

5. The custom module will also need to be added to the `getPackages` array in the `MainApplication.java` file, as follows:

```java
protected List<ReactPackage> getPackages() {
    return Arrays.<ReactPackage>asList(
        new MainReactPackage(),
        new MediaPackage()
    );
}
```

6. As covered in the *Exposing Custom Android Modules* recipe earlier in this chapter, we must add the requisite boilerplate to `MediaPackage.java` for our `MediaManager` custom module to be exported to the React Native layer. Refer to that recipe for a more thorough explanation. Add the requisite boilerplate as follows:

```java
import com.facebook.react.ReactPackage;
import com.facebook.react.bridge.NativeModule;
import com.facebook.react.bridge.ReactApplicationContext;
import com.facebook.react.uimanager.ViewManager;

import java.util.ArrayList;
import java.util.Collections;
import java.util.List;

public class MediaPackage implements ReactPackage {
    @Override
    public List<ViewManager>
createViewManagers(ReactApplicationContext reactContext) {
        return Collections.emptyList();
    }

    @Override
    public List<NativeModule>
createNativeModules(ReactApplicationContext reactContext) {
        List<NativeModule> modules = new ArrayList<>();

        modules.add(new MediaManager(reactContext));

        return modules;
    }
}
```

7. The JavaScript layer for the Android app is identical to that found in the previous iOS recipe. Use *step 7* to *step 12* of this recipe to complete the final portion of the app.

13
Integration with Native Applications

In this chapter, we will cover the following recipes:

- Combining a React Native app and a Native iOS app
- Communicating from an iOS app to React Native
- Communicating from React Native to an iOS app container
- Handle being invoked by an external iOS app
- Combining a React Native app and a native Android app
- Communicating from an Android app to React Native
- Communicating from React Native to an Android app container
- Handle being invoked by an external Android app

Introduction

React Native was introduced as a solution to build native applications using JavaScript, with the goal of granting more developers the ability to build truly native applications for multiple platforms. As a consequence of building a React Native application with a team, it can be common for JavaScript developers and native developers to work closely together.

One of the advantages of React Native's ability to render native UI views is that they can be easily embedded inside existing native apps. It is not uncommon for companies to already have sophisticated native apps that are critical to their line of business. There may be no immediate need to rewrite their entire codebase in React Native if the app is not broken. In such a case, React Native can be leveraged by both JavaScript and native developers to write React Native code that can be integrated into an existing app.

This chapter will focus exclusively on using React Native inside existing native iOS and Android applications. We will cover rendering a React Native app within a native app, how to communicate between the React Native app and its native parent app, and how our React Native app can be invoked with other apps on a user's device.

When working on the Android recipes, it is recommended that you enable the auto-import settings in Android Studio or use *Alt+Enter* to perform a quick fix code completion for the class import.

Combining a React Native app and a Native iOS app

In the event that you work for a company or have a client that has an active iOS app out in the world, it may not be advantageous to rewrite it from scratch, especially if it is well-built, used frequently, and praised by its users. If you just want to build new functionality using React Native, the React Native app can be embedded and rendered inside an existing native iOS app.

This recipe will walk through creating a blank iOS app and adding it to a React Native app so that the two layers can communicate with each other. We will cover two ways of rendering the React Native app: embedded inside the application as a nested view, and another as a full-screen implementation. The steps that are discussed in this recipe serve as a baseline for rendering React Native apps, along with native iOS apps.

Getting ready

This recipe will be referencing a native iOS application named `EmbeddedApp`. We will walk through creating the sample iOS application in this section. If you already have an iOS app you intend on integrating with React Native, you can skip ahead to the recipe instructions. You will, however, need to be sure that you have `cocoapods` installed. This library is a package manager for Xcode projects. It can be installed via Homebrew using the following command:

```
brew install cocoapods
```

With `cocoapods` installed, the next step is creating a new native iOS project in Xcode. This can be done by opening Xcode and choosing **File | New | Project**. In the window that follows, choose the default **Single View Application** iOS template to get started, and hit **Next**.

In the options screen for the new project, be sure to set the **Product Name** field to `EmbeddedApp`:

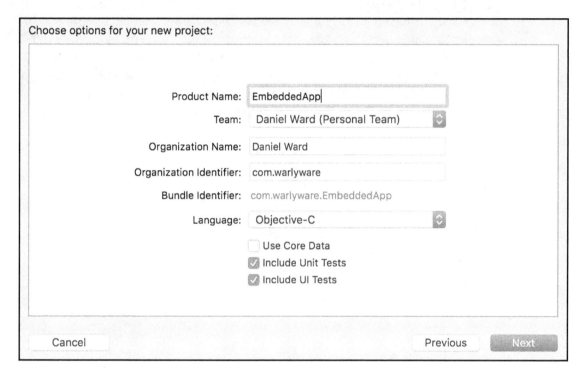

How to do it...

1. We'll begin by creating a new vanilla React Native app that will serve as the root of our project. Let's name the new project `EmbedApp`. You can create the new React Native app with the CLI using the following command:

```
react-native init EmbedApp
```

2. By creating the new app with the CLI, the `ios` and `android` subfolders will be automatically created for us, holding the native code for each platform. Let's move the native app we created in the *Getting ready* section to the `ios` folder so that it lives at `/EmbedApp/ios/EmbeddedApp`.

3. Now that we have the basic structure we need for the app, we'll need to add a Podfile. This is a file, similar to `package.json` in web development, that keeps track of all of the cocoapod dependencies (called pods) that are used in a project. The Podfile should always live in the root of the vanilla iOS project, which in our case is `/EmbedApp/ios/EmbeddedApp`. In a Terminal, `cd` into this directory and run the `pod init` command. This generates a base Podfile for you.

4. Next, open the Podfile in your favorite IDE. We'll be adding the pods that are needed for the app to this file. The following is the contents of the final Podfile, with the newly added React Native dependencies in bold:

```
target 'EmbeddedApp' do
  # Uncomment the next line if you're using Swift or would like to
use dynamic frameworks
  # use_frameworks!

  # Pods for EmbeddedApp

  target 'EmbeddedAppTests' do
    inherit! :search_paths
    # Pods for testing
  end

  target 'EmbeddedAppUITests' do
    inherit! :search_paths
    # Pods for testing
  end

  # Pods that will be used in the app
  pod 'React', :path => '../../node_modules/react-native',
:subspecs => [
    'Core',
    'CxxBridge', # Include this for RN >= 0.47
    'DevSupport', # Include this to enable In-App Devmenu if RN >=
0.43
    'RCTText',
    'RCTNetwork',
    'RCTWebSocket', # Needed for debugging
    'RCTAnimation', # Needed for FlatList and animations running on
native UI thread
    # Add any other subspecs you want to use in your project
  ]
```

```
# Explicitly include Yoga if you are using RN >= 0.42.0
  pod 'yoga', :path => '../../node_modules/react-
native/ReactCommon/yoga'

# Third party deps podspec link
  pod 'DoubleConversion', :podspec => '../../node_modules/react-
native/third-party-podspecs/DoubleConversion.podspec'
  pod 'glog', :podspec => '../../node_modules/react-native/third-
party-podspecs/glog.podspec'
  pod 'Folly', :podspec => '../../node_modules/react-native/third-
party-podspecs/Folly.podspec'

end
```

Notice how each of the paths listed in the React Native dependencies that we're adding point to the `/node_modules` folder of the React Native project. If your native project (in our case, `EmbeddedApp`) was at a different location, these references to `/node_modules` would have to be updated accordingly.

5. With the Podfile in place, installing the pods themselves is as easy as running the `pod install` command from the Terminal in the same directory we created the Podfile.

6. Next, let's return to the React Native app at the root directory of the project, `/EmbedApp`. We'll start by removing the generated code in `index.js`, and replacing it with our own simple React Native app. At the bottom of the file, we'll use the `registerComponent` method on the `AppRegistry` component to register `EmbedApp` as the root component of the React Native app. This will be a very simple app that just renders the text `Hello in React Native` so that it can be distinguished from the native layer in later steps:

```
import React, { Component } from 'react';
import {
  AppRegistry,
  StyleSheet,
  View,
  Text
} from 'react-native';

class EmbedApp extends Component {
  render() {
    return (
      <View style={styles.container}>
        <Text>Hello in React Native</Text>
      </View>
```

```
      );
    }
  }

  const styles = StyleSheet.create({
    container: {
      flex: 1,
      justifyContent: 'center',
      alignItems: 'center',
      backgroundColor: '#F5FCFF',
    }
  });

  AppRegistry.registerComponent('EmbedApp', () => EmbedApp);
```

7. Now that we have a React Native app, we can move to the native code. When we initialized cocoapods in *step 3*, it also generated a new `.xcworkspace` file. Be sure to close the `EmbeddedApp` project in Xcode, then re-open it in Xcode using the `EmbeddedApp.xcworkspace` file.

8. In Xcode, let's open `Main.storyboard`:

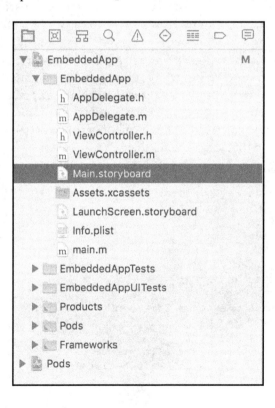

9. In the storyboard, we'll need to add two buttons: one labeled **Open React Native App** and one labeled **Open React Native App (Embedded)**. We'll also need a new container view below the two buttons. The resulting storyboard should look something like this:

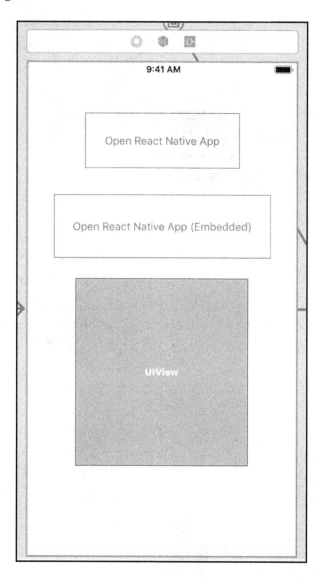

10. Next, we'll need a new a new Cocoa Touch Class. This can be created from the menus by choosing **File | New | File.** We'll name the class `EmbeddedViewController` and assign it a subclass of `UIViewController`:

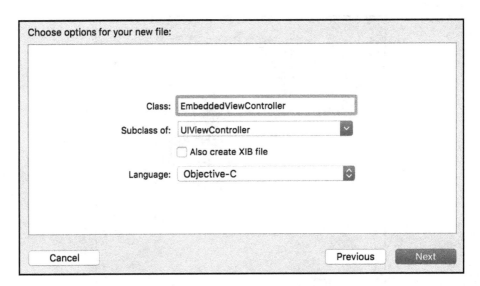

11. Let's return to `Main.storyboard`. In the new scene that's created by adding the class in the previous step (second **View Controller Scene**), select the **View Controller** child. Make sure that the **Identity inspector** is open in the right-hand panel:

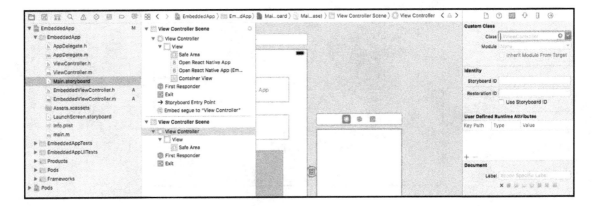

With the **View Controller** selected, change the **Class** value to our newly created class, EmbeddedViewController:

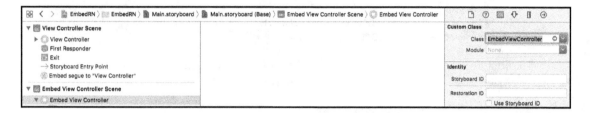

12. Next, in the top **View Controller Scene**, select the **Embed segue** object:

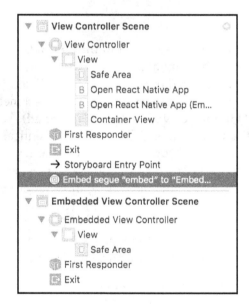

13. With the segue selected, select the Attributes inspector from the right-hand panel, and update the **Identifier** field to the **embed** value. We will use this identifier to embed the React Native layer within the native app:

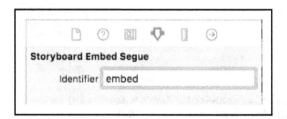

14. We're ready to build out the `ViewController` implementation. Open
    the `ViewController.m` file. We'll start with the imports:

    ```
    #import "ViewController.h"
    #import "EmbeddedViewController.h"
    #import <React/RCTRootView.h>
    ```

15. Just beneath the imports, we can add an interface definition to point to the
    `EmbeddedViewController` we created in *step 10*:

    ```
    @interface ViewController () {
        EmbeddedViewController *embeddedViewController;
    }

    @end
    ```

16. Following is the `@interface`, we'll add the methods we need to the
    `@implementation`. The first method, `openRNAppButtonPressed`, will be wired
    to the first button we created in the storyboard, labeled **Open React Native App**.
    Likewise, the `openRNAppEmbeddedButtonPressed` method will be wired to the
    second button, **Open React Native App (Embedded)**.
    You'll likely notice that the methods are almost identical, with the second method
    referencing `embeddedViewController`, the same `EmbeddedViewController`
    class we created in step 10 (`[embeddedViewController
    setView:rootView];`). Both methods define `jsCodeLocation` with the value
    of `http://localhost:8081/index.bundle?platform=ios`, which is the
    URL that the React Native app will be served from. Also, take note that
    the `moduleName` property in both methods is set to `EmbedApp`, which is the name
    that the React Native app is exported as, which we defined in *step 6*:

    ```
    @implementation ViewController

    - (void)viewDidLoad {
        [super viewDidLoad];
        // Do any additional setup after loading the view, typically
    from a nib.
    }

    - (void)didReceiveMemoryWarning {
        [super didReceiveMemoryWarning];
        // Dispose of any resources that can be recreated.
    }

    - (IBAction)openRNAppButtonPressed:(id)sender {
        NSURL *jsCodeLocation = [NSURL
    ```

```
URLWithString:@"http://localhost:8081/index.bundle?platform=ios"];
    RCTRootView *rootView =
    [[RCTRootView alloc] initWithBundleURL : jsCodeLocation
                            moduleName : @"EmbedApp"
                            initialProperties : nil
                            launchOptions : nil];
    UIViewController *vc = [[UIViewController alloc] init];
    vc.view = rootView;
    [self presentViewController:vc animated:YES completion:nil];
}
- (IBAction)openRNAppEmbeddedButtonPressed:(id)sender {
    NSURL *jsCodeLocation = [NSURL
URLWithString:@"http://localhost:8081/index.bundle?platform=ios"];
    RCTRootView *rootView =
    [[RCTRootView alloc] initWithBundleURL : jsCodeLocation
                            moduleName : @"EmbedApp"
                            initialProperties : nil
                            launchOptions : nil];
    [embeddedViewController setView:rootView];
}

// Defined in next step

@end
```

17. We'll also need to define the `prepareForSegue` method. Here, you can see `segue.identifier isEqualToString:@"embed"`, which refers to the **embed** identifier we gave the segue in *step 13*:

```
// Defined in previous steps

- (void) prepareForSegue:(UIStoryboardSegue *)segue
sender:(id)sender {
    if([segue.identifier isEqualToString:@"embed"]) {
        embeddedViewController = segue.destinationViewController;
    }
}

@end
```

18. With our implementation of `ViewController` in place, we now we need to wire up our button actions to the buttons themselves. Let's return to `Main.storyboard`. *Ctrl* + click on the first button to get a menu of actions that are assignable to the button, select the **Touch Up Inside** action by clicking and dragging from **Touch Up Inside** back to the storyboard, and map the button to the `openRNAppButtonPressed` method we defined in *step 15*. Repeat these steps for the second button, linking it instead to the `openRNAppEmbeddedButtonPressed` method:

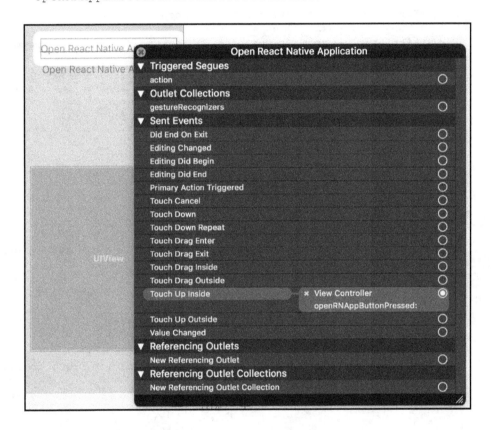

19. For the React Native layer to be able to communicate with the native layer, we also need to add a security exception, which will allow our code to communicate with localhost. Right-click on the Info.plist file and select **Open As | Source Code**. Within the base <dict> tag, add the following entry:

```
<key>NSAppTransportSecurity</key>
<dict>
  <key>NSExceptionDomains</key>
  <dict>
    <key>localhost</key>
    <dict>
      <key>NSTemporaryExceptionAllowsInsecureHTTPLoads</key>
      <true/>
    </dict>
  </dict>
</dict>
```

20. Our app is complete! From the /EmbedApp root directory, start up the React Native app using the CLI with the following command:

```
react-native start
```

21. With the React Native app running, let's also run the native app EmbeddedApp from Xcode. Now, pressing the **Open React Native App** button should open the React Native app we created in *step 6* in full screen, and the same React Native app should open within the container view we created in *step 9* when pressing the **Open React Native App (Embedded)** button.

How it works...

In this recipe, we covered rendering a React Native app within a native iOS app via two different methods. The first method replaces the application's main UIViewController instance with the React Native app, referred to in the native code as RCTRootView. This was accomplished in the openRNAppButtonPressed method. The second and slightly more involved method is rendering the React Native app inline with the native app. This was accomplish by creating a container view that links to a different UIViewController instance. In this case, we replaced the contents of embedViewController with our RCTRootView instance. This is what happens when the openRNAppEmbeddedButtonPressed method is fired.

See also

For a better understanding of the role cocoapods plays in Xcode/React Native development, I recommend Google's *Route 85 Show* episode covering the subject on YouTube. The video can be found at `https://www.youtube.com/watch?v=iEAjvNRdZa0`.

Communicating from an iOS app to React Native

In the previous recipe, we learned how to render a React Native app as part of a larger native iOS app. Unless you're building a glorified app container or portal, you'll likely need to communicate between the native layer and the React Native layer. This will be the subject matter of the next two recipes, one recipe for each direction of communication.

In this recipe, we will cover communicating from the native layer to the React Native layer, sending data from the parent iOS app to our embedded React Native app, by using a `UITextField` in the iOS app that sends its data to the React Native app.

Getting ready

Since this recipe requires a native app with a nested React Native app within it, we'll be beginning at the end of the previous recipe, effectively picking up where we left off. This will help you understand how basic cross-layer communication works so that you can use the same principles in your own native app, which may already exist and have complex features. Therefore, the easiest way to follow along with this recipe is to use the endpoint of the previous recipe as a starting place.

How to do it...

1. Let's start by updating the `ViewController.m` implementation file in the native layer. Be sure to open the project in Xcode via the `.xcworkspace` file in the `EmbeddedApp`, which we placed in the `/ios/EmbeddApp` directory of the project in the previous recipe. We'll start with the imports:

```
#import "ViewController.h"
#import "EmbeddedViewController.h"
#import <React/RCTRootView.h>
#import <React/RCTBridge.h>
#import <React/RCTEventDispatcher.h>
```

2. The next step is to add a reference to the React Native bridge via the `ViewController` interface, effectively linking the native controller with the React Native code:

```
@interface ViewController () <RCTBridgeDelegate> {
    EmbeddedViewController *embeddedViewController;
    RCTBridge *_bridge;
    BOOL isRNRunning;
}
```

3. We will also need an `@property` reference of `userNameField` that we will use in a later step to wire to the `UITextField`:

```
@property (weak, nonatomic) IBOutlet UITextField *userNameField;

@end
```

4. Directly below this reference, we'll begin defining the class methods. We'll begin with the `sourceURLForBridge` method, which defines where the React Native app will be served from. In our case, the app URL should be `http://localhost:8081/index.bundle?platform=ios`, which points at the `index.js` file of the React Native app once it is run with the `react-native start` command:

```
- (NSURL *)sourceURLForBridge:(RCTBridge *)bridge {
    NSURL *jsCodeLocation = [NSURL
URLWithString:@"http://localhost:8081/index.bundle?platform=ios
"];
    return jsCodeLocation;
}
```

5. We'll leave the `viewDidLoad` and `didReveiveMemoryWarning` methods as is:

```
- (void)viewDidLoad {
    [super viewDidLoad];
}

- (void)didReceiveMemoryWarning {
    [super didReceiveMemoryWarning];
    // Dispose of any resources that can be recreated.
}
```

6. Next, we'll need to update the `openRNAppEmbeddedButtonPressed` method. Notice how the `moduleName` property is set to `FromNativeToRN`. This is a reference to the name that we give the React Native app when it is exported, which we'll define in a later step. This time, we are also defining a property of `userName` for passing data to the React Native layer:

```
- (IBAction)openRNAppEmbeddedButtonPressed:(id)sender {
    NSString *userName = _userNameField.text;
    NSDictionary *props = @{@"userName" : userName};
    if(_bridge == nil) {
        _bridge = [[RCTBridge alloc] initWithDelegate:self
        launchOptions:nil];
    }
    RCTRootView *rootView =
    [[RCTRootView alloc] initWithBridge :_bridge
                            moduleName : @"FromNativeToRN"
                      initialProperties : props];
    isRNRunning = true;
    [embeddedViewController setView:rootView];
}
```

7. We'll also need an `onUserNameChanged` method. This is the method that will do the actual sending of data across the bridge to the React Native layer. The event name we're defining here is `UserNameChanged`, which we'll reference in the React Native layer in a later step. This will also pass along the text that's currently in the text input, which will be named `userNameField`:

```
- (IBAction)onUserNameChanged:(id)sender {
    if(isRNRunning == YES && _userNameField.text.length > 3) {
        [_bridge.eventDispatcher
sendAppEventWithName:@"UserNameChanged" body:@{@"userName" :
_userNameField.text}];
    }
}
```

8. We'll also need `prepareForSegue` for configuring `embeddedViewController` just before it is displayed:

```
- (void) prepareForSegue:(UIStoryboardSegue *)segue
sender:(id)sender {
    if([segue.identifier isEqualToString:@"embed"]) {
        embeddedViewController = segue.destinationViewController;
    }
}
@end
```

9. Back in the `Main.storyboard`, let's add that **Text Field**, along with a **Label** that defines what the input is for. You can also name the input **User Name Field** so that everything is easier to recognize in the **View Controller Scene**:

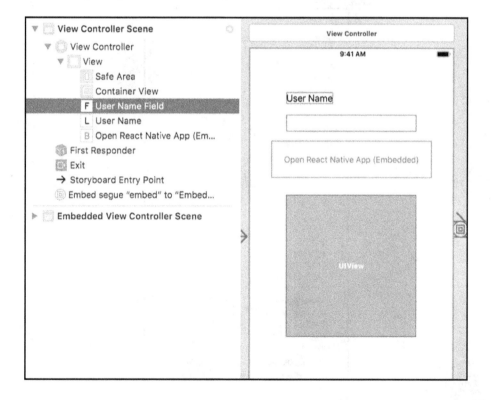

10. Next, we'll need to wire an event for when the text changes in the **User Name Field** text input, and a referencing outlet so that the **View Controller** knows how to reference it. These can both be done via the **Connections Inspector**, which is accessible via the last button along the top of the right-hand side panel (the icon is a right pointing arrow in a circle). With the text input selected, click and drag from **Editing Changed** to the **View Controller** (represented via the main storyboard), and choose the onUserNameChange method we defined in *step 7*. Then, create the following wirings by dragging the item to the ViewController. Similarly, add a new **Referencing Outlet** by clicking and dragging from the **New Referencing Outlet** back to the **View Controller**, this time choosing the **userNameField** value we targeted in *step 7*. Your **Connections Inspector** settings should now look like this:

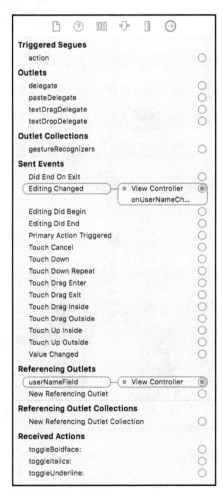

11. We've now completed the steps needed in the native app. Let's move on to the React Native layer. Back in the `index.js` file, we'll start with imports. Notice how we're now including the `NativeAppEventEmitter`.

12. Put the following functions inside the class definition:

```
import React, { Component } from 'react';
import {
  AppRegistry,
  StyleSheet,
  View,
  Text,
  NativeAppEventEmitter
} from 'react-native';
```

13. We'll name the app `FromNativeToRN` to match the module name we defined in the native layer in *step 6*, using `AppRegistry.registerComponent` to register the app with the same name. We'll also leave the basic styles in place:

```
class FromNativeToRN extends Component {
 // Defined in following steps
}

const styles = StyleSheet.create({
  container: {
    flex: 1,
    justifyContent: 'center',
    alignItems: 'center',
    backgroundColor: '#F5FCFF',
  }
});

AppRegistry.registerComponent('FromNativeToRN', () =>
FromNativeToRN);
```

14. We'll set an initial `state` object with a `userName` string property for storing and displaying the text that's received from the native layer:

```
class FromNativeToRN extends Component {
  state = {
  userName: ''
  }

  // Defined in following steps
}
```

15. The userName value passed into the React Native layer will be received as a property. When the component mounts, we want to do two things: set the userName state property if it's already defined by the native layer, and wire an event listener to update userName when the text field in the native layer is updated. Recall in *step 7* that we defined the event's name to be UserNameChanged, so that's the event we'll listen for. When the event is received, we update the state.userName to the text that's passed along with the event:

```
componentWillMount() {
  this.setState({
    userName : this.props.userName
  });

  NativeAppEventEmitter.addListener('UserNameChanged', (body) =>
{
      this.setState({userName : body.userName});
  });
}
```

16. Finally, we can add the render function, which simply renders the value stored in state.userName:

```
render() {
  return (
    <View style={styles.container}>
      <Text>Hello {this.state.userName}</Text>
    </View>
  );
}
```

17. It's time to run our app! First, in the root of the project, we can start up the React Native app with the React Native CLI with the following command:

```
react-native start
```

We follow this by running the native app in the simulator via Xcode:

Communicating from React Native to an iOS app container

The last recipe covered communication between layers in the direction of native to React Native. In this recipe, we will cover communicating in the opposite direction: from React Native to native. This time, we will render a user input element inside our React Native app and set up a one-way binding from React Native to a UI component rendered in the native app.

Getting ready

Just like the last recipe, this recipe depends on the final product of the first app in this chapter, in the *Combining a React Native app and a Native iOS app* recipe. To follow along, be sure you've finished that recipe.

How to do it...

1. Let's begin in the native layer. Open the `EmbeddedApp` native app in Xcode via the `.xcworkspace` file. We'll first add imports to `ViewController.m`:

```
#import "ViewController.h"
#import "EmbeddedViewController.h"
#import <React/RCTRootView.h>
#import <React/RCTBridge.h>
#import <React/RCTEventDispatcher.h>
```

2. As we did in the last recipe, we need to add a reference to the React Native bridge via the `ViewController` interface, providing a bridge between the native controller and the React Native code:

```
@interface ViewController () <RCTBridgeDelegate> {
    EmbeddedViewController *embeddedViewController;
    RCTBridge *_bridge;
    BOOL isRNRunning;
}
```

3. We will also need a @property reference of userNameField that we will use in a later step to wire to the UITextField:

```
@property (weak, nonatomic) IBOutlet UITextField *userNameField;

@end
```

4. Let's move on to defining the @implementation. Again, we must provide the source of the React Native app, which will be served from localhost:

```
@implementation ViewController

- (NSURL *)sourceURLForBridge:(RCTBridge *)bridge {
    NSURL *jsCodeLocation = [NSURL
URLWithString:@"http://localhost:8081/index.bundle?platform=ios"];
    return jsCodeLocation;
}
```

5. Using the viewDidLoad method, we can also connect the controller to the method that opens the React Native app in our container view (openRNAppEmbeddedButtonPressed). We'll leave the didReveiveMemoryWarning method as is:

```
- (void)viewDidLoad {
    [super viewDidLoad];
    [self openRNAppEmbeddedButtonPressed:nil];
}

- (void)didReceiveMemoryWarning {
    [super didReceiveMemoryWarning];
    // Dispose of any resources that can be recreated.
}
```

6. Like the last recipe, we'll need to update the openRNAppEmbeddedButtonPressed method. This time, the moduleName property is set to FromRNToNative to reflect the name that we will give the React Native app when it is exported, as defined in a later step. We also define a property of userName for passing data to the React Native layer:

```
- (IBAction)openRNAppEmbeddedButtonPressed:(id)sender {
    if(_bridge == nil) {
        _bridge = [[RCTBridge alloc] initWithDelegate:self
launchOptions:nil];
    }
    RCTRootView *rootView =
    [[RCTRootView alloc] initWithBridge :_bridge
```

```
                                    moduleName : @"FromRNToNative"
                                    initialProperties : nil];
            isRNRunning = true;
            [embeddedViewController setView:rootView];
        }
```

7. The last two methods we'll need in this file are `prepareForSegue` for configuring the `embeddedViewController` just before it is displayed, and an `updateUserNameField` method that will be fired when our text input in the native layer is updated with new text from the user:

```
- (void) prepareForSegue:(UIStoryboardSegue *)segue
sender:(id)sender {
    if([segue.identifier isEqualToString:@"embed"]) {
        embeddedViewController = segue.destinationViewController;
    }
}

-(void) updateUserNameField:(NSString *)userName {
    [_userNameField setText:userName];
}
@end
```

8. Unlike the previous recipe, we'll need to also update the `ViewController` header file (`ViewController.h`). The method referenced here, `updateUserNameField`, will be used when we define the `ViewController` implementation:

```
#import <UIKit/UIKit.h>

@interface ViewController : UIViewController
- (void) updateUserNameField:(NSString *)userName;

@end
```

9. Next, we're going to need to create a new `UserNameManager` native module. First, create a Cocoa Touch class named `UserNameManager`. Once created, let's open the implementation file (`UserNameManger.m`) and add our imports:

```
#import "UserNameManager.h"
#import "AppDelegate.h"
#import "ViewController.h"
#import <React/RCTBridgeModule.h>
```

> For a more in-depth look at creating native modules, refer to the
> *Exposing Custom iOS Modules* recipe in `Chapter 11`, *Adding Native*
> *Functionality*.

10. Next, we'll define the class implementation. The main takeaway here is
    the `setUserName` method, which is the method that we're exporting from the
    native layer for use in the React Native app. We'll use this method in the React
    Native app to update the value in the native **Text Field**. However, since we are
    updating a native UI component, the operation must be performed on the main
    thread. This is the purpose of the `methodQueue` function, which instructs the
    module to execute on the main thread:

```
@implementation UserNameManager
RCT_EXPORT_MODULE();

- (dispatch_queue_t)methodQueue
{
    return dispatch_get_main_queue();
}

RCT_EXPORT_METHOD(setUserName: (NSString *)userName) {
    AppDelegate *delegate = (AppDelegate *)[[UIApplication
sharedApplication] delegate];
    ViewController *controller = (ViewController
*)delegate.window.rootViewController;
    [controller updateUserNameField:userName];
}
@end
```

11. We'll also need to update the `UserNameMangager.h` header file to use the React
    Native bridge module:

```
#import <Foundation/Foundation.h>
#import <React/RCTBridgeModule.h>

@interface UserNameManager : NSObject <RCTBridgeModule>

@end
```

12. Like the last recipe, we'll need to add a **Text Field** and **Label** for the **User Name** input:

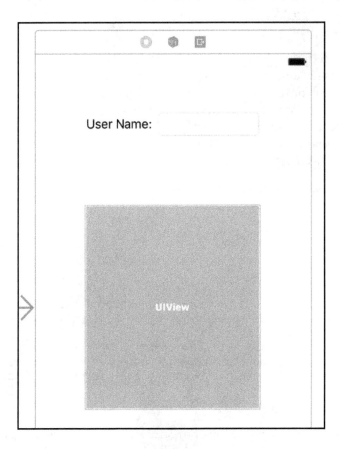

13. We'll also need to add a **Referencing Outlet** from the **Text Field** we created in the last set to our `userNameField` property:

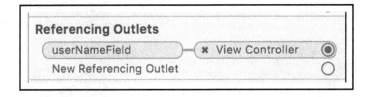

TIP

> If you need more information on how to create a **Referencing Outlet**,
> view *step 10* of the previous recipe.

14. We're finished with the native portion of this project, so let's turn to our React
    Native code. Let's open the `index.js` file at the root of the project. We'll start
    with our imports:

```
import React, { Component } from 'react';
import {
  AppRegistry,
  StyleSheet,
  View,
  Text,
  TextInput,
  NativeModules
} from 'react-native';
```

15. Let's define the app with the name `FromRNToNative` to line up with the
    `moduleName` we declared in the native code in *step 6*, and register the component
    with the same name. The `state` object only needs a `userName` string property
    for hold the value that's saved to the `TextInput` component, which we'll add in
    the component's `render` function:

```
class FromRNToNative extends Component {
  state = {
    userName: ''
  }

  // Defined on next step
}

AppRegistry.registerComponent('FromRNToNative', () =>
FromRNToNative);
```

16. The app's `render` function uses a `TextInput` component to take input from the user, which it will then send to the native app via the React Native bridge. It does this by calling the `onUserNameChange` method when the value of the `TextInput` changes:

```
render() {
  return (
    <View style={styles.container}>
      <Text>Enter User Name</Text>
      <TextInput
        style={styles.userNameField}
        onChangeText={this.onUserNameChange}
        value={this.state.userName}
      />
    </View>
  );
}
```

17. The last thing we need to do is define the `onUserNameChange` method that's used by the `onChangeText` property of the `TextInput` component we defined in the previous step. This method updates `state.userName` to the value in the text input, and also sends the value along to the native code by using the `NativeModules` component in React Native. `NativeModules` has the `UserNameManager` class we defined as a Cocoa Touch class in the native layer in *step 9*. We call the `setUserName` method that we defined on the class in *step 10* to pass the value along to the native layer, where it will be displayed in the **Text Field** we created in *step 12*:

```
onUserNameChange = (userName) => {
  this.setState({userName});
  NativeModules.UserNameManager.setUserName(userName);
}
```

18. The app is done! Return to the root of the project to start up the React Native app with the following command:

```
react-native start
```

Then, with the React Native app started, run the native `EmbeddedApp` project from Xcode. Now, the input in the React Native app should communicate its value to the input in the parent native app:

How it works...

To communicate from our React Native app to the parent native app, we created a native module named `UserNameManager` with a `setUserName` method, which we exported from the native layer, and used in the React Native app, in its `onUserNameChange` method. This is the recommended way of communicating from React Native to native.

Handle being invoked by an external iOS app

It is also a common behavior for native apps to communicate between one another via linking, and are usually prompted to the user with the phrase **Open in...**, along with the name of an app that can better handle an action. This is done by using a protocol that is specific to your app. Just like any website link has a protocol of either `http://` or `https://`, we can also create a custom protocol that will allow any other app to open and send data to our app.

In this recipe, we will be creating a custom protocol called `invoked://`. By using the `invoked://` protocol, any other app can use it to run our app and pass data to it.

Getting ready

For this recipe, we'll be starting from a new vanilla React Native app. Let's name it `InvokeFromNative`.

How to do it...

1. Let's start by opening the native layer of the new project in Xcode. The first thing we need to do is adjust the project's **Build Settings**. This can be done by selecting the root project in the left panel, then choosing the **Build Settings** tab along the top of the middle panel:

2. We'll need to add a new entry to the **Header Search Paths** field:

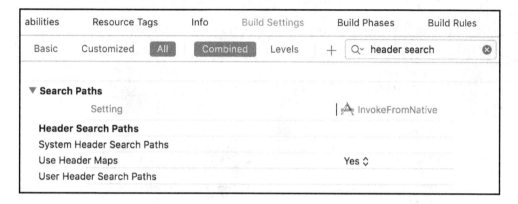

For the project to know the location of the React Native JavaScript, it needs the `$(SRCROOT)/../node_modules/react-native/Libraries` value. Let's add it as a recursive entry:

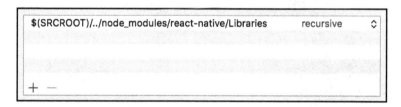

3. We also need to register our custom protocol, which will be used by other apps. Open the `Info.plist` file as source code (right-click then **Open As | Source Code)**. Let's add an entry to the file that will register our application under the `invoked://` protocol:

```
<key>CFBundleURLTypes</key>
<array>
  <dict>
    <key>CFBundleTypeRole</key>
    <string>Editor</string>
    <key>CFBundleURLSchemes</key>
    <array>
      <string>invoked</string>
    </array>
  </dict>
</array>
```

4. Next, we need to add the `RCTLinkingManager` to the `AppDelegate`
   implementation, which lives in `AppDelegate.m`, and wire it to our app:

```objc
#import "AppDelegate.h"

#import <React/RCTBundleURLProvider.h>
#import <React/RCTRootView.h>
#import <React/RCTLinkingManager.h>


@implementation AppDelegate

// The rest of the AppDelegate implementation

- (BOOL)application:(UIApplication *)application
  openURL:(NSURL *)url
  options:(NSDictionary<UIApplicationOpenURLOptionsKey, id>
*)options
{
  return [RCTLinkingManager application:application openURL:url
options:options];
}

@end
```

5. Now, let's move on to the React Native layer. Inside `index.js`, we'll add our
   imports, which includes the `Linking` component:

```javascript
import React, { Component } from 'react';
import {
  AppRegistry,
  StyleSheet,
  Text,
  View,
  Linking
} from 'react-native';
```

6. Next, we'll create the class definition and register the component as `InvokeFromNative`. We'll also define an initial `state` object with a `status` string property set to the value `'App Running'`:

```
class InvokeFromNative extends Component {
 state = {
 status: 'App Running'
 }

 // Defined on following steps
 }

AppRegistry.registerComponent('InvokeFromNative', () =>
InvokeFromNative);
```

7. Now, we'll use the mount and unmount life cycle hooks to add/remove the event listener for the `invoked://` protocol. When the event is heard, the `onAppInvoked` method, which is defined in the next step, will be fired:

```
componentWillMount() {
  Linking.addEventListener('url', this.onAppInvoked);
}

componentWillUnmount() {
  Linking.removeEventListener('url', this.onAppInvoked);
}
```

8. The `onAppInvoked` function simply takes the event from the event listener and updates `state.status` to reflect that invocation has happened, displaying the protocol via `event.url`:

```
onAppInvoked = (event) => {
  this.setState({
    status: `App Invoked by ${ event.url }`
  });
}
```

9. The `render` method's only real purpose in this recipe is to render the `status` property on state:

```
render() {
  return (
    <View style={styles.container}>
      <Text style={styles.instructions}>
        App Status:
      </Text>
      <Text style={styles.welcome}>
        {this.state.status}
      </Text>
    </View>
  );
}
```

10. We'll also add a few basic styles to center and size the text:

```
const styles = StyleSheet.create({
  container: {
    flex: 1,
    justifyContent: 'center',
    alignItems: 'center',
    backgroundColor: '#F5FCFF',
  },
  welcome: {
    fontSize: 20,
    textAlign: 'center',
    margin: 10,
  },
  instructions: {
    textAlign: 'center',
    color: '#333333',
    marginBottom: 5,
  },
});
```

11. Our app is finished. Once you've started running the app, you should see something like this:

12. With the app running, we can simulate the action of another app opening our React Native app using the `invoked://` protocol. This can be done with the following Terminal command:

```
xcrun simctl openurl booted invoked://
```

Once invoked, the app should update to reflect the invocation:

How it works...

In this recipe, we covered how to register a custom protocol (or URL schema) for allowing our app to be invoked by other apps. The aim of this recipe was to keep our example as simple as possible, so we did not build out the handling data we passed to an app via the linking mechanism. However, it is entirely possible to do so if the needs of your app require it. For a deeper dive on the `Linking` component, check out the official documents at `https://facebook.github.io/react-native/docs/linking`.

Combining a React Native app and a native Android app

Since the Android platform still holds the majority stake in the smartphone market space, it's likely that you'll want to build the app for both Android as well as iOS. A large advantage of React Native development is making this process easier. But what happens when you want to write a new feature using React Native for a working Android app that's already been published? Fortunately, React Native makes this possible as well.

This recipe will cover the process of embedding a React Native app inside an existing Android app by displaying the React Native app inside a container view. The steps here are used as a baseline for the recipes that follow, which involve communication with a React Native app.

Getting ready

In this section, we will create a sample Android application using Android Studio called `EmbedApp`. If you have a base Android application you would like to work with, you can skip these steps and proceed to the actual implementation:

1. Open Android Studio and create a new project (**File | New Project**)
2. Set the application name to `EmbeddedApp` and fill out your company domain. Press **Next**
3. Leave **Empty Activity** selected as the default and press **Next**
4. Leave the **Activity** properties as they are by default and press **Finish**

How to do it...

1. At this point, our app has no references to React Native, so we'll start by installing it. In the app's root folder, in the Terminal, install React Native from the command line using `yarn`:

```
yarn add react-native
```

Alternatively, you can use `npm`:

```
npm install react-native --save
```

2. We'll also need a Node.js script for starting the React Native app. Let's open `package.json` and add the following property as a member of the scripts object:

```
"start": "node node_modules/react-native/local-cli/cli.js start"
```

3. We only need a very simple React Native app for this recipe. Let's create an `index.android.js` file with the following boilerplate app:

```javascript
import React, { Component } from 'react';
import { AppRegistry, StyleSheet, View, Text } from 'react-native';

export default class EmbedApp extends Component {
  render() {
    return (<View style={styles.container}>
      <Text>Hello in React Native</Text>
    </View>);
  }
}

const styles = StyleSheet.create({
 container: {
   flex: 1,
   justifyContent: 'center',
   alignItems: 'center', backgroundColor: '#F5FCFF'
   }
});

AppRegistry.registerComponent('EmbedApp', () => EmbedApp);
```

Naming this file `index.android.js` indicates to React Native that this code only applies to the Android version of this app. This is recommended by the official docs when platform-specific code is more complex. You can read more about it at `https://facebook.github.io/react-native/docs/platform-specific-code#platform-specific-extensions`.

4. Let's return to Android Studio and open the `build.gradle` file (from the app module) and add the following to the dependencies:

```
dependencies {
    implementation fileTree(dir: "libs", include: ["*.jar"])
    implementation "com.android.support:appcompat-v7:27.1.1"
    implementation "com.facebook.react:react-native:+" // From
node_modules
}
```

5. We'll also need a reference to the local React Native maven directory. Open the other `build.gradle` and add the following line to the `allprojects.repositories` object:

```
allprojects {
  repositories {
    mavenLocal()
      maven {
        url "$rootDir/../node_modules/react-native/android"
      }
    google()
    jcenter()
  }
}
```

6. Next, let's update the app's permissions to use the internet, and the system alert window. We'll open `AndroidManifest.xml` and add the following permissions to the `<manifest>` node:

```
<?xml version="1.0" encoding="utf-8"?>
 <manifest
xmlns:android="http://schemas.android.com/apk/res/android"
    package="com.warlyware.embeddedapp">

    <uses-permission android:name="android.permission.INTERNET" />
    <uses-permission
android:name="android.permission.SYSTEM_ALERT_WINDOW"/>

    <application
```

```xml
            android:name=".EmbedApp"
        android:allowBackup="true"
        android:icon="@mipmap/ic_launcher"
        android:label="@string/app_name"
        android:roundIcon="@mipmap/ic_launcher_round"
        android:supportsRtl="true"
        android:theme="@style/AppTheme">
        <activity android:name=".MainActivity">
            <intent-filter>
                <action android:name="android.intent.action.MAIN"
/>

                <category
android:name="android.intent.category.LAUNCHER" />
            </intent-filter>
        </activity>
    </application>

</manifest>
```

7. We're ready to update the `MainApplication` Java class. The `getUseDeveloperSupport` method here will enable the development menu. The `getPackages` method is a list of packages used by the app, and only includes `MainReactPackage()` since we are only using the main React package. The `getJSMainModuleName` method returns the `index.android` string, which refers to the `index.android.js` file in the React Native layer:

```java
import android.app.Application;

import com.facebook.react.ReactApplication;
import com.facebook.react.ReactNativeHost;
import com.facebook.react.ReactPackage;
import com.facebook.react.shell.MainReactPackage;

import java.util.Arrays;
import java.util.List;

public class MainApplication extends Application implements
ReactApplication {
  private final ReactNativeHost mReactNativeHost = new
ReactNativeHost(this) {
    @Override
    public boolean getUseDeveloperSupport() {
      return BuildConfig.DEBUG;
    }
```

```
    @Override
    protected List<ReactPackage> getPackages() {
      return Arrays.<ReactPackage>asList(
        new MainReactPackage()
      );
    }
  };

  @Override
  public ReactNativeHost getReactNativeHost() {
    return mReactNativeHost;
  }
  @Override
  protected String getJSMainModuleName() {
    return "index.android";
  }
}
```

8. Next, let's create another new Java class with the name `ReactFragment`. This class needs three methods: `OnAttach` is called when the fragment is attached to the main activity, `OnCreateView` instantiates the view for the fragment, and `OnActivityCreated` is called when the activity is being created:

```
import android.app.Fragment;
import android.content.Context;
import android.os.Bundle;
import android.view.LayoutInflater;
import android.view.ViewGroup;

import com.facebook.react.ReactInstanceManager;
import com.facebook.react.ReactRootView;

public abstract class ReactFragment extends Fragment {
  private ReactRootView mReactRootView;
  private ReactInstanceManager mReactInstanceManager;

  // This method returns the name of our top-level component to
show
  public abstract String getMainComponentName();

  @Override
  public void onAttach(Context context) {
    super.onAttach(context);
    mReactRootView = new ReactRootView(context);
    mReactInstanceManager =
      ((EmbedApp) getActivity().getApplication())
        .getReactNativeHost()
```

```
        .getReactInstanceManager();
    }

    @Override
    public ReactRootView onCreateView(LayoutInflater inflater,
ViewGroup group, Bundle savedInstanceState) {
        super.onCreate(savedInstanceState);
        return mReactRootView;
    }


    @Override
    public void onActivityCreated(Bundle savedInstanceState) {
        super.onActivityCreated(savedInstanceState);
        mReactRootView.startReactApplication(
          mReactInstanceManager,
          getMainComponentName(),
          getArguments()
        );
    }
}
```

10. Finally, create a Java class called `EmbedFragment` that will
    extend `ReactFragment`:

    ```
    import android.os.Bundle;

    public class EmbedFragment extends ReactFragment {
      @Override
      public String getMainComponentName() {
        return "EmbedApp";
      }
    }
    ```

11. Let's open `MainActivity.java` and add `implements`
    `DefaultHardwareBackBtnHandler` to the class definition for
    handling hardware back button events. You can view the annotated source code
    for this React Native class here: https://github.com/facebook/react-native/
    blob/master/ReactAndroid/src/main/java/com/facebook/react/modules/
    core/DefaultHardwareBackBtnHandler.java.

12. We'll also be adding a few methods to the class. The `onCreate` method will set the content view to the Main Activity and add a FAB button that, when clicked, will instantiate a new instance of the `EmbedFragment` we defined in *step 10*. That instance of `EmbedFragment` is used by the fragment manager to add the React Native app to the view. The remaining methods handle the events that occur when the device's system buttons are pressed (such as the back, pause, and resume buttons):

```
import android.app.Fragment;
import android.os.Bundle;
import android.support.design.widget.FloatingActionButton;
import android.support.v7.app.AppCompatActivity;
import android.support.v7.widget.Toolbar;
import android.view.KeyEvent;
import android.view.View;

import com.facebook.react.ReactInstanceManager;
import
com.facebook.react.modules.core.DefaultHardwareBackBtnHandler;

public class MainActivity extends AppCompatActivity implements
DefaultHardwareBackBtnHandler {
  private ReactInstanceManager mReactInstanceManager;

  @Override
  protected void onCreate(Bundle savedInstanceState) {
    super.onCreate(savedInstanceState);
    setContentView(R.layout.activity_main);
    Toolbar toolbar = (Toolbar) findViewById(R.id.toolbar);
    setSupportActionBar(toolbar);

    FloatingActionButton fab = (FloatingActionButton)
findViewById(R.id.fab);
    fab.setOnClickListener(new View.OnClickListener() {
      @Override
      public void onClick(View view) {
        Fragment viewFragment = new EmbedFragment();
getFragmentManager().beginTransaction().add(R.id.reactnativeembed,
viewFragment).commit(); }
    });

    mReactInstanceManager = ((EmbedApp)
getApplication()).getReactNativeHost().getReactInstanceManager();
  }


  @Override
```

```java
public void invokeDefaultOnBackPressed() {
  super.onBackPressed();
}

@Override
protected void onPause() {
  super.onPause();

  if (mReactInstanceManager != null) {
    mReactInstanceManager.onHostPause(this);
  }
}

@Override
protected void onResume() {
  super.onResume();

  if (mReactInstanceManager != null) {
    mReactInstanceManager.onHostResume(this, this);
  }
}

@Override
protected void onDestroy() {
  super.onDestroy();

  if (mReactInstanceManager != null) {
    mReactInstanceManager.onHostDestroy(this);
  }
}

@Override
public void onBackPressed() {
  if (mReactInstanceManager != null) {
    mReactInstanceManager.onBackPressed();
  } else {
    super.onBackPressed();
  }
}

@Override
public boolean onKeyUp(int keyCode, KeyEvent event) {
  if (keyCode == KeyEvent.KEYCODE_MENU && mReactInstanceManager
!= null) {
    mReactInstanceManager.showDevOptionsDialog();
    return true;
  }
  return super.onKeyUp(keyCode, event);
```

```
    }
  }
```

13. The last step is to add some settings for the layout when the fragment is loaded.
We'll need to edit the content_main.xml file, which is located in the /res
folder. This is the main content of the view. It holds the container view
(FrameLayout) that we will attach the fragment to, and the other native elements
should be displayed:

```
<FrameLayout
    android:layout_width="match_parent"
    android:layout_height="300dp"
    android:layout_centerVertical="true"
    android:layout_alignParentStart="true"
    android:id="@+id/reactnativeembed"
    android:background="#FFF">
</FrameLayout>
```

14. In the Terminal, run the following command:

```
react-native start
```

This builds and hosts the React Native app. Now, we can open the app in
the Android emulator. You will see the following after pressing the **FAB** button:

How it works...

To accomplish rendering React Native inside of our Android application, we had to perform a few steps. First, we had to define an `Application` class that implements the `ReactApplication` interface. Then, we had to create a `Fragment` that would be responsible for instantiating and rendering the `ReactRootView`. With a fragment, we are able to render the React Native view in our `MainActivity`. In this recipe, we added the fragment to our fragment container view. This essentially replaces all of the application content with the React Native application.

We covered a lot of integration code in this recipe. For a more in-depth look at how each of these pieces work, you can read the official documentation at `https://facebook.github.io/react-native/docs/integration-with-existing-apps.html`.

Communicating from an Android app to React Native

Now that we have covered how to render our React Native app inside an Android app in the *Combining a React Native app and a native Android app* recipe, we're ready to take the next step. Our React Native application should be more than a dummy UI. It should be able to react to actions that are going on in its parent application.

In this recipe, we will accomplish sending data from our Android application to our embedded React Native app. The React Native application can accept data when it is first instantiated, and then at runtime. We will be covering how to accomplish both methods. This recipe will use `EditText` in the Android app and set up one-way binding to the React Native app.

Getting ready

For this recipe, please ensure that you have an Android app with a React Native app embedded. If you need guidance to accomplish this, please complete the *Combining a React Native app and a native Android app* recipe.

How to do it...

1. In Android Studio, open the Android portion of the React Native app. First, we'll need to edit `content_main.xml`.

2. We'll only need a very simple layout for this app. You can edit the file by pressing the **Text** tab on the bottom to open the source editor and add/replace the following nodes:

```
<TextView android: layout_width = "wrap_content"
android: layout_height = "wrap_content"
android: text = "Press the Mail Icon to start the React Native
application"
android: id = "@+id/textView" />
<FrameLayout android: layout_width = "match_parent"
android: layout_height = "300dp"
android: layout_centerVertical = "true"
android: layout_alignParentStart = "true"
android: id = "@+id/reactnativeembed"
android: background = "#FFF" >
</FrameLayout>
<LinearLayout android:orientation="horizontal"
android:layout_width="match_parent"
android:layout_height="75dp"
android:layout_below="@+id/textView"
android:layout_centerHorizontal="true">
  <TextView
  android:layout_width="wrap_content"
  android:layout_height="wrap_content"
  android:text="User Name:"
  android:id="@ + id / textView2"
  android:layout_weight="0.14 " />
  <EditText android:layout_width="wrap_content"
  android:layout_height="wrap_content"
  android:id="@ + id / userName"
  android:layout_weight="0.78"
  android:inputType="text"
  android:singleLine="true"
  android:imeOptions="actionDone"/>
</LinearLayout>
```

3. Open `MainActivity.java` and add the following class fields:

```
private ReactInstanceManager mReactInstanceManager;
private EditText userNameField;
private Boolean isRNRunning = false;
```

4. Inside the `onCreatemethod`, set the `userNameField` property with the following code:

```
userNameField = (EditText) findViewById(R.id.userName);
```

5. We'll be using a FAB button to update the content of the Android app to be our React Native app. We will need to replace `FloatingActionButtononClickListener` with the following:

```
fab.setOnClickListener(new View.OnClickListener() {
  @Override public void onClick(View view) {
    Fragment viewFragment = new EmbedFragment();
    if (userNameField.getText().length() > 0) {
      Bundle launchOptions = new Bundle();
      launchOptions.putString("userName",
      userNameField.getText().toString());
      viewFragment.setArguments(launchOptions);
    }
getFragmentManager().beginTransaction().add(R.id.reactnativeembed,
viewFragment).commit();
    isRNRunning = true;
  }
});
```

6. Next, we need to add a `TextChangedListener` to our `userNameField` in the `onCreate` method:

```
userNameField.addTextChangedListener(new TextWatcher() {
  @Override public void beforeTextChanged(CharSequence s, int
start, int count, int after) {}
  @Override public void onTextChanged(CharSequence s, int start,
int before, int count) {}
  @Override public void afterTextChanged(Editable s) {
    if (isRNRunning) {
      sendUserNameChange(s.toString());
    }
  }
});
```

7. The last change we need to make for our `Activity` is to add methods that will send the event across the React Native bridge:

```
private void sendUserNameChange(String userName) {
  WritableMap params = Arguments.createMap();
  params.putString("userName", userName);
```

```
    sendReactEvent("UserNameChanged", params);
}

private void sendReactEvent(String eventName, WritableMap params) {
    mReactInstanceManager.getCurrentReactContext()
.getJSModule(DeviceEventManagerModule.RCTDeviceEventEmitter.class)
        .emit(eventName, params);
}
```

8. Let's return to the JavaScript layer. We'll use the `addListener` method of the `NativeAppEventEmitter` component to listen to the `UserNameChanged` event that was sent from the native Android code, and update `state.userName` with the data from the event:

```
import React, { Component } from 'react';
import {
  AppRegistry,
  StyleSheet,
  View,
  Text,
  NativeAppEventEmitter
} from 'react-native';

export default class EmbedApp extends Component<{}> {
  componentWillMount() {
    this.setState({
      userName : this.props.userName
    });

    NativeAppEventEmitter.addListener('UserNameChanged', (body) =>
{
        this.setState({userName : body.userName});
    });
  }
  render() {
    return (
      <View style={styles.container}>
        <Text>Hello {this.state.userName}</Text>
      </View>
    );
  }
}

const styles = StyleSheet.create({
  container: {
    flex: 1,
    justifyContent: 'center',
```

```
        alignItems: 'center',
        backgroundColor: '#F5FCFF',
    },
    welcome: {
        fontSize: 20,
        textAlign: 'center',
        margin: 10,
    },
    instructions: {
        textAlign: 'center',
        color: '#333333',
        marginBottom: 5,
    },
});

AppRegistry.registerComponent('EmbedApp', () => EmbedApp);
```

9. Now, if you run the application, you can enter text in the **User Name** field and start the React Native application:

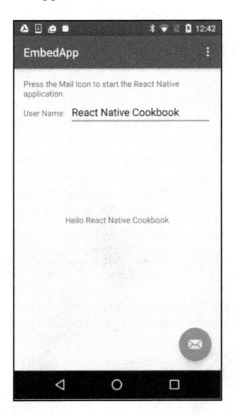

How it works...

In this recipe, we rendered the fragment as an inline view. In *step 2*, we added an empty `FrameLayout` that we targeted in *step 5* to render the fragment. The binding functionality was accomplished by using the React Native bridge via `RCTDeviceEventEmitter`. This was originally designed to be used with native modules, but as long as you have access to the `ReactContext` instance, you can use it for any communication with the React Native JavaScript layer.

Communicating from React Native to an Android app container

As we discussed in the previous recipe, it is extremely beneficial for our embedded application to be aware of what's going on around it. We should also make an effort so that our Android parent application can be informed about what goes on inside the React Native application. The application should not only be able to perform business logic – it should be able to update its UI to reflect changes in the embedded app.

This recipe shows us how to leverage native modules to update the native UI that's created inside the Android application. We will have a text field in our React Native app that updates a text field that is rendered in the host Android application.

Getting ready

For this recipe, please ensure that you have an Android application with a React Native app embedded. If you need guidance to accomplish this, please complete the *Combining a React Native app and a native Android app* recipe.

How to do it...

1. Open Android Studio to your Project and open `content_main.xml`.
2. Press the **Text** tab on the bottom to open the source editor and add/replace the following nodes:

```
<?xml version="1.0" encoding="utf-8"?>
<RelativeLayout
xmlns:android="http://schemas.android.com/apk/res/android"
```

```
    xmlns:app="http://schemas.android.com/apk/res-auto"
    xmlns:tools="http://schemas.android.com/tools"
    android:layout_width="match_parent"
    android:layout_height="match_parent"
    android:paddingBottom="@dimen/activity_vertical_margin"
    android:paddingLeft="@dimen/activity_horizontal_margin"
    android:paddingRight="@dimen/activity_horizontal_margin"
    android:paddingTop="@dimen/activity_vertical_margin"
    app:layout_behavior="@string/appbar_scrolling_view_behavior"
    tools:context="com.embedapp.MainActivity"
    tools:showIn="@layout/activity_main">

    <TextView
        android:layout_width="wrap_content"
        android:layout_height="wrap_content"
        android:text="Press the Mail Icon to start the React Native
application"
        android:id="@+id/textView" />

    <FrameLayout
        android:layout_width="match_parent"
        android:layout_height="300dp"
        android:layout_centerVertical="true"
        android:layout_alignParentStart="true"
        android:id="@+id/reactnativeembed"
        android:background="#FFF"></FrameLayout>

    <LinearLayout
        android:orientation="horizontal"
        android:layout_width="match_parent"
        android:layout_height="75dp"
        android:layout_below="@+id/textView"
        android:layout_centerHorizontal="true">

    <TextView
        android:layout_width="wrap_content"
        android:layout_height="wrap_content"
        android:text="User Name:"
        android:id="@+id/textView2"
        android:layout_weight="0.14" />

    <EditText
        android:layout_width="wrap_content"
        android:layout_height="wrap_content"
        android:id="@+id/userName"
        android:layout_weight="0.78"
        android:inputType="text"
        android:singleLine="true"
```

```
                    android:imeOptions="actionDone"/>
        </LinearLayout>
    </RelativeLayout>
```

3. Create a Java class named `UserNameManager`. This will be a native module that will serve the purpose of updating the `EditText field` we added to the layout.

> If you are not familiar with creating a native module for React Native, please refer to the *Exposing custom Android modules* recipe in `Chapter 11`, *Adding Native Functionality*.

4. Most of the work in `UserNameManager.java` is being done in the `setUserName` method. Here, the Android layer updates the text contents of the view based on what it's sent from the React Native layer. The React method isn't necessarily going to run on the main UI thread, so we use `mainActivity.runOnUiThread` to update the view when the main UI thread is ready:

```
public class UserNameManager extends ReactContextBaseJavaModule {
  public UserNameManager(ReactApplicationContext
reactApplicationContext) {
    super(reactApplicationContext);
  }
  @Override public String getName() {
    return "UserNameManager";
  }
  @ReactMethod public void setUserName(final String userName) {
    Activity mainActivity =
getReactApplicationContext().getCurrentActivity();
    final EditText userNameField = (EditText)
mainActivity.findViewById(R.id.userName);
    mainActivity.runOnUiThread(new Runnable() {
      @Override public void run() {
        userNameField.setText(userName);
      }
    });
  }
}
```

5. To export the `UserNameManager` module, we'll need to edit the `UserNamePackage` Java class. We can export it to the React Native layer by calling `modules.add`, passing in a new `UserNameManager` that takes the `reactContext` as a parameter:

```java
public class UserNamePackage implements ReactPackage {
  @Override public List < Class << ? extends JavaScriptModule >>
createJSModules() {
      return Collections.emptyList();
  }
  @Override public List < ViewManager >
createViewManagers(ReactApplicationContext reactContext) {
      return Collections.emptyList();
  }
  @Override public List < NativeModule >
createNativeModules(ReactApplicationContext reactContext) {
      List < NativeModule > modules = new ArrayList < > ();
      modules.add(new UserNameManager(reactContext));
      return modules;
  }
}
```

6. Add the `UserNamePackage` in the `getPackages` method in `MainApplication`:

```java
@Override
protected List<ReactPackage> getPackages() {
 return Arrays.<ReactPackage>asList(
  new MainReactPackage(),
  new UserNamePackage()
 );
}
```

7. Now, we need to have our React Native UI render a `TextField` and call our `UserNameManager` native module. Open `index.android.js` and import the `TextInput` and `NativeModules` modules from `'react-native'`.

8. Create a variable reference for the `UserNameManager`:

```javascript
const UserNameManager = NativeModules.UserNameManager;
```

9. The React Native app will simply need a `TextInput` for manipulating a `userName` property on the `state` object:

```javascript
let state = {
  userName: ''
}
```

```
onUserNameChange = (userName) => {
  this.setState({
    userName
  });

  UserNameManager.setUserName(userName);
}

render() {
  return (
    <View style={styles.container}>
      <Text>Embedded RN App</Text>
      <Text>Enter User Name</Text>
      <TextInput style={{styles.userNameField}
        onChangeText={this.onUserNameChange}
        value={this.state.userName}
      />
    </View>
  );
}
```

10. After running the application, starting the React Native embedded app, and adding text to the text field, you should see something similar to what's shown in the following screenshot:

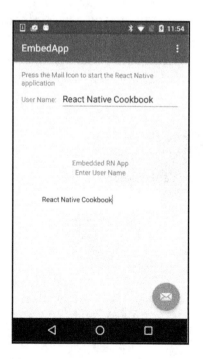

How it works...

To get our React Native app to update the native app containers, we created a native module. This is the recommended way of communicating from JavaScript to the native layer. However, since we had to update a native UI component, the operation had to be performed on the main thread. This is achieved by getting a reference to `MainActivity` and calling the `runOnUiThread` method. This is done in the `setUserName` method of *step 4*.

Handle being invoked by an external Android app

Earlier in this chapter, we covered how to handle invocation from an external app in iOS in the *Handle being invoked by an external Android app* recipe. In this recipe, we'll cover the same concept of deep linking in Android.

How to do it...

1. Let's begin by opening the React Native Android project in Android Studio and navigating to `AndroidManifest.xml`.

2. For our example, we will register our application under `invoked://scheme`. We'll update the `<activity>` node to the following:

```
<activity
android:name=".MainActivity"
android:label="@string/app_name"
android:configChanges="keyboard|keyboardHidden|orientation|screenSi
ze"
android:windowSoftInputMode="adjustResize"
android:launchMode="singleTask">
  <intent-filter>
    <action android:name="android.intent.action.MAIN" />
    <category android:name="android.intent.category.LAUNCHER" />
  </intent-filter>
</activity>
```

For more information on how this `intent-filter` works, refer to the official Android documentation at https://developer.android.com/ training/app-links/deep-linking.

3. Next, we'll need to create a simple React Native app whose UI reacts to being invoked. Let's open the `index.android.js` file. We'll start by importing the `Linking` module in the `import` block from `'react-native'`:

```
import React from 'react';
import { Platform, Text, Linking } from 'react-native';
```

4. Let's build out the `App` class for the React Native app. When the component mounts, we'll register a `Linking` event listener with an event we'll name `url`. When this event occurs, `onAppInvoked` will be fired, updating the `status` property of state, along with the event that's passed to the callback:

```
export default class App extends React.Component {
  state = {
    status: 'App Running'
  }
  componentWillMount() {
    Linking.addEventListener('url', this.onAppInvoked);
  }
  componentWillUnmount() {
    Linking.removeEventListener('url', this.onAppInvoked);
  }
  onAppInvoked = (event) => {
    this.setState({ status: `App Invoked by ${event.url}` });
  }
  render() {
    return (
      <View style={styles.container}>
        <Text style={styles.instructions}>
          App Status:
        </Text>
        <Text style={styles.welcome}>
          {this.state.status}
        </Text>
      </View>
    );
  }
}
```

5. Running the application and invoking it from another app will look something like this:

How it works...

In this recipe, we registered our URL schema for linking by editing the `AndroidManifest.xml` file in *step 2*. An important thing to note is the change of the `launchMode` to `singleTask`. This prevents the operating system from creating multiple instances of our React activity. This is important if you want to be able to properly capture the data that's passed along with the intent.

14
Deploying Your App

In this chapter, we will cover the following recipes:

- Deploying development builds to an iOS device
- Deploying development builds to an Android device
- Deploying test builds to HockeyApp
- Deploying iOS test builds to TestFlight
- Deploying production builds to the Apple App Store
- Deploying production builds to the Google Play Store
- Deploying Over-The-Air updates
- Optimizing React Native app size

Introduction

If you're an independent developer, you're likely to go through a few different stages of development. The first stage will find you testing your app on your personal iOS or Android device. After exhausting this stage, you're probably going to want to share it with a select group of people to get user feedback. Eventually, you're going to reach a point where your app is ready to be released into the world via app stores. This chapter will walk through each one of these stages and cover pushing updates to your app, along with a few optimization tips.

Deploying development builds to an iOS device

During development, you'll likely spend much of your time testing your iOS app using the iOS Simulator that comes installed with Xcode. While the iOS Simulator is by far the best performing and closest method to running our application on an iOS device, it's still not the same as the real thing. The iOS Simulator uses the computer's CPU and GPU to render the simulated OS, so depending on your development machine, it may end up performing better (or worse) than the actual device.

Thankfully, Expo's ability to test running code on an actual device comes one step closer to the real end product, but there are still differences between a final app and a development app running in Expo. And if you're building a pure React Native app, you won't have the luxury of using Expo to easily run the app on a device.

Either way, you'll eventually want to test the real app on a physical device so you can experience the actual UX and performance of the end product.

In this recipe, we will walk you through taking a React Native app and deploying it to an iPhone or iPad.

Getting ready

We'll just need a new pure React Native app, which we'll name `TestDeployApp`. You can create the app via the following command:

```
react-native init
```

Also, make sure your iOS device is connected to your development machine via USB.

How to do it...

1. Let's first open the newly created React Native iOS project in Xcode. Open the Project Editor by selecting the root of the project in the left panel.
2. Under the **General** tab of the **Project Editor**, select the iOS app in the **TARGETS** section on the left. Under the **Signing** section, select your **Team**, as follows:

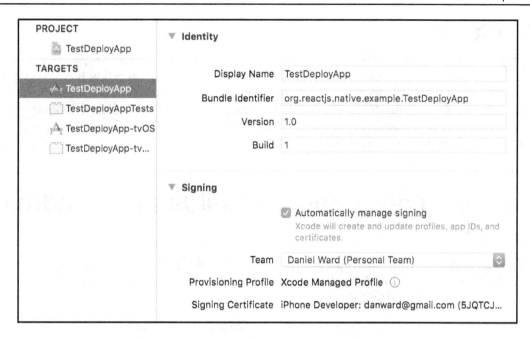

3. Repeat this step for two each of the entries in the **TARGETS** list.

4. Select your device in the destination selector, as follows:

5. To start running the app on your connected device, just press the Play button. You'll have to make sure your device is plugged in, unlocked, and trusted for it to show up in the devices list in Xcode. If this is the first time running an app you've developed on this device, you'll also need to adjust the settings to trust apps from your developer account. On the iOS device, this setting can be found in **Settings** | **General** | **Device Management**.

How it works...

Deploying our development build to the device simply involves designating a Team, then running the app as you would for use on the Xcode simulator, but targeting the plugged in device instead. We use the localhost packager to create our bundle file. This file then gets saved locally on the device for the future. Note that, since this is a development build, the code is not yet as optimized as it will be in a final release. You will see a significant performance increase when moving to a production release.

Deploying development builds to an Android device

While developing an Android application, you'll most often probably be running the app on an Android emulator. While convenient, an emulator will have poor performance when compared with a real Android device.

The best way to test an app is to use a physical Android device. This recipe will walk through deploying a React Native app to a physical Android device.

Getting ready

We'll just need a new pure React Native app, which we'll name `TestDeployApp`. You can create the app via this command:

```
react-native init
```

Also, make sure your iOS device is connected to your development machine via USB.

How to do it...

1. Let's start by opening our React Native Android project in Android Studio.
2. Next, press the run button, as follows:

3. Make sure the **Choose a running device** radio button is selected, and that your device is displayed in the list. Press **OK** to continue, as follows:

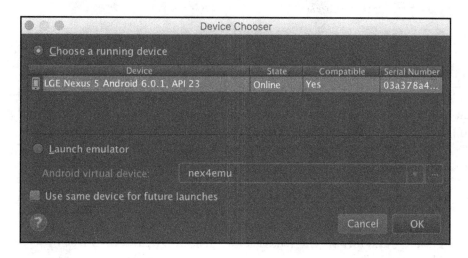

There's more...

The React Native packager should start when you run the application. If it doesn't, you'll have to manually start the packager. If you see an error screen with the message **Could not get BatchedBridge, please make sure your bundle is packaged correctly** or **Could not connect to development server**, you should be able to fix this by running the following command in the Terminal:

```
adb reverse tcp:8081 tcp:8081
```

How it works...

Much like Xcode, we can run our app by simply plugging in a real device, pressing **Run**, and selecting the device the app should run on. The only complication that might arise is setting up communication between the device and the development machine. These problems can often be solved with the command:

```
adb reverse
```

This establishes a port forward from the device to the host computer. This is a development build, and the code is not yet optimized, so there will be a performance increase once the app is built as a production release.

Deploying test builds to HockeyApp

Before releasing an app into the wild, it's important to stress test your app and to get user feedback when possible. To accomplish this, you need to create a signed build of your app that you can share with a group of test users. For a robust test build, you'll need two things: analytics/reporting on app performance, and a mechanism for delivery. HockeyApp provides this and more for your test builds on both iOS and Android. While both of the official platforms for releasing applications to the Apple App Store and Google Play Store provide functionality for testing and analytics, HockeyApp provides a unified place for handling these concerns, and a secondary source of metrics, crash reporting, and more.

It should be noted that HockeyApp was recently acquired by Microsoft. They have announced that the HockeyApp product will be discontinued in favor of Microsoft's App Center in November of 2019. You can read more about it on the product transition page at `https://hockeyapp.net/transition`. This recipe will walk through deploying a React Native app to HockeyApp for testing purposes. We will walk through both iOS and Android releases.

Getting ready

For this recipe, we will be using the same empty, pure React Native app from the last two recipes, which we named `TestDeployApp`. For iOS deployments, you will need to be enrolled in the Apple Developer Program, and you'll need to have `cocoapods` installed. The easiest way to install `cocoapods` is to use homebrew, via this command:

```
brew install cocoapods
```

You'll also need to have a HockeyApp account, which you can sign up for at their website at `https://hockeyapp.net/`

How to do it...

1. First, we need to install the `react-native-hockeyapp` module in our application. Open the Terminal, go to your application's root project directory, and enter the following command:

   npm install react-native-hockeyapp --save

2. Go into your `ios/` directory and initialize your Podfile:

   pod init

3. Open your Podfile and add `pod "HockeySDK"` to your target.
4. Back in the Terminal, install the Podfile, as follows:

   pod install

5. Now, let's open up Xcode and open our React Native project: (`ios/TestDeployApp.xcodeproj`).
6. I recommend changing your **Bundle Identifier** to something more meaningful than the default, so please change it in your **General Settings** dialog, as follows:

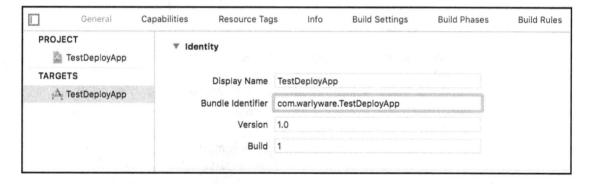

7. Drag and drop `./ios/Pods/Pods.xcodeproj` into the **Libraries** group in your project navigator, as follows:

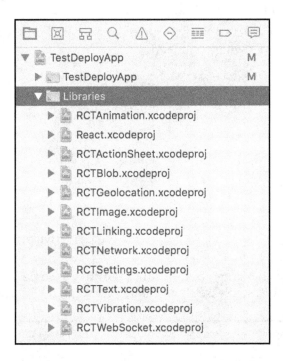

8. Drag and drop the `RNHockeyApp.h` and `RNHockeyApp.m` files located in `./node_modules/react-native-hockeyapp/RNHockeyApp/RNHockeyApp` into the same **Libraries** group.

9. Next, we'll go to the HockeyApp site and create our app there. Log in and click the **New App**.

10. Since we do not have our build ready yet, click **manually** in the phrase **Don't want to upload a build? Create the app manually instead** in the following modal.

11. When filling out the fields in the **Create App** form, be sure to match the **Title** and **Bundle Identifier** that we defined earlier in *step 6*, then press **Save**, as follows:

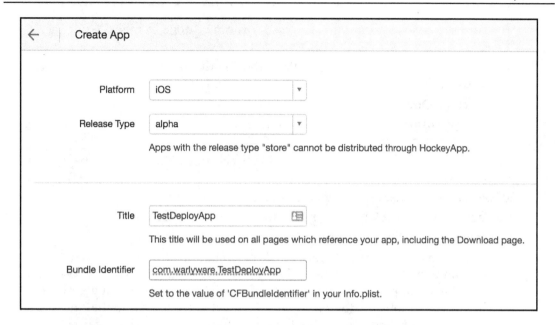

12. Make a note of the **App ID** since we'll be using it in the next step.

13. Open `App.js` and add the following code:

```
import HockeyApp from 'react-native-hockeyapp';

export default class
TestDeployApp extends Component {
  componentWillMount() {
    HockeyApp.configure(YOUR_APP_ID_HERE, true);
  }

  componentDidMount() {
    HockeyApp.start();
    HockeyApp.checkForUpdate();
  }
}
```

14. Back in Xcode, set **Generic iOS Device** as your destination target and build (**Product | Build**) the app, as follows:

15. Now, we need to create our `.ipa` file. This can be done from the Xcode menu via **Product | Archive**.

16. This will open the **Archives** list. Press the **Distribute App** button to start the process of creating the `.ipa`.

17. Select the **Development** option and press **Next**.

18. Your provisioning team should automatically be selected. With the correct Team selected, press **Next**.

19. Leave the default **Export** settings and press **Next**. On the summary page, also press **Next**.

20. Select the destination directory and press **Export**.

21. Back in the *HockeyApp* browser window, click **Add Version**.

22. Drag the `.ipa` file we just exported into the modal window.

23. We can leave the settings here set to their defaults, so continue pressing **Next** until the last modal screen, then press **Done** at the summary screen. That's it for the iOS app. You can add users to your *HockeyApp* app, and your testers should then be able to download your app. Let's switch over to the Android side of things. Open Android Studio, then open the Android folder in our React Native.

24. Repeat *step 8* to *step 11*, changing the **Platform** to **Android**, as follows:

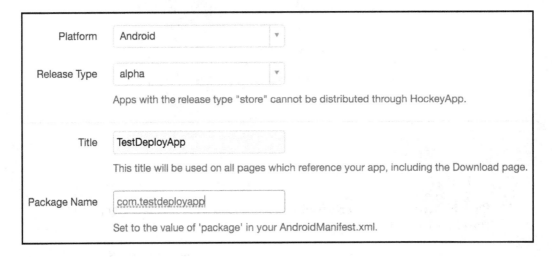

25. Now, we need to build our `.apk` file. You can find the most up-to-date method for building the `.apk` in the React Native documentation, located at:

    `https://facebook.github.io/react-native/docs/signed-apk-android.html`

26. Repeat *step 21* and *step 22* for the `.apk` generated from our Android project.

How it works...

For this recipe, we used *HockeyApp* for its two main features: its beta distribution and its HockeySDK (which supports crash reporting, metrics, feedback, authentication, and notifications for updates). For iOS, beta distribution is done through the OTA enterprise distribution mechanism hosted by *HockeyApp*. When you sign your app, you control which devices can open it. *HockeyApp* just sends notifications and provides the URL for beta testers to download your app through its enterprise app store. Android is simpler since there is no need to worry about how apps are transferred. This means *HockeyApp* hosts the `.apk` file on a web server that testers can download and install.

For more info on setting up *HockeyApp* on Android, you can read the official documentation at `https://support.hockeyapp.net/kb/client-integration-android/hockeyapp-for-android-sdk`.

Deploying iOS test builds to TestFlight

Before *HockeyApp* came along, the most popular service for beta testing mobile apps was TestFlight. In fact, it was so good at doing just that, that Apple purchased its parent company and integrated it into iTunes Connect. TestFlight now serves as the official app testing platform for Apple. There are a few differences between TestFlight and *HockeyApp* to consider. First and foremost, TestFlight became iOS only when it was purchased by Apple. Second, there are two styles of testing in TestFlight: internal and external. **Internal testing** involves sharing the application with Developer or Admin role members of your team, and limits distribution to 25 testers across 10 devices each. **External testing** allows you to invite up to 2,000 testers who do not have to be members of your organization. This also means that these testers do not use up your device quota. External testing applications go through the **Beta App Review** performed by Apple, which is not quite as rigorous as Apple's review for releasing an app to the App Store, but it is a good first pass.

This recipe focuses on taking our React Native app and deploying a test build to TestFlight. We will be setting up an internal test, since we do not want Apple reviewing our example React Native app, but the procedure is the same for both internal and external testing.

Getting ready

For this recipe, we will be using the same boilerplate React Native app from previous recipes, which we've named `TestDeployApp`. You will also need to be enrolled in the Apple Developer Program, you'll need to have your development and distribution certificates set up in Xcode, and your app will need to have its AppIcon set.

How to do it...

1. Let's start by opening our project in Xcode via the `ios/TestDeployApp.xcodeproj` file.

2. As stated in the last recipe, I also recommend changing your **Bundle Identifier** to something more meaningful than the default, for example:

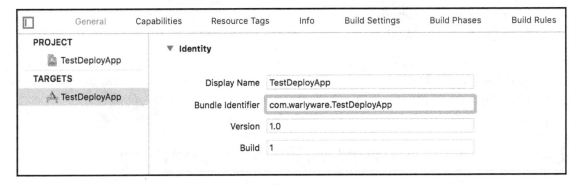

3. Next, let's log in to the Apple Developer Program and navigate to the App ID registration page, located
at `https//:developer.apple.com/account/ios/identifier/bundle`.

4. Here, fill out the **Name** and **Bundle ID** for your project, then press the **Continue** button, followed by the **Register** button, and finally the **Done** button to complete registration of the app.

5. Next, we'll log in to the iTunes Connect site, located
at `https://itunesconnect.apple.com`.

6. In iTunes Connect, navigate to **My Apps**, then press the Plus (+) button and select **New App** to add a new app.

7. In the New App dialog, fill out the **Name** and **Language**. Select the **Bundle ID** to match the one you created previously, and add a unique app reference in the SKU field, then press **Create**.

8. Next, navigate to the TestFlight section for your app and be sure to fill out the **Localizable Information** section.

9. Let's return to Xcode to create the `.ipa` file. Select **Generic iOS Device** for the active scheme, then create the file via the Xcode menu (**Product | Archive**). This will open the **Archives** list, where you can press the **Upload to App Store** button to upload the app.

10. Your provisioning team should automatically be selected. Be sure the correct team is selected and press **Choose**. Once the archive is created, press the **Upload** button.

11. After uploading the app, you'll need to wait until you receive an email from iTunes Connect informing you that the build has completed processing. Once processing is complete, you can return to the iTunes Connect page and open the **Internal Testing** view.

12. In the **Internal Testing** section, click **Select Version to Test** and select your build, then click the **Next** button. At the **Export Compliance** screen, press **OK**.

13. We're ready to add internal testers. Select the users you would like to test the app, then click the **Start Testing** button and confirm your selection in the following modal. Your users should now get an invitation email to test your app!

How it works...

TestFlight serves as a first-class citizen in the App Store publishing pipeline. Apple has integrated its support for application beta testing distribution directly into iTunes Connect, creating a smooth and seamless process for developers. This procedure is largely the same as deploying to the App Store, except that when using iTunes Connect, you must enable and configure testing.

It is a seamless experience for the tester as well. As soon as you add test users in iTunes Connect, they are notified to install the TestFlight app, where they will have easy access to the apps they can test. TestFlight also makes the process easier for developers by not requiring them to add any extra third-party libraries or code to support TestFlight, as would be needed with *HockeyApp*.

Deploying production builds to the Apple App Store

Once you've thoroughly tested your app, you're ready to move on to the next (and likely the most exciting) step in the iOS app making process: releasing to the Apple App Store.

This recipe will walk through the process of preparing your production build and submitting it to the Apple App Store. We won't actually be submitting the app to the store, since we're working with an example app instead of a production-ready one. The last few steps in the process, however, are very straightforward.

Getting ready

For this recipe, we will again be using the simple React Native example app from earlier recipes, TestDeployApp. You'll of course also need to be enrolled in the Apple Developer Program, and have your development and distribution certificates set up in Xcode as discussed earlier in this chapter. For a real production app deployment, you will also need to have both the AppIcon set and screenshots of the app ready for use in iTunes.

How to do it...

1. Let's start by opening up Xcode using the ios/TestDeployApp.xcodeproj file.
2. As stated before, it's recommended that you change your **Bundle Identifier** to something more meaningful than the default, so be sure to change it in the **General Settings** dialog.
3. It's also a good idea to test your app in Production Mode on your device. This can be done by changing your app scheme's **Build Configuration** (found via the **Product** | **Scheme** | **Edit Scheme** menus) to **Release**, as follows:

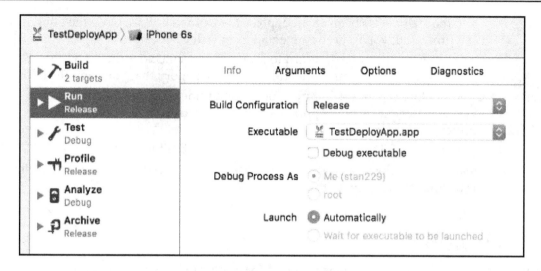

4. Next, you'll need to register the app on the App ID registration page, located at:

   `https://developer.apple.com/account/ios/identifier/bundle`

   This step requires an active Apple Developer Program account.

5. Fill out the **Name** and **Bundle ID** fields for your project and press the **Continue** button.

6. Next, we'll log in to the iTunes Connect site, located at `https://itunesconnect.apple.com`. In the **My Apps** section, press the Plus (+) button and select **New App**.

7. You'll need to fill out the **Name** and **Language** in the following dialog, then select the **Bundle ID** matching the one you created earlier in the recipe. Also, add a unique app reference for the **SKU** and press the **Create** button.

8. Let's return to Xcode and create the `.ipa` file. Select **Generic iOS Device** for the active scheme, and create the file via the menus (**Product | Archive**), which will open the **Archives** list. Finally, press **Upload to App Store**.

9. Select your Provisioning Team, then press **Choose**.

10. Once the archive has been created, press the **Upload** button. Once the build has been processed, you'll receive an email from iTunes Connect.

11. Once the app is processed, return to iTunes Connect. Under the **App Store** section, open **App Information** and select the category that your app fits into.

12. Open the **1.0 Prepare for Submission** section under **iOS APP**. Fill out all the required fields, including **App Screenshots**, **Description**, **Keywords**, and **Support URL**.

13. Next, under the **Build** section, select the `.ipa` we built in *step 8*.

14. Finally, fill out the **Copyright** and **App Review Information** sections, then click the **Submit for Review** button.

How it works...

In this recipe, we covered the standard process for publishing iOS apps to the App Store. There are no React Native-specific steps we needed to follow in this case, since the final product (the `.ipa` file) contains all of the code needed to run the React Native packager, which will in turn build the `main.jsbundle` file in release mode.

Deploying production builds to Google Play Store

This recipe will walk through the process of preparing a production build of our app and submitting it to the Google Play Store. As in the last recipe, we'll stop right before actually submitting to the App Store, since this is only an example React Native app, but the rest of this process is also straightforward.

Getting ready

For this recipe, we will be using the same simple React Native app we've used throughout this chapter, `TestDeployApp`. You will need to have a Google Play Developer account in order to submit an app to the store, and you'll also need to have all the icons and screenshots ready for the Play Store if you want to actually publish your app.

How to do it...

1. Let's start by opening the React Native project in Android Studio. The first step is building the `.apk` file. As mentioned earlier in this chapter, the process of creating a production Android app from a React Native project is involved and prone to change. Visit the React Native Documentation for creating the `.apk` at `https://facebook.github.io/react-native/docs/signed-apk-android.html`.

2. Next, let's open the Google Play Developer Console in a web browser, located at `https://play.google.com/apps/publish/`.

3. Let's kick off the process by clicking **Add new application**. Fill out the **Title** field, and click the **Upload APK** button, as follows:

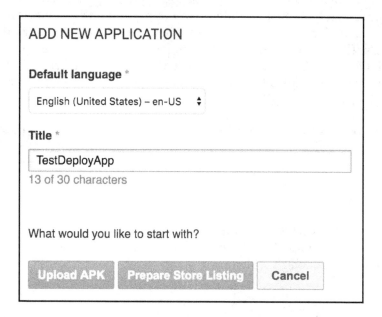

4. You'll see the **APK** section of the **Publish** screen next. Click **Upload your first APK to Production**, then drag and drop (or select) your `.apk` file.

5. A series of self-explanatory modals will follow. Go through each of the categories in the side menu on the left (**Store Listing**, **Content Rating**, and so on). and fill out all of the information accordingly.

6. Once you have satisfied all the requirements, press the **Publish App** button.

How it works...

In this recipe, we covered the process for publishing Android apps to the Google Play Store. By following the directions linked to in *step* 2, your React Native app will have been through the Gradle `assembleRelease` process. The `assemble` process runs the packager to create the JavaScript bundle file, compile the Java classes, package them together with the appropriate resources, and finally allow you to sign the app into an `.apk`.

Deploying Over-The-Air updates

One useful side effect of our React Native app being written in JavaScript is that the code is loaded at runtime, which is similar to how Cordova hybrid applications work. We can leverage this functionality to push updates to our application using **Over-The-Air** (**OTA**). This allows for adding features and bug fixes without having to go through the App Store approval process. The only limitation to OTA updates for React Native is that we cannot push compiled (Objective-C or Java) code, which means the update code must be in the JavaScript layer only. There are a few popular services that provide cloud-based OTA app updates. We will be highlighting `CodePush`, a service by Microsoft.

This recipe will cover setting up and pushing updates using `CodePush` for our React Native app on both iOS and Android.

Getting ready

For this recipe, we will be using the same simple React Native app we've used throughout this chapter, `TestDeployApp`. We'll be deploying the apps to physical devices running in production/release mode, which will allow the app to receive updates from the CodePush servers.

How to do it...

1. In order to use CodePush, we will need to install the CodePush CLI and create a free account. This can be done in a Terminal by running the following two commands:

```
npm install -g code-push-cli
code-push register
```

2. The next step is to register our app with CodePush. Make a note of the deployment keys for the app provided by the output from running `code-push register`. We will be using the **staging key** for this recipe. The documentation suggests adding one app per platform, with an `-IOS` or `-Android` suffix for each. To add the app to CodePush, use this command:

```
code-push app add TestDeployApp-IOS
code-push app add TestDeployApp-Android
```

3. We're also going to need the React Native CodePush module installed in the React Native project directory. This can be done with `npm`, as follows:

```
npm install --save react-native-code-push
```

Or, with `yarn`:

```
yarn add react-native-code-push
```

4. The next step is linking the CodePush native modules with our project. When prompted for your deployment key for Android and iOS, use the staging key discussed in *step 2*. Linking the native modules can be done with the following command:

```
react-native link react-native-code-push
```

5. Next, we need to set our React Native app up to use CodePush. Inside of `index.js`, we'll need to add three things: the CodePush import, an options object, and a call to the imported `codePush` module when registering the app via `AppRegistry.registerComponent`. Set up the app as follows:

```
import {AppRegistry} from 'react-native';
import App from './App';
import codePush from 'react-native-code-push';

const codePushOptions = {
  updateDialog : true
}

AppRegistry.registerComponent('TestDeployApp',
  () => codePush(codePushOptions)(App)
)
```

6. To test out our changes in the iOS app, let's deploy to our iOS device. Open the React Native project in Xcode, change your scheme's **Build Configuration** (**Product | Scheme | Edit Scheme...**) to **Release**, then press **Run**, as follows:

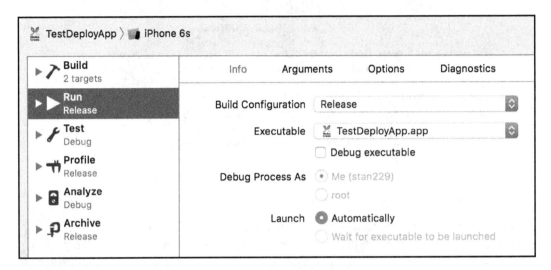

7. Next, make some sort of arbitrary change to the React Native code in the app, then in the Terminal, run the following command to update the app with the new code:

```
code-push release-react TestDeployApp ios -m --description
"Updating using CodePush"
```

8. Next, close and reopen the app on your iOS device. You should see the following prompt:

9. After continuing past the prompt, the app will update itself to the latest version!

10. Let's also test the feature on Android. You'll need to have made your Android app into a `.apk` file by following the steps outlined in the React Native documentation at `https://facebook.github.io/react-native/docs/signed-apk-android.html`.

11. With your Android device plugged into your development machine, run the following command in the Terminal from the `android/` directory:

```
adb install
app/build/outputs/apk/app-release.apk
```

12. Next, make a change to the React Native JavaScript code. As long as new code is added, we can use that changed code to update the app. Then, run the following command in the Terminal:

```
code-push release-react TestDeployApp android -m --description
"Updating using CodePush"
```

13. Once again, close and reopen your app on your Android device to get the following prompt:

14. After proceeding past the prompt, the app will update itself to the latest version.

How it works...

CodePush (as well as other cloud-hosted OTA update platforms) works by using the same technique that has existed in React Native since its inception. React Native loads a JavaScript bundle when the app is initialized. During development, this bundle is loaded from `localhost:3000`. Once we've deployed an app, however, it will look for a file named `main.jsbundle` that has been included in the final product. By adding the call to `codePush` in `registerComponent` in *step 5*, the app will check in with the CodePush API to see if there is an update. If there is a new update, it will prompt the user about it. Accepting the prompt downloads the new `jsbundle` file and restarts the app, causing the code to be updated.

Optimizing React Native app size

Before deploying our app to production, it's always a good idea to shrink the app bundle size to as small a file as possible, and there are several techniques we can leverage to do so. These can involve supporting fewer devices or compressing included assets.

This recipe will cover a few techniques for limiting production package file sizes in both iOS and Android React Native apps.

Getting ready

For this recipe, we will be using the same simple React Native app we've used throughout this chapter, `TestDeployApp`. You'll also need to have code signing working for iOS, and the ability to create `.apk` files as covered in previous recipes.

How to do it...

1. We will start off with some simple optimizations performed on our bundled assets, which often includes images and external fonts:
    - For PNG and JPEG compression, you can use a service such as `http://www.tinypng.com` to reduce the file size with little to no reduction in image quality.

- If you use the `react-native-vector-icons` library, you will notice that it bundles eight different font icon sets. It's recommended that you remove any of the icon font libraries that are not being used by your app.
- SVG files can also be compressed and optimized. One service for this purpose is `http://compressor.io`.
- Any audio assets packaged with your app should be using a file format that can leverage high quality compression, such as MP3 or AAC.

2. For iOS, there's not much that can be done to further reduce file size beyond the settings that are enabled by default on the release scheme. These include enabling Bitcode for app thinning and setting the compiler optimization to **Fastest, Smallest [-Os]**.

3. For Android, there are two things you can do that could improve file size:
   - In Android Studio, open `android/app/build.gradle` and locate the following lines, then update their values to the following:

```
def enableSeparateBuildPerCPUArchitecture = true
def enableProguardInReleaseBuilds = true
```

4. If you plan to only target ARM-based Android devices, we can prevent it from building for x86 altogether. In the `build.gradle` file, locate the `splits abi` object and add the following line to not include x86 support:

```
include "armeabi-v7a"
```

You can read more about ABI management in the Android docs at:

```
https://developer.android.com/ndk/guides/abis
```

How it works...

In this recipe, we covered techniques that can be used to reduce app file size. The smaller the JavaScript bundle is, the faster the JavaScript interpreter will be able to parse the code, translating into faster app load times, and quicker OTA updates. The smaller we can keep our `.ipa` and `.apk` files, the faster our users will be able to download the app.

15
Optimizing the Performance of Your App

In this chapter, we will cover the following recipes:

- Optimizing our JavaScript code
- Optimizing the performance of custom UI components
- Keeping animations running at 60 FPS
- Getting the most out of ListView
- Boosting the performance of our app
- Optimizing the performance of native iOS modules
- Optimizing the performance of native Android modules
- Optimizing the performance of native iOS UI components
- Optimizing the performance of native Android UI components

Introduction

Performance is a key requirement of almost every single piece of technology in software development. React Native was introduced to solve the issue of poor performance that existed in hybrid apps that wrap web applications in a native container. React Native has an architecture that lends itself to both flexibility and excellent performance.

When considering the performance of a React Native app, it is important to think about the big picture of how React Native works. There are three major parts to a React Native app, and their relative performance is depicted in the following diagram:

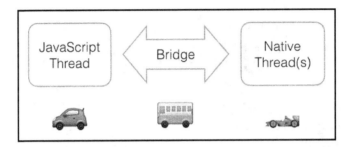

The recipes in this chapter focus on using lower-level functions that take up less memory and have fewer operations, thus lowering the time it takes for a task to complete.

Optimizing our JavaScript code

It's safe to say that your React Native apps will probably be written mostly in JavaScript. There may be some native modules and custom UI components, but for the most part, all of the views and business logic will likely be written in JSX and JavaScript. And if you're using modern JavaScript development techniques, you'll also be using language constructs introduced with ES6, ES7, and beyond. These may be available natively as part of the JavaScript interpreter bundled with React Native (JavaScriptCore) or polyfilled by the Babel transpiler. Since JavaScript probably constitutes the majority of any given React Native app, this should be the first part we optimize in order to squeeze extra performance out of the app.

This recipe will provide some helpful tips for optimizing JavaScript code to make it as performant as possible.

Getting ready

This recipe is not necessarily dependent on React Native, since it focuses on the JavaScript that's used to write any React app. Some of these suggestions are micro-optimizations that will probably only improve performance on older/slower devices. Depending on which devices you intend to support, some tips will go further than others.

How to do it...

1. The first optimization to look at is speeding up iterations. Often, you'll likely be using functions that take iterator functions as arguments (`forEach`, `filter`, and `map`). As a rule of thumb, these will be slower than doing a standard `for` loop. If the size of the collection you're iterating over is very large, this could make a difference. Here's an example of a faster filter function:

```
let myArray = [1,2,3,4,5,6,7];
let newArray;

// Slower:
function filterFn(element) {
  return element > 2;
}
newArray = myArray.filter(filterFn);

// Faster:
function filterArray(array) {
  var length = array.length,
    myNewArray = [],
    element,
    i;

  for(i = 0; i < length; i++) {
    element = array[i];
    if(element > 2) {
      myNewArray.push(array[i]);
    }
  }
  return myNewArray;
}

newArray = filterArray(myArray);
```

2. When optimizing iterations, it can also be more performant to ensure that you store the variables you are accessing on the iteration, somewhere close by:

```
function findInArray(propertyerties, appConfig) {
  for (let i = 0; i < propertyerties.length; i++) {
    if (propertyerties[i].somepropertyerty ===
    appConfig.userConfig.permissions[0]) {
      // do something
    }
  }
}
```

```
function fasterFindInArray(propertyerties, appConfig) {
    let matchPermission = appConfig.userConfig.permissions[0];
    let length = propertyerties.length;
    let i = 0;

    for (; i < length; i++) {
        if (propertyerties[i].somepropertyerty === matchPermission)
{
            // do something
        }
    }
}
```

3. You can also optimize your logical expressions. Keep your fastest and closest executing statements on the left:

```
function canViewApp(user, isSuperUser) {
    if (getUserPermissions(user).canView || isSuperUser) {
        return true;
    }
}

function canViewApp(user, isSuperUser) {
    if (isSuperUser || getUserPermissions(user).canView) {
        return true;
    }
}
```

4. While modern JavaScript (ES6, ES7, and so on) constructs can be more enjoyable to develop with, some of their features execute more slowly than their ES5 counterparts. These features can include `for of`, `generators`, `Object.assign`, and others. A good reference for performance comparisons can be found at https://kpdecker.github.io/six-speed/.

5. It can be helpful to avoid `try-catch` statements, since they can affect the optimization made by the interpreter (as is the case in V8).

6. Arrays should have members that are all of the same type. If you need to have a collection where the type can vary, use an object.

How it works...

JavaScript performance is a topic of constant debate. It is sometimes difficult to keep up with the latest in performance metrics, since Google, Apple, Mozilla, and the global open source community is always hard at work improving their JavaScript engines. For React Native, we focus on WebKit's JavaScriptCore.

Optimizing the performance of custom UI components

While building your React Native app, it's a safe bet that you will be creating custom UI components. These components can either be compositions of several other components or a component that builds on top of an existing component and adds more functionality. With added functionality, complexity also increases. This increased complexity leads to more operations, and in turn, the potential for slowdowns. Fortunately, there are some ways to make sure that our custom UI components are performing the best they can. This recipe shows several techniques for getting the most out of our components.

Getting ready

This recipe requires that you have a React Native app with some custom components. As these performance suggestions may or may not provide value to your app, use discretion when you choose to apply these to your code.

How to do it...

1. The first optimization we should look at is what is tracked in the `state` object of a given component. We should make sure that all the objects we have in the `state` are being used, and that each can potentially change, causing a desired re-render.
2. Take a look at the `render` function of each component. The overall goal is to keep this function performing as fast as possible, so try to ensure that no long-running processes occur within it. If you can, cache computations and constant values outside the `render` function so that they are not instantiated every time.

3. If you have conditional JSX that may return in the render function, return as early as possible. Here's a trivial example:

```
// unoptimized
render() {
  let output;
  const isAdminView = this.propertys.isAdminView;

  if(isAdminView) {
    output = (<AdminButton/>);
  } else {
    output = (
      <View style={styles.button}>
        <Text>{this.propertys.buttonLabel}</Text>
      </View>
    );
  }
  return output;
}

// optimized
render() {
  const isAdminView = this.propertys.isAdminView;

  if (isAdminView) {
    return (<AdminButton/>);
  }
  return (
    <View style={styles.button}>
      <Text>{this.propertys.buttonLabel}</Text>
    </View>
  );
}
```

4. The most important optimization we can make is to skip the render method altogether if it isn't needed. This is done by implementing the shouldComponentUpdate method and returning false from it, making it a pure component. Here's how we can make a component a PureComponent:

```
import React, { PureComponent } from 'react';

export default class Button extends PureComponent {

}
```

How it works...

The majority of your React Native apps will consist of custom components. There will be a mix of stateful and stateless components. As highlighted in *step 2*, the overall goal is to render our component in the shortest amount of time possible. Another gain can be achieved if a component can be architected to only have to render the component once and then be left untouched, as covered in *step 4*. For more information on how pure components are used and how they can be beneficial, check out `https://60devs.com/pure-component-in-react.html`.

See also

You can find some more information about React component performance optimizations in the official documentation at `https://reactjs.org/docs/optimizing-performance.html`.

Keeping animations running at 60 FPS

An important aspect of any quality mobile app is the fluidity of the user interface. Animations are used to provide a rich user experience, and any jank or jitter can negatively affect this. Animations will likely be used for all kinds of interactions, from changing between views, to reacting to a user's touch interaction on a component. One of the most important factors in creating high-quality animations is making sure that they do not block the JavaScript thread. To keep animations fluid and not interrupt UI interactions, the render loop has to render each frame in 16.67 ms, so that 60 FPS can be achieved.

In this recipe, we will take a look at several techniques for improving the performance of animations. These techniques focus in particular on preventing JavaScript execution from interrupting the main thread.

Getting ready

For this recipe, we'll assume that you have a React Native app that has some animations defined.

How to do it...

1. First and foremost, when debugging animation performance in React Native, we'll want to enable the performance monitor. To do so, show the **Dev Menu** (shake the device or *cmd + D* from the simulator) and tap **Show Perf Monitor**. The output in iOS will look something like the following screenshot:

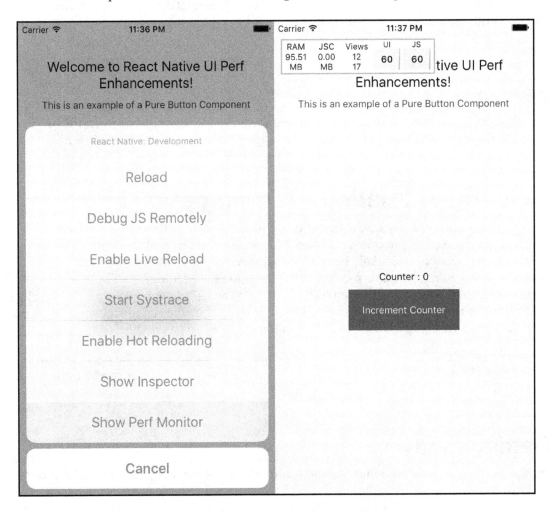

The output in Android will look something like the following screenshot:

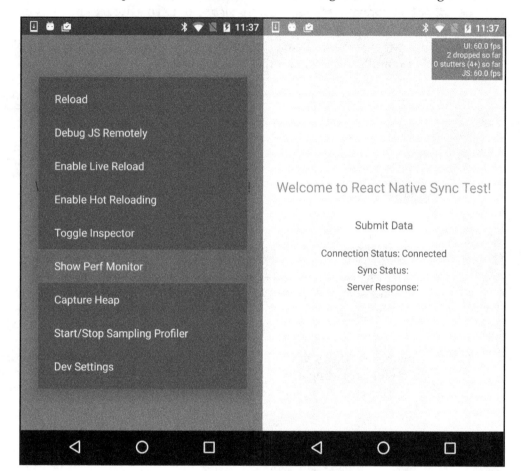

2. If you are looking to animate a component's transition (opacity) or dimensions (width, height), then make sure to use LayoutAnimation. You can find an example of using LayoutAnimation in Chapter 6, *Adding Basic Animations to Your App*, in the *Expanding and collapsing containers* recipe.

If you want to use LayoutAnimation on Android, you need to add the following code when your application starts: UIManager.setLayoutAnimationEnabledExperimental && UIManager.setLayoutAnimationEnabledExperimental(true).

3. If you need finite control over the animations, it is recommended that you use the `Animated` library that comes with React Native. This library allows you to offload all of the animation work onto the native UI thread. To do so, we have to add the `useNativeDriver` property to our `Animated` call. Let's take a sample `Animated` example and offload it to the native thread:

```
componentWillMount() {
  this.setState({
    fadeAnimimation: new Animated.Value(0)
  });
}

componentDidMount() {
  Animated.timing(this.state.fadeAnimimation, {
    toValue: 1,
    useNativeDriver: true
  }).start();
}
```

Currently, only a subset of the functionality of the Animated library supports native offloading. Please refer to the *There's more...* section for a compatibility guide.

4. If you are unable to offload your animation work onto the native thread, there is still a solution for providing a smooth experience. We can use the `InteractionManager` to execute a task after the animations have completed:

```
componentWillMount() {
  this.setState({
    isAnimationDone: false
  });
}
componentWillUpdate() {
  LayoutAnimation.easeInAndOut();
}

componentDidMount() {
  InteractionManager.runAfterInteractions(() => {
    this.setState({
      isAnimationDone: true
    });
  })
}

render() {
```

```
            if (!this.state.isAnimationDone) {
              return this.renderPlaceholder();
            }
            return this.renderMainScene();
        }
```

5. Finally, if you are still suffering from poor performance, you'll have to either rethink your animation strategy or implement the poorly performing view as a custom UI view component on the target platform(s). This would mean implementing both your view and animation natively using the iOS and/or Android SDK. In `Chapter 11`, *Adding Native Functionality*, we covered creating custom UI components in the *Rendering custom iOS view components* and *Rendering custom Android view components* recipes.

How it works...

The tips in this recipe focus on the simple goal of preventing the JavaScript thread from locking. The moment our JavaScript thread begins to drop frames (lock), we lose the ability to interact with our application, even if it's for a fraction of a second. It may seem inconsequential, but the effect is felt immediately by a savvy user. The focus of the tips in this recipe is to offload animations onto the GPU. When the animation is running on the main thread (the native layer, rendered by the GPU), the user can interact with the app freely without stuttering, hanging, jank, or jitters.

There's more...

Here's a quick reference for where `useNativeDriver` is usable:

Function	iOS	Android
`style`, `value`, `propertys`	√	√
`decay`		√
`timing`	√	√
`spring`		√
`add`	√	√
`multiply`	√	√
`modulo`	√	
`diffClamp`	√	√
`interpoloate`	√	√
`event`		√

| division | √ | √ |
| transform | √ | √ |

Getting the most out of ListView

React Native provides a pretty performant list component out of the box. It is extremely flexible, supports rendering almost any component you can imagine inside of it, and renders them rather quickly. If you'd like to read some more examples of how to work with ListView, there are a couple of recipes in this book, including *Displaying a list of items* in Chapter 2, *Creating a Simple React Native App*, that use it. The React Native ListView is built on top of ScrollView to achieve the flexibility of rendering variable-height rows with any view component.

The major performance and resource drawback of the ListView component occurs when you are working with an extremely large list. As the user scrolls through the list, the next page of rows is rendered at the bottom. The invisible rows at the top can be set to be removed from the render tree, which we will cover shortly. However, the references to the rows are still in memory as long as the component is mounted. Naturally, as our component uses up the available memory, there will be less room for quickly accessible storage for the upcoming components. This recipe will cover dealing with some of these potential performance and memory resource issues.

Getting ready

For this recipe, we assume that you have a React Native app that is making use of a ListView, preferably with a large dataset.

How to do it...

1. Let's start with some optimizations we can make to our vanilla ListView component. If we set the initialListSize property to 1, we can speed up the initial rendering.
2. Next, we can bump up the pageSize if the component being rendered in each row is not complex.

3. Another optimization is setting the `scrollRenderAheadDistance` to a comfortable value. If you can expect users to rarely scroll past the initial viewport, or that they're likely to scroll slowly, then you can lower the value. This prevents the `ListView` from rendering too many rows in advance.

4. Finally, the last optimization we can make use of is the `removeClippedSubviews` property. However, the official documentation states the following:

   "The feature may have bugs (missing content) in some circumstances - use at your own risk."

5. Combining *steps 1 to step 4* can be seen in the following example code:

```
renderRow(row) {
  return (
    <View style={{height:44, overflow:'hidden'}}>
      <Text>Item {row.index}</Text>
    </View>
  )
}

render() {
  return (
    <View style={{flex:1}}>
      <ListView
        dataSource={this.state.dataSource}
        renderRow={this.renderRow}
        pageSize={10}
        initialListSize={1}
        pageSize={10}
        scrollAheadDistance={200}
      />
    </View>
  )
}
```

How it works...

As with developing any app, the more flexible and complex something is, the slower it performs. ListView is an excellent example of this concept. It is extremely flexible, since it can render any View in a row, but it can quickly bring your application to a halt if not used carefully. The result of the optimizations defined in *step 1* to *step 4* will vary across different situations based on what you are rendering and the data structure that is being used by the ListView. You should experiment with these values until you find a good balance. As a last resort, if you are still unable to achieve the required performance benchmark, you can look at some of the community modules that provide new ListView implementations or alternatives.

See also

The following is a list of some of the third-party ListView implementations that promise increased performance:

- recyclerlistview: This library is the most robust alternative to ListView, boasting a long list of improvements and features, including support for staggered grid layouts, horizontal mode, and footer support. The repository is located at https://github.com/Flipkart/recyclerlistview.
- react-native-sglistview: This takes removeClippedSubviews to the next level by flushing the memory when the offscreen rows are removed from the render tree. The repository is located at https://github.com/sghiassy/react-native-sglistview.

Boosting the performance of our app

The reason for React Native's existence is building native apps with JavaScript. This is different than similar frameworks such as Ionic or Cordova hybrid applications, which wrap a web application written in JavaScript and attempt to emulate native app behavior. Those web applications only have access to native APIs for performing processing, but cannot render native views inside their apps. This is one major benefit to React Native apps, thus making them inherently faster than hybrid apps. Since it's so much more performant out of the box, we generally do not have to worry about overall performance as much as we would with a hybrid web app. Still, with a little extra effort, a slight improvement in performance might be achievable. This recipe will provide some quick wins that we can use to build faster React Native apps.

How to do it...

1. The simplest optimization we can make is to not output any statements to the console. Performing a `console.log` statement is not as trivial a task as you'd imagine for the framework, so it's recommended to remove all console statements when you are ready to bundle your final app.

2. If you use a lot of console statements during development, you can have Babel automatically remove them when creating the bundle by using the `transform-remove-console` plugin. This can be installed into the project via the Terminal using `yarn`:

```
yarn add babel-plugin-transform-remove-console
```

3. Alternatively, you can use `npm`:

```
npm install babel-plugin-transform-remove-console --save
```

   With the package installed, you can add it to the project by adding a `.babelrc` file containing the following code:

```
{
  "presets": ["react-native"],
  "env": {
    "production": {
        "plugins": ["transform-remove-console"]
    }
  }
}
```

4. Next, make sure that when you're analyzing your performance, your app is running in production mode, preferably on a device. If you are curious about how to do this, you can refer to the *Deploying test builds to HockeyApp* recipe in `Chapter 13`, *Deploying Our App*.

5. Sometimes, when you are animating the position or layout of a `View`, you may notice performance dips in the UI thread. You can mitigate this by setting the `shouldRasterizeIOS` and `renderToHardwareTextureAndroid` properties to true for iOS and Android platforms. Be mindful that this may increase memory usage significantly, so be sure to test the performance after these changes as well.

6. If you find that you need to transition views using a navigation state change while also performing synchronous, potentially long-running processes, it can become a performance bottleneck. This commonly occurs when building a `DataSource` for a `ListView` or when transforming data to power the upcoming view. You should experiment with processing only an initial subset of the data, enough to render the UI quickly enough. Once the animation completes between page transitions, you can use `InteractionManager` to load the rest of the data. You can refer to the *Keeping animations running at 60 FPS* recipe for more information on how to use `InteractionManager`.

7. Finally, if you have identified a particular component or task that is slowing down your app, and cannot find a viable solution, then you should consider moving it to the native thread by creating a native module or native UI component to implement this piece of functionality.

How it works...

This recipe covers some higher-level and broader-scoped tips for all React Native apps. The most significant performance gains you will likely see from these tips are from moving a component to the native layer, as covered in *step 7*.

Optimizing the performance of native iOS modules

Often, when building a React Native app, you will need to work with native Android and iOS code. You may have built these native modules to expose some extra functionality provided by a native API, or perhaps your app needed to perform an intensive background task.

As was touched on earlier, working in the native layer really allows you to make use of a device's full capacity. However, it doesn't mean that the code we write will automatically be the fastest it could be. There's always room to optimize and achieve performance gains.

In this recipe, we will provide some tips on how to make your Objective-C code run a bit faster using the iOS SDKs. We will also consider how React Native and the React Native bridge, which is used to communicate between the JavaScript and the native layers, fit into the bigger picture.

Getting ready

For this recipe, you should have a React Native app that uses native modules that have been created for iOS. If you need help with writing native modules, take a look at the *Exposing custom iOS modules* recipe in `Chapter 11`, *Adding Native Functionality*.

How to do it...

1. First and foremost, when working with native modules, we have to be mindful of the data going through the React Native bridge. Keeping the data in cross-bridge events and callbacks to a minimum is always the goal, since the data serialization between Objective-C and JavaScript is very slow.

2. If you need to keep data cached in memory for consumption by the native module, keep it stored in a local property or field variable. Native modules are singletons. Do this instead of returning a large object to store in the React Native component.

3. Sometimes, we have to leverage classes that are large because they are robust in their feature set. For the Objective-C and iOS side of things, instead of instantiating something like `NSDateFormatter` in your method each time that you expose the feature via `RCT_EXPORT_METHOD`, store the reference of this class as a property or an instance variable.

4. Furthermore, native methods such as `NSDateFormatter` are often extremely heavy, so avoiding them is advisable where possible. For instance, if your application can deal with just UNIX timestamps, then you can easily get an `NSDate` object from a timestamp with the following function:

   ```
   - (NSDate*)dateFromUnixTimestamp:(NSTimeInterval)timestamp {
       return [NSDate dateWithTimeIntervalSince1970:timestamp];
   }
   ```

5. The most significant performance optimization you can make, if the situation presents itself, is spawning asynchronous background threads to handle intensive processing. React Native fits this model well, since it uses an asynchronous messaging/event system to communicate between the JavaScript and native threads. When your background process is complete, you can either invoke a callback/promise or fire an event for the JavaScript thread to pick up. To learn how to create and leverage background processes in React Native iOS native modules, check out the *Background processing on iOS* recipe in `Chapter 11`, *Adding Native Functionality*.

How it works...

Objective-C code executes very quickly – almost as quickly as vanilla C. Therefore, the optimizations we perform do not have much to do with executing tasks but rather with how things are instantiated and by not blocking native threads. The biggest performance boost you'll see is by property using the **Grand Central Dispatch** (**GCD**) to spawn background processes, as described in *step 5*.

Optimizing the performance of native Android modules

While developing your React Native application, you may find yourself writing native Android modules to either create cross-platform features on both iOS and Android or to make use of native APIs that have not been wrapped as first-party modules for Android but that do exist on iOS. Hopefully, you found some useful advice on working with native modules in `Chapter 11`, *Adding Native Functionality*.

In this recipe, we will cover several techniques for speeding up our React Native Android native modules. Many of these techniques are limited to general development on Android, and a few will address communicating with the React Native JavaScript layer.

Getting ready

For this recipe, you should have a React Native app that makes use of the native modules you created for Android. If you need help with writing native modules, please take a look at the *Exposing custom Android modules* recipe in `Chapter 11`, *Adding Native Functionality*.

How to do it...

1. First and foremost, just as with iOS native modules, you'll want to limit the amount of data crossing the React Native bridge. Keeping the data that's in events and callbacks to a minimum will help to avoid slowdowns caused by the serialization between Java and JavaScript. Also, as with iOS, try to keep data cached in memory to be used by the native module; keep it stored in a private field. Native modules are singletons. This should be leveraged instead of returning a large object to store in the React Native component.

2. When writing Java code for Android, you should do your best to avoid creating short-term objects. If you can, use primitives, especially for datasets such as arrays.

3. It is better to reuse objects instead of relying on the garbage collector to pick up an unused reference and instantiate a new object.

4. The Android SDK provides a memory-efficient data structure for replacing the use of a `Map`, which maps integers to objects, called `SparseArray`. Using it can reduce memory usage and improve performance. Here's an example:

```
SparseArray<SomeType> map = new SparseArray<SomeType>();
map.put(1, myObjectInstance);
```

> There is also `SparseIntArray`, which maps integers to integers, and `SparseBooleanArray`, which maps integers to Boolean values.

5. While it may sound counterintuitive to developers used to OOP development in Java, avoiding the use of getters and setters by accessing the instance field directly can also improve performance.

6. If you're ever working with `String` concatenation, make use of `StringBuilder`.

7. Lastly, the most significant performance optimization you can make, if possible, is spawning asynchronous background threads to perform heavy computations by leveraging React Native's asynchronous messaging/event system to communicate between the JavaScript and native threads. When your background process is complete, you can either invoke a callback/promise or fire an event for the JavaScript thread to pick up. To learn how to create background processes in React Native Android native modules, please read the *Background processing on Android* recipe in `Chapter 11`, *Adding Native Functionality*.

How it works...

The majority of the tips in this recipe revolve around efficient memory management. The Android OS uses a traditional-style garbage collector similar to the desktop Java VM. When the garbage collector kicks in, it can take anywhere between 100-200 ms to free memory. *Steps 3-6* all provide suggestions that reduce the app's memory usage.

Optimizing the performance of native iOS UI components

React Native provides us with an excellent foundation to build almost any kind of user interface using built-in components and styling. Components built in Objective-C using the iOS SDK, OpenGL, or some other drawing library will generally perform better than composing the prebuilt components using JSX. When using these native view components, there are some use cases that may have a negative impact on app performance.

This recipe will focus on getting the most out of the iOS UIKit SDK when rendering custom views. Our goal is to render everything as quickly as possible for our application to run at 60 FPS.

Getting ready

For this recipe, you should have a React Native app that renders custom native UI components you have written for iOS. If you need help with wrapping UI components in React Native, please take a look at the *Exposing custom iOS view components* recipe in `Chapter 11`, *Adding Native Functionality*.

How to do it...

1. As mentioned previously, only pass data across the React Native bridge when it is unavoidable to do otherwise, since data serialization between Objective-C and JavaScript types is slow.
2. If there is data that you need to store for referencing sometime in the near future, it's better to store it in the native class that you initialized. Depending on your application, you can either store it as a property on the `ViewManager`, a singleton that serves instances of the `View`, or a property on the `View` itself.
3. If your view component involves rendering multiple `UIView` instances as children of a parent `UIView` container, make sure all the instances have the `opaque` property set to `true`.
4. If you are rendering an image inside your view component (not using the React Native `Image` component), then setting your image to be the same dimension as the `UIImageView` component can help performance. Scaling, and other image transformations, are heavy operations that can impact frame rate.

5. One of the most impactful tweaks in writing iOS view components is avoiding offscreen rendering. Avoid doing the following with SDK functionality if possible:

   - Using classes that start with the **Core Graphics** (**CG**) library
   - Overriding the `drawRect` implementation of `UIView`
   - Setting `shouldRasterize=YES`, or using `setMasksToBounds` or `setShadow` on your `UIView` instance's `layer` property
   - Custom drawings using `CGContext`

6. If you need to add a shadow to your view, make sure to set the `shadowPath` to prevent offscreen rendering. Here's an example of how the initialization and shadow definition should look:

```
RCT_EXPORT_MODULE()

- (UIView *)view {
  UIView *view = [[UIView alloc] init];

  view.layer.masksToBounds = NO;
  view.layer.shadowColor = [UIColor blackColor].CGColor;
  view.layer.shadowOffset = CGSizeMake(0.0f, 5.0f);
  view.layer.shadowOpacity = 0.5f;

  view.layer.shadowPath = [[UIBezierPath
bezierPathWithRect:view.bounds] CGPath];

  return view;
}
```

How it works...

This recipe focused on some helpful tips that allow the GPU to do as much of the work as it can. The second part discussed how to keep the load on the GPU as low as possible. Enforcing the `opaque` property in *step 3* tells the GPU not to worry about checking the visibility of other components so that it can calculate transparency. *Steps 5* and *step 6* prevent offscreen rendering. Offscreen rendering generates bitmap images using the CPU (which is a slow process) and, more importantly, it keeps the GPU from rendering the view until the images have been generated.

Optimizing the performance of native Android UI components

Over the last few years, Android native UI performance has improved significantly. This is primarily due to its ability to render components and layouts using GPU hardware acceleration. In your React Native app, you may find yourself using custom view components, especially if you want to use a built-in Android feature that has not yet been wrapped as a React Native component. Even though the Android platform has made a conscious effort to increase the performance of its UI, the way components are rendered can quickly negate all of these benefits.

In this recipe, we'll discuss a few ways to get the best performance out of our custom Android view components.

Getting ready

For this recipe, you should have a React Native application that renders custom native UI components you have written for Android. If you need help with wrapping UI components in React Native, check out the *Exposing custom Android view components* recipe in `Chapter 11`, *Adding Native Functionality*.

How to do it...

1. As stated previously, only cross the React Native bridge with data when necessary. Keep the data in events and callbacks to a minimum as the data serialization between Java and JavaScript is slow.

2. If there is data that you need to store for referencing sometime in the near future, it's better to store it in the native class that you've initialized. Depending on your application, you can either store it as a property on the `SimpleViewManager`, a singleton that serves instances of the `View`, or a property on the `View` itself.

3. When building out views, consider that components often consist of other child components. These components are held in a hierarchy of layouts. Over-nesting layouts can become a very expensive operation. If you are using multi-level nested `LinearLayout` instances, try to replace them with a single `RelativeLayout`.

4. You can analyze the efficiency of your layout using the **HierarchyViewer** tool that's bundled inside the Android Device Monitor. To open it from the Android Device Monitor, click **Window** | **Open Perspective...** | **Hierarchy View** and select **OK**.

5. If you are performing repeated animations on your custom view natively in Java (not using the React Native Animated API), then you can leverage hardware layers to improve performance. Simply add a `withLayer` method call to your `animate` call. For example:

```
myView.animate()
  .alpha(0.0f)
  .withLayer()
  .start();
```

How it works...

Unfortunately, there aren't that many optimizations you can perform when it comes to rendering Android UI components. They generally revolve around not over-nesting layouts, since this increases complexity by orders of magnitude. When you have layout performance issues, the app is most likely suffering from overusing the GPU, or overdrawing. Overdrawing occurs when the GPU renders a new view over an existing view that is already rendered. You can enable **GPU Overdraw Debugging** in the Android **Developer Settings** menu. The order of severity of overdrawing is No Color -> Blue -> Green -> Light Red -> Dark Red.

In *step 5*, we provided a quick tip for improving the performance of animations. This is particularly true for repeated animations, since it caches the animation output on the GPU and replays it.

Other Books You May Enjoy

If you enjoyed this book, you may be interested in these other books by Packt:

Hands-On Design Patterns with React Native
Mateusz Grzesiukiewicz

ISBN: 9781788994460

- Explore the design Patterns in React Native
- Learn the best practices for React Native development
- Explore common React patterns that are highly used within React Native development
- Learn to decouple components and use dependency injection in your applications
- Explore the best ways of fetching data from the backend systems
- Learn the styling patterns and how to implement custom mobile designs
- Explore the best ways to organize your application code in big codebases

React and React Native - Second Edition
Adam Boduch

ISBN: 9781789346794

- Learn what has changed in React 16 and how you stand to benefit
- Craft reusable components using the React virtual DOM
- Learn how to use the new create-react-native-app command line tool
- Augment React components with GraphQL for data using Relay
- Handle state for architectural patterns using Flux
- Build an application for web UIs using Relay

Leave a review - let other readers know what you think

Please share your thoughts on this book with others by leaving a review on the site that you bought it from. If you purchased the book from Amazon, please leave us an honest review on this book's Amazon page. This is vital so that other potential readers can see and use your unbiased opinion to make purchasing decisions, we can understand what our customers think about our products, and our authors can see your feedback on the title that they have worked with Packt to create. It will only take a few minutes of your time, but is valuable to other potential customers, our authors, and Packt. Thank you!

Index

creating 36, 37, 39, 40, 41, 42

U

UI components
  styling, glamorous-native used 353, 354, 355,
    358, 359
universal applications
  dealing with 101, 102, 103, 104, 105, 107, 108,
    110, 111, 112
Unsplash 160

V

vector-icons library
  reference 99
vector-icons package
  reference 99
video player
  mimicking, images used 31, 32, 34, 35
view
  store, connecting to 323, 325, 326, 327, 329,
    330, 331

W

Watchman
  installing 19
websites
  linking to 129, 131, 132, 133, 134
WebSockets
  real-time communication, establishing 277, 278,
    280, 281, 282, 284
WebView props
  reference 129
WebView
  used, for embedding external websites 121,
    122, 123, 124, 125, 126, 127, 128, 129
workflow
  selecting 340, 341, 343

X

Xcode
  download link 10
  installing 10, 12

CPSIA information can be obtained
at www.ICGtesting.com
Printed in the USA
LVHW061602030722
722680LV00004B/34